Teaching

Teaching

Strategies and Methods for Student-Centered Instruction

Hellmut R. Lang
UNIVERSITY OF REGINA

Arthur McBeath
Professor Emeritus
UNIVERSITY OF REGINA

Jo Hébert

HARCOURT
BRACE

Harcourt Brace & Company
Toronto Montreal Fort Worth New York Orlando
Philadelphia San Diego London Sydney Tokyo

Canadian Cataloguing in Publication Data

Lang, Hellmut
    Teaching : strategies and methods for student-centered instruction

Includes bibliographical references and index.
ISBN 0-03-922866-5

1. Teaching. I. McBeath, A. (Arthur).
II. Hebert, Jo. III. Title.

LB1025.3.L36 1994   371.1'02   C94-930999-0

Publisher: Heather McWhinney
Editor and Marketing Manager: Joanna Cotton
Projects Co-ordinator: Laura Paterson Pratt
Director of Publishing Services: Jean Davies
Editorial Manager: Marcel Chiera
Supervising Editor: Semareh Al-Hillal
Production Editor: Laurel Parsons
Production Manager: Sue-Ann Becker
Production Supervisor: Carol Tong
Copy Editor: Darlene Zeleney
Cover Design: Opus House
Cover Photo: Jose L. Pelaez/Masterfile
Interior Design: Avril Orloff
Typesetting and Assembly: Pixel Graphics Inc.
Technical Art: Michael Kelley, Pixel Graphics Inc.
Printing and Binding: Data Reproductions

This book was printed in the United States of America.

    2 3 4 5   99 98 97 96 95

■ ■ ■ ■ ■

PREFACE

Teaching: Strategies and Methods for Student-Centered Instruction responds to the frustrations expressed over decades by teacher–education students who have found it difficult to transfer their teacher–training experience into successful classroom practice. We have written this book to help you, whether you are a novice or an experienced instructor. It is hoped that you will gain personal meaning from its contents and transpose that meaning into a repertoire of instructional skills, deriving from career-long professional development, which will increase your satisfaction and success in your chosen field of education.

Teaching presents an up-to-date, comprehensive, and balanced profile of modern instructional methods. The book contains a wealth of information, expressed in straightforward language, that will help you meet with confidence the challenges of teaching young people in today's classrooms. Its organization and content promote a "theory to action to reflection" approach to the learning and practice of instructional skills, thereby helping you to

- analyze your motives for becoming a teacher;
- learn to identify your strengths, foster your innate capabilities, and develop effective interpersonal skills as you prepare to teach;
- study and observe teaching principles and techniques while gradually learning to apply them, first in the "safety" of the microteaching laboratory and later in "real" classrooms;
- grow in confidence through a cycle of acquiring theoretical knowledge, gaining practical experience, and consolidating your professional development through a process of critical reflection;
- foster constructive feelings and emotions that support your development of a mature and positive self-concept;
- create a classroom climate that is conducive to the professional process of teaching/learning, supportive of your students' growth in knowledge, skills, self-esteem, and positive interactions with others, and that is multicultural in its dimensions;
- master effective classroom-management techniques and instructional strategies, methods, skills, and processes to acquire, with practice, holistic-teaching expertise;
- plan and present effective lessons that meet a broad range of learners' needs, using a variety of techniques to motivate your students to take increasing responsibility for their own learning and development;

◆ reflect on and evaluate your role and performance in the classroom;
◆ promote your students' increasing independence by using, as appropriate, direct, indirect, experiential, interactive, and individual instructional strategies;
◆ consistently and constructively observe, monitor, and evaluate students while gradually giving them more responsibility for self-monitoring and self-evaluation;
◆ encourage them to transfer and apply knowledge gained through study and experience to performance in other school and life situations;
◆ keep abreast of developments in the field of education and make a commitment to foster your own professional growth throughout your career.

To promote these aims, we have made the content of *Teaching* applicable to instruction at a broad range of educational levels: elementary, secondary, adult, vocational, and business education. We have developed the content from a rich base of conceptual thought applied to empirical research and tested in school and university classrooms for over twenty years. The sequence in which we present topics, case studies, practical applications through activities, and feedback instruments is tried and true. It is the result of direct experience in teaching and training teachers at every level of the academic system, as well as knowledge of special fields of instruction, such as aboriginal teacher-training and foreign-language teaching. Other expert practicing teachers and educational administrators have also contributed to the preparation of this book, thus enriching its content.

"Knowledge is power." We thank you, the reader, for giving us the opportunity to pass on knowledge that we prize and that, wisely handled, should serve you, your students, and your profession well.

Hellmut Lang
Arthur McBeath
Jo Hébert

Acknowledgments

Teaching represents the contributions and interactions, over two decades, of many people at the Faculty of Education of the University of Regina and elsewhere, who took a developmental-team approach to its planning, delivery, and evaluation. Art McBeath and Hellmut Lang designed the original manuscript. Art conceived the idea and Hellmut contributed additional ideas, created protocols, designed graphics, and spent innumerable hours creating a manuscript and making many revisions. Jo Hébert contributed further ideas and molded the revised version into a user-friendly, state-of-the-art, instructional tool.

Errol Young contributed in a number of ways and was particularly helpful in devising and designing parts of the content. Sandra Blenkinsop and Louise

Kozey helped to develop ideas and material, and tested much of the content in their own classroom teaching.

The topics, protocols, activities, and instruments that *Teaching* presents have been extensively tested in microteaching labs on campus, in in-service teaching situations, and in classrooms. Over the years, the content has been continuously refined. Donna Scarfe helped significantly by writing elementary classroom case studies and later, as a member of Hellmut's team, by teaching much of the material developed, as well as instructing in complementary professional studies and educational psychology classes. Others involved in the developmental and instructional processes were Ron Richmond, Mark Taylor, Cyril Kesten, Helen Christiansen, Bill Hromyk, Nancy Hicks, Dave Friesen, Ray Petracek, and Larry Lang. Fred Bessai, with his extensive knowledge of learning theory, made invaluable suggestions.

Donald Kauchak of the University of Utah, Virginia Richardson of the University of Arizona, Arlene Saretsky of Chicago State University, and Douglas Smith of the University of Saskatchewan reviewed the text and made helpful comments and suggestions during many stages of the book's development.

The insight and persistence of Heather McWhinney made the book a reality. Joanne Weaver and Tracy Knapper made many useful suggestions. Joanna Cotton gave welcome assistance. Laura Paterson Pratt deserves special mention for her patient editing and professional expertise.

A NOTE FROM THE PUBLISHER

Thank you for selecting *Teaching: Strategies and Methods for Student-Centered Instruction*, by Hellmut R. Lang, Arthur McBeath, and Jo Hébert. The authors and publisher have devoted considerable time to the careful development of this book. We appreciate your recognition of this effort and accomplishment.

We want to hear what you think about *Teaching: Strategies and Methods for Student-Centered Instruction*. Please take a few minutes to fill out and mail the stamped student reply card at the back of the book. Your comments and suggestions will be valuable to us as we prepare new editions and other books.

BRIEF CONTENTS

■ ■ ■ ■ ■
CONTENTS

PART 2 · THE LEARNING ENVIRONMENT

PART 3 — MASTERING THE BASICS — 151

PART 1

Becoming an Effective Teacher

■ ■ ■ ■ ■

Part 1 of *Teaching* deals with your personal and professional development as a teacher. In order to become an effective teacher, you will need to consider your motives for making this career decision, identify the factors that make for effective teaching, and undertake a process of personal professional development. Chapters 1 to 3 will help you start on this process of discovery and development.

Chapter 1 reviews the characteristics of effective teaching and outlines a plan for your professional development. You will begin by assessing your current attitudes to teaching, and your current knowledge about lesson planning and classroom instruction. When you have made this assessment, the text will launch you on a practical professional development process that includes forming "helping" teacher–student relationships, combining teaching sessions with "reflection" (inquiry into and assessment of practice), and developing a lesson-planning and "feedback" cycle for classroom use.

Chapter 2 presents teaching as an "interactive" profession that involves communication; that is, giving and receiving messages through behavior as well as verbal and body language. These messages relate to the learning (cognitive) process, but they also relate to feelings, attitudes, and values. Three aspects of teacher–student relations are

♦ communication (behavioral, verbal, and nonverbal);
♦ interpersonal relationships (evolving from our attempts to understand others and help them to understand us);
♦ group relationships.

Chapter 3 introduces the process of instructional planning. Lesson planning, which includes choosing and analyzing appropriate topics, is based on an orderly review of learning goals and instructional procedures. A good lesson plan provides for modeling and teaching effective "people skills" while making presentations that motivate (establish set), link a lesson's parts, maintain students' attention by engaging them in activities, keep them on task, evaluate their task performance and give feedback, and effect appropriate closure. Preparing careful lesson plans will also help you to reflect on and learn from your own performance after you have taught your lessons.

Building on the foundation of these first three chapters, you will begin to develop professionally by using your own experiences and insights into the theories and practice of effective education.

CHAPTER 1

TEACHING FOR LEARNING

■ ■ ■ ■ ■

Teaching is one of those things ... that everybody thinks he or she can do better than the experts ... Teachers can do something, and do something; they teach. Like any other professional activity, teaching requires a cultivated ability. To be done exceptionally well, it also requires a special talent and a sense of vocation. There are "born" teachers just as there are "born" statesmen" or "born musicians."

(ROYAL BANK, 1989, P. 1)

■ ■ ■ ■ ■

OVERVIEW

In choosing to become a teacher, you have decided to enter a "helping" profession. Through a professional development process, which really began with your interest in entering this profession, you can become a successful "learning facilitator." To achieve this goal, you will need to master curriculum subject matter, and acquire excellent "people skills" (i.e., communication and interpersonal/group skills). You will also need to develop an empathetic perception (i.e., consciously sharing the values and feelings of others from *their* point of view) of the needs and goals of your community, the parents of the children and young people in its education system, your colleagues, and, above all, your students.

This chapter will introduce you to various practical techniques of professional development. You will learn and record more about yourself and your motivations as a learning facilitator; you will become more familiar with the principles and practice of student-centered education; you will begin to target specific teaching competencies in practice teaching sessions, both in the microteaching lab and in community classrooms; and you will form the foundation of a habit of "reflective teaching."

■ ■ ■ ■ ■

TO BE OR NOT TO BE ... A TEACHER?

Years ago or more recently, you made a big decision: you decided to become a teacher. Your decision involves accepting heavy responsibilities, since after a student's home environment, the teacher is the next most important factor in her or his development. Of course, you did not make your decision to teach "cold," for you have had years of exposure to teachers who used different approaches and methods. Your perception of teaching will change, however, when you move from a place in front of "the desk" to a place behind it.

At this point, it may help you clarify your thinking to define the term *teacher*, first in the broadly understood sense of the word and, second, in its personal significance for you.

What Makes a Teacher?

Teachers function in many capacities, and as your experience in teaching grows, you will need to become familiar with performing a broad range of roles, all of which bear an important relation to your professional development. Some of these roles are discussed below.

THE TEACHER AS CONSTRUCTIVE SELF-ANALYST

One important part of becoming a teacher is expanding your self-knowledge (getting to know more about yourself) through constructive self-analysis. Self-knowledge is extremely important for anyone who wishes to become a member of a helping profession, for without sound self-knowledge, no one can truly help others. By practicing constructive self-analysis, you should learn more about several aspects of your mental and emotional life. Consider the following possibilities.

Personal Motivation

It is important for you to determine why you want to become a teacher/learning facilitator. You may be motivated, for instance, by a particular ideology or set of beliefs. Such motivation can be persuasive and powerful, but it can also be dangerous. An extreme of missionary zeal might limit your understanding of some students and induce you to impose your own values on them, since in helping others, we all tend to use ourselves and our own perceptions and needs as points of reference.

Personal Beliefs and Values

Foisting your beliefs or values on others, whether knowingly or not, may be an ineffective way of teaching, at best, and a harmful way, at worst. This approach to teaching can impede empathy, which is the basis of effective helping.

Personal Needs and Feelings

Are you trying to fulfill your personal needs by becoming a teacher/helper? Being an effective helper requires awareness and control of your personal needs and feelings, which should prevent your projecting them onto others. To help others without impeding their development, you must set your personal interests aside.

The Power of Personal Modeling

Intentionally or not, every teacher is a model who influences students. This means that teachers have a professional responsibility to provide positive **modeling** in their general behavior and approach to **learning**.

Personal Ethics

Ethical beliefs about people and society should serve to guide human actions. Teachers who value the welfare of their students will do nothing to harm them. Teachers' professional organizations establish codes of ethics that reflect common values relating to teacher—student relationships and serve as formal guidelines for professional behavior.

Limits of Personal Responsibility

Teachers must learn to set realistic limits for the personal responsibility they assume for themselves and others, by balancing their own, their students', and society's expectations and needs. The most committed teacher cannot "be all things to all persons"!

Points to ponder . . .

- ❏   What do I believe are my responsibilities as a teacher?
- ❏   What responsibilities shall I resign to parents? to others?

THE TEACHER AS RESEARCHER

Learning for teaching requires, among other activities, the reading of a range of educational materials relating both to theory and to practice, for "There now exists a body of knowledge and a fresh set of conceptions about teaching on which to base teacher education ... many advances in pedagogical knowledge can now ... provide teacher education with a scientific foundation" (Berliner, 1985, p. 4). Theories about teaching come from disciplines such as psychology, sociology, and philosophy, as well as from the study of the science and art of **pedagogy** (effective teaching and training of children), and from the wisdom gained in the practice of these disciplines. Although it is important for you to become familiar with major theories of education and instruction, such knowledge, by itself, will not ensure effective teaching. To teach effectively, you must know the subjects you will teach and be able to translate theoretical knowledge into action.

Learning to teach also involves a type of research that has been described as "critical reflection," or "inquiring into and making sense of practice" (Friesen,

1991, pp. 10–11). In our sense of the term, reflection goes beyond personal mental exercise: it often involves writing and conversing, and so is practiced by both individuals and groups. Group reflection is based on nonjudgmental, open-ended questions (i.e., questions that have no prescribed "right answer") and thoughtful responses (Wilson, 1990).

Reflection, of course, should lead to implementation: that is, your reflections should lead to decisions that you will put into practice in the microteaching lab or the classroom, for "Without action, reflection leads nowhere" (Houston, 1988, p. 8). This cyclical approach of inquiry, reflection, and action, which brings the process of lifelong professional learning-through-inquiry into teaching practice, can provide you and your fellow teachers-in-training with "ample opportunity to participate in the role of teachers-as-researchers, producers as opposed to consumers of professional knowledge" (Friesen, 1991, p. 14).

THE TEACHER AS LEARNER

One of the factors that can strongly affect your future teaching style is the highly individual matter of your preferred learning style. To this point, you may have taken your own **learning-style preferences** very much for granted, but as you begin to teach, you will find that some students prefer to learn, and respond best in, teacher-centered whole-class settings, while others learn best in a small group, and still others prefer to work alone. Learners who learn best in teacher-centered situations have been termed **field dependent** (Good and Brophy, 1990). Field-dependent learners perceive globally, generally taking an overview of situations, and they tend to require the classroom structure and extrinsic (external) **reinforcement** that a teacher supplies. Their counterparts, **field-independent** learners (Good and Brophy, 1990), perceive analytically, generally taking rather impersonal views so that they can identify, analyze, and relate the parts of a situation to form a whole picture. They tend to be self-directed and to be more comfortable working individually than in groups.

Teachers, too, have learning-style preferences. Field-dependent teachers may prefer impersonal teaching situations, emphasize the purely academic and theoretical aspects of content, prefer teacher-centered learning methods, set and emphasize their own standards and principles, and give negative feedback when their students fail to meet their expectations. By contrast, field-independent teachers may try to create a warm and positive classroom environment, establish good group dynamics, interact readily with their students, use class discussion and student-centered activities, and supply positive feedback to encourage students' efforts (Good and Brophy, 1990). They involve students in organizing lesson content and use questions to verify their students' understanding of lesson presentations.

Points to ponder . . .

- ❏ What is my learning-style preference?
- ❏ Am I field dependent or field independent?
- ❏ How might my learning-style preferences affect my teaching-style choices?
- ❏ How might I balance my teaching-style choices to meet all my students' needs?

Once you have recognized your own learning-style preferences, you should be better able to recognize those of your students (see Chapter 3). Your awareness should help you to build on your students' strengths, without letting your personal learning-style preferences lead you to overemphasize their use or to dislike students whose preferences differ from yours. Instead, use a balanced approach to teaching, and help your students to become comfortable with and to operate well in both styles of learning.

THE TEACHER AS LEARNING FACILITATOR

In earlier days, most people saw teachers solely as instructors whose job was to transfer knowledge from their own heads to those of their students. More recently, people have been viewing teachers as *learning facilitators*, members of a "helping" profession. This view parallels the widely held view that learning takes place only *within* a student—that is to say, teachers can help students to learn, but they cannot learn for them. Your task as a teacher will be to *help* students grow toward the achievement of their personal goals.

Your role as teacher, then, is to be a learning facilitator; that is, a resource person who is sensitive to the self-concept of individual students and to the development of group health and effectiveness. To be a successful learning facilitator, you must be or become

- ✦ empathetic
- ✦ warm and caring
- ✦ a provider of specific, descriptive, and nonjudgmental feedback
- ✦ positive and respectful of others
- ✦ open and genuine
- ✦ a capable communicator
- ✦ interested in enlarging your own and your students' knowledge
- ✦ productively introspective

Students learn best when they are actively involved in the learning process. They need opportunities to hone their interpersonal ("people") skills to achieve the various educational objectives that are part of the curriculum. In classes in which learning is mainly teacher-centered and focuses on lectures, essays, and examinations, students are unlikely to "bond" into cohesive cooperative groups that share responsibility for developing their learning potential. In such circumstances, neither the role of the teacher as learning facilitator nor the power of the group to promote learning will be fully realized.

THE TEACHER AS DEVELOPING PROFESSIONAL

An effective teacher must possess a broad range of readily usable areas of knowledge and instructional skills. One of the chief purposes of teacher education is to help teachers-in-training acquire knowledge and become skillful in the use of the **generic principles and practices of teaching**. Though people sometimes speak of "born teachers," in reality, teachers who use appropriate methods of instruction and produce positive results are continually learning to observe, select, plan, and implement a variety of teaching approaches and methods. Such teachers present course content in ways that their students can understand, while actively involving themselves and their students in the process of learning. In other words, the successful teacher is constantly "learning on the job."

The major components of teacher education are academic, professional, and practical learning. Only by combining these three aspects of teacher education will you enrich your ability to form useful concepts that you can apply successfully as a developing professional. The learning process involves the following elements.

Introduction to a Theory

First, your instructor, this text, or some other learning resource will present a theory relating to a targeted professional skill. Your instructor will model the skill and discuss with you its application in the classroom. You will find it helpful to note in a personal professional journal the impact (the resulting knowledge and feelings) that this new experience makes on you.

Microteaching-Lab Sessions

Next, you and your peers may each present a mini-lesson, targeting the same skill in a microteaching-lab (peer practice-teaching) session. Your peers and your instructor will provide you with feedback on your use of the targeted skill. When all members of the group have taught a mini-lesson, you will participate in a general "debriefing" discussion about the professional target. You will then record in your journal your observations and reflections about your lab experience.

Practice Teaching in the Classroom

Following a microteaching-lab session, you and a teaching partner will teach a lesson in a school classroom, targeting the same professional skill. You and your partner will observe each other and, along with the cooperating (classroom) teacher, each of you will provide feedback about the other's use of the targeted skill.

Recording and Reflecting on Observations and Experience

The notes you make about your observations and reflections may clarify your intent to adjust your professional target or adopt a new one, and so the cycle continues. By reflecting on the quality of your developing teaching skills and by participating in innovative methods and practices, you will continue to develop professionally throughout your teaching career.

■ ■ ■ ■ ■

TRAINING FOR TEACHING

Training for teaching, then, is a complex process that includes many aspects. You would find it frustrating and unproductive to try to master every aspect at once: it makes much more sense to develop your analytical skills by observing carefully, targeting particular teaching skills in sequence, identifying specific learner goals and achievements, reflecting logically on your growing experience, and recording your conclusions for maximum recall and professional growth.

Targeting Personal Professional Growth

In *Teaching* the term **target** refers to a personal professional improvement to which you are directing your intentions and energies, whereas the terms *objective* and *goal* refer to an intended learner outcome. As a teacher-in-training, you will target (aim at) the following five areas of professional growth:

✦ *Personal development.* As a learning facilitator, you must expand your self-knowledge; take increasing responsibility for your own behavior; respond positively to feedback; view yourself more objectively and critically, while maintaining a positive self-concept and building self-esteem; and enlarge your concern for others and your ability to promote their growth.

✦ *Knowledge of subject matter.* You must prepare yourself to teach by acquiring a thorough knowledge of pertinent course materials and curriculum content. Your knowledge must extend beyond the content of class texts so that you can restructure that content into teaching units that fit the curriculum and promote your students' experience and knowledge.

✦ *Teaching procedures.* You will need to acquire and use appropriately a variety of teaching and classroom-management strategies and skills.

- ◆ *Interpersonal communication.* You will learn to talk and listen more productively with students, colleagues, and parents.
- ◆ *Level of conceptualization.* You will learn to identify areas of your own teaching capability that need improvement, to apply instructional theories and ideas that will modify your teaching methods, and to design effective plans for your own professional development.

No successful teacher can afford to neglect any one growth area because all these areas are interrelated. Working with your fellow students and faculty members, you should continue to grow in all these areas over the entire period of teacher training, and beyond.

Targeting Teaching Competencies

As you pursue your teacher-training course, you will target and develop a variety of teaching competencies, several of which you may need to use simultaneously. You must learn, for instance, to instruct and respond to your students in keeping with their individual and cultural differences; to communicate productively with students, parents, and colleagues, both individually and in groups; and to manage your class effectively, using **discipline** techniques as necessary. To this end, working with a partner or a small group, you will take an active part in practice-teaching sessions that require you and your partner(s) to prepare, deliver, and analyze the lessons you teach, while taking turns at acting as "helper and helpee." As you focus on and practice each new target, you will continue to practice previous ones, thus building a repertoire—a personal fund—of teaching competencies.

In becoming a successful teacher, you will evolve through three stages of professional development, or expanding skill levels. First, you will master the basic instructional techniques, such as asking questions and giving directions, needed to provide daily teaching and to take routine action. Next, you will master effective decision making, a skill that will allow you to evaluate, either "on the spot" or during short- or long-term planning sessions, options for taking action. Finally, you will practice critical reflection. The goal of reflective practice is to help you become a self-analyzing, self-actualizing teacher and decision maker by developing a lifelong habit of systematic reflection.

Figure 1.1 illustrates these three levels of professional competencies. As you become competent at each level, you will find your interests and capabilities rising toward the next level.

Of course, as we have suggested above, you will not set out to develop a large number of competencies at one time. Instead, as each topic is introduced, you should focus on a specific target relating to that topic rather than on everything you might do or say during a lesson. No teacher-in-training can focus on all the

FIGURE 1.1

Development of Teaching Capabilities

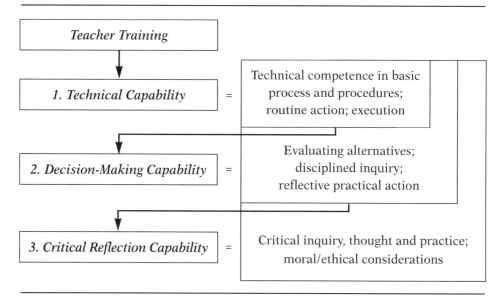

Source: Derived from "Reflectivity: The Edsel of Education?" by J. Moore, S. Mintz, and M. Berriman, in H. Waxman, H. Frieberg, J. Vaughen, and M. Weil (Eds.), *Images of Reflection in Teacher Education*, Reston, VA: Association of Teacher Educators.

components of teaching at once, any more than a beginning golfer taking a swing at a ball can think simultaneously of improving his or her golf grip, stance, body turn and thrust, back swing, stroke, and follow-through.

The competencies you will develop in the beginning are the stepping stones to practicing the art of teaching. When you choose and use them thoughtfully, they become part of your professional repertoire. Gradually, you will find that the targets you choose and practice separately do not fall into a vacuum. As you acquire a number of specific competencies, your understanding of the whole art of teaching will deepen, and the targeted skills will meld. As the process enlarges your teaching competencies, it should also extend your capability for self-analysis and help you to take increasing responsibility for your own professional growth.

Targeting Reflective Teaching

Driving the complex process of your professional development will be your growing practice of reflective decision making. To become competent at reflection, you must:

- acquire a broad understanding of the material world in which you are working;
- realize that technical teaching skills are essential to providing meaningful **learning experiences** for students;
- learn how to promote effective classroom learning experiences;
- remember that reflective teaching requires much practical activity, such as caring and nurturing;
- recognize and participate in a continuous cycle of development in which theory shapes practice and practice shapes theory.

You will use reflective decision making to assess the likely practical, ethical, and moral outcomes of your plans, and to review logically your decisions and actions. In practice,

- before and after you have tried to meet a target, reflect on what you wish to learn or what you have learned;
- consider the targets you will try to meet in the future, and how each fits into the entire teaching process.

Reflective practice will help you to base your decisions and actions on keen observation, reasoned analysis, and good judgment.

PRACTICE *and Projects*

1. Educators often find it useful to introduce a new topic of study with a "pretest" that informs both students and teachers of what students already know about the topic. A pretest identifies learning needs and suggests the setting of specific targets; it also provides a tool for measuring progress as learning advances.

   Using Data Collection Form 1.1 (Appendix A), prepare a professional profile as a pretest. Although you will likely have to score some competencies as "not rated" (NR), developing a professional profile at this stage can help you to make personal professional development plans later on, during and after your practice teaching opportunities.

■ ■ ■ ■ ■

THE PROFESSIONAL DEVELOPMENT PROCESS

The **professional development** process is a complex set of procedures that involve deciding on lesson content (what you will teach) and format (how you will teach it), putting those decisions to work (in **microteaching** labs or classroom practice-teaching sessions), and evaluating the results.

To prepare for effective teaching, you will need to learn about educational theory, enlarge your ability to implement your theoretical knowledge in practical ways, and acquire decision-making and reflective thinking skills. It is important for you to keep in mind this combination of theory, action, and reflection, for professional teaching requires combining the practices and principles of teaching, and applying their elements in the classroom. In other words, you must become a well-informed and reflective decision maker who can carry out your decisions in the classroom in a professional way.

Preparing for Effective Teaching

A successful professional development process combines three interrelated features:

◆ a helping (supportive, facilitating, and nonjudgmental) relationship among participants;
◆ a pre- and post-teaching conferencing procedure relating to your achievement of a specific professional target and your pupils' achievement of lesson objectives;
◆ the practice of a range of teaching competencies in a learning cycle that is illustrated in Figure 1.2.

FIGURE 1.2

Professional Development Process

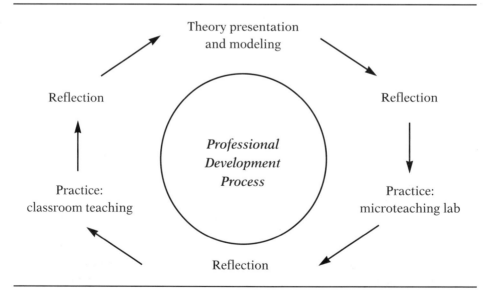

MICROTEACHING: TARGET TEACHING IN THE MICROTEACHING LAB

Microteaching will be a critical part of your professional development process. Microteaching labs (peer practice-teaching sessions) are an excellent means of building **helping relationships** that will promote professional development. During these microteaching sessions, you will practice many teaching skills: **conferencing**, observing and collecting descriptive data, delivering **effective feedback**, and practicing reflective action. These skills are critical parts of the repertoire of professional teachers.

Before you begin a microteaching session, you will have watched your instructor present and model the specific teaching competency that you should target during your lesson. You will have had opportunities to observe, to record your observations and feelings about the model lesson, and to note how you intend to use the targeted teaching skill in microteaching your lesson.

You will find the microteaching lab a controlled and "safe" environment for practicing professional teaching among your peers. If you were to practice first in an actual classroom, you might find it hard to concentrate on a specific professional target since coping with the many **variables** of a classroom while targeting a specific teaching skill might prove distracting. In a microteaching session, in which the overall success of your lesson is not critical, you are free to focus on the target teaching skill.

In microteaching sessions, you will have a teaching partner with whom you will share responsibilities for planning the lesson, observing, recording observations, and receiving and giving feedback. Since the main purpose of microteaching is to practice and receive feedback relating to a professional target in a supportive atmosphere, you can safely concentrate on your target. Microteaching sessions should reduce the pressure of delivering your first lessons and prepare you to practice the same targets later on in the more complex setting of a classroom.

CONFERENCING FOR PROFESSIONAL TEACHING

The conferencing procedure begins with a preteaching session (**preconferencing**), during which you and your "lab" partner will select a professional development target. Remember that the purpose of microteaching lessons is to practice professional development targets and to reflect on that practice. Whatever topic you choose should give you opportunities to practice your chosen target: for example, if you target effective questioning, the lesson content and teaching method should allow you to ask many questions. For your early practice sessions, you should choose topics that are relatively simple, have no demanding depth of subject matter, and can be taught in ten minutes at most. For instance, you might choose to prepare a lesson on one aspect of a favorite hobby or of a subject that you hope to teach later on.

You might also use a preteaching conferencing session to revise a lesson plan to meet a particular target and to plan for target-related data collection while you are teaching. During your lesson, your partner will observe and collect data relating to the target you have chosen.

GIVING AND RECEIVING FEEDBACK

After a practice lesson, **postconferencing** (debriefing following a lesson) will allow you and your partner to share feedback relating to the targeted teaching skill, the data collected during the lesson, and your students' learning experience. Giving feedback is a way of providing information to another person about what he or she has been doing or saying, or about the effect of those actions or words on others. Instructors, teaching partners, and cooperating teachers are responsible for promoting professional growth by providing useful feedback, which is often based on data collected on a standard data-collection sheet provided by an instructor.

Effective feedback is

◆ solicited, not imposed;
◆ specific, accurate, and complete;
◆ given in a nonthreatening and nonjudgmental way;
◆ provided at the earliest opportunity;
◆ descriptive, clear, and nonevaluative;
◆ focused on behavior that can be controlled;
◆ owned by the receiver, not the giver.

This type of feedback allows you and your peers to grow and learn from **deferred successes** (attempts that do not meet with immediate success but contribute to later success), without feeling threatened or overwhelmed by competition. To benefit from feedback, you must reflect on the information given, analyze and interpret it, and decide how to apply it in teaching your next lesson. In doing this, you take responsibility for your own professional growth.

You can use the experience and information obtained through practicing this cycle in your next preteaching conference session, thereby starting the cycle anew. Data Collection Form 1.2 (Appendix A) provides a checklist for your use in pre- and post-teaching conferences.

KEEPING A PROFESSIONAL JOURNAL

Since becoming a professional teacher is a cyclical experience that involves learning about educational theory and then putting that theory into practice, you will find it helpful to keep a personal **professional development journal** to describe your learning/teaching experiences and your reflections on them. Such a journal will help you to think about and learn from your teaching experiences, and to plan for future activities. It is important to make your journal entries as *personal* as possible: this is *your* journal, *your* personal professional development tool. Merely to write what you think your instructor may want to hear defeats the purpose of keeping such a record.

Writing down your reflections on your professional development experiences can be a powerful and valuable means of requiring you to think, in a very precise way, about your teaching activities and your corresponding responses and revised targets. To do this productively, you will need to recall, analyze, synthesize, evaluate, and plan. As you make successive entries, a record of your professional growth emerges that will help you to visualize where you have been, where you are, and what targets you hope to reach. This record should increase your understanding of the teaching process as a constant reordering. To make this record as useful as possible, consider the following elements.

Format

Prepare a title page for your journal, followed by a table of contents and then by a "Record of Targets" that will list a target for every lesson you teach, either in a microteaching lab or in a school classroom. You might use dividers to separate the body of your journal into its three main parts: "Part A. Impressions," "Part B. Targets," and "Part C. Stocktaking and Career Choices."

This record will provide you with a profile of your progress, and clearly show which aspects of the targets need more attention and practice. Such a record can be useful as you move to higher levels of preparation or begin to teach on your own.

Journal Entries

Typical journal entries should occupy about one page for each on-campus class; one to one and a half pages for each microteaching lab (before you insert your lesson plan and all feedback); and two to two and a half pages for each school classroom day (before you insert your lesson plan and all feedback). **Stocktaking** and Career Choices sections will require about one page each. Special investigations may require one to three pages.

Part A of your journal should contain unstructured or free-flowing notes of your general observations on broad philosophic or moral issues, questions or concerns relating to your professional development, specific tips from your cooperating teacher, and nontarget-related feedback. There is no need to aim at any particular format in this section. Just enter the date in the margin and "Go for it!" Ask yourself, "What, if anything, gave me a hit today?" "What did I observe that impressed/excited me?" "I'm annoyed. What should I do?" When you have identified these issues, set yourself a professional target.

In Part B, which you should organize by target topics, you will enter target-related information acquired in class, then in microteaching labs, and, finally, in school classrooms. In the "Class" sections of Part B, comment on your readings in the text, as well as your experiences in class. Identify a professional development target, and outline specific plans to meet that target in the following microteaching lab. You will find it helpful to use the "Description (Desc)/Impact (Imp)/Intent (Int)" formula illustrated in Figure 1.3.

In the "Lab" sections, record your reflections on your successes in meeting the target set for your microlesson. Record, too, any deferred successes (i.e., those that you hope to achieve later by changing an approach that did not work well initially). Note your observations of your partner's and other classmates' experiences in meeting their targets, and the salient points of the general discussion of the target that follows the lab teaching sessions. Conclude by noting specific plans for reaching the target set for your classroom lesson.

In the "School" section, record your reflections about your deferred successes in meeting your target, your partner's experiences in meeting the target, and your cooperating teacher's use of target skills. Try to record all the target-related data available on the lessons you teach. If you find blanks or noninformative entries on your data collection forms, ask your partner or cooperating teacher to recall their observations so that you can update your notes. Record any target-related verbal feedback that your partner, your lab instructor, or the cooperating teacher gives you. Conclude by noting specific plans for achieving your target the next time you teach.

Use Part C of your journal to assess your professional growth. To do this, take stock twice in each semester, at the mid and end points. At the mid point, use your professional profile pretest (Data Collection Form 1.1, in Appendix A) to remind you of what you knew and could do as a teacher at the beginning of the term. Compare your pretest profile with an updated professional profile that identifies what you now know and can do, and what you still need to learn and to practice. At the end of term, compare your midterm profile with an end-of-term profile. At the end point, review your choice of a teaching career.

Points to ponder . . .

- ❑ Do I still wish to teach? At what grade level? In what major and minor subject areas?
- ❑ What are my reasons?
- ❑ What other options might I pursue?
- ❑ What are my plans for my future?

FIGURE 1.3

Sample Page of Personal Professional Development Journal, Part B

Target: Giving Directions

[Desc = Describe; Imp = Impact; Int = Intention]

Class

(Desc) [Target-related topics presented in text/lecture or discussed in class?] _____

_____

_____

[Activities in which you participated?] _____

_____

_____

(Imp) [What did you learn? How do you feel about it?] _____

_____

_____

(Int) [When and how do you intend to use your knowledge as you practice the target in a microteaching lab?] _____

_____

_____

Microteaching Lab

(Desc) [Summarize events in lab. To what extent did you achieve the target? To what extent did your partner achieve the target? What did you learn about the target during the lab?]

_____

_____

(continued)

(Figure 1.3 continued)

(Inp) [What did you learn and how do you feel about your target because of your lesson? (Consider the feedback you received.) Your partner's lesson? The rest of the lab?]

_____

_____

_____

(Int) [What will you do because of your experience and feelings when you practice the target in a school classroom?] _____

_____

_____

[*Note:* Attach your lesson plan and the feedback that you received.]

School

(Desc) [How did you practice your target? How did your partner practice the target? How did your cooperating teacher use the target skill?] _____

_____

_____

(Inp) [What did you learn? How do you feel about your practice of the target? (Consider the feedback you received.) Your partner's practice of the target? What did you learn about the target skill from the cooperating teacher?] _____

_____

_____

(Int) [What will you do when you next have an opportunity to practice the target?] _____

_____

_____

[*Note:* Attach your lesson plan and the feedback that you received.]

TARGET TEACHING IN THE SCHOOL CLASSROOM

After you have studied the theory and rationale of a target skill, have seen it modeled, and have practiced it in a microteachinglab, you are ready to practice the skill while teaching "real" pupils in a school classroom.

The main purpose of classroom placement is to give you an opportunity to practice specific professional targets in a realistic setting. You and your microteaching-lab partner may be placed with a cooperating teacher to begin your classroom practice. Cooperating teachers should not be viewed as experts who tell you what to do, but as helpers who provide you with opportunities to teach lessons that lend themselves to the practice of specific professional targets. As in your microteaching-lab sessions, you will be putting theory into practice, and ownership and responsibility for learning continue to rest with you. Your lesson content should be straightforward and simple, and your lesson should require relatively little preparation time. Again, you will receive feedback, this time from your cooperating teacher, as well as from your classroom-placement partner.

PUBLIC RELATIONS FOR TEACHERS-IN-TRAINING

Suggestions for forming and maintaining positive relations in your practice-placement classroom are offered in Table 1.1.

TABLE 1.1

Teacher-in-Training Public Relations in School Classrooms

Making telephone contact	Before your first visit to the school where you will be practice teaching, phone your cooperating teacher to introduce yourself and arrange your first meeting.
Entering the building	When you enter the school, go directly to the administration office to let staff know who you are and why you are visiting.
Arrival times	Arrive at least half an hour before classes begin.
Departure times	Make sure to allow ample time for postconferencing, and ask your cooperating teacher if you can help in any way before you leave the school.

(continued)

(Table 1.1 continued)

Dress	On your first visit to the school, wear business clothing, and note the staff's dress norms. If they seem unusual to you, ask your cooperating teacher's advice on dress. Follow the norms on your subsequent visits.
Staff room	Remember that staff must share chairs, tables, hangers, and other equipment. Ask which items, including cups, are available for visitors, or bring your own cup. Be prepared to pay for the coffee and other supplies that you use.
Parking	Before driving to the school, ask whether guest or public/street parking facilities are available. On your arrival, be careful not to park in someone else's space.
Observing school rules	Be sure to observe all school rules. Remember that you, like the teachers on staff, are a model for pupil behavior.
Preparing lesson plans	Make sure that your lesson plans are complete *before* you arrive at school, and that you have the target data collection sheets you need to supply your teaching partner and cooperating teacher.
Ethics	Observe the applicable professional code of ethics in your interactions with school administrators, teachers, and pupils. You must treat with professional confidentiality your classroom observations and the information you gather about pupils.

PRACTICE *and Projects*

1. Prepare a personal profile, as described below, to introduce yourself to your fellow teachers-in-training and to find out more about them.

    a. On a sheet of bristol board, draw a large stick-figure picture of yourself.

    b. Starting in the upper left-hand corner, add pictures and symbols supplemented by single words or short phrases that provide answers to the following questions:

    ◆ What are your feelings at this moment?

    ◆ What are two of your favorite activities?

(continued)

(continued)

- What has been your greatest personal achievement to date?
- What is an issue on which you are determined never to change?
- What one thing can other people do to make you happy?
- What two characteristics would you most like to develop?

2. When you have chosen or been assigned a lab partner, interview her or him, using the following questions:
   - What is your name?
   - What are your major and minor fields of specialization?
   - What are your hobbies?
   - What is your all-time favorite movie? recording artist/group?
   - What work experience have you had?
   - What schools and colleges have you attended?
   - What has been the most meaningful event for you in the past year or so?
   - Have you sisters? brothers? a spouse? If so, what do they do?
   - Why have you decided to become a teacher?
   - What are your feelings about the practice-teaching experiences to come?
   - If you could make one change in the school system, what would it be?

SUMMARY

- Preparing for teaching begins with your decision to become a teacher.
- The effective teacher combines the functions of constructive self-analyst, researcher, learner, learning facilitator, and developing professional.
- Effective training for teaching involves targeting specific, sequential, personal goals for professional growth.
- Successful professional growth requires a helping relationship among participants, pre- and postconferencing based on careful observation and impartial feedback and reflection, and the practice of a range of competencies in microteaching-lab and school-classroom sessions.
- Keeping a personal professional journal promotes effective reflection and professional growth.
- Successful target teaching in the classroom requires teachers-in-training to practice considerate professional public relations in their placement schools.

KEY WORDS

conferencing	microteaching-lab	practice teaching
empathy	session	professional
learner	personal beliefs and	development
field-dependent	values	target
field-independent	needs and feelings	journal
learning facilitator	modeling	reflective teaching
learning-style	motivation	self-analysis
preference	responsibility	teacher as researcher

RECOMMENDED READING

Teachers as "Helping Professionals"

Brammer, L. (1985). *The helping relationship: Process and skills* (3rd ed.). Englewood Cliffs, NJ: Prentice-Hall.

Professional Development

Brooks, J., & Brooks, M. (1993). *In search of understanding: The case for constructivist classrooms.* Alexandria, VA: Association for Supervision and Curriculum Development.

Cohen, A. (1993). A new educational paradigm. *Phi Delta Kappan, 74*(10), 791–95.

Dill, D., et al. (1990). *What teachers need to know: The knowledge, skills and values essential to good teaching.* San Francisco, CA: Jossey-Bass.

Eisner, E. (1991). What really counts in schools. *Educational Leadership, 48*(5), 10–17.

Henderson, J. (1993). *Reflective teaching: Becoming an inquiring educator.* New York: Macmillan.

Zemelman, S., Daniels, H., & Hyde, A. (1993). *Best practice: New standards for teaching and learning in America's schools.* Portsmouth, NH: Heinemann.

CHAPTER 2

COMMUNICATION:
PROMOTING "PEOPLE SKILLS"

■ ■ ■ ■ ■

Contemporary life places a premium on citizens' abilities to relate well to others ... schools have an increased responsibility for helping students learn behavioral skills that will equip them to fill responsible and useful roles in society and contribute maximally to the productivity of groups ... this means that concurrent with the academic curriculum, schools must concern themselves with developing interpersonal skills in their students. ...
(SCHMUCK & SCHMUCK, 1992, PP. 8–9.)

■ ■ ■ ■ ■

OVERVIEW

Effective human communication and interaction depend on successful use of "people skills" that enable the user to communicate and interact productively with others. Basic communication depends on nonverbal (body language) and verbal (speaking, listening) skills, and on use of time and space. Successful interaction depends on communication, interpersonal, and group skills that emphasize cooperation. Learning more about yourself and others promotes these skills. This chapter discusses teaching and modeling all these skills, and providing practice in their development, beginning with the presentation of the "Johari Window," a useful device for helping one "open up" to others.

Clear communication, both verbal and nonverbal, reduces any "perception (understanding) gap" between the giver of a message and its receiver. Effective interpersonal skills promote clear two-way communication, reduce the "interpersonal gap," and help groups to perform effectively. Group skills promote and support cooperative work and learning. You will find these skills particularly helpful for forming and maintaining sensitive and "helping" interpersonal and group relationships with your teaching partners.

■ ■ ■ ■ ■

TEACHING AS A "PEOPLE BUSINESS"

Teaching is first and foremost a "people business," for teacher–student relationships are a key factor in keeping students in school. Since students comprise much more than an intellect, teaching involves more than promoting students' intellectual growth: it must address the "whole person," stimulating cognitive (intellectual) development, psychomotor development (relating to all movement controlled by mental activity), and affective development (relating to values and attitudes). Every person with whom you will work as a teacher, whether it be a student, a faculty member, an administrator, a parent, or a member of the public, has unique needs, feelings, **attitudes**, **values**, and life experiences. To relate cooperatively to these varied groups of human beings and to participate productively in their interactions, you will need strong communication and interactive skills. Perhaps the most important aspect of teacher training is learning, practicing, and teaching people skills. Table 2.1 lists some of them.

TABLE 2.1

Communication, Interpersonal, and Group Skills

Communication Skills	Interpersonal Skills	Group Skills
Verbal		
Paraphrasing	Participating	Brainstorming
Word choice	Making clear statements	Problem solving
Clarity	Describing own behavior	Goal setting
Enunciation	Describing others' behavior	Resolving conflicts
Tone variation	Describing feelings	Consensus seeking
Pausing	Perception checking	Monitoring group effectiveness
Nonverbal		
Eye contact		
Facial expression		
Body position and motion		
Gestures		

Subskills of Interpersonal and Group Skills		
Listening	Interpreting	Collecting data
Participating	Encouraging	Organizing data
Interacting	Summarizing	Trusting
Seeking information	Clarifying	Being open
Sharing information	Soliciting feedback	Observing
Deferring judgment	Giving feedback	Coding
Being genuine	Setting goals	Imagining
Taking responsibility	Trying provisionally	Criticizing
Compromising	Seeking consensus	Analyzing
Collaborating	Hypothesizing	Diagnosing
Mediating	Categorizing	Initiating
Including	Comparing	Accepting
Recording	Contrasting	
Reporting	Classifying	

Two factors that can help you to teach and practice effective people skills are self-knowledge and knowledge of your own and other **cultures**, for cultural background tends to shape everyone's behavior and expectations in all situations.

Expanding Your Self-Knowledge

The foundation for good interpersonal skills is self-understanding. To become a successful teacher, therefore, you must learn more about yourself. In general, there are two ways in which people learn about themselves: by chance and by making a conscious effort. The latter way is usually the more effective.

THE "JOHARI WINDOW"

One means of learning more about yourself—and others—is to construct a "Johari Window" (sometimes called a "Johari Awareness Model"), illustrated in Figure 2.1. The **Johari Window** (Luft, 1969) can help you give and receive information about yourself as a means of developing positive classroom and staff room relationships and interactions.

The "Public" (open) area of the Johari Window represents information (e.g., physical characteristics, group behavior, outline of personal history) that you know about yourself, and that most of your associates (e.g., your instructors and

FIGURE 2.1

The Johari Window: Giving and Receiving Information about Oneself

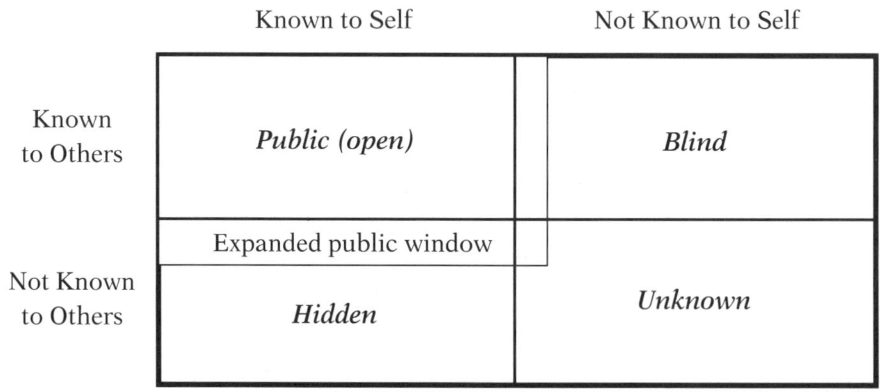

	Known to Self	Not Known to Self
Known to Others	*Public (open)*	*Blind*
Not Known to Others	Expanded public window *Hidden*	*Unknown*

Source: Adapted from *Of Human Interaction*, by J. Luft, 1969, Palo Alto, CA: National Press Books.

fellow students) know about you. The "Blind" area represents information about you that you do not know but that others do (e.g., speech mannerisms), since others observe things about us of which we ourselves are unaware. The "Hidden" area represents information about yourself that you know but that others do not (e.g., that you become uncomfortable in a social situation when others seem to be excluding you from the conversation). The "Unknown" area represents information about yourself that neither you nor anyone else knows (e.g., you have the potential to become a good photographer, but you have not yet owned a camera).

Since "opening up" to others generally encourages them to open up to you, by working to enlarge your Public window, you may learn more about others and how to help them, and become more effective in doing so. To open up, you must transfer information from your other "window" areas into the Public area. You can do this by revealing more about yourself to others, by inviting and accepting feedback from others about yourself, or by taking part in activities that show you more about your own behavior and motives.

Learning About Others

The shape that a society takes is largely determined by learning, which is generally a social process greatly facilitated by clear **communication**, that is, "the exchange or sharing of thoughts and feelings through symbols that represent approximately the same conceptual experience for everyone involved" (Johnson & Johnson, 1975, p. 100). Such communication is the basis of interpersonal and group relationships.

COMMUNICATING FEELINGS

The process of human interaction, or dealing with others, begins with one person's attempt to send a message—that is, to communicate a meaning or a feeling—to another. The "sender" has a mental image that he or she encodes in spoken language, in print or writing, in a drawing or diagram, and/or in body language. Each sender's method of encoding depends on his or her background, circumstances, interests, values, intent, and ways of interpreting and communicating. All these factors may differ somewhat from the corresponding factors affecting the "receiver" of the message. Thus, the sender often needs to check with the receiver to discover whether he or she has received and understands the message as the sender intended it.

The following are some of the most critical factors in sending and receiving messages in the classroom:

- open, trusting, and supportive teacher–student relationships;
- clarity of expression;
- use of relevant pictures/objects to support verbal messages;
- obvious sincerity about the message;
- adapting the message to the learner's level of understanding;
- checking that the learner has understood the message.

■ ■ ■ ■ ■

BASIC COMMUNICATION SKILLS

Although **communication skills** include body language, speaking, listening/observing, writing, and reading, we shall focus here on verbal and nonverbal communication skills, which we shall term the **basic communication skills**.

Verbal Communication Skills

When you hear the term *communication*, you are likely to think first of spoken language, for the human voice brings words to life. The words you speak, their meanings, and your manner of delivery—the firmness and modulation of your tone (timbre and resonance) and the tempo, pitch, and loudness of your voice—will shape the messages you send to your students, stimulating their thoughts and feelings, and helping them to frame concepts. The words you choose and the way you use them should promote positive feelings, clear understanding, and the process of learning.

Many variables determine the "teaching power" of verbal messages. These variables include how well the message is organized, what strength of feeling it delivers, and at what point in a lesson it is presented. Students remember more clearly those messages that are specific, that are delivered at the beginning or end of a lesson, and that present opposing views, or are positive or negative (rather than neutral) in feeling and tone. To send effective oral messages to your pupils, you will need to develop good speaking skills that incorporate the following features:

- *Audibility.* Speak loudly enough for all to hear, but not so loudly that you irritate your listeners.
- *Clarity.* Use words and sentence structures that are descriptive, concise, and suited to the listeners' level of understanding. Avoid "run-on," fragmented, or incomplete statements and questions.
- *Precise enunciation.* Pronounce each word distinctly, with crisp initial and final sounds. Avoid sloppy run-ons such as "gonna," "kinda," and "won'tya." Use phrasing to clarify meaning.
- *Variety and emphasis.* Vary your rate of speaking and the volume, inflection, and tone of your voice. Avoid slipping into a monotone.

◆ *Correct language*.   Use correct grammar and sentence structure, and avoid slang.

◆ *Lack of mannerisms*.   Eliminate mannerisms of speech that distract or annoy listeners, such as frequent repetitions of "OK? … Uh-huh … and-uh … you know," and throat clearing.

Nonverbal Communication Skills

Rarely do we communicate by means of words alone: we use nonverbal messages to reinforce the meaning of our words, and to convey our feelings and preferences. We convey these nonverbal messages through posture, facial expression or color, gestures, body movement, or even touching. Learners "read" a teacher's shoulder shrug, frown, lift of an eyebrow, or hand movement, though the teacher may be unaware of the nonverbal message that he or she is sending. Messages that reflect lower expectations and negative attitudes of teachers can hinder the social and intellectual development of children from minority cultures. By contrast, teachers can use nonverbal messages to show that they believe their students are worthy, can be trusted, and can and will succeed. To this end, you should learn to recognize and make positive use of nonverbal messages, including those listed below.

◆ *Eye contact*.   Make each student feel that you are personally noticing, addressing, or including him or her. Look at the person you are addressing rather than directing your gaze to your notes, the chalkboard, or a particular spot or object in the room.

◆ *Facial expression*.   Use appropriate facial expressions to support your verbal messages. Censor blank, bored looks, but show your enthusiasm.

◆ *Motion*.   In walking about your classroom, you may show your interest—or lack of it—in your students by moving toward or away from them. Make sure that you use your motion to support your spoken messages. Circulate among your students, recognizing and communicating with them. Create a variety of stimuli by moving about the room to attend to individuals or groups of pupils who need assistance. Focus attention on the lesson by approaching the chalkboard or other teaching aids while maintaining eye contact with your students.

◆ *Gestures*.   To emphasize a point or promote understanding, use gestures in ways that promote rather than distract attention. Avoid distracting or annoying mannerisms, such as scratching, playing with a pencil, wetting your lips, swaying, or cracking your knuckles.

◆ *Physical contact*.   Use physical contact in group situations to promote learning (e.g., by guiding a student's hand movement) or to gain attention. Show approval in this way only with great discretion, when the students' age level or gender makes such contact appropriate.

◆ *Silence*.   Use silence to gain attention, to emphasize a point, to provide students with thinking time, or to deal with a minor disruption (see Chapter 5).

SPACE AND TIME AS COMMUNICATION TOOLS

The positions of your desk and your students' desks are territory indicators. Some teachers may unconsciously use their desk as a psychological barrier that protects them from students or as a symbol of authority: a room arranged in straight rows, with the teacher's desk "front and center," sends one nonverbal message, whereas a room arranged in a semicircle sends quite another (Moore, 1989).

The amount of time you spend on a topic will suggest to your students how important you consider that topic to be. Your use of pauses and "thinking time" after you ask a question, and the patience you show when students are answering questions or contributing to a discussion, also send messages.

Communication Congruence

Above all, verbal and nonverbal messages should be congruent: that is, they should mean the same thing to the sender and the receiver. When messages are not congruent, communication breakdowns can create an "interpersonal gap," which may become a primary cause of misunderstandings that result in anger and mistrust. Consider the situations presented in For Example 2.1.

In these situations, the message sent is not the message received, and a communication gap causes frustration or even anger. You risk creating such gaps if you assume—and fail to check—that senders' and receivers' interpretations of messages are congruent. You will avoid communication gaps by stating clearly any message you wish to convey, ensuring that your nonverbal messages support your words, and checking that the message received is the message you sent.

PRACTICE *and Projects*

1. Create a personal Johari Window. Develop a personal plan for expanding your Public area to enlarge your self-knowledge and improve your communication skills.

2. Form groups of five persons with different teaching majors or fields of specialization. Each member will speak to the group for three to five minutes, using the stems provided below. Listeners will use a copy of Data Collection Form 2.1 (Appendix A) to record their observations on the speaker's use of two or three communication skills. (Divide the skills to be observed as equally as possible among the group members.) After the session, listeners will provide the speakers with descriptive nonjudgmental feedback.

(continued)

(continued)

STEM: "I think that [*subject of specialization*] is important because ... "

"I think that the study of [*subject of specialization*] is fascinating because ... "

"Some students do not like [*subject of specialization*] because ... "

"Teaching [*subject of specialization*] could be improved by ... "

3. a. Using the professional development process outlined in Chapter 1, plan a microteaching-lab lesson that targets effective basic verbal and nonverbal communication.

b. Teach the lesson to your peers while your teaching partner observes and records his or her observations, using Data Collection Form 2.1 (Appendix A).

c. Keep the written feedback you receive so that you can later plan and teach a classroom lesson, targeting the same skills and being observed by a cooperating teacher.

If a partner or cooperating teacher is not available, fill out a copy of the data collection form yourself after you teach your lesson.

FOR EXAMPLE 2.1

Communication Breakdowns

SITUATION 1. You and a friend have agreed to meet in an hour. You are now waiting for your friend on one street corner, while your friend waits for you on another. Each of you is becoming more angry by the minute.

SITUATION 2. On a Tuesday evening, you receive a phone call from a friend who tells you, with obvious annoyance, that he is waiting for you to return his book as you promised. You believe that you agreed to return the book on Tuesday of next week.

SITUATION 3. On a Monday morning, you ask your class to hand in their assignments. No one has finished the assignment, and you respond with exasperation, while your students respond with confusion and frustration, claiming that the assignment is not due till Friday.

What causes ineffective communication? How might you have avoided the communication breakdowns described above? What might you have done to promote effective communication?

■ ■ ■ ■ ■

HUMAN INTERACTIONS

A teacher's work involves a steady stream of interactions—more than a thousand a day (Jackson, 1968, p. 121)—with individuals, small groups, and the class as a whole. The success of these interactions depends largely on the level of interpersonal skills that teachers practice and teach their students to practice.

Interpersonal Skills

In working with colleagues, students, or parents, good teachers tend to use two kinds of **interpersonal skills**: those that help them understand others and those that help others understand them. People who practice effective interpersonal skills are genuine and empathetic, have a positive but realistic self-concept, and respect others as individuals. They are not patronizing, judgmental, or negatively critical, and they do not ridicule or belittle others. They listen, help their students identify and explore problems, help students to understand the consequences of choices, and suggest alternative methods for finding solutions.

SKILLS TO HELP YOU UNDERSTAND OTHERS

Some interpersonal skills are primarily helpful for understanding others. Examples include the following.

Listening

Effective two-way communication can occur only if both parties listen—for feelings, as well as for words—and if listening is responsive. Every failure to listen attentively to a message can cause mistakes, hurt feelings, frustration, or anger. Responsive listening involves the use of several important skills for understanding others: paraphrasing (rephrasing the substance of what a speaker has said to check your perceptions and ensure that you have correctly understood the message), accepting the speaker's feelings, and asking for clarification as necessary. By modeling these skills and teaching your students how to use them, you can show that you expect them to use the skills as you do.

Points to ponder ...

❑ How often have you caught yourself paying less than full attention when another person was speaking?

❑ Were you using the other person's "air time" to think about what you were going to say next?

(continued)

(continued)
❏ Have you ever thought that others have been only half-listening to you?
❏ If so, how did their behavior make you feel?

Paraphrasing

Paraphrasing consists of restating in your own words the substance of a message sent by another person, or providing an example that reflects your understanding of that message. Restating the sender's message confirms your perception of his or her assertion and can help to increase your understanding of the feelings behind the words by setting the message into your personal frame of reference. Paraphrasing also offers the sender an opportunity to clarify any misperception expressed in the receiver's response, and so close a communication gap. Paraphrasing is a powerful way of saying, "You are important. I have time for you. I respect your ideas. I want to understand."

In framing a paraphrase, remember to do the following:

◆ Concentrate on the message that the sender is trying to communicate. Appear attentive, interested, and open to the sender's ideas and feelings.
◆ Listen for the feelings behind the sender's words.
◆ Preface your paraphrase with leads such as

"You think ..."   "Do you think that ...?"
"Your position is ..."   "It seems to me that ..."
"Do you mean ...?"   "I heard you saying ..."

◆ Put the sender's statement into your own words without quoting or mimicking.
◆ Match your nonverbal message to your verbal message.
◆ Make no judgments. Express neither approval nor disapproval.
◆ Pursue the interchange until sender and receiver agree on the meaning.

For Example 2.2 provides a sample of paraphrasing.

Perception Checking

Listeners often draw inaccurate impressions from a speaker's words or body language. The reason may be that we unconsciously interpret others' words and body language from our own point of view, projecting our own feelings, attitudes, or desires. **Perception checking** is a useful skill for making sure that you are interpreting a speaker's feelings accurately. Like paraphrasing, it is a means of avoiding misunderstandings that could cause frustration or anger.

Perception checking requires that you both listen to a message and observe nonverbal clues carefully to form a basis for drawing a tentative inference. You then describe, clearly and unemotionally, the sender's feelings as you perceive or infer them. You express neither approval nor disapproval of those feelings or motives, but simply offer your perception/inference as a **hypothesis** (a tentative conclusion)

FOR EXAMPLE 2.2

Paraphrasing

COOPERATING TEACHER: In our next lesson, I'd like you to present examples of appeals that advertisers use to persuade consumers to buy their products. Show lots of examples of the use of color in your presentation.

STUDENT TEACHER: Do you mean that you want me to teach about the various ways color can be used in advertising?

COOPERATING TEACHER: Not quite. I'd like you to present some examples of the emotional appeals advertisers use to influence consumer choice, and I'd like you to support each category of appeal with real samples.

STUDENT TEACHER: Oh! You want me to teach a lesson about the psychological appeals advertisers use, and I should show actual examples from the media, preferably ones that are colorful.

COOPERATING TEACHER: That's it!

and not a statement of fact. This allows the sender to confirm or correct your interpretation. In doing this, you let the sender know that you care enough to want to understand his or her feelings and to avoid making or acting on false assumptions. For Example 2.3 illustrates perception checking.

SKILLS TO HELP OTHERS UNDERSTAND YOU

While it is important that you understand others, it is just as important that you help others to understand you. **Behavior description** (to help others understand

FOR EXAMPLE 2.3

Perception Checking

SPEAKER: I get the impression that I have made you angry. Have I?
Am I right in thinking that you are disappointed with what happened?
I get the impression that you are pleased with the results.
It seems to me that I hurt your feelings. Did I?
You look bewildered. Are you?
You seemed to agree with the way I handled the situation. Did you?
You appeared to be nervous when I asked you to speak. Were you?
I'm not sure whether you were pleased or displeased with the results.

what behavior you are responding to) and **feelings description** (to help others understand how you are feeling) are two skills you can use to help others understand you.

Behavior Description

Sometimes you respond in certain ways to your observations of others and their behavior. When you explain your response by describing that behavior clearly, you offer those others information that they can confirm or confute. Your description should be as specific, nonaccusatory, and nonevaluative as possible, to avoid making the listener feel inadequate or attacked and, even perhaps, leading him or her to become defensive and to try to retaliate. An apt description of behaviour reduces the receiver's need to raise defenses and increases the likelihood of understanding. The description should focus on specific observable actions, and show that you are stating hypotheses to be checked, and not presenting established facts. Its message should be, "You are important. I want to understand you." To relate your descriptions to specific actions, you might use stems such as "I see that ... ," "What I saw happen was ... ," "I noticed that ... ," "I observed ...." For Example 2.4 provides a sample behaviour description.

Feelings Description

How often have you said or heard, "If only I had known! ... I wish that you had told me ... "? Everyone has feelings, and freedom to describe those feelings in a

---

F O R   E X A M P L E   2 . 4

Behavior Description

COMMENT 1: "Nathan, you seem to support the opposite view of whatever I say today."

Not: "Nathan, you're just trying to show off!"

COMMENT 2: "Mae, you began to speak before Leroy had finished his comment."

Not: "Mae, you deliberately cut Leroy off!"

COMMENT 3: "Joe, when I was telling the story, you were smiling. I'm puzzled."

Not: "Joe, why were you leering at me when I was telling the story?"

sensitive, nonaccusatory way promotes communication. Conversely, feelings that are not expressed may be misinterpreted. Tears, for example, may signify fear, anger, pain, joy, or hay fever. An observer may not be able to identify the cause or may jump to a wrong conclusion.

Many people find it hard to express feelings. Some may believe that they should be tough, "keep a stiff upper lip," and repress their emotions; others—particularly those with low self-esteem—may fear that observers will discount any feelings they show and put them down. But although expressing feelings does involve risk, it is often far better to express them than to allow them to eat away at us or cause us to build resentment against another person.

Often, the purpose of describing feelings is to start a discussion that improves a relationship. People need to know how you feel in order to take your feelings into account: the accusation, "If you loved me, you'd understand!" is seldom fair, for people who are to understand one another and improve their relationships must share their "inner state." In most settings, describing feelings is productive: describing your feelings to another person carries the cryptic message, "I trust you. You are important to me. I need you to understand." It also suggests that "by disclosing myself to you, I create the potential for trust, caring, commitment, growth and self-understanding" (Johnson, 1986). By contrast, unexpressed feelings can impede communication and damage relationships.

To express your feelings accurately, you must be aware of them, accept them, and know how to communicate them effectively. People generally communicate their feelings through verbal statements or through nonverbal actions, or both. You might express your feelings verbally by making an assertion ("I feel very nervous"), by using a metaphor ("I have butterflies in my stomach"), or by stating a preference ("I'd rather run away!"). Nonverbal actions such as sighing, falling silent, turning away, frowning, smiling, or keeping someone waiting can also express feelings, but since it is particularly easy to misinterpret nonverbal actions, it is often better to express feelings verbally. Ignoring negative feelings is like ignoring the low-oil warning light in your car. Serious damage can result!

In any case, it is important to find ways of expressing feelings that do not make other persons feel guilty or coerced. Try always to describe your feelings in a matter-of-fact, information-giving way. It is possible that your feelings have resulted from faulty perceptions. A person you resent may not have intended to hurt or annoy you, and may be quite unaware of the effect of his or her words or actions. Bringing feelings into the open can initiate a problem-solving process and lead to a stronger relationship.

For Example 2.5 provides four illustrations of effective descriptions of feelings.

PRACTICE and Projects

1. a. As a class, play the old "telegraph game" by relaying a message from person to person. The first person in line relays the message to the next person, who relays it to the next, and so on. The last person in line announces to the whole group the message that he or she has received. In a debriefing session, compare the original and final forms of the message, and trace the changes in the message back to the person who first heard it.

    b. Discuss the effect of one-way communication. Review evidence that feelings or emotions are part of all messages.

2. Sit back to back, opposite your partner. One of you will receive a diagram and the other a pencil and paper. As partner A describes the diagram, partner B draws it from A's description. Ask no questions for clarification during this process, but compare the finished diagrams. Debrief on your experience, including your feelings.*

3. Form a triad consisting of a "message sender," a "perception checker," and an observer. The message sender chooses a picture from a magazine, holds the picture up so that the perception checker can see it, and makes a brief statement about it. The checker then states what he or she believes the sender's feeling is about the picture. If the checker's impression is incorrect, the observer makes a perception-checking statement. Each person in turn should take the roles of message sender, perception checker, and observer. Debrief after each round.*

4. Use Data Collection Form 2.2 (Appendix A) to analyze your own or your teaching partner's use of interpersonal skills in teaching a microlab or classroom lesson.

These activities have been adapted from the manual Internship Seminars for Interns and Cooperating Teachers, *by the Faculty of Education, University of Regina, 1988, Regina, SK.*

FOR EXAMPLE 2.5

Feelings Description

SITUATION 1. A blurts out, "Oh, shut up!"

    Better: "I feel angry with you when you …"

       "I feel hurt by what you are saying, and I wish you'd stop."

       "I know what you are going to tell me, and you're right."

               (continued)

(continued)

SITUATION 2. B says, "You shouldn't have done that!"

          Better: "I really like your gift to me."

                  "Your gift makes me feel obligated to you."

                  "I feel mean because I gave you a far smaller gift."

SITUATION 3. C suddenly falls silent.

          Better: "It seems to me that you're putting me down."

                  "What you said reminded me of a close friend who died."

                  "I'm worried about teaching tomorrow's lesson."

SITUATION 4. D accuses, "You're always, always late!"

          Better: "I'm upset with you because I had to wait so long in the cold."

                  "I was worried that something had happened to you."

                  "You won't have time now to pick up the filmstrip we need, and that means I'll have to change my lesson plan."

Group Skills

So far, we have considered primarily the use of one-on-one communication skills. In classroom teaching, however, you will often need to model and teach **group skills**—that is, interpersonal skills that apply to group situations.

BUILDING EFFECTIVE CLASS GROUPS

Effective class groups rarely occur by chance, but you can foster their development by using appropriate teaching methods, prescribing the structure of tasks, monitoring group performance, gently securing or helping to modify group expectations, and promoting trust. Encourage group development by promoting group "togetherness" and sensitivity to individual members' needs, and by intervening, when appropriate, to provide group maintenance activities. Teach your students the interpersonal skills of expressing acceptance and support as they interact, of rejecting nonsupportive self-serving behaviors such as ridicule or blaming, and of seeking ways of working more cooperatively. Encourage them to contribute openly information, ideas, feelings, and reactions, as well as to share resources and materials.

When appropriate, plan learner-centered rather than teacher-centered lessons, helping students to cover the content in as personal a way as possible. Encourage

active participation and productive interaction. Practice supportive listening; use **critical thinking skills**, but accept and support individuals while encouraging group maintenance and development. Provide nonjudgmental feedback on the group's skills practice, productivity, and health, encouraging students to share this responsibility by teaching them how to collect and report group-effectiveness data. Table 2.2 lists activities and interventions that you can use to promote cooperative learning in your classroom.

TEACHING/LEARNING GROUP SKILLS

Most teaching and learning in schools takes place in group settings. Each class group develops a personality of its own, for "the classroom is a complex social system that is affected by many social forces, including friendships, communication patterns, power and influence, perceived leader/group member roles, and peer group norms" (Lang & Scarfe, 1988, p. 227). **Group dynamics** (i.e., the "people power" exercised within a group), which strongly affect **classroom climate**, can help or hinder your teaching and your students' learning. When you ask questions or assign a task, peer friendship patterns and group, subgroup, and individual attitudes, as well as your relationship with individuals, will affect student responses. It is important, therefore, for you to learn about the effects of group processes and dynamics, and to learn, use, and teach the skills of sharing information and encouraging positive and productive interaction.

Teaching effective people skills requires modeling them, for no matter what you *say*, your students will tend to practice what you *do*. To teach and model group skills, therefore, you must foster open and courteous give and take, showing and encouraging originality, spontaneity, and sensitivity to the needs of others. Be sure to set a nonstressful, supportive, emotional tone. Provide opportunities for students to be leaders and followers, exchanging those roles as appropriate to the situation and to the experience required.

You will find that your class group needs to learn and practice various specific group behaviors and skills throughout the term. It is the *consistent* application of communication, trust, leadership, and **conflict resolution** skills that makes a group effective. You should teach these skills as specifically as you teach reading or math skills. Make sure that your students clearly understand what a given skill is, and why they need to learn and practice it until it is part of their repertoire.

Students can help one another to succeed academically and personally. Each group member should be responsible for helping others, who, in turn, are responsible for helping him or her (see Chapter 15). Teachers should stress their expectation that the class will establish a fertile climate for this group support function and carry

TABLE 2.2

Group Activities and Teacher Interventions for Cooperative Learning

Orientation Phase
1. Teacher modeling of the skills and behavior expected of students.
2. Providing get-acquainted activities: making name cards, using peer introductions, and initiating "ice-breaking" games.
3. Describing and expecting the practice of group support for individual growth.
4. Clear description of course/unit/lesson objectives, content, and evaluation.
5. Using teaching methods that require interaction and use of positive norms.
6. Teaching and having the class practice rules and routines.
7. Teaching and providing practice in developing interpersonal and group skills.
8. Introducing and practicing group-monitoring techniques.
9. Using activities (as appropriate) to promote personal disclosure (with students mature enough to exercise discretion).

Group-Maintenance Phase
1. Fostering, as appropriate, further disclosure and openness (with discretion).
2. Using positive, constructive norms.
3. Practicing participation skills such as seeking information, sharing information, listening, interacting, including and encouraging, clarifying, summarizing, and concluding.
4. Extending interpersonal skills.
5. Practicing leadership and participation, and monitoring group effectiveness.
6. Practicing shared leadership, cooperation, and consensus seeking.
7. Practicing brainstorming, buzzing, problem solving, and decision making.
8. Practicing negotiation skills such as listening, proposing, analyzing, diagnosing, interpreting, criticizing, compromising, and resolving conflict.
9. Practicing systematic and nonjudgmental observation, reporting, soliciting/giving and receiving feedback, and interpreting data.

Pre-Termination Phase
1. Recalling and reviewing group experiences and achievements.
2. Identifying acquired individual and group skills.
3. Identifying termination as a phase that leads to future growth.
4. Identifying ways the current group or its members might continue to support one another in the future.

Source: Much of the information in this table is derived from "Group Support during Student Teaching" by H. Lang and D. Scarfe, 1988, in P.Holborn, M. Wideen, and I. Andrews (Eds.), *Becoming a Teacher* (pp. 238–239), Toronto: Kagen and Woo.

it out. When the group "pulls for" the individual and sees that group success is tied to individual successes, self-concepts blossom, and learning tends to increase.

Supportive class groups exercise communication and interpersonal skills to produce trusting and nonjudgmental interchanges. Members are responsible, aware of the effect of their behavior on others, and willing to risk, face, and learn from difficulties and problems. They accept personal differences, and explore problems with sympathy and understanding, sharing their capabilities and combining information from their diverse backgrounds to produce creative solutions (see Chapter 6). They express feelings openly, seeking solutions to problems in an objective and goal-centered (rather than self-centered) manner. They achieve goals and maintain the group by involving each member, valuing contributions, attending to feelings, and resolving conflicts as they monitor and evaluate their own and the group's performance.

Students who learn to exercise effective interpersonal skills feel less threatened, and are less defensive and more comfortable with one another. They learn better because they feel free to participate actively in class; as a result, group interaction increases, and peer influence strengthens, rather than hinders, the individual. As the group develops, its members become more self-disciplined, interact more positively, and participate more spontaneously and actively in discussion. You benefit by developing effective class-management skills; your class benefits from improved self-concepts, greater social maturity, better grades, and better interpersonal and group relationships and skills that will help them, later, to participate more effectively in adult society.

THE ABCs OF CLASS GROUPS

The class group is a *work* group. Effective teacher–student class groups work toward the following goals:

A. *Task achievement*: Academic goals
B. *Group maintenance*: Interpersonal and group skills to strengthen the group
C. *Group effectiveness*: Reacting to changing tasks and to the needs of members and of the group itself.

Task Achievement

Effective and cohesive class groups best achieve common curriculum objectives and academic goals. Various individuals and bodies set these common goals: society in general, school officials, teachers, the student body, a particular class, or one or more individuals. One of a teacher's most difficult tasks is to harmonize a variety of goals. If goal setters differ in their objectives, conflict and trouble can result. To avoid conflict, it is best, when practicable, to discuss with your students what the common classroom goals should be and to try to achieve **consensus** (the support of the group for a common position).

Teachers use academic tasks to help students reach curriculum goals that will promote their achievement of higher academic and employment goals. Group skills required for academic **task achievement** include following directions, asking questions, obtaining and sharing information and ideas, summarizing, checking for understanding, directing the group's attention to matters in hand, and budgeting time.

Group Maintenance

Effective **group maintenance** requires identifying and dealing positively with the feelings and interpersonal relationships of one's class members. Group maintenance skills include active listening, responding to ideas, paraphrasing, sharing feelings, encouraging others, and checking for consensus.

The object of teaching group maintenance skills is to build a strong, cohesive, and stable work group whose members help and support one another in achieving academic tasks. Part of the challenge of group maintenance lies in the fact that membership in some class groups is not voluntary: elementary school students, for example, do not select their class group, though as students move through high school, their choice of options increases. A secondary school class group may have several teachers and programs that provide various social settings. Membership in adult education classes may or may not be fully optional, depending on employers' and the job's requirements.

Group norms. Every group has norms (accepted rules of behavior). Rules established by the teacher may or may not be norms, depending on whether or not the group accepts and follows them. Norms may include the language used in class, the kind of clothing and hair styles worn in school, subjects of conversation, the persons one talks to, and the amount of work students do. Each subgroup within a class group has its own norms that may or may not be identical with class norms. Norms can either facilitate or impede the achievement of curriculum objectives. A student's deviation from accepted norms may lead to disapproval or rejection by group members, a reprimand or punishment by the teacher, or even expulsion by the school board.

Group Effectiveness

Group effectiveness depends, in part, on the group's structure—that is, the patterns of relationships determined by the positions that members in the group occupy. Structure is affected by the following three factors.

Roles. A person's **role** is the sum of the functions that he or she is expected to perform within a group. In a classroom situation, the two major roles—culturally defined but adapted by members of the class—are those of "teacher" and "student." The teacher's role may range from that of knowledge disseminator and disciplinarian to that of learning facilitator and friend. The role of each student may vary from that of competitor to that of helper or cooperative learner.

Status. The **status**, or position, of a group member reflects the degree of influence and power that the group attributes to her or him. Of course, some individuals and subgroups exercise more influence and power than others do. The teacher of a class enjoys the highest formal status and is usually accepted as the group's leader. The way in which the teacher (or other person of high status) behaves toward an individual affects the class's view of that person. If, for example, a teacher shows high regard for a certain student, that student may enjoy a higher status. Alternatively, the teacher's preference may cause resentment, and class members may view the student as a "browner" or "teacher's pet."

Attraction. **Attraction** patterns influence the way individuals interact and communicate and, consequently, affect the extent of their achievement. Attraction determines how much group members like one another and the extent to which they choose to work or play together. Almost every class group has subgroups made up of friends or members of cliques, though some students do not belong to a subgroup. Deliberate effort is needed to build a constructive and cohesive class group. The reward for such effort will be your and your students' productive reactions to the changing needs of individuals and to the group's changing tasks.

MONITORING GROUP WORK

To **monitor** group work effectively, position yourself so that you can see everyone in the room. Be sensitive to indications of off-task behavior, but quietly check before you intervene to see if your observations are correct. Whenever possible, use nonverbal communication to **redirect** students' attention to their task or unobtrusively deter inappropriate behavior (see Chapter 5). When a question is asked, turn it back to the group; trust and value their help. Support and prize the contributions of group members, build on their efforts, and celebrate group successes. Use "probes" (a series of questions to take students step by step through a reasoning process) and "redirects" (passing on a question to the class or to another student), and seek or, if necessary, provide elaboration on student responses (see Chapter 7). Make each learner feel valued by you and the group (see Chapter 6). Remember always that the behavior you model and encourage can make a big difference to the success of group learning.

GROUP DEVELOPMENT STAGES

Class groups tend to move through relatively predictable stages from their first meeting to their last. These typical group development stages progress through the following cycle:

- ✦ *Orientation*: adjusting to the group;
- ✦ *Conflict*: an inherent part of the process of reconciling personal wishes and group demands;
- ✦ *Productivity*: achieving common learning goals;
- ✦ *Termination*: a process of closure, phasing into a new period of orientation.

Orientation

During the group orientation phase, group members may show personal uncertainty and teacher dependency as they try to sort out their roles and identify group norms. Group members are likely to ask themselves, if not others, "Do I want to be here? ... What is expected of me? ... How do I fit? ... Will I make a fool of myself? ... Will the others like me? ... Will I succeed?" Leaders and sources of influence have yet to be identified, but gaining the approval of classmates is important, and individuals may fear disapproval or rejection. Little by little, however, students begin to establish relationships and to participate in group activity, at least tentatively or superficially.

You can promote group development at this stage by recognizing and respecting the needs of your students as individuals. You should provide clear information about class objectives, procedures, and the **evaluation** process. You can help your students get to know and feel comfortable with one another through "icebreaking" and other group activities. Depending on the experience and maturity of the group, you can teach the characteristics of an effective group, its leaders and participants, and have your students discuss and propose norms such as acceptance, openness, empathy, trust, respect, risk taking, and commitment. You should also teach and provide practice in classroom rules and routines.

Conflict

Some anxiety, tension, and disagreement are normal parts of growth in the early period of new group situations. These feelings arise from increased participation and interaction as group members get to know one another better: "Why does *that* bunch do all the talking? ... Why do I and a few others have to do *everything*? ... Nobody cares what *I* think! ... Should I really say what I think? If I do, will I look dumb? ... He's such a nerd! ... What a sucker!"

Individuals may jockey for influence, leadership, and control, and will likely test their leader and one another before they really settle in. Disputes may arise over group and individual responsibilities, individual roles, and group norms, goals, and expectations. Interpersonal differences may occur, and cliques may form. During this period, you should reassure the group that conflict is normal, and emphasize that positive experiences can result from learning how to reconcile differences and resolve disagreements. You may need to identify the underlying dynamics of differences that arise, and deal with these in constructive ways. At first, this may mean helping individuals to recognize and express negative feelings, but the process should lead to more positive feelings and greater group cohesion as you teach and promote the use of interpersonal and group skills, and establish a productive learning climate. In overcoming its conflicts, the group will build a more secure identity and move into a phase of more cohesive development. Ways of working together will emerge, and members will establish cooperative **behavioral norms** (see Chapter 16).

Productivity

As group conflict decreases, group cohesion—the primary characteristic of a well-functioning group—and productivity increase. Class members develop proficiency in attaining goals, and become more flexible and adaptive in their modes of working together. Roles, attraction, status, and norms are established. Common goals are accepted. Members recognize that it is normal to have "ups and downs," but trust is high, and most interpersonal conflicts are handled constructively. Members' attitudes become more positive: "If I have something to say, I don't mind saying it ... Most of the people in this class are OK ... We're one of the best classes in the school!"

Even in this phase, however, group health tends to fluctuate, and members may even revert to the conflict stage. You must intervene, as appropriate, to ensure that potential and actual conflicts are handled constructively. You must continually decide whether task achievement or group maintenance should be stressed at any given point, and facilitate productivity by remaining sensitive to individual and group needs and by reinforcing the use of communication, interpersonal, and group skills.

Termination

As the school year or semester approaches its end, the group approaches its dissolution. If the group has been a healthy one, anxieties, lethargy, and conflicts may surface, and productivity may decrease. There is a time of grieving over the dissolution of a secure support system and of uncertainty about an unknown future: "I really don't want to change classes! ... Do we *have* to? ... Will my friends and I be in the same class next year?"

Early in the life of the group, you should begin to prepare your students for the group termination stage by helping them to see it as a phasing into future interpersonal and group situations (Lang & Scarfe, 1988). Reassure your students that established friendships need not terminate with the group, and help them to see this phase as a maturation process that leads to the formation of future groups and to future growth. To this end, you might have your class review its successful group experiences and identify skills still to be mastered.

PRACTICE *and Projects*

1. List the groups to which you belong. Use the descriptions of group stages provided on pages 46–48 to determine the stage of development of each group.

2. Using a copy of Data Collection Form 2.3: My Behavior in Groups (Appendix A), assess the group membership behavior you normally display.

3. a. Recall a teacher who was particularly effective in establishing a productive class group. List some of the things that teacher did and said that promoted group effectiveness.
   b. Form groups of three. Have each member tell about his or her teacher. As a group, prepare a list of productive teacher behaviors.
   c. Form groups of six to prepare a single list of behaviors that includes all the behaviors your group has listed. Select the twelve most important productive behaviors, combining points where possible.

Source: These activities are derived from the manual *Internship Seminars for Interns and Cooperating Teachers* (1988) by the Faculty of Education, University of Regina, 1988, Regina, SK.

SUMMARY

* Education is a "people business," in which success depends on communication, interpersonal, and group skills that emphasize cooperation.
* In order to become a successful teacher, you must learn more about yourself and others.
* Basic communication skills include body language, speaking, listening, observing, reading, writing, and use of time and space.
* For successful communication, verbal and nonverbal messages must be congruent.

◆ Positive human interactions depend on good interpersonal skills, including listening, paraphrasing, perception checking (to help you understand others), and nonjudgmental description of behavior and feelings (to help others understand you).

◆ Teachers can foster effective class groups by using appropriate teaching methods, prescribing the structure of tasks, monitoring group performance, gently securing and/or modifying group expectations, and promoting trust.

◆ Effective class groups cooperatively pursue task achievement, group maintenance, and group effectiveness.

◆ Class groups have a predictable life span, progressing through consecutive stages of orientation, conflict, productivity, and termination. Effective teachers help students to prepare for, work through, and accept the termination of these stages as preparation for the next phase of their education or life experience.

KEY WORDS

communication
    nonverbal (body
        language)
    verbal
communication
    congruence
description of
    behavior, feelings
development
    affective

cognitive
psychomotor
group
    task achievement
    maintenance
    effectiveness
    orientation
    conflict
    productivity
    termination

RECOMMENDED READING

Brammer, L. (1985). *The helping relationship: Process and skills* (3rd ed.). Englewood Cliffs, NJ: Prentice-Hall.

Civikly, J. (1992). *Classroom communication: Principles and practice*. Dubuque, IA: Wm. C. Brown.

Kagan, S. (1992). *Cooperative learning*. San Juan Capistrano, CA: Resources for Teachers.

Knapp, M. (1972). *Nonverbal human communication*. New York: Holt, Rinehart & Winston.

CHAPTER 3

PLANNING FOR TEACHING

■ ■ ■ ■ ■

If teachers are to make a significant difference, they must know what they want their students to accomplish.

(TENBRINK, 1986)

■ ■ ■ ■ ■

OVERVIEW

In the teaching/learning cycle, successful lessons rarely "just happen." Such lessons are generally the result of careful planning for the three major phases of effective lessons—set (motivation), development/delivery, and closure—which should flow naturally from one into another. This planning evolves from an orderly review of learning objectives and instructional procedures, and includes choosing and analyzing appropriate topics.

As an effective teacher, you will begin your planning by writing lesson objectives that specify what learners should know or be able to do as a result of your lesson. Starting from this point, you will consider how to motivate your students to learn about a particular topic. You may choose from three different kinds of motivation (learning "set"): orientation, transition, and evaluation.

In planning a lesson's development, you must take into account three domains of learning: cognitive (intellectual: see Chapters 8 and 10), psychomotor (relating to intellectually directed physical skills: see Chapter 9), and affective (relating to values and attitudes: see Chapter 11).

To create and maintain students' interest, you should involve them as actively as possible in your lesson delivery. Delivering a lesson involves making presentations that establish set (motivate), link the sequential parts, maintain students' attention by engaging them in activities, keep them on task, evaluate and give feedback on their task performance, provide appropriate closure, and encourage them to reflect on and learn from their own performance. It also includes modeling and teaching effective people skills (see Chapters 2 and 15).

You will vary your delivery through shifts in focus (directing attention), movement, sense interaction (providing experiences that call for seeing, hearing, touching, smelling, or tasting), and pausing (using silence).

Budgeting time and setting a mental alarm clock to allow for a stimulating closure can give you and your students significant satisfaction. You can use this procedure to highlight key ideas, and to reinforce, synthesize, and summarize information.

■ ■ ■ ■ ■

PLANNING A LESSON

"Prepare a lesson plan for ... !"

Does planning a lesson—any lesson—seem a daunting assignment? "So little time to plan! So many things to think of! So much classroom time to fill!" **Lesson planning** *is* a complex procedure that must take into account both teaching and learning components, and for that reason it is important that you see and understand how these components fit together. Figure 3.1 illustrates the congruence, or fit, of the various elements that provide the foundation of lesson planning.

Identifying Instructional Objectives

Before you can teach a successful lesson, you must determine what you want your students to know as a result of your teaching. In other words, effective lesson planning begins with identifying **instructional objectives**, also referred to as *instructional goals*, *learning goals*, and *learning objectives*, terms that professional educators use to signify the knowledge and/or skills they wish students to acquire as a result of participating in a lesson.

Since even the most skillful of teachers cannot look directly into their students' minds, the most practical way to identify learning objectives is to decide what your students should be able to *show you they can do*, through specific behaviors and performance, when they have participated in a lesson. Thus, professional teachers think of learning objectives in terms of observable student behaviors and performance, and the statements they prepare describing them are called **behavioral objectives**.

FIGURE 3.1

Congruence in Lesson Planning

CONGRUENCE

Course Objectives

Unit Objectives

Lesson Objectives
(Outcomes)

Instructional Procedures

Evaluation Procedures

CONGRUENCE

⑤

By reflecting on Figure 3.1, you will realize that every lesson plan can be based on a careful review of sequential objectives and procedures that help the planner to arrange and deliver lesson elements in a logical order.

Preparing Instructional Objectives

Useful instructional objectives are clear statements that specify the knowledge, skills, or attitudes and the level of performance that students should be able to demonstrate as a result of one instructional session. As you begin to identify instructional objectives, you will find it helpful to classify them as primarily cognitive, psychomotor/procedural, or affective. In preparing instructional objectives, be sure, as well, to specify three components:

- ◆ the content you wish your students to learn;
- ◆ the conditions (such as the time and materials required) that will help them show their grasp of the content;
- ◆ the degree of learning you expect them to achieve.

WRITING INSTRUCTIONAL OBJECTIVES

To organize your thoughts into clear and specific statements, you should write out your lesson objectives. Your focus should be on your students' responsive behavior and observable behavior. Do not be satisfied with stating what you wish your students to learn, or how they should think or feel. Such statements are too vague to support evaluation of your lesson or your student's learning.

Be certain, too, to distinguish instructional objectives from **learning activities**. Learning activities are those actions or experiences in which you will have your students engage in order to learn content or practice a skill or develop values and attitudes. Figure 3.2 demonstrates the difference between activities and objectives. Responsive behavior demonstrates that those activities have paid off in the achievement of knowledge, skill performance, or acting out of values or attitudes.

Evidence shows that, although writing objectives is hard work, it produces a number of advantages: better instruction, more efficient learning, and more accurate evaluation of both teacher and student performance.

PROFESSIONAL DEVELOPMENT OBJECTIVES

Besides aiming to ensure that your students will achieve the topic-related lesson objectives that you set, you should also aim to practice a professional development target. Your lesson plan should record this target, along with a plan for achieving it that is just as specific as your plan to achieve your topic-related target. If, for example, your professional development target is the equal distribution of questions, try to express more than a good intention such as, "I shall try to spread my questions to all parts of the room, and direct them to as many students as possible." Instead, specify a definite procedure such as, "I shall use a

FIGURE 3.2

Distinguishing between Activities and Objectives

Activities	*Objectives*
#1 "Students will view a film on pollution and record key causes of pollution in their notebooks."	#1 "After viewing and discussing a film about pollution, all students will be able to list in their notebooks the key causes of pollution."
#2 "Students will read three short Native American legends and discuss the significance of Native American cultures."	#2 "After reading three short Native American legends and holding small-group discussions on their significance, each student will be able to list three reasons why legends are important in Native American cultures."

seating chart and place a check mark beside the name of each student to whom I direct a question."

Your microteaching-lab instructors and cooperating teachers will expect you to present and discuss written lesson plans with them before you microteach a lesson. Only when you have made this practice routine should you begin to make your written plans more concise.

Preparing Detailed Lesson Plans

Once you have observed the relation between instructional objectives and particular lesson plans, you will find it helpful to follow a procedure for preparing detailed plans that helps you think through each lesson's essential elements, identifying and considering these elements in the order of their use. Figure 3.3 illustrates an approach to lesson planning that stresses the key steps and factors of this procedure.

CHOOSING A LESSON TOPIC

Course or unit objectives, which are usually laid down in prescribed curricula, form a frame on which lesson topics should be hung. But these objectives, though

FIGURE 3.3

Framing a Lesson Plan

1. Set: advance organizers or outline or general principles or questions	4. Frequent checks for student understanding to ensure mastery
2. Brief description of learning objectives and new or key concepts	5. Closure: review of main points and how they fit together
3. Presentation of material in small, organized, sequenced steps	6. Follow up with questions or provide assignment for understanding and application of learnings

Source: Adapted from *Educational Psychology: A Realistic Approach* (3rd ed.) (pp. 219–220) by T.L. Good and J.E. Brophy, 1986, New York: Longman. Adapted by permission.

necessary guiding principles, may be stated in terms too general to help you plan specific lessons. Your first step in preparing to teach a lesson, therefore, will be to choose a topic that relates to a particular unit: you might, for example, decide to teach a lesson on "horses" as part of a unit on "mammals" prescribed in a science curriculum.

If you are asked to choose a lesson topic, you will find ideas easy to come by: you might find your topic in a curriculum outline, a student text, or a demonstration lesson that you have observed; a film or other media product might suggest a topic; or a test framed to assess students' progress might indicate a need for a lesson on a particular point or procedure. Whatever its source, the lesson topic you choose will help you to determine the instructional objectives of your lesson.

FRAMING LESSON OBJECTIVES

Once you have chosen a topic, the most practical way for you to begin preparing a lesson plan is at the "far end" of the process: in other words, with the lesson objectives. To establish these objectives, try asking yourself, "What do I want my students to know as a result of this lesson? What skills do I want them to master? What values, attitudes, and appreciation do I want them to acquire?" These are the broad "landscape" questions that should frame lesson plans.

Topic-Related Objectives

When you have answered the landscape questions, ask yourself a number of more detailed ones. These might include the following.

Points to ponder ...

- ❏ How will the lesson I plan to teach fit the course and unit of study?
- ❏ How will I begin the lesson? develop it? conclude it?
- ❏ How will I determine whether my students have acquired the knowledge and skills objectives that I have identified?

Your answers to these questions will help you to select specific content and to target student learning and skills objectives; they should also help you to choose appropriate presentation strategies and methods, student activities, and evaluation techniques. Therefore, they should also specify the working conditions (such as time and materials available) that relate to these factors. All this information will help you decide on your time allocation, lesson structure and pacing, methods of monitoring student activities, expected success rate, means of evaluation, and ways to obtain feedback.

Data Collection Form 3.1 (Appendix A) will help you develop a format for your early lesson plans. Attach a copy to your lesson plan, and provide a copy for your teaching partner and/or the cooperating teacher who will be observing and assisting you. Though you may feel awkward and slow in your early attempts to write instructional objectives, it is worth the effort to persevere. Objectives well planned are evaluation half planned!

PLANNING LESSON CONTENT

In planning your early lessons, define carefully the material that you intend to cover. Keep your lesson content simple, but remember that **content** represents a broad range of learning objectives, and that, as your experience increases, so will your perceptions of its importance and your plans for its use. To help your students reach the learning goals you have planned, you must always choose content that is meaningful and logically organized. Consider your students' developmental levels, and remember that content should challenge but not frustrate learners.

Identify Prerequisite Learnings

Review your lesson objectives to identify all the prerequisite learnings—prior knowledge or skills—that your students must have in order to learn the content you are planning to teach. If you do not know whether your students already have this knowledge or these skills, you should use some form of inquiry or pretest to determine how basic your lesson introduction should be. This is important, since you can lead your students into further knowledge or skills *only by beginning at the point where they are*, not at the point where they are supposed to be.

Set Level of Student Performance

To meet your professional development targets, you will need to describe your students' degree of success (i.e., level of performance) in meeting the learning objectives set. The key to describing performance successfully is to use verbs that express observable action. Verbs such as *understand, know, comprehend, learn, remember, evaluate, feel, value,* and *appreciate* do not describe *observable* action. By contrast, verbs such as *list, name, select, write, draw, outline, match, pronounce, solve,* and *form* record performance that is easy to observe and evaluate.

Set Conditions of Student Performance

Part of establishing objectives is determining the conditions under which your students will perform. Conditions relate to the circumstances governing students and to the nature of the materials students use when they perform the procedures prescribed for attaining the objectives.

Think out the conditions and contexts associated with your lesson objectives. To express these conditions clearly and specifically, ask yourself the question, "Under what circumstances is the objective to be performed?" The answer to this question often relates to the information or materials that you will provide for your students. For Example 3.1 focuses on conditions for meeting objectives.

PRACTICE *and Projects*

1. List the letters identifying the following statements. Write "V" beside the letters of the statements that include verbs describing observable student performance.
   a. Students will name the capital cities of the European countries.
   b. Students will appreciate Mozart operas.
   c. Students will know how to subtract two-digit numbers.
   d. Students will match the anmes of athletes with athletes' pictures.
   e. Students will know the sounds symbolized by *b* and *v*.
   f. Students will list the causes of the War of 1812.
   g. Students will remember how an internal combustion engine works.

2. List the letters identifying the following statements. Write "C" beside the letters of the statements that identify the conditions (or givens) for meeting objectives.
   a. Students will know how to prepare a Caesar salad.

(continued)

(continued)

　　b. As students view twelve slides showing foreign cars, they will write the brand name of the car in each slide on a slip of paper with twelve numbered blank spaces.

　　c. Students will identify upper- and lower-case letters of the alphabet.

　　d. When provided with a diagram of a human hand, students will label the various bones.

　　e. Students will appreciate the complexities of the rules of the game of tennis and the tennis strokes.

　　f. As they write a paragraph containing five or more sentences, students will enter the appropriate punctuation.

　　g. Given a list of words, students will identify the adjectives.

3.　Identify the performance objectives, conditions, and degree of sources targeted in each of the following instructions.

　　a. Given a diagram of a human eye, students, in three meintes or less, will correctly label 75 percent of its principal parts, including the cornea, iris, pupil, retina, lens, vitreous body, optic nerve, and fovea.

　　b. When given an exercise containing ten sentences, students will underline the subject of each sentence. They will correctly identify at least eight.

　　c. When given, in order of occurrence, the names of five incidents that took place during the Riel Rebellion, students will be able to list the significant events for which those incidents are known and identify at least two contributing factors for four of the five.

4.　Rewrite the following instructional objectives to state clearly the performance objectives, conditions, and degree of success targeted.

　　a. Students will be able to recognize the topic sentences of paragraphs.

　　b. Students will know the different kinds of triangles.

　　c. Students will appreciate the pros and cons of free trade.

　　d. Students will cover the causes of acid rain.

　　e. Students will know the fundamentals of cross-skiing.

　　f. Students will be able to write good footnotes.

　　g. Students will enjoy reading Canadian poetry.

　　h. Students will cover the different kinds of clouds: cirrus, stratus, cumulus, and nimbus.

　　i. Students will be less prejudiced against ＿＿＿＿＿＿ (Name a minority group).

　　j. Students will show fair play at the next basketball game.

FOR EXAMPLE 3.1

Conditions for Meeting Objectives

Students will serve a tennis ball **[performance objective]** into the serving area **[condition]**, six times out of then **[level of performance]**, using the American twist style **[condition]**, and without presence of a receiving player **[condition]**.

Now consider the following instructional objectives listed by a teacher-in-training:

EXAMPLE 1. "Given ten newspaper advertisements, students will name the nature of the emotional appeal in each ad."

EXAMPLE 2. "Students will name the emotions appealed to in newspaper ads."

EXAMPLE 3. "On a map of Canada showing provincial borders, students will mark and label the capital cities of the ten provinces. They will complete this task within ten minutes."

Examples 1 and 3 outline conditions for meeting the stated objective.

Why would you not find Example 2 useful as it stands? Could you salvage Example 2 by rewriting it? If so, how?

■ ■ ■ ■ ■

SETTING THE SCENE

Once you have planned your lesson objectives and content, you should consider a number of practical factors that will help you to deliver the content smoothly and your students to achieve the learning objectives you have identified.

Selecting Teaching Aids

As an addendum to your lesson plan, you should list the teaching or demonstrating aids (e.g., overhead or movie projector, charts, models, maps, texts) and student learning materials that your plan calls for. You should also note your plans for obtaining equipment, practicing its use as necessary, and distributing student materials as required. Jot down a reminder to yourself to check in advance that suitable teaching/learning areas will be available for your use.

Planning Set

Planning lesson **set** (or finding a way to "turn students on" to particular learnings) gives you an opportunity to motivate your students to learn new information or skills and to discover their significance. Inducing a positive set should be a deliberate part of your lesson planning, for students whose teachers are skillful in **set induction** learn more and retain their learning longer. Think of ways to catch your students' interest and to forge positive links between the new material you plan to teach and what they have already learned.

Planning Presentation

Advice on making an effective presentation can be compared to the advice often given for delivering a good speech: "Tell your listeners what you are going to tell them. Tell them. Tell them what you have told them."

To plan your presentation, list in sequence what observable actions your students will perform to achieve the objectives you have set. Consider and choose the teaching methods you will use to present your lesson (Chapters 4–15). Plan to provide opportunities, too, for checking your students' understanding of the lesson you will teach, for encouraging students to participate directly by engaging in appropriate activities, and for practicing what they will learn. You will find Data Collection Forms 3.1 and 3.2 useful for organizing your lesson plans, and for recording those plans as they relate to your presentation, your students' performance objectives, and your professional targets.

Planning for Data Collection and Feedback

Data collection and feedback are important parts of the teaching/learning cycle. Make arrangements to provide for these elements, both in practice-teaching sessions and later on in your own classroom.

You may use Data Collection Form 3.1 to record your observations and give feedback on the evidence of planning in microteaching-lab and classroom lessons that you observe. When you receive a teaching assignment, arrange to share your lesson plans with your lab or classroom partner(s) and your instructor or the cooperating teacher. Remember that your lesson plans and the feedback you receive on their use will form an important part of your professional journal entries.

Planning Evaluation

Evaluation is an important factor both in teaching and in personal development. Throughout your teacher-training course, you will benefit by planning for continuous, in-progress evaluation of your own teaching and your students' learning (performance) (see Chapter 17). To evaluate productively the lessons you teach, you will need to listen carefully to the feedback provided by your peers and instructors, and to spend time in reflection. To provide feedback to your students and evaluate their performance, you should use periodic question-and-answer check-ups, solicit student contributions, ask students to display their work, and move about the room as students are working to monitor their performance by watching for nonverbal clues such as a quizzical look, frown, smile, or nod, and provide help as needed. You will also give a test occasionally or ask students to hand in completed worksheets.

Planning Closure

Allot sufficient time for **closure** (bringing your lesson to a productive end), to leave your students with a sense of satisfaction in what they have accomplished. Use their satisfaction to promote interest in future activities and experiences that will relate in some way to the lesson they have just completed.

Adjusting Your Lesson Plan

The outline above is not meant to imply that you should always follow exactly the same steps in planning a lesson, for lesson planning is rarely that linear or lockstep a process. The important point is that your finished lesson plan should contain all the elements that apply, and that all these elements be congruent (fit logically) with one another.

Remember, too, that you will not always be able to follow rigidly the lesson plan that you have prepared. At times, circumstances will dictate that you revise your lesson plans on the spot to meet students' needs. Be prepared to deviate from a lesson plan *for good reason*. You may discover, for example, that your students have not mastered prerequisite learnings to the degree that you had anticipated, that an activity may not be producing the required result, or that your class is covering the activities you have planned faster than you had estimated. None of these discoveries will be reason for panic if you have considered them as possibilities and have "overplanned" accordingly.

PRACTICE *and Projects*

1. a. While your instructor teaches a model lesson of about ten minutes in length, think about the various parts of the lesson and the planning that they required. At the close of the lesson, try to identify the essential lesson elements and "discover" the preplanning that was needed.

    b. Join a subject-specialization group. Working with your group, choose a simple topic relating to your special subject. Design a lesson plan, including a suitable professional target.

    c. Choose a representative to describe your lesson plan to the rest of the class. Ask for questions, comments, and constructive suggestions.

2. a. Working with your teaching partner, plan, prepare, and teach a lesson to your microteaching-lab group that targets inclusion of the lesson elements described above.

    b. As soon as possible, teach a classroom lesson, using the same target.

■ ■ ■ ■ ■

DELIVERING A LESSON: FROM SET TO CLOSURE

There are, of course, many types of lessons, and many ways to organize them, but teachers of effective lessons usually

- ◆ induce set by beginning with a memorable **focusing** event, and previewing what is to come;
- ◆ present new information or procedures sequentially, and link them logically to familiar content, making frequent checks for student understanding, and providing opportunities for student participation and practice;
- ◆ close with a statement or event that "pulls things together," summarizes learnings, and points out what students have achieved.

The following sections will discuss the elements that are common to delivery of a lesson.

Inducing Set

"Where did we leave off yesterday? ... Turn back to page 87, and we'll go on from there ... Open your texts at Chapter 3 on page 99." The teacher who hopes to interest students in the subjects he or she is teaching will seldom, if ever, introduce a lesson in this way. Bored or disgruntled students who have no chance to observe their teacher's enthusiasm for a subject or hear comments on the purpose or expected outcomes of a lesson are likely to wonder, "Why do I have to study this stuff? When will I ever need it? What good is it?"

Your lesson introductions should "grab" your students' interest and induce a positive set that will motivate and facilitate learning. You should use set induction to

- orient your students to new material and focus their attention on the lesson;
- create a framework in which your students can organize the information or skills that you will present;
- encourage your students' involvement in the lesson;
- help your students to make the transition from known to new material by using examples and analogies (parallel cases);
- promote your students' interest and involvement in the lessons that will follow.

ADAPTING SET

It is clear that you should induce set at the beginning of your lessons, but lessons often have a number of parts, or stages, and students can benefit from a positive set (focusing, previewing, and linking) as they begin each segment. Use set induction at appropriate points to send your class messages that you are interested in and value the content of your lessons, and that you feel positively about your students and their achievements, and are confident that they can and will continue to succeed.

To introduce a lesson segment, teachers generally choose one of three basic kinds of set: orientation, transition, and evaluation.

Orientation Set

The purpose of establishing an **orientation set** is to create a receptive attitude for the introduction of new material, to focus students' attention, and to motivate them to learn. An orientation set can also make students more receptive to lesson objectives by stimulating them to visualize new content or participate willingly in new activities. You might use an activity, event, puzzle, anecdote or joke, illustration, map, chart, or object to interest and motivate your students.

Transition Set

By inducing **transition set**, teachers predispose students to link information or skills that they already know to elements of the new content that they are about to learn, thus bolstering their confidence that they will continue to succeed as they advance. Transition set relies primarily on analogies, examples, or interesting and familiar activities to introduce new information.

Evaluation Set

In inducing **evaluation set**, you will be preparing your students for—and involving them in—review and/or assessment of newly acquired knowledge and skills. To determine the degree to which students have grasped the lesson content, you will use questions, quizzes, tests, and activities that are heavily student-centered or -generated. You should also use evaluation set to remind your students of what they have already accomplished.

Developing a Lesson

After you have induced positive set, you are ready to develop your lesson. Lesson development creates possibilities for you to function as an "organizer of success experiences," providing your students with opportunities to win a series of small successes by guiding and supporting them as they learn.

INVOLVE STUDENTS ACTIVELY

Students should be as actively involved as possible throughout the lesson, and confident about themselves and their accomplishments. To ensure their—and your—confidence and success, you must develop effective instructional skills (see Chapters 7–15) and class management procedures (see Chapter 5), and choose appropriate resources and teaching aids, teaching strategies and methods, student activities, and evaluation procedures. You cannot, of course, attend immediately to all these aspects of developing successful lessons, but you can be confident that as you continue to "teach for learning," you will develop professionally from observing your instructors' and cooperating teachers' modeling of teaching techniques, your microteaching-lab and classroom teaching experiences (see Chapter 1), and the textbook and library resources available to you.

VARY PRESENTATION

Think of a class that, as a student, you always looked forward to and enjoyed. How did your teacher gain and hold your attention? In contrast to teachers in whose classes you were often bored, this teacher probably varied the way she presented different segments of the lesson, appealing to a variety of your senses. She would have moved about the room, varied her manner of speaking and the length of pauses she made, used visuals and other types of teaching aids, had you handle materials, asked questions, encouraged you to interact with your peers, and—to vary the pace and method of learning—organized times for listening, speaking, and writing.

By contrast, you may have had instructors who remained at the front of the room, droning on and on and on or, worse still, mumbling incessantly from a set of notes on which they steadily focused their gaze. They used no visuals, rarely interacted with the students—expecting them just to sit and listen—and did not encourage them to interact with one another. Their presentation never varied: the stimulus—if it existed—was constant. The result was boredom.

The effective teacher creates interest through careful planning "designed to develop and maintain a high level of student attention during the course of a lesson by varying the presentation" (Shostak, 1982, p. 121). He or she knows how and when to vary stimulus in order to direct and keep students' attention on the lesson, emphasize key points and provide refreshing changes of pace, facilitate learning, and promote retention and transfer of new content.

Varying your mode of presentation is important for the following reasons:

◆ Students—particularly young children, but older children and adults as well—tend to remain interested in listening, watching, or performing an activity only for a limited period of time. A wise old sociology professor used to say, "If you don't strike oil after five or ten minutes, quit boring."

◆ People receive information through all their senses. We have learned about 1 percent of what we know through taste, 2 percent through touch, 4 percent through smell, 10 percent through hearing, and 83 percent through sight. In learning, we retain 10 percent of what we read, 20 percent of what we hear, 30 percent of what we see, 50 percent of what we hear *and* see, 70 percent of what we say, and 90 percent of what we say *and* do simultaneously (Murgio, 1969). Obviously, then, a multisensory approach to learning increases learners' retention.

◆ For a variety of reasons, including previous experience and cultural background, we all have preferred learning styles (see Chapter 1). Individual learning-style preferences vary in every group of students. Therefore, a teacher who varies the presentation of subject matter reaches and interests more students.

Depending on your students' background, some presentations should be highly concrete, or "hands-on," to promote **enactive (participatory) learning**; others should involve the use of pictures or other visual materials, to promote **iconic learning** (learning related to visual images); and still others should involve the use of spoken or written language or other symbols, to promote **symbolic learning**. These three "levels" of learning form a useful step-by-step learning process. Remember, however, that using a symbolic mode of teaching before students have learned through a concrete mode (using "hands-on" materials) or a pictorial mode may well be a waste of your time and theirs.

◆ Variety for the sake of variety is unproductive in many situations, but in selecting **teaching/learning** strategies, variety pays dividends. The superiority of one teaching strategy or method over another has not been demonstrated, but it is known that the use of a variety of strategies and methods increases learning. Students of all ages are bound to become bored in an unchanging environment.

CASE STUDY **3.1**

VARYING LESSON PRESENTATION

Miss Chadwick is teaching a Grade 2 class to count by fives. She asks the children to move to the carpeted area at the back of the classroom, where she has set up a stand that displays a 1–100 chart.

When she has made sure that all the children can see the chart, she tells them what the lesson will be about and explains that it is important to know how to count by fives because it makes telling time and counting money quicker and easier. Then, pointing to the chart, Miss Chadwick shows how, when counting by fives, she uses the fifth number, finding and circling each. When she has circled several fifth numbers, she asks the children, "What number comes next? ... How do you know?"

After the children have identified several more numbers in the "fives" progression, Miss Chadwick says, "I'm going to ask you a question. I want you to think hard and put up your hands when you have an answer. Close your eyes and listen while I read the numbers we have circled. Listen for a pattern."

As Miss Chadwick reads "5, 10 ... 40," hands begin to go up. After pausing a few seconds, Miss Chadwick asks Manuel to describe the pattern. Manuel says that the pattern is made up of numbers ending in 5, then 0, then 5, then 0.

"How may of you agree with Manuel?" Miss Chadwick asks. The children raise their hands, and several nod, as well. "Can anyone guess what the next number will be?" She selects Tanya from many volunteers to give the answer. The class then identifies the rest of the numbers on the chart.

Miss Chadwick asks the children to let their left hand be the " '5' numbers" and their right hand be the " '0' numbers." As the children, in unison, count by fives to 100, they are to raise their hands alternately, keeping time together. They then move into a circle, and each becomes a living part of a "counting by fives" procedure by putting up their left hand, then their right hand, in turn. One child says "5, 10," the next says "15, 20," the next "25, 30," and so on, to 100.

(continued)

(continued)

Next, Miss Chadwick asks the children to form pairs.

"I see that you can all count by fives," she says. "In your pair, think of a way to count by fives so that each partner is doing some counting. It's important to count correctly, and you should help each other with that. See if you can think of a way to share the counting."

One pair alternates numbers; another does two numbers each; another does a pattern of three numbers, then one: "5, 10, 15" "20" "25, 30, 35" "40," and so on. After a few minutes, Miss Chadwick asks several pairs to show the class how they shared the counting. To close the lesson, the children work at their desks on a dot-to-dot activity that provides individual practice in counting by fives.

VARY STIMULI

Your professional repertoire should include a number of **stimulus variation** techniques. These techniques all relate to the skill of focusing (deliberately controlling the direction of) a learner's attention.

Focusing

Have you ever walked down a city street and seen someone staring up at a tall building? Did *you* look up, as well? This method of focusing someone's attention probably works with most people. It is even easier to rouse another person's curiosity and focus his or her attention by pointing. Among the means you can use to focus others' attention are

- ◆ your voice, with its variations in audibility, tone, and emphasis;
- ◆ audio equipment;
- ◆ pictures, charts, maps, print materials, chalkboard materials, films;
- ◆ movement, gestures, facial expressions;
- ◆ blocks, rods, models, displays, and other concrete teaching materials, many of which can be examined visually, handled, smelled;
- ◆ silence.

Making Statements

Giving clear directions (see Chapter 9) helps students to focus. To provide this help and clarify students' understanding, try the following:

◆ *Support statements with gestures.*   Gestures can carry messages that reinforce the spoken word and stimulate imagination. You might use a pointer to show your students, *"This* is the direction in which the water will flow," or bring your hand gently down from above your head while saying, "The glider gently followed the air currents and landed on the ground."

◆ *Use movement* **(kinesthetic variation).** The eye tends to be attracted to and follow movement. Skillful directors make effective use of movement in plays or movies to draw attention, hold interest, and emphasize key aspects of plot development. Effective teachers move smoothly, freely, and purposefully to various parts of the classroom. Their movement focuses their students' attention and improves communication. They also involve their students in movement when this is practicable.

◆ *Shift sense stimuli.* Students' ability to take in and process information increases significantly when the senses of sight, hearing, and touch are shifted (used in combination or in sequence). You might shift sense stimuli during the course of a lesson by

- ◆ explaining a dance step, demonstrating it, and then having students practice it;
- ◆ showing a transparency on a screen, turning the projector off to comment, showing the transparency once more, turning the projector off again, and having students sketch what they have seen;
- ◆ telling students about the differences in texture between wool and silk, having them feel samples of the two materials, and then describing the differences more specifically;
- ◆ telling your students about sound waves, demonstrating by means of a tuning fork and a pith ball on a string, and then using a diagram on the chalkboard to explain the principle involved.

Shifting Interactions

A teacher who lectures without involving students promotes no overt interaction. When he directs a question to the class rather than to specific students, he centers the interaction on himself. When he directs questions to specific students, he involves them directly in the development of the lesson, using teacher-directed (not teacher-centered) interaction. When a teacher redirects a student's question from himself to another student, the focus of interaction shifts from teacher to students.

Using Questions

By using questions and answers to shift interactions, you will involve your students more actively in their lessons (see Chapter 7). Students pay closer attention if they are likely to be asked a question because they enjoy interacting with one another and helping to develop the lesson. Peers sometimes perceive one another's feelings or problems more quickly than do adults, and explain things to one another better at their own level than a teacher can. Such "at-task" peer interaction can be highly motivating (see Chapter 13).

Pausing or Silence

Though everyone has heard the proverb "Silence is golden," some teachers seem to believe that they are failing to earn their salary unless they are constantly talking. By contrast, entertainers have long known the value of the dramatic pause. You, too, can learn to use pauses very effectively during the course of a lesson to

◆ emphasize an important point and let it "sink in";
◆ promote comprehension by breaking information into smaller parts;
◆ create a dramatic effect such as inducing suspense;
◆ provide time for students to think a process through before they respond;
◆ promote class participation by providing the opportunity for more students to add comments or ask questions;
◆ draw attention to a statement by using silence as contrast;
◆ give students time to make notes while lecturing or dictating;
◆ show disapproval of minor disruptions (see Chapter 5);
◆ recognize and participate in the multicultural nature of the class (see Chapter 6).

PROMOTE TRANSFER

As you begin to teach, you will soon find that promoting transfer—that is, the adaptation of information or skills learned in one context to a new context—is helpful to students. "Telling" students information is rarely enough to make it available for transfer. You can promote transfer by checking to make sure that students understand what they are learning; by identifying the general circumstances and/or particular aspects and attributes that make a situation what it is; by providing enough practice so that students "overlearn" (easily remember and use) information or skills; by pointing out the similarities and differences between two or more items or contexts; and by having students practice transfer.

PRACTICE *and Projects*

1. a. Join a subject-specialization group to brainstorm examples of each kind of **stimulus variation** outlined above.
    b. Working with the same group, write and present a case study of your own, illustrating stimulus variation. Ask the rest of your class to observe and to collect data, using Data Collection Form 3.3 (Appendix A). Your instructor may ask specific questions relating to this procedure.

PROVIDE CLOSURE

Closure consists of the statements or actions you use to bring a lesson to a productive conclusion. Its purpose is to "help students bring things together in their own minds, to make sense out of what has been going on" (Shostak, 1986, p. 128). You should plan for closure that provides time for students to review what they have learned, enjoy a feeling of accomplishment, grasp new insights or connections, or project links between material that they have just learned and what they will learn in the next lesson.

Closure can consist of or combine three aspects of learning experience: review, transfer, and serendipity. **Review closure** can "tie up" a lesson or lesson segment concisely, by drawing students' attention to the major points and their sequence or to the closing point; by summarizing discussion; or by relating the lesson to a concept or generalization taught earlier.

You can use **transfer closure** to reinforce or consolidate learnings, encouraging your students to apply content learned in new contexts. Draw your students' attention to a closing point and facilitate transfer by providing for the point's immediate practice; then ask your students to apply the point to other contexts or to develop new knowledge from it.

Serendipity closure is based on a "natural" but unplanned opportunity that allows you to close a lesson productively near the end of the allotted time. A particularly apt student response or key question, an unusual event, or a sudden insight that occurs to you might provide a fitting opportunity for serendipity closure.

Plan to have your students participate actively in a lesson's closure rather than simply listening to a long summary. You might include in closure two instructional procedures: overview (a capsule of the framework) and practice (application or repetition). You might also have your students recall the main ideas presented or, occasionally, challenge them to consider what they have learned and be prepared to discuss it at the beginning of the next lesson. After closure, you might assign homework.

Try to organize all the segments of your lesson so that you do not "run out of time" and have to race through closure or omit it entirely, for closure is a very important part of a successful lesson.

You may use Data Collection Form 3.4 (Appendix A) for recording data relating to set and closure.

PRACTICE *and Projects*

1. Watch your instructor or cooperating teacher deliver a model lesson that illustrates set, development, and closure.

2. a. Working with a subject-specialization group, brainstorm esamples of orientation, transition, and evaluation set induction.
   b. In the same group, brainstorm examples of review, transfer, and serendipity closures.

3. Using Data Collection Form 3.4 (Appendix A), analyze Case Study 3.2. Your instructor may ask specific questions as you proceed.

4. Working with a subject-specialization group, choose a topic and design a lesson plan that has an appropriate and motivating set, an interesting development, and an effective closure. Your plan must flow smoothly from one phase to the next. Be prepared to describe your plan to your class, and ask the members to identify the kind of set and closure chosen.

5. a. Plan and microteach a lesson that targets appropriate set, development, and closure.
   b. Plan and teach a classroom lesson with the same targets.

CASE STUDY 3.2

SET AND CLOSURE

Orientation

coop

Ms. Holmberg began her lesson on stereotyping, discrimination, and racism by dividing her Grade 11 Social Studies class into five numbered groups of six. As the groups were forming, she wrote on the chalkboard the headings "Black," "Indian (North American)," "Japanese," "Spanish," and "White."

Transitions *Link to prior* 4. "You remember the rules for brainstorming," she began. "When it's your turn to speak, just state whatever comes to mind. Each group will start with the heading on the chalkboard that has the same number I've given the group. You'll have ten minutes to brainstorm all the characteristics of the people mentioned in your heading. Choose a recorder to record the points your group mentions. Use the space under your heading on the chalkboard, and write so that the people in the back row can read."

Jason raised his hand. "Ms. Holmberg, should we say anything that's not nice, like—uh—'lazy' or 'smelly'?"

(continued)

(continued)

"I'm glad you asked," Ms. Holmberg replied. "It shows that your are a very sensitive person. At this stage, we're not going to judge whether the characteristic is true or false, or good or bad. But when the ten minutes are up, you'll separate the statements that are plainly descriptive from those that are generalizations that don't apply to all, or even most, people in your category."

After ten minutes, Ms. Holmberg gave a presentation about beliefs, attitudes, stereotyping, discrimination, and racism. She reminded the class *Transition* of what they had learned about critical thinking, particularly checking assumptions. The students then rejoined their groups to discuss the lists they had made on the chalkboard and decide which of the characteristics they would now reject. Then each group reported on the characteristics they had listed. Finally, with the students' help, Ms. Holmberg summarized their learnings about discrimination.

Evaluation

CLOSURE (Review) NO SERENDIPITY

INSTRUCTIONAL ACTIVITIES
1) Brainstorming 4) Coop Learning
2) Discussion 5) Summarizing
3) Critical thinking

SUMMARY

+ Planning a lesson must take into account both teaching and learning components.
+ Effective lesson planning begins with identifying instructional objectives in terms of observable student procedures (performance).
+ Step 1 in lesson planning is to choose a topic that relates to a particular instructional unit.
+ Step 2 is to frame lesson objectives by determining what knowledge, skills, attitudes, and values you want your students to acquire as a result of the lesson.
+ Step 3 involves identifying more specific particulars relating to topic-specific content, student learning, and skills objectives and to the choice of appropriate presentation strategies, teaching methods, student activities, and evaluation techniques.
+ Step 4 involves planning lesson content, taking into account prerequisite student learnings, and the level and conditions of student performance.
+ Practical factors that make for successful lesson delivery include preselecting teaching aids, providing positive set, choosing appropriate teaching methods, arranging for data collection and feedback, and planning lesson evaluation and closure.

◆ Lesson plans may and should be adjusted "on the spot" for good reason.
◆ A complete review of successful lesson delivery advises
    ◆ induce and adapt set;
    ◆ involve students actively;
    ◆ vary presentation;
    ◆ vary stimuli;
    ◆ promote transfer;
    ◆ provide closure.

KEY WORDS

closure
  review
  transfer
  serendipity
conditions of
  performance
instructional
  objectives
learning
  enactive
  iconic
  symbolic

lesson content
  planning
  topics
  presentation
  evaluation
observable actions
  and procedures
performance
  level
  objective
prerequisite learnings

set
  orientation
  transition
  evaluation
stimuli
teaching aids
transfer

RECOMMENDED READING

Bellon, J., Bellon, E., & Blank, M. (1992). *Teaching from a research knowledge base: A development and renewal process*. New York: Merrill.

Gronlund, N., & Linn, R. (1990). *Measurement and evaluation in teaching* (6th ed.). New York: Macmillan.

Mager, R. (1984). *Preparing instructional objectives* (2nd ed.). Palo Alto, CA: D.S. Lake.

PART 2

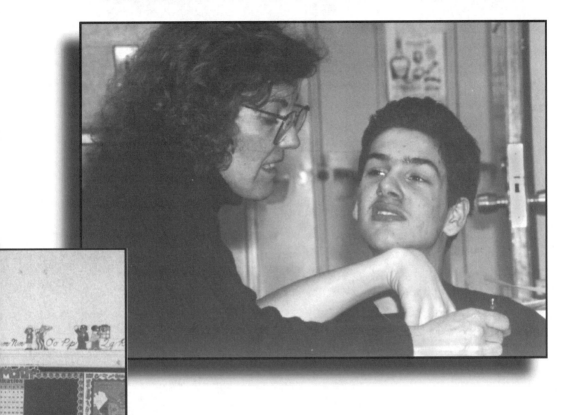

The Learning Environment

■ ■ ■ ■ ■

Classroom climate and environment—the psychological and physical elements that make up classroom "surroundings"—largely determine how children regard their educational experience. Chapter 4, which deals with classroom climate and student motivation, shows that the most productive classroom atmosphere is based on a high level of student involvement in the learning process and of cooperation between teacher and students and among the students themselves. Successful teachers show warmth and interest while retaining leadership, managing movement, maintaining group focus, and handling minor disruptions unobtrusively. Studying these basic skills and their interrelationships and applying them in the classroom are fundamental factors of good instruction.

Motivation, a highly stimulating factor in the learning process, informs all aspects of a lesson: delivery, task assignment, maintaining task involvement, using competition, providing feedback, and devising rewards. When classroom climate and environment are positive, teachers usually succeed in motivating their students to assume more responsibility for their own learning.

Chapter 5 discusses classroom management from the point of view of both students and teachers, and shows how management style can combine the perceived needs and goals of both groups. It describes the broad spectrum of management styles that range from complete authoritarianism to virtually total permissiveness, and suggests strong arguments in favor of an eclectic approach that adapts to a range of situations and learning needs. Successful teachers are sensitive to individual and group responses and needs, and show warmth and interest while retaining leadership, managing movement, and maintaining group focus. They keep order by means of preventive discipline, keeping minor disruptions to a minimum and handling unobtrusively those that inevitably occur. They also understand how to use reactive discipline positively, dealing promptly and professionally with any major disturbance.

Today's "cosmic classrooms" must meet the broadest range of learner needs so far identified. Chapter 6 points out that multicultural communities are the norm, and students within them range from gifted to severely challenged. Since students are individuals with widely diverse backgrounds, teachers must make strong and consistent efforts to meet many different types of learning needs. These needs will relate to natural abilities, preferred learning styles, divergent cultural norms and linguistic patterns, different developmental stages, diverse family and societal patterns, varying economic conditions, and many other variables. The important constant is for you to train yourself to be sensitive in observing each student's needs and to develop teaching skills that will help you to meet individual needs while continuing to promote both personal and group learning in a cooperative setting.

CHAPTER 4

CLASSROOM CLIMATE AND STUDENT MOTIVATION

■ ■ ■ ■ ■

The combination [of] the physical facilities and organization of the class room ... [the] interpersonal communications, and the classroom management techniques that are employed ... can create a [climate] where students are motivated and encouraged to learn in a variety of ways.

(SASKATCHEWAN EDUCATION, 1984, P. 37)

[Motivation] energizes and directs behavior ... arouses a person to initiate some action [or] ... causes a person to try to reach a certain goal ... [or not to] give up trying to reach a goal.

(WOOLFOLK, 1990, P. 302)

■ ■ ■ ■ ■

OVERVIEW

Classroom climate evolves from the atmosphere and environment in which teachers and students work, interact, and learn. In its broadest sense, classroom climate includes group organization, interpersonal communication, and classroom management. A positive and productive classroom climate evolves from a warm and caring attitude that begins with the teacher's use of effective "people skills" to establish an atmosphere and environment in which students and teachers work together and interact positively.

The effective classroom provides a climate that is conducive to learning: positive, challenging, and relevant. In such a climate, students "feel good about themselves" and become caring and supportive of one another so that they can take risks and learn both from successes and "deferred successes." Much of their development comes about from following the example set by an empathetic teacher who values and enjoys learning, is knowledgeable and skilled, and has earned their respect.

Each student has a unique learning-modality preference—visual, auditory, kinesthetic, or tactile—influencing his or her responses to different instructional approaches. Teachers, too, prefer different approaches to learning/teaching, but they should help their students, as they foster the development of their natural abilities, to adapt to a range of instructional approaches and learning styles.

Motivation should be the purpose underlying every aspect of lesson planning and delivery. A positive classroom climate, efficient classroom management, and good teacher–student rapport are essential for effective motivation, as are the use of a broad range of teaching strategies and methods that induce and maintain interest.

Elements that promote motivation include modeling and teaching enthusiasm for learning, interesting subject matter and lesson delivery, a variety and choice of tasks appropriate to students' learning levels, and prompt feedback. Competition and extrinsic rewards may motivate some students, but teachers should also model and promote experiences of the personal satisfaction in achievement that is the basis of self-motivation and its intrinsic reward. Motivated students show interest, perceive their learning as relevant, anticipate success, and experience satisfaction and increased self-esteem.

■ ■ ■ ■ ■

SCHOOL CLIMATE AND STUDENT ACHIEVEMENT

Today's parents and teachers and the community in general tend to judge a school's effectiveness by its students' achievements. Schools that are more than dispensers of knowledge—that focus on meeting the personal needs of students by providing a healthy classroom climate and positive learning environments—are remarkable places and can achieve remarkable results: higher-than-average academic performance, better attendance, a more stable staff, and higher student morale; fewer discipline problems, lower drop-out rates, less vandalism, and lower delinquency rates. These schools are communities in which students and teachers treat one another with respect, and where students are happy, confident, productive, and proud of their school.

Such healthy school environments combine several interrelated variables (Drefs, 1989, pp.18–28), including

◆ clean, well-maintained, and attractive physical facilities;
◆ clearly communicated and consistently enforced rules that create order and good discipline without being oppressive (see Chapter 5);
◆ teachers who model desired behavior, using preventive rather than reactive discipline (see Chapter 5);
◆ care and support for individual students, pervading every aspect of the school;
◆ administrative ingenuity in freeing teachers to concentrate on instruction and professional development through extensive use of outside facilities and resources, and creative problem solving;
◆ meaningful participation in learning experiences by students and the community.

Classroom Climate: Atmosphere and Environment

Speaking generally, **classroom climate** might be defined as a compound of the atmosphere (ambiance, ethos) and environment (or ecology) in which students and teachers work and interact. Children learn best in a climate in which the atmosphere nurtures their bodies, minds, and spirits.

The term *climate* should be viewed broadly: it includes physical facilities and group organization, interpersonal communication and classroom management. It also covers the expectations that the administrative and teaching staff have of their students, the teaching methods used to promote student performance of those expectations, and the evaluation methods applied to assess their own and their students' learning and performance.

CLASSROOM CLIMATE AND THE PHYSICAL ENVIRONMENT

Your classroom's physical environment, with its arrangement of equipment and materials, influences the intellectual, social, and emotional climate, and helps to determine how easy or difficult you will find it to teach effectively, and how well your students will learn. Your classroom should be a pleasant and interesting place in which to work, well organized for teaching and learning activities. It should support and promote effective instruction and management, accommodate different seating arrangements, allow for a variety of teaching strategies, and take traffic patterns into account. It is best to arrange your classroom furniture and equipment in a way that allows you to see each student. Supplies should be easy for you and your students to obtain. Such arrangements can conserve class time, and reduce interruptions and delays.

To check the suitability of your classroom's physical environment, ask yourself the following questions (Jacobsen, Eggen, Kauchack & Dulaney, 1985):

- Can you see all your students from your desk, and can they all see you? (If not, you cannot be aware of what is going on, and some students may become inattentive or misbehave.)
- Can all your students easily see your presentations and visuals? (Inability to see and understand invites inattention and misbehavior.)
- Are teaching materials and student supplies easily accessible? (Such arrangements reduce confusion and loss of time.)
- Are high-traffic areas separate and uncongested? (If so, there will be less jostling and misbehavior, traffic will move more quickly, and you will find it easier to see and control your students' activities.)

Figure 4.1 summarizes the characteristics of a positive classroom climate.

FIGURE 4.1

Characteristics of a Positive Classroom Climate

Positive Expectations

- Expecting students to succeed
- Matching the nature and pacing of instruction with learner needs and interests

Positive Teacher Behaviors

- Academically focused
- Businesslike but caring
- Convivial, encouraging, and stimulating

Positive Classroom Climate

Positive Classroom Management

- Effective room arrangement
- Reasonable rules/procedures
- Positive accountability

High Level of Success

- 70+% success for questions and 95+% for seatwork
- Using student ideas and matching student interests

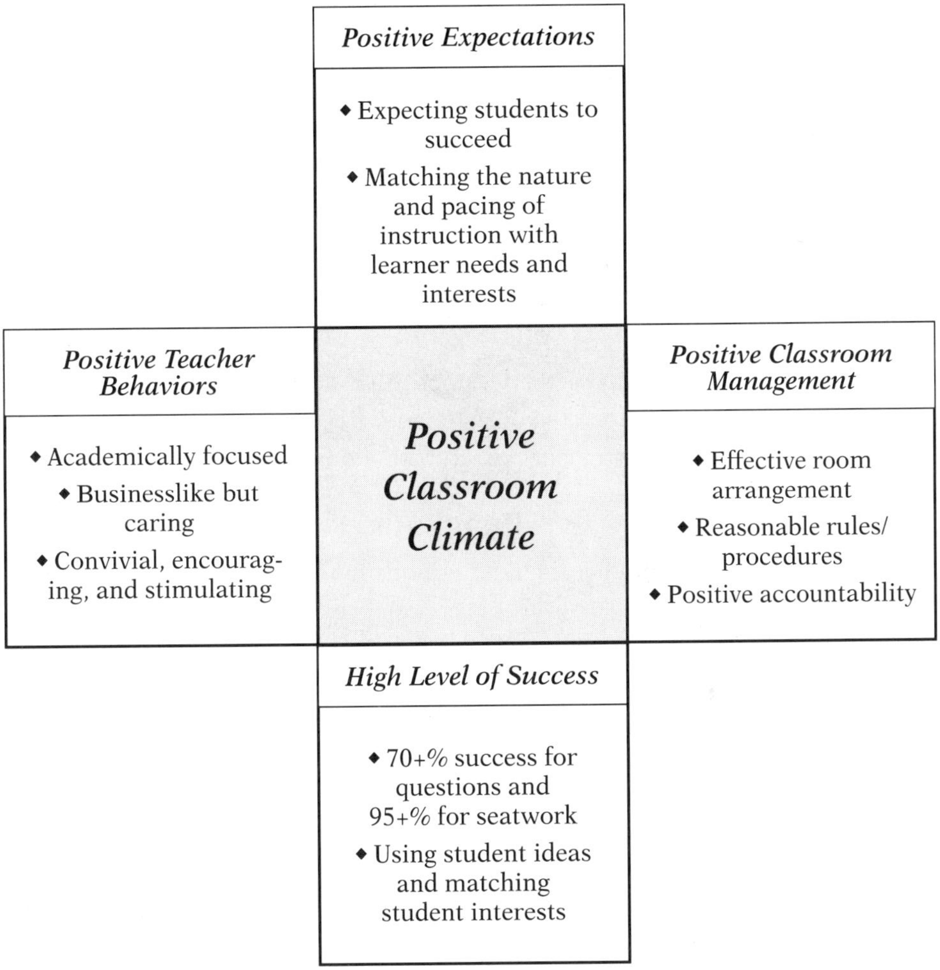

Source: The statistics relating to levels of success in this figure are taken from *Educational Psychology: A Realistic Approach* (3rd ed.) (pp. 360–361) by T.L. Good and J.E. Brophy, 1986, New York: Longman.

CLASSROOM CLIMATE AND THE LEARNING ENVIRONMENT

To create a positive classroom climate that supports your professional development and your students' educational achievement, you should focus on two elements: your role as teacher and your students' learning goals.

Classroom Climate and Your Role as Teacher

Teacher behavior relates closely to classroom climate and, in turn, to student achievement, which is highest when instructors show that they expect students to master the curriculum (Good & Brophy, 1986, p. 360). You can do much to create a positive learning climate by ensuring that your classroom is a safe, orderly, harmonious, and friendly place to work. You can accomplish this by

- modeling positive and constructive attitudes and behaviors to colleagues, students, and parents;
- exercising authority fairly;
- offering warmth and support;
- encouraging independent thought or cooperation, as appropriate;
- motivating your students to learn, and allowing them a measure of choice in the learning process;
- ensuring a reasonable balance between positive and negative feedback;
- seeking opportunities to make your students feel liked, included, supported, accepted, valued, successful, special, and emotionally secure.

ESTABLISHING RULES AND PROCEDURES

Exercising your role as teacher includes establishing classroom **rules** (i.e., statements of standards that specify or forbid certain behaviors) and **procedures** (i.e., prescribed steps for helping students to participate in class activities and accomplish particular learning tasks). It is essential for you to establish workable rules and procedures very early in the school year, and to impress on your students their accountability (through accepting consequences) for following them. It is just as important for your students to understand and see these rules and procedures— and consequently the associated behavioral norms (the behaviors expected of students)—as fair and important. Therefore, you will want to think very carefully about the rules and procedures you plan to establish before communicating them to or developing them with your students.

Many teachers believe that involving students in setting rules promotes "ownership" and responsibility. Students who have shared in the decision-making process of setting rules may be better able to understand the reasons behind them and more willing to uphold them. If you invite students to share in rule making, however, you must differentiate between rules that they must accept on your authority and those that they can have a say in forming.

You should not simply state rules and procedures but teach them explicitly: in fact, you might spend up to one-third of the first few days of school teaching them. Even high school teachers should teach rules and procedures, and discuss the consequences of their infraction. The rewards and penalties inherent in the system of consequences you develop (see Chapter 5) should encourage your students to engage in learning tasks and build a sense of personal worth. Effective consequences are rooted in a positive caring climate and an attitude of curiosity and excitement about learning.

Rules

Good rules are based on the Golden Rule: "Always treat others as you would like them to treat you" (Matthew 7:12, *New English Bible*). Rules should be worded positively, defining what should be done rather than what should not. Begin by stating some "givens," such as "All students and teachers must follow school rules." There is no point, however, in confusing your students with a lifetime supply of specific regulations: do not expect them to remember and practice more than five to seven general rules. "Respect others and their property," for example, covers a multitude of specifics, and is easily accepted and remembered.

Procedures

Specifying procedures by means of clear and explicit directions often removes much of the uncertainty that plagues beginning teachers as to how to create and maintain a productive classroom climate. Perhaps the most important factor in establishing effective classroom learning procedures is giving clear directions (see Chapter 9) that promote student accountability for routine procedures such as recording attendance and promptness, entering and leaving the classroom, taking out and putting away equipment and materials, participating in question-and-answer sessions or group or class discussions, beginning and completing seatwork, obtaining help from you or from peers, and completing assignments (Woolfolk, 1990, p. 357).

By contrast, students cannot respond productively to directions they do not understand. Confused or frustrated students may become indifferent, or angry. Belief that their failure is "their fault" (because they are "too stupid" to understand what they are hearing) may damage their self-concept. The result of misunderstanding may be inappropriate work performed in the wrong way, off-task behavior such as daydreaming or disruption, and the loss of opportunities for productive learning.

MAINTAINING FLEXIBILITY

While rules and procedures are important, effective teachers do not lose sight of the need for a sensible degree of flexibility in the classroom. One team of researchers (Dunn & Dunn, 1987) found, for example, that not all students learn best

- when sitting perfectly still in a "proper" position, at a desk or table, in a well-lit and completely quiet setting. (Contrary to popular belief, reading in low light does not damage eyesight, though it may induce eyestrain and headaches.);
- when classroom temperature ranges from 19°C to 20°C (68°F to 70°F);
- early in the morning (in fact, most learners perform better in the late morning or early afternoon);
- through whole-group instruction;
- when teaching involves a sequence of clearly stated objectives and detailed, step-by-step explanations.

Some students learn well when they

- have suitable classroom furniture;
- eat, drink, or chew on objects;
- can move about and use their own perceptual strengths.

In determining the degree of flexibility you will maintain in your classroom, consider the "point of balance" between individual freedom and the right of the group to optimal learning conditions.

Classroom Climate as a Growth Factor

Professional teachers know that nothing succeeds like success, and nothing stultifies like continual failure! People like to do the things they do well, but soon lose interest in doing the things they do badly, for no one likes activities that damage self-concept. This does not mean that students must always be successful, but it does mean that students who make a reasonable effort should achieve success most of the time. If necessary, add or even replace curriculum content (without losing sight of overall goals) to meet those needs, and let your students— both the capable and the less capable—know that you believe they can master the learning goals you have set.

PRACTICE *and Projects*

1. a. Working in groups of six, brainstorm for ten minutes things a teacher can do or encourage students to do, to foster a positive classroom climate for learning.
    b. As a group, complete the following statement:
       "A classroom with a positive learning climate is one in which ... "
    c. Report and debrief as a class.

■ ■ ■ ■ ■

SETTING LEARNING GOALS

If your students are to develop a positive attitude toward meeting learning goals, you must set goals that are challenging but achievable. To do this, you will need to become familiar with your students individually, and to discover their preferred learning modalities.

Learning Modalities: An Overview

Learning modalities (ways of learning), charted in Figure 4.2, are classified as visual (learning by seeing), auditory (learning by hearing), tactile (learning by touching or manipulating), or kinesthetic (learning through movement).

FIGURE 4.2

Learning Modalities

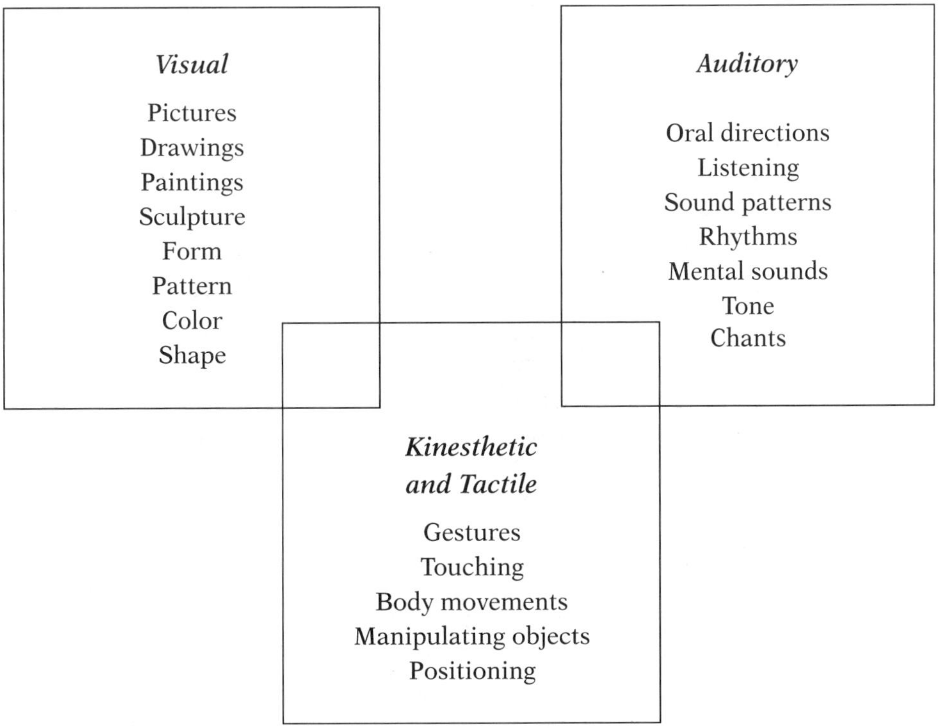

Visual

Pictures
Drawings
Paintings
Sculpture
Form
Pattern
Color
Shape

Auditory

Oral directions
Listening
Sound patterns
Rhythms
Mental sounds
Tone
Chants

Kinesthetic and Tactile

Gestures
Touching
Body movements
Manipulating objects
Positioning

LEARNING-STYLE PREFERENCES

Each student has unique **learning-style preferences,** or ways in which he or she naturally learns most readily (see Chapter 1). These innate preferences influence the ways in which students approach learning—intuitive, imaginative, theoretical, or practical—and the modalities and kinds of stimuli—visual, auditory, kinesthetic, or tactile—that make learning most meaningful for them. Such "perceptual preferences affect more that 70 percent of school-age youngsters" (Dunn, Beaudry, & Klavas, 1989, p. 52). Barbe and Swassing (1979), in a study of students from kindergarten to Grade 6, showed the following ratios of learning modalities: visual dominance 33 percent; auditory dominance 24 percent; kinesthetic or tactile dominance 14 percent; and mixed modalities 29 percent. Modality preferences evolve from many factors, including gender, race, culture, experience, and right- or left-handedness. Modality strengths occur singly or in combination, change over time, and tend to become integrated as students mature.

Visual Learners

Visual learners learn by watching, seeing, or imagining; they tend to prefer the visual arts and often think in "pictures" based on descriptions, visualizing or imagining information as it is presented. Visual disorder may distract these learners, who tend to be quiet, neat, orderly, and well planned and organized. Many focus on details rather than on a whole task, doodling or finding something to watch during a presentation. They remember faces rather than names and may need to write facts down in order to recall them.

Auditory Learners

Auditory learners learn through listening and talking. They particularly enjoy talking—even to themselves—and when learning, they may vocalize silently, sometimes moving their lips or even humming. They like listening to plays and dialogs, but avoid long descriptions. They remember names, but may forget faces. They tend to focus on the whole, sometimes missing details, and may choose to solve problems by talking them through. They prefer music to the visual arts, but extraneous sounds may distract them.

Kinesthetic and Tactile Learners

Some people learn best through physical processes of touching or moving. Tactile learners learn by touching or manipulating objects, and kinesthetic learners by making a prescribed set of movements (e.g., performing a procedure for themselves). These learners are action oriented, remembering information better when they can be physically involved in the learning process. They may be poor listeners, for they tend to fidget, seem to need to move often, and may supplement their words with gestures. They often respond to music by moving and want to touch pictures or sculptures.

LEARNER DIVERSITY

As you observe your students' learning-modality preferences, you will discover that learner diversity is an important reality of classroom experience (see Chapter 6). Learner diversity means that no single curriculum or way of teaching works equally well for everyone. Thus, all learners in a classroom do not always benefit from conventional instruction, for learners respond differently to different instructional approaches. Biological and developmental characteristics make some learners open to a given teaching method and others not.

Some researchers stress the importance of recognizing and adapting teaching strategies to accommodate a variety of learning styles (see For Example 4.1). Ken Henson (1988), of the University of Alabama, also maintains that matching teaching and learning styles "consistently increases academic achievement, improves attitudes toward school, and reduces discipline problems" (p. 157).

There are two ways to achieve such a match:

◆ match teachers with students who have similar personalities;
◆ have teachers pick teaching methods that correspond to students' learning styles.

PROMOTING "STYLE FLEX"

Though you will find it helpful to identify and foster your students' preferred learning styles, it is not realistic for you always to try to match instruction to individual students' preferences, for although each person has unique ways of

---

FOR EXAMPLE　4.1

Matching Teaching and Learning Styles

Robert Sternberg (1990b), a professor of psychology and education at Yale, observes that

> styles of learning and thinking are every bit as important as levels of ability ... we ignore students' thinking styles at our peril—and theirs ... Whenever possible, most people choose styles of managing themselves with which they are comfortable ... *any subject can be taught in a way that is congruent with any style.* (p.367)

learning, people also share similar learning styles. Recognizing these similarities will help you to plan effective learning experiences for your class. Moreover, although most people have one predominant style of learning, they also have a secondary style and should be encouraged to develop it. It is important to expose your students to a variety of teaching and learning styles and different learning modalities. "Style flex" (adaptation to a range of learning styles) can be developed, and you should promote it.

Your own learning-style preferences will influence the way you teach, but you can help your students by recognizing your preferences and their influence on your choice of teaching techniques, and consciously varying your instructional approaches. In fact, every teacher should develop a repertoire of teaching strategies and methods that will suit *all* students' learning styles some of the time and help learners to adapt to a range of learning styles (see Chapter 1).

PRACTICE *and Projects*

1. Working in small groups, discuss the following questions:
   a. What value is there in knowing more about learning styles?
   b. How might we vary stimuli to respond to a number of learning styles?
   c. What advantage is there in varying teaching style, regardless of learning-style preferences?
   d. What kind of learning experiences do I, as a student, prefer? Why?

2. a. Working in subject-area groups, develop a lesson plan for a class of learners predominantly of one style.
   b. Share your lesson plan and its rationale with your whole class.
   c. Invite class members to challenge your rationale and explore a variety of other approaches.

■ ■ ■ ■ ■

MOTIVATING YOUR STUDENTS

Much of your job as a teacher is to create conditions and structure activities that will **motivate** your students to achieve their full performance potential. Your target should be to motivate your students by being "encouraging, energetic, exciting and stimulating" (Kindsvatter, Wilen, & Ishler, 1988, p. 108). To attain these professional targets, you will need to structure some essential preconditions:

◆ a positive learning climate that is supportive and relaxed, but businesslike;
◆ reasonable and efficient classroom management routines, organization, and procedures;

♦ good relationships and positive rapport with your students, based on your encouragement, understanding, and patience.

The Teacher as Model

To promote these ends, it is important for you to model interest in learning and to project enthusiasm, for enthusiasm "rubs off." You can show by your manner, as well as by your words, that the course material is important. Make it plain that you expect your students to be interested in learning, to be curious, to want to understand content and master skills, and to try their best to do so. Explain that you value learning because it is personally fulfilling and intrinsically rewarding. Encourage your students to tell you about things that they find interesting, unusual, or surprising, and to ask questions about them. Point out how content relates to personal interests and applies to everyday life. Let your students know that you believe they want to transfer their school learnings to their everyday lives. Show that you enjoy your students: try to be a guide, an enabler, and a fellow-learner, not a boss or a judge. You will find your support, love, and example to be valuable student motivators.

The Teacher as Motivator

Remind yourself, at each stage of the teaching process, that achieving effective motivation is at least half the task of involving your students in learning and applying content and skills. Form a habit of approaching each element of lesson planning, preparation, and delivery with the intent to motivate your students. By forming such a habit, you will come to see how you can use "the tasks students are assigned, students' perceptions of these tasks, [your] rapport with students, and the **reward structures** [you] introduce" (Good & Brophy, 1990, p. 403) to achieve this target.

Your reactions to students and classroom incidents will make a difference in the way your students respond. Train yourself to recognize your students' feelings accurately—this is a critical teaching skill—and to accept them positively. Since word choice and intonation send their own messages, use accepting rather than rejecting language: try "Good morning! Good to see you!" rather than "Not *you* again!"

Affective messages are communicated nonverbally as well as verbally (see Chapter 2). Nonverbal communication consists largely of facial expressions and body language. Monitor your nonverbal responses carefully, since they may speak even more clearly to your students than your words. A smile or a nod at a critical point can work wonders! A shrug or a dismissive gesture can discourage a student from making the effort needed to succeed. Remember, too, that your feelings or moods affect your students' behavior: your enthusiasm can "vitalize" your students just as any show of apathy or boredom may "infect" them. Guidelines (Kindsvatter et al., 1988) to help you motivate your students are summarized in Table 4.1.

PLANNING FOR MOTIVATION

Since students' attitudes toward their learning tasks can be shaped, professional teachers do not leave motivation to chance: they plan carefully to use a range of teaching competencies to provide their students with encouraging evidence of progress and improvement (feedback), to praise their efforts and achievements when they can do so sincerely, and to use appropriate rewards. By such planning, you will raise your students' confidence and self-esteem, and help to maintain their enthusiasm for learning, while focusing on ultimate goals.

To maximize your students' motivation, you should always plan and structure lessons and assignments that match your students' tasks with their abilities: tasks should challenge, but not threaten, and success should be attainable by reasonable effort. This is vital, since students who are regularly assigned tasks too difficult for them to perform well soon stop trying, and their self-esteem declines. Plan activities that your students like, and offer choices of activities or tasks. Base your grading on descriptive, accurate records that reflect individual progress and class completion rates.

TABLE 4.1

Motivating Your Students

1. Foster and show warmth and caring.
2. Model desired student behavior.
3. Inform students of the goals you expect.them to achieve, the reasons for your expectations, and the procedures they should follow to achieve those goals.
4. Expect the best from your students.
5. Involve students actively in your lessons.
6. Make learning seem worth while.
7. Capitalize on your students' interests.
8. Capitalize on your students' ideas.
9. Capitalize on your students' curiosity.
10. Cultivate your students' self-esteem.
11. Challenge students to do their best.
12. Use positive reinforcement.
13. Individualize instruction to meet your students' needs, interests, and abilities.
14. Use cooperation and competition as appropriate.
15. Reduce your students' anxiety.

Source: The information in this table is based on *Classroom Teaching Skills: A Primer* (pp. 201–203) by K. Moore, 1989, New York: Random House.

Whenever possible, capitalize on your students' interests by choosing related topics and examples, and by adapting learning tasks to include them. Data Collection Form 4.1 (Appendix A) will help you to record your students' interests. From these records, you will obtain clues to choosing or developing activities and tasks that will motivate your students to learn willingly. Data Collection Form 4.2 will help you to record your plans systematically.

TEACHING FOR MOTIVATION

Positive motivation is critical to students' success. Since all teaching should motivate learners, there is no need, at this point, to change your professional targets for lesson delivery.

Motivation through Lesson Delivery

Your success in motivating students by your style of lesson delivery will depend largely on the degree of interest you can rouse and maintain. The following tips may help you to plan and monitor motivational delivery skills:

- Try to plan lesson introductions that will get all your students off to a good start, since some students find getting started the hardest part of a task.
- To promote your students' understanding, you might introduce a new topic or activity by taking them through an **advance organizer** (or overview) to give them a general sense of the whole topic or task before them and to show them the organization or structure of the material to be learned. State learning goals clearly, and focus your students' attention on elements that require special concentration.
- Maintain teaching momentum by organizing smooth transitions from one lesson segment to another.
- Pace your lessons slowly enough for all your students to follow, but rapidly enough to keep their interest high and minimize wasted time: the pace should seem unhurried, but momentum should be maintained.
- Give clear, concise, step-by-step information and achievable directions for learning procedures and activities to your whole class, checking after each step that *all* students understand.
- If material is complex or lengthy, try to break it down into "bite-size" pieces that you can present serially, allowing students to digest one piece before you add the next. This approach leads by smooth transitions to a review of the new information or process, perhaps followed by seatwork or a homework assignment.
- Introduce suspense or rouse curiosity by building up to a "punch line" or including an element of surprise.

Encourage your students to learn more about things with which they are already familiar, while introducing moderate amounts of new and unfamiliar material. The familiar ideas and examples that you introduce in teaching new material will shed light on the new content, and the new ideas you present will shed light on familiar material. At the same time, do not allow your students to assume that they already have "the answer" to new ideas or problems that you are introducing. Accustom them to question any preconceived notions they may have by pointing out exceptions to general rules, and by noting and discussing mysteries, paradoxes (seeming contradictions), and contradictions.

MOTIVATION AND TASK ASSIGNMENTS

Build on your students' strengths and levels of functioning. Plan for individual success by gearing your expectations and class activities to your students' potential level of achievement. Make use of your students' interests by discussing with them interesting activities and areas for study, and by developing topics and providing examples that motivate them to learn. Involve your students in choosing learning activities, discussing what they consider fair assignments, and setting limits.

Vary the nature and elements of the tasks you assign: their level of difficulty, the length of time allowed for their completion, the work setting, and the number of students directly involved. When tasks involve listening or reading, use stories, anecdotes, or other devices that help to "personalize" content. Guide and encourage your students to listen actively, asking questions and making comments on what they hear. Use fantasy experiences and simulations to encourage participation through imagination and to provide vicarious experiences that personalize learning.

Structure new and unexpected first-hand experiences that involve direct participation and challenge or provoke conflict. Some activities should include game-like features to provide fun and allow students to explore, discover, solve puzzles, and engage in nonthreatening, "nongraded" competition. Be sure, however, not to stress games to the point where your students remember the fun but forget the lesson content.

Maintaining Task Involvement

To maintain high-quality task involvement and help your students to expect success, give clear and concise explanations and directions so that they will understand precisely what you expect them to do, and how you expect them to do it. To promote understanding, fill in or explain details that are unclear or missing in texts, and make abstract content more concrete, familiar, and personal by using anecdotes or examples that involve familiar or personal elements.

Check to ensure that each student understands your explanations and directions. If you find that some students are confused, explain or demonstrate again. Remind your students that you expect them to remain on task, and that you intend to check their work. Ensure that your students finish tasks that involve a product (e.g., maps, drawings, models, essays). Completing tasks helps students to understand their purpose and meaning, and gives them a sense of accomplishment. When tasks involve understanding content rather than producing a product, have your students complete the learning process by discussing or debriefing, linking new to familiar content, and transferring the information they have acquired to other situations.

MOTIVATION THROUGH COMPETITION

Competition, used appropriately, can motivate and stimulate students to try harder. It can also supply a useful incentive for students to master specific skills when speed of performance and quantity of output are important, though it is not particularly useful for tasks that require discovery, creativity, or intensive thought.

Be sensitive to your students' comfort with competition: for those who respond well to the challenge of competition, arrange suitable opportunities to compete, setting high but attainable standards. For those students who find individual competition stressful, however, you might substitute team competition (see Chapter 15), or de-emphasize competition with peers and emphasize self-competition instead.

MOTIVATION THROUGH FEEDBACK

As your students work at or complete assignments, provide prompt feedback that will benefit them by guiding their current or later efforts. In giving verbal feedback, you might say, for instance, "I understand what makes you feel frustrated," but then go on to communicate confidence in the student's ability to learn and grow: "You can do it! Let's work through this example together, and then you can try the next one by yourself." Vary the types of feedback by using programmed learning materials, answer keys, computer-assisted instruction, and peer interaction (see Chapters 4 & 5).

Provide **positive reinforcement** for gains. Encourage students who are working diligently by recognizing and reinforcing reasonable effort, even though it may not have been successful. Correct without criticism: you might say, for example, "That's not exactly right, but close … Let me show you another way … Have you thought of trying this? … How do you think this might work? … Here's another way of trying to find the answer." Remind your students of their previous successes: they want to discover and believe in their capabilities and strengths, but they may require emotional support or "coaching" to achieve this. By showing confidence in their capabilities and openly anticipating that they will make honest efforts, you will help them to succeed. If, on the other hand, you introduce negative warnings that they will find their tasks difficult, they probably will!

MOTIVATION THROUGH REWARDS

Ideally, students will gladly engage in activities because they like them, or because they are already interested in the content. In practice, however, rewards given for improved or successful performance can often motivate students to "try harder," thus helping them to connect effort with achievement. Initially, rewards are likely to be extrinsic (i.e., external). Marks are the most obvious form of **extrinsic reward**: about half the students in a typical class will respond positively to the motivation of better marks for higher performance. Other forms of reward are tokens of achievement (e.g., gold stars or a listing on an honor roll), a teacher's verbal approval, free time, play time, a choice of activities, or even a prize.

Rewards need not be associated only with individual competition. Group rewards for strong effort or performance can be used to promote cooperation and interactive skills (see Chapter 15). Appropriate rewards help all students to develop positive social behaviors, self-concepts, and affective skills.

As students mature, they can be taught to value and seek **intrinsic rewards** (i.e., internal rewards). Encourage your students to view learning tasks positively, focusing, whenever possible, on the internal satisfaction to be gained from challenges met and tasks well done.

Identifying Motivated Students

Monitoring your methods of motivating your students is part of reflecting on your own professional progress. Your skill in meeting the professional target of student motivation will, of course, improve with practice. From the beginning, however, you should be alert to any—or any combination—of four responses that mark motivated learners. They are as follows:

◆ *Interest.* Motivated learners will pay attention to the lesson or activity, showing interest and curiosity.
◆ *Perception of relevance.* Learners will find instruction relevant to their interests, and to their perceived personal needs and goals.
◆ *Anticipation.* Learners will anticipate success in assimilating instruction.
◆ *Satisfaction.* Learners will experience appropriate intrinsic (internal) or extrinsic (external) rewards.

PROMOTING EXPECTATIONS OF SUCCESS

Students who set themselves reasonable goals, make an effort to achieve them, and expect to succeed are more likely to succeed than are students who fear failure. Each success provides a student with practice in using learning skills effectively, raises self-confidence, and leads to expectations of other successes. You can promote your students' success in the following ways:

- Make sure that your students are well prepared for tasks of appropriate difficulty.
- Divide learning tasks into manageable parts.
- Teach your students to analyze each task they are set, to identify personal goals for each stage of each task, and to assess their progress according to their own (not others') past performance.
- Help your students to see the connection between effort and success, and to concentrate on the task at hand rather than on fear of failure.
- Teach students to "backtrack" to find the cause of any mistakes they may have made, instead of giving up in frustration.
- Teach your students to set personal rewards (e.g., treating themselves to a five-minute break after completing ten math problems).
- Provide discouraged students with additional (perhaps peer) help.
- Help your students to feel less anxious about tests by teaching and providing practice in effective study methods and test-taking skills.

PRACTICE *and Projects*

1. a. Recall a favorite teacher who "turned you on" to a particular subject. List things that the teacher did or said that induced high motivation.
   b. In a group of three peers, share your list, and try to reach consensus on the top six motivational characteristics or strategies identified.
   c. Join another group of three peers to reach consensus on the top eight motivational characteristics or strategies identified. Report your findings to your class.

2. Using the material in this chapter and other sources, analyze Case Study 4.1, and devise a tentative motivation plan for Grant.

3. a. Join a subject-interest group. Use Data Collection Form 4.1 (Appendix A) to record members' subject-related interests.
   b. On the basis of responses, choose an appropriate grade level, and plan a lesson to motivate students to investigate a subject-related topic.

CASE STUDY **4.1**

MOTIVATION

Seven-year-old Grant is one of just five minority students in his Grade 1 class at Davin School. He is not a difficult child to handle, for he is neither ill-tempered nor disruptive in class, but he seems to live in a world of his own. He rarely completes his work, and Ms. James, his teacher, has to tell him things at least three or four times before he seems to take them in.

Grant's attention span is usually very short: during "sharing time" or Ms. James's presentations, he seldom sits still for more than five minutes. Instead of paying attention, Grant wanders about the classroom, draws on the chalkboard, or plays at his desk. Once he does get involved in a task, however, it is hard for him to put it away and begin something else. When he joins the class circle, he fights, fidgets, fusses, plays with himself, moves about, and talks to others. He rarely contributes or answers questions during circle time.

Grant is not an ESL student; he speaks English well, but he appears to be shy. When he first arrived at Davin School in September, he was put into a Grade 2 class at his mother's request. After a month of constant failure, he told his teacher that he really should have been placed in Grade 1. He has recently been transferred to Ms. James's Grade 1 class. Ms. James has noticed that whenever she assigns the children a task, Grant behaves as though it does not apply to him.

SUMMARY

- Classroom climate is a compound of psycho-social atmosphere and physical environment.
- A logically arranged, interesting, and pleasant classroom environment promotes effective teaching and learning.
- A school that provides a healthy classroom climate and positive learning environments can achieve superior performance by both teachers and students.
- To create a positive classroom climate, instructors should focus on their own role as teacher and on their students' learning goals.

- To promote a positive student attitude toward academic achievement and the attainment of learning goals, try to ensure that those students who make a reasonable effort will achieve success most of the time.
- Observe your students' preferred learning modalities carefully. Foster their innate learning strengths, but ensure that they develop and use a range of learning modalities.
- To ensure positive student motivation, plan carefully to provide students with encouraging evidence of progress and improvement (feedback), praise their efforts and achievements when you can do so sincerely, and use appropriate rewards.
- Model interest in learning and project enthusiasm, showing by your words and manner that the course material is important, and that you expect your students to want to understand its content and master its skills.
- Plan and structure lessons and assignments that your students like, and that offer them choices. Tasks should challenge, but not threaten your students, and success should be attainable by reasonable effort.
- In planning lesson delivery, frame interesting introductions, provide advance organizers, state learning goals clearly, and direct your students' attention to elements that require special concentration. Link new information to familiar material. Introduce suspense or rouse curiosity by building up to a "punch line" or including an element of surprise.
- Vary the length and complexity of tasks assigned. Encourage your students to ask questions, and provide a strong component of **experiential learning**.
- Provide prompt and varied feedback on student performance.
- Use appropriate rewards to reinforce your students' will to succeed, progressing from extrinsic to intrinsic forms of reward. Rewards may be applicable to individuals or groups.
- Monitor your own success in motivating your students by observing the extent to which students demonstrate the following factors: interest and curiosity; perception of relevance to personal needs and goals; anticipation of success in assimilating instruction; experience of satisfaction in extrinsic and intrinsic rewards.
- Promote your students' expectations and achievement of success by ensuring that they are well prepared for tasks of appropriate difficulty, and that they are trained to analyze each task set and to concentrate on that task rather than on fear of failure. Provide discouraged students with any additional help they might need and lower students' anxiety levels by teaching and providing practice in effective study methods and test-taking skills.

KEY WORDS

achievement
advance organizer
classroom climate
   atmosphere
   environment
directions
flexibility
learner diversity
learning goals
learning modalities
   visual

auditory
tactile
kinesthetic
lesson delivery
motivated learner
   interest
   perception of
      relevance

anticipation
satisfaction
procedures
rules
[learning] "style flex"
teacher as model
teacher as motivator

RECOMMENDED READING

Gallen, V., & Bold, J. (1989). *Saskatchewan Teachers' Federation study of teaching*. Saskatoon: Saskatchewan Teachers' Federation.

Martin, J. (1983). *Mastering instruction*. Boston: Allyn & Bacon.

CHAPTER 5

CLASSROOM MANAGEMENT

■ ■ ■ ■ ■

Different teacher personalities, teaching styles, and management practices will create very different classroom atmospheres ... Classroom atmosphere influences student achievement, satisfaction with the class, and feelings toward the teacher.
(DAVIS, 1983, P. 37)

■ ■ ■ ■ ■

OVERVIEW

Effective classroom management, which begins with efficient lesson planning and preparation, helps free teachers to teach and students to learn. Students thrive in a positive, personalized, and supportive classroom climate and an environment in which they feel safe, cared for, and involved.

Approaches to classroom management range from intimidation to almost total permissiveness, but it is best to avoid both extremes by teaching, monitoring, and enforcing reasonable classroom rules, routines, and procedures. Students learn best from teachers who keep them on task by combining positive reinforcement with "preventive discipline." To do this, teachers must master effective direction giving and practice the basic classroom skills of awareness, "overlapping," movement management, and group focus.

It is critical that, as a beginning teacher, you get off to a good start in managing your classroom. To avoid being trapped in the "nice gal/guy syndrome," you should begin by establishing—ideally in consultation with your students—five to seven broad rules and the consequences of their infringement. Enforcing these rules requires that you routinely monitor desired classroom activity to deter minor disruptions, and deal fairly but firmly with negative classroom behavior.

There are practical ways of dealing with those minor disruptions that occasionally occur in every classroom. Major disruptions must be handled calmly and professionally, with help, if necessary, from the administrative staff and/or parents.

■ ■ ■ ■ ■

MANAGING YOUR CLASSROOM

Classroom management is a complex set of behaviors that teachers use to establish and maintain "conditions that will enable students to achieve their instructional objectives efficiently—that will enable them to learn" (Weber, 1983, p. 272). No other aspect of teaching is of more concern to teachers-in-training, for appropriate classroom management is a critical part of effective instruction. For Example 5.1 elaborates on this point.

Classroom Management: A Student Perspective

We often read or hear about classroom management from the perspective of educators. It may be useful to look at classroom management from "the other side of the desk," for unless teachers can remember to walk in their students' shoes, negative student experiences may result in negative learning.

A study conducted by James Allen (1986) has shown that students tend to have two major classroom goals: to "socialize" with their peers and to "pass the course." In classrooms in which academic demands are low, students tend to focus on "having fun" (socializing) to reduce boredom. In classes in which instruction is fast paced and academic demands are high, students tend to focus on passing the course. They like best those classes that give them opportunities to socialize while learning interesting content.

Points to ponder . . .

❑ Without ever losing sight of instructional objectives, how might I introduce classroom activities that involve participation?

❑ Meeting the same condition, how might I introduce classroom activities that involve socializing?

FOR EXAMPLE   5.1

A Study of Teacher Effectiveness

A landmark study conducted by Jacob Kounin and his associates (Kounin, 1970; Kounin & Doyle, 1975; Doyle 1977) reviewed classroom management by comparing effective teachers and their well-behaved students with ineffective teachers whose classrooms were beset with many behavioral problems. These studies identified four skills that marked the effective teachers of well-managed classrooms: "withitness," "overlapping," movement management, and maintaining group focus.

Classroom Management: A Teacher Perspective

Smoothly running and productive classrooms in which students are highly involved in learning activities and there is little disruption or off-task behavior do not evolve by chance. Three basic elements of teaching that combine to achieve such classrooms are effective management, preventive discipline, and interesting instruction. In such classrooms, discipline, in the form of established rules and procedures (see Chapter 4), produces appropriate student behaviors, and well-planned instruction promotes successful learning experiences, as described below:

- Teachers who *manage effectively* create and maintain conditions in which students can learn efficiently. They organize the classroom area and its supplies to promote learning, and set a positive classroom climate (see Chapter 4); they establish productive classroom and group norms, routines, and procedures, while teaching lessons, organizing and monitoring learning, maintaining good student behavior, and evaluating classroom management and student achievement (Emmer, Evertson, Sanford, Clements, & Worsham, 1989; Evertson, Emmer, Clements, Sanford, & Worsham, 1984).
- Teachers who use *preventive management* (Jacobsen, et al., 1985) set rules (preferably by consensus) and procedures, and enforce them by establishing the consequences of certain behaviors (see Chapter 4).
- Teachers who provide *interesting instruction* promote learning by diagnosing learner needs, planning lessons to meet those needs, motivating student participation by means of a variety of teaching strategies and skills (see Chapter 4), and regularly assess students' progress and their own professional development (see Chapters 1 and 17).

It is scarcely possible to separate these three elements of teaching, for effective classroom management and preventive discipline are the foundation of productive instruction, while excellent teaching and classroom management skills facilitate preventive discipline.

APPROACHES TO CLASSROOM MANAGEMENT

Approaches to classroom management may be classified by the degree of teacher intervention and control that each approach requires. The following outline represents a continuum of strategies, beginning with the strongest element of teacher intervention and ending with the strongest element of student self-direction (Weber & Roff, 1983).

Intimidation

Intimidation attempts to control students' behavior through strategies that create fear. These strategies include threats, sarcasm, ridicule, disapproval, psychological coercion, and physical force.

Authoritarianism

Authoritarianism sets and enforces rules in a dictatorial way, using obtrusive discipline as necessary. Authoritarian teachers seek to control students' behavior by issuing commands, orders, and directives supplemented by careful monitoring.

Behavior Modification

Behavior modification attempts to promote desirable behavior and eliminate undesirable behavior through the use of praise, rewards, modeling, contingency contracting, prompts (clues), signals, **response costs** (a kind of fine that can cost a student a reward that has already been earned), **negative reinforcement**, and **punishment**. (Note that the safe and successful use of behavior modification requires a special setting and a specially trained staff.)

Instruction

Instruction based on students' needs and interests can motivate them to focus on their work, greatly reducing the incidence of problem behavior. This approach requires a positive climate that promotes planning for student success (see Chapter 3), selection of relevant content (see Chapter 16), competent use of appropriate teaching and learning strategies and skills (see Chapters 2 and 7–15), and use of reasonable routines and procedures (see Chapter 4).

"Cookbook" Management

Cookbook classroom management is an eclectic approach that may consist of applying a prescription of "do's and dont's," without any obviously consistent rationale. Alternatively, it may consist of adapting a number of the most effective aspects of other approaches to the requirements of unique groups or individuals.

Socio-Emotional Management

The **socio-emotional** approach to management calls for building healthy inter-personal relationships that support a positive classroom climate. Teachers model and promote empathy, genuineness, acceptance, active listening, and humor, while applying logical consequences to student behavior.

Group Processes

Group processes use the class (a social system) to support and promote appropriate individual behavior and learning. Effective group action is promoted by the teacher's competent application of *withitness* (a term coined by Jacob Kounin [1970] to signify a state of constant alertness to all classroom activity), reasonable expectations, sharing of leadership, and use of group-maintenance activities (see Chapters 13 and 15).

Permissiveness

Permissiveness is the extreme opposite of intimidation. The permissive teacher promotes maximum student freedom in order to foster natural development of each individual's full potential. He or she acts as a consultant rather than an authority figure, encouraging students to take responsibility for their own learning.

SELECTING A MANAGEMENT STYLE

The intimidation, cookbook, and permissive approaches to classroom management are difficult to defend, and few educationists now support pure authoritarianism. It is easier to advocate the other approaches—none of which has so far been proved best—for there is strong empirical (experiential) evidence that some elements, at least, of each of them produce positive results. But since each individual and class group is unique, the most sensible approach to class management is likely to be an eclectic one that uses selectively those techniques that best fit a particular situation.

Acquiring Basic Management Skills

You should make basic management skills, illustrated in Figure 5.1, part of your professional repertoire. By learning and practicing these skills, identified by Kounin and Doyle (Kounin, 1970; Kounin & Doyle, 1975; Doyle, 1977) and confirmed by other researchers (Emmer et al., 1989; Weber & Roff, 1983), you can greatly reduce the number and severity of any classroom management problems that you may face.

DEVELOPING "WITHITNESS"

Teachers who have developed **withitness** seem to have "eyes in the back of their heads" to spot quickly what students are doing—or not doing—an almost uncanny ability to time interventions so that they "nip problems in the bud." This faculty seems to convince their students that any misbehavior will be noticed promptly, a healthy conviction that tends to keep them on task. "Withitness" also guards teachers from blaming the wrong person for misbehavior or punishing a group for the misbehavior of one or a few students (Kounin, 1970).

To develop this faculty, stand where you can see all your students when you are presenting a lesson. Make frequent eye contact with as many of them as possible by glancing often at all parts of the room. Use "stage" turns (i.e., face your class as you turn) so that you can maintain eye contact with your students as you move toward the chalkboard; stand at an angle to write on the chalkboard so that you can see as many students as possible. Circulate to various parts of the room

FIGURE 5.1

Basic Classroom Management Skills

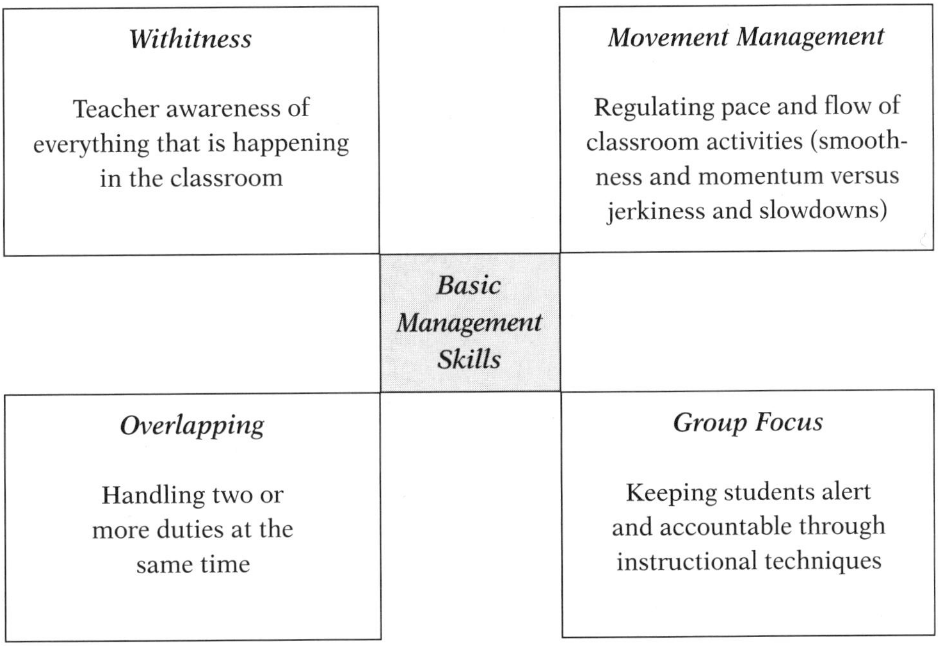

Withitness		*Movement Management*
Teacher awareness of everything that is happening in the classroom		Regulating pace and flow of classroom activities (smoothness and momentum versus jerkiness and slowdowns)
	Basic Management Skills	
Overlapping		*Group Focus*
Handling two or more duties at the same time		Keeping students alert and accountable through instructional techniques

Source: Based on *Discipline and Group Management in Classrooms* by J. Kounin, 1970, New York: Holt, Rinehart and Winston, and "The Uses of Nonverbal Behaviors: Toward an Ecological Model of Classrooms" by W. Doyle, 1977, *Merrill–Palmer Quarterly, 23,* pp. 179–192.

when opportunity offers and, as you stop to help one student, stand where you can see as many others as possible.

"OVERLAPPING"

Skilled teachers train themselves to **overlap** (handle two or more situations or activities simultaneously), allowing the flow of productive classroom activity to continue uninterrupted while they deal with a particular need. They avoid becoming so immersed in one activity that they neglect another that requires immediate attention. The effective use of overlapping depends, of course, on constant "withitness."

You might apply overlapping skills by

♦ making eye contact with, moving closer to, or standing beside a misbehaving student or group of students to deter their off-task behavior while continuing to direct other activities;

- directing a question to a student who has not been paying attention to regain his or her attention;
- acknowledging raised hands with nods or other nonverbal signals to avoid distracting students who are quietly on task;
- removing an object a student is playing with without interrupting a presentation to focus the "player's" attention without slowing the pace of your lesson;
- gesturing to deter a misbehaving student from pursuing an inappropriate activity to avoid focusing the attention of other students on the misbehavior.

MANAGING MOVEMENT

Skilled teachers use **movement management** to regulate the pace and flow of classroom activities, keeping "dead time" to a minimum. To manage movement effectively,

- organize your demonstration materials, teaching aids, or learning centers (see Chapter 14) so that they are ready for immediate use;
- train your students to take out their books or materials promptly so that they are ready to begin work when you are;
- teach and use efficient routines for distributing materials and supplies;
- establish efficient routines for moving students promptly from room to room or from one part of the room to another.

FOSTERING GROUP FOCUS

Group focus keeps you aware of *all* your students—not just one or two—and keeps each student "actively involved, alert, and accountable for [his or her] performance" (Weber, Roff, Crawford, & Robinson, 1983, p. 25); it also contributes to peer learning. Fostering group focus involves the use of "withitness," "overlapping," and productive movement management. To foster group focus,

- pace your lessons quickly enough to maintain your students' interest, but not so quickly as to confuse and discourage them;
- frame questions at a variety of levels, and distribute them widely to keep students alert (see Chapter 7);
- accept responses only from students whom you have recognized: since **call-out answers**—unsolicited responses that are blurted out—can be a major source of classroom management problems, it is worth establishing at the beginning of the year that you will not accept them. (**Choral responses** have a place, however, with shy pupils or in classes in which students are practicing the sounds of a language.);

◆ circulate during seatwork in order to ensure that your students understand and are learning, to help individuals, and to see to it that your students hand in assignments and receive prompt feedback and reinforcement.

Management and Instruction

Teaching presents a constant challenge to make optimum use of class time—that is, to maximize students' **academic learning time**—by keeping them on task and accountable. To achieve this target, you will need to address the following areas of "routine" classroom management.

BUILDING POSITIVE RELATIONSHIPS

Establishing positive relationships with students (see Chapter 4) while enforcing reasonable discipline is a constant challenge to teachers. To achieve such relationships, you must gain respect as a teacher and as a person. You may encounter classes that think it "fun" to test the authority of a student teacher; or you may feel uncertain as to how far you should go in joking or speaking informally with students, in case they take advantage of your approach. Until you develop an effective personal discipline style, you may wonder how—and when—to act, without being too hard on students. These challenges become formidable indeed if you find that you must reverse inappropriate behavior patterns and poor attitudes.

Change *is* possible, however: in classes in which some students need to make behavioral changes, you can help them to achieve instructional goals while you achieve professional targets by setting reasonable rules and developing efficient procedures and routines that all students can understand and follow. Explain these routines to your students, demonstrate or illustrate them (see Chapter 9), and give your class time to practice them.

Motivation, productive instruction, and good organization are key factors in building positive relationships:

◆ *Motivation* is the key to keeping students interested and on task (see Chapter 4). This can be a challenge, especially in a class unprepared to find the subject matter fascinating, and ready to drop off to sleep. You may need to plan different tasks for students of different abilities, since some will finish an assignment while others are still working slowly (see Chapter 14). You will need tact to control students who are excited about what they are doing without dampening their spirits.

◆ *Instruction* that results in learning must maintain a high level of student interest. You can make instruction interesting by using success-oriented teaching techniques and by pacing delivery as appropriate to learners' needs (see Chapter 6). Willingly accept students' ideas, clearly state work requirements and assignments, and provide regular feedback on students' behavior, as well as on their work (see Chapter 4).

- *Organization* can present a challenge when circumstances demand that you work with your entire class, while an individual wants—and needs—your attention (see Chapter 6). You may be well aware that if you direct your attention to a few students, the others will begin a social chat, but your awareness alone will not solve the problem. Arrange to monitor students' practice of skills you have taught. Peer coaching or "partnerships" may be useful in some situations (see Chapter 15).

ORGANIZING GROUP AND INDIVIDUAL WORK

Group organization allows you to arrange for students to work at their current levels of achievement and needs (see Chapter 15). At times, you may need to organize group activities to engage some of your students while you attend to the special needs of those of a different cultural background, finding ways to integrate the latter, as far as possible, into class activities (see Chapter 6).

Set an appropriate level of challenge for assignments and seatwork, and explain clearly how and when you expect your students to get help with difficulties, and what options they can pursue when they have finished their work (see Chapter 14). Individuals should make continuous progress in (usually) small, achievable steps, involving a minimum of confusion or frustration. Success rates should be high: about 75 percent for questions and 100 percent for seatwork (Good & Brophy, 1986, pp. 360–361).

MONITORING CLASSROOM ACTIVITY

As soon as possible, establish fair and consistent classroom rules and procedures based on group needs and **individual accountability** (see Chapter 4). Choose learning objectives thoughtfully, and communicate them clearly. Systematically foster and monitor appropriate behavior, and follow through on behavioral consequences. Such classroom management and monitoring should prevent students from becoming anxious, confused, or resentful, and help them to achieve success.

Controlling the Instruction Process

Control of classroom behavior patterns, lesson content, learning experiences, and other procedures can be viewed along a continuum of teacher-to-student responsibility/control as shown:

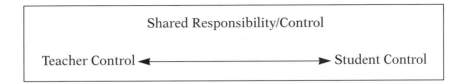

Shared Responsibility/Control

Teacher Control ◀——————————▶ Student Control

The balance of responsibility/control patterns may vary, depending on factors such as the type of lesson content and the degree of readiness on the part of the students to take responsibility for their own learning (see Chapter 14).

When a teacher determines the learning objectives, content, pacing, learning activities, classroom rules and procedures, and assessment, with little or no input from students, teacher control in a classroom is high. A high level of teacher control suggests that students may be only passively involved in their learning process.

Although a high level of student control may suggest the opposite—that students are actively involved in the teaching/learning process—it is very demanding of the teacher. It requires that the teacher determine students' command of knowledge and skills in relation to the topic to be studied, identify their learning needs and, to meet those needs, teach student-selected content and activities, using student-selected methods and means of evaluation. The teacher's role becomes that of facilitator and resource person rather than that of presenter or instructor.

Direct instruction strategies and methods (e.g., lecture, assigned questions, and explicit teaching—see Chapter 12) are generally considered highly teacher-centered and -controlled, whereas indirect strategies and methods (e.g., inquiry, cooperative learning, **group investigation**, and some experiential learning—see Chapters 13 to 15) are generally considered strongly student-centered and -controlled. Despite these general perceptions, opportunities exist for varying the balance of control in both types of instruction, and the locus of control can—and often should—shift during the teaching of any unit or lesson.

THE ISSUE OF CONTROL

How much control should students exercise over what they learn and how they learn? Can students be trusted to learn diligently the content and skills they need? Ethically and legally, how much control can teachers relinquish?

Few educators disagree that teachers should seek and value the opinions of their students. Knowing that a teacher seeks their opinion motivates students to learn (see Chapter 4). Students do not respect or like teachers who are indifferent to or scorn their feelings and judgments (see Chapter 3). In addition, knowing what students think helps you to make adjustments and clear up misconceptions. A more complex question is the amount of voice students should have in selecting lesson content, learning methods, and modes of evaluation.

Factors to consider when deciding the degree of control you should entrust to your students include

• the degree to which you have already established positive classroom management;
• the level of interpersonal and group skills your students have acquired;
• the need for increased motivation through promotion of student ownership;
• the availability of print and nonprint resources needed to make student-directed instruction practical (see Chapters 13, 14);
• the degree of student control with which you can be comfortable.

PRACTICE *and Projects*

1. a. Think of a teacher who managed his or her classroom very well. Record the things this teacher did or said to keep students on task and learning. Tell two partners about your teacher.
    b. Working with your two partners, identify five characteristics that made the teacher you described a successful classroom manager. Join another group, and again agree on five characteristics. Choose a spokesperson from your group of six to report to the whole class.

2. Form groups of five or six. Take turns recalling examples you have noticed of teachers using each of the basic management skills outlined above.

3. Use Data Collection Form 5.1 (Appendix A) to help you analyze Case Study 5.1. Your instructor may pose specific questions for your response.

4. a. Form groups of seven or eight. Compose and deliver a skit representing a teacher's use in class of one of the management skills outlined above.
    b. Ask the other members of your class to use Data Collection Form 5.1 to record their observations.
    c. Debrief as a class.

■ ■ ■ ■ ■

MANAGING CLASSROOM BEHAVIOR

In all effectively managed classrooms, students follow reasonable rules and procedures consistently applied (see Chapter 4). Effective classroom-behavior management depends largely on motivation and problem prevention. From the very beginning, your students should know that you mean business, have a sense of humor, will be fair and consistent but firm, and expect them *all* to behave

CASE STUDY 5.1

USING BASIC MANAGEMENT SKILLS

Mr. Agropolis is presenting a lesson on volcanic action to his Grade 6 class. He is standing behind a table at the side of the room, using a model of a volcano to explain the causes and effects of a volcanic eruption. All the students can see the model as they stand in a semicircle around the table. While Mr. Agropolis is speaking, Beulah makes a remark to her neighbor, Yoko. Mr. Agropolis catches Beulah's eye and without stopping his explanation, raises his finger to his lips. Beulah stops talking, and both she and Yoko pay attention.

Mr. Agropolis keeps his students' attention by varying his voice pattern, asking questions at random, and occasionally drawing their attention to the model for clarification of some detail. When asking questions he phrases the question first, looks around for a few seconds and then asks a specific student to respond.

When the demonstration is over, Mr. Agropolis motions to John and Sasha near the front. They begin to distribute the worksheets that are on the side table. He tells the other students not to begin working until he has given directions and then signals them to return to their desks. When everyone is seated and has a worksheet, he calls for attention, waits briefly until the class is quiet and looking at him, and then explains the assignment. As he explains, he moves around the room, approaching nonattending students, sometimes pointing at a worksheet or staying nearby until a child is attending again. He unobtrusively gives a "thumbs up" signal to a shy child who is attending carefully.

appropriately and to succeed scholastically. There is no substitute for starting the term by showing that you will do your best to provide lessons that are relevant and interesting, and by sending the message, through your professional attitude, "I care about you. I know that you can behave and learn well. I want to help you develop into a *more mature you.*"

Discipline in the Well-Managed Classroom

The primary aim of **discipline** in the well-managed classroom is to train students to take responsibility for positive self-discipline. The first approach to achieving this target is likely to be the constructive use of extrinsic and intrinsic rewards and penalties to motivate or deter students as appropriate. Subsequent steps will probably involve the use of preventive discipline. Inevitably, there will be occasions when responsive discipline is required, but these should become fewer as students learn to accept more responsibility for their own learning.

USING REWARDS AND PENALTIES

A **reward** is a desirable consequence of suitable behavior, effort, or achievement. Rewards should be attainable by reasonable effort, for if they are too easy or too hard to earn, they lose their motivational value. Depending on the age and stage of your students, rewards might include grades or other symbols (e.g., gold stars); teacher approval given publicly or privately; recognition in the form of certificates, posting of work, prizes (e.g., equipment, games, books, or money), or privileges (e.g., socializing time, elective reading, or playing a game).

A **penalty** is an undesirable consequence of inappropriate behavior. Penalties should "fit the crime" and be neither trivial nor harsh. When penalties must be imposed, they should be administered "without malice" in a matter-of-fact, unblaming way, as if to say, "I still like you, but the consequence you have chosen will happen." Angry and attacking ways of punishing may result in further misbehavior.

Penalties might include reduction of grades (for failing to do assignments), demerits, loss of privileges, confiscation of forbidden possessions, referral to an administrator, isolation (in or after class), restitution (e.g., replacement of stolen or damaged goods, or cleaning up a deliberately or carelessly made mess), suspension and, in extreme situations, expulsion.

The concept of individual "choice" and accountability is critical to the effective use of rewards and penalties: the student must choose to work and behave well or to be idle and misbehave. In making the choice, the student—not you—chooses the consequence of reward or punishment.

Encouraging Desirable Behavior

Since people tend to behave in ways that yield rewards, you will find it useful to make a point of encouraging students who are behaving appropriately or to reward a disruptive student who adopts desired forms of behavior. Praise and encouragement are powerful stimulants! Effective praise is sincere, contingent on effort and achievement, and appropriate to the value and particulars of the accomplishment. In giving recognition, be sure to specify the praiseworthy behavior or achievement and to give praise at times and places that will not embarrass the recipient or others.

AVOIDING THE "NICE GAL/GUY" SYNDROME

Make sure that from the beginning, your students understand the consequences of their actions; then, dispassionately enforce those consequences, for students neither respect nor particularly like teachers who cannot control a class. Be firm to be kind!

Do not fall into the trap that imprisons so many beginning teachers: the "nice gal/guy syndrome." These teachers want their students to like them and so remit— or, worse still, apply inconsistently—the consequences of misbehavior or late assignments. Because they fear to put a stop to disruptions, the disruptive behavior spreads, and before they know it, they have lost control of their class. Failure to nip minor disruptions in the bud results in the very thing that beginning teachers fear most: almost inevitably, such "nice guys/gals" lose the respect of their students, and misbehavior escalates.

EXERCISING PREVENTIVE DISCIPLINE

"An ounce of prevention is worth a pound of cure!" Whenever possible, use preventive-discipline skills to establish and maintain classroom conditions that promote positive student behavior and free you for instruction and your students for learning.

Preventive discipline, which embraces what is known as assertive discipline, comprises a number of strategies for heading off minor classroom disruptions and greatly reducing the likelihood of major ones. At the outset, tell your students plainly that you cannot tolerate misbehavior because it interferes with the rights of other students to learn and grow, and with your right and duty to teach. Follow through on your statement: consistency is important, for students learn quickly whether or not a teacher will continue to enforce the rules, procedures, and routines laid down.

Well-planned classroom activities reduce disruptions and the time needed to deal with them, for the more time students spend diligently learning and practicing, the more they achieve, and the less likely they are to misbehave. The proportion of time students are engaged in constructive, interesting, and meaningful work should be high, though there should be "play" time as well. Organize the procedures of handling materials and supplies, moving students from one spot to another or having them change from one activity to another so that little time is available for disruptive or off-task behavior.

EXERCISING RESPONSIVE DISCIPLINE: DEALING WITH MINOR DISRUPTIONS

Minor disruptions occur in every classroom, and you will have to deal with some, for there never has been, nor ever will be, a classroom where no disruptions occur. Your students may seek attention or test limits by inattention, tardiness or absenteeism, talking out of turn, neglecting assignments, using profanity or making crude or smart remarks, ignoring instructions, moving about at will, socializing persistently, or disturbing others. Even when you have developed excellent classroom management skills, you will encounter such problems occasionally, but you can learn how to keep them to a minimum. You should handle undesirable incidents patiently, calmly, nonjudgmentally, and kindly, avoiding actions that might have adverse effects on your students. Handling such incidents might involve the following steps.

Deter Unacceptable Behavior

Recall a class in which one person started to giggle, then another, and another until the giggles caused a **ripple effect** around the room (Kounin, 1970). Your ways of handling disruptions can cause ripple effects that may be positive or negative. The ripple effect is positive when you cause other students to observe a rule by dealing calmly, reasonably, and effectively with a student who has broken it. By contrast, to let a student "get away with" an infraction can have a negative ripple effect, for it can lead the rule breaker or others to repeat the offense.

Though you should not normally ignore violations of rules and procedures that may spread, or "ripple," it is best to ignore some minor misbehaviors of short duration, since **reacting** to them may only distract students' attention and interrupt the flow of the lesson/activity. If a student violates a rule, you must use your common sense and good judgment: Has the misbehavior occurred often in the past? Is it likely to persist? Has it interrupted the flow of the lesson? Was it an accident, such as the inadvertent dropping of a book? Accidental disruptions should usually be ignored or handled with sympathy or supportive humor.

Your students should discover very early, however, that you cannot allow inattention or misbehavior to continue. When a student's attention lapses or is distracted by something other than the assignment given, redirect it to the task (e.g., "Brian, go on with the problems on page 33"). Use "overlapping" to handle minor disruptions without drawing undue attention. In dealing with a disruptive student, make extended eye contact, pause, or move toward the student. Use cues, prompts, and signals to deter the student and to remind him or her of appropriate behavior. If silent signals fail, quietly but firmly ask the student to stop, make it clear what positive action he or she is to take, and ensure that the student understands your directions. Later, when the rest of the class is working, quietly tell the student of the consequence incurred.

Issue a Direct Desist

Issue a direct desist when necessary. When one student deliberately disrupts the activities of others, you may need to rebuke that student verbally or by gesture, and turn his or her behavior in a positive direction. If you must give a verbal reprimand, be calm, firm, and objective, clearly stating the behavior that must stop and the desired behavior. If possible, handle the matter discreetly, on a one-to-one basis. Remember that, in disciplining a student,

- *personal responses are critical*: Teaching calls for consistent self-control. You must keep your temper and follow a professional pattern of management, even if your students test the limits of your authority with a show of disrespect. Issues with colleagues, including differences in approaches taken by you and your cooperating teachers, must be negotiated privately in a professional manner;
- *staying in control is essential*: Never overreact, and never attack the personal worth of any individual. Your approach should be positive, sending the message, "Your behavior is not acceptable, but even though it must stop, I still like you!" Do not take misbehavior as a personal attack: make it plain that you will not hold a grudge or resort to "put-downs" or sarcasm that damage self-concept. Handle any problems that occur in a professional way: keep your ego out of it!
- *monitoring and checking task performance will deter repetition of minor disruptions*: The procedures suggested above should normally cause little interruption to class activities and should quickly return a misbehaving or off-task student to task. Some students, however, may resume disruptive behavior when you turn your eyes away, and it is wise to check that they are remaining on task. Use "overlapping" to do this without interrupting the normal course of classroom activities.

DEALING WITH MAJOR DISRUPTIONS

Major disruptions caused by serious behavior problems can create difficulties, especially for new teachers. Overt defiance requires a prompt response. Such behavior includes drinking, substance abuse, cheating, being absent without reason, or refusal or failure to bring books to class, participate in class activities, follow a direct order, answer a question, or do assignments. Seriously disruptive students may throw objects, be physically aggressive to the point of terrorizing other students, or create a chaotic class situation that is completely out of control.

Your students' safety and your own should be your primary concern in seriously disruptive situations. If possible, isolate the disruptive student immediately; in any case, try to defuse the situation promptly and quietly, and do *not* try to settle issues in front of a class, since the student might feel that he or she must remain defiant in order to "save face." A brief cooling-off period may be helpful to you and your student, but serious issues *must* be resolved in consultation with your student and, if necessary, with a member of the Guidance staff, the principal or vice-principal, and/or the student's parent(s).

CASE STUDY 5.2

HANDLING A MINOR DISRUPTION

Ms. Kim Bear's students are working in pairs to make Christmas wreaths from clothes hangers and colored plastic. Ms. Bear has given instructions and is circulating about the room. She nods to Sharim and Joseph, who are sharing the tasks involved. To Janice and Peter, she says, "Good work! I like the way you're tying the pieces close together. May I show the others how you're doing it?" She shows the partly finished wreath to the other children.

Ms. Bear spends more time in the part of the room where children are having difficulty sharing the task. Occasionally, she asks a question or makes a suggestion to a pair about how they might cooperate. When everyone is on task, she says, "I wish everyone in the school could see how well you're all sharing, taking turns, and deciding together how to finish your wreath. Give yourselves a pat on the back." Giggling, the children give themselves a pat on the back and then continue their work.

Julia quickly loses interest in the task and makes threatening gestures at her partner with her scissors. Ms. Bear says, "Julia, will you please take the waste basket around to collect the scraps, and bring it back to me?" When Julia returns the waste basket, Ms. Bear says quietly, "It's your turn to cut now, Julia. Please be careful with the scissors. If you wave them around, you might hurt someone." She helps Julia restart her task, monitoring the proper procedure, and comments, "That's the safe way to use scissors. Good for you!"

Ms. Bear moves away, but stands where she can still observe Julia's behavior. Julia notices and says, "See! I'm still cutting nicely!"

A number of approaches to dealing with seriously disruptive behavior are discussed briefly below. In all of these approaches, it is essential to keep your ego out of it! A professional teacher does not take student misbehavior as a personal attack any more than a physician whose patient does not take the medication prescribed sees his or her noncompliance as a personal attack.

Reality Therapy

Many professional educators advocate an approach to handling disruptions developed by William Glasser, known as *reality therapy*. This problem-solving process, which is based on care and concern, stresses the importance of creating a positive facilitative atmosphere in the school and the classroom.

Reality therapy is intended to help students change unacceptable behavior. It begins with a classroom meeting at which students set rules for themselves and their peers; in subsequent meetings, they adjust rules or develop new ones as needed, and deal with problems that have occurred. At these meetings, the teacher functions as discussion facilitator and group member, explaining school and group rules, and enforcing them as necessary. The meetings are held to facilitate teacher–student and student–student involvement so that students can take responsibility for controlling themselves and following school rules, thus becoming more accountable for their own behavior and learning (Weber & Roff, 1983).

When a problem occurs, the teacher intervenes, using a process introduced by Glasser (Good & Brophy, 1990) that includes the following steps:

- Before meeting with the student, describe the disruptive behavior and teachers' typical reactions.
- Analyze the description, and decide which responses work and which do not. Avoid repeating responses that do not work.
- Try to improve your personal relationship with the student. Take the initiative to show concern and provide encouragement.
- Confer with the student to help her analyze her disruptive behavior by asking her to describe it. When the student has done this, ask her to stop the disruptive behavior.
- If the problem continues, hold a short conference with the student, and ask her to describe the disruptive behavior again. Ask whether the behavior is breaking a rule or an unstated expectation, and whether it is reasonable. Have the student state how the behavior should be changed. Be warm and supportive, but persistent and firm.
- If the disruptive behavior persists, call another conference with the student. Have her focus on the behavior and state the specific actions that she will take to eliminate the problem. Agree on what these actions will be, and how they will be carried out.
- If the above process fails, isolate the student temporarily. Have her spend the time in isolation devising a plan to ensure that she will follow the rules. Do not allow the student to rejoin the class/group until she has formulated the plan, and you and she have agreed on it.
- The next consequence of noncompliance is in-school suspension. The student must now deal directly with the principal or person responsible for school discipline. She will be permitted to return to the classroom only when she has made a workable plan that is acceptable to all parties. Parents should be notified if suspension continues for longer than one day.

◆ This step—which applies only if the student remains out of control and the in-school suspension continues—consists of calling parents to remove the student from school. The next day, the student returns, and the process begins again.

◆ The last step is removal from school and referral to another agency. Even at this point, a student is allowed to return to school if she makes and clearly commits to a specific acceptable plan.

Points to ponder ...

❑ What do I consider "professional behavior" in face of a student behavior problem?

❑ How can I keep my ego out of it?

PRACTICE *and Projects*

1. a. Working in a group of five, ask each person to suggest a concern relating to classroom management that beginning teachers might have. Discuss these hypothetical concerns, and suggest positive ways of handling them.

   b. Report to the class your group's suggestion for handling one of the situations you have discussed. Your report might take the form of a role play or skit.

2. a. On separate file cards, write two personal concerns relating to classroom management. Collect the cards, and appoint a "facilitator" to read the concerns aloud, in turn, while "recorders" write them on the chalkboard. Duplications are not written out but represented by a check mark beside concerns already written. When the contents of all cards have been recorded, do a frequency count of the concerns listed.

   b. Beginning with the problems of highest frequency, problem solve by groups. When all groups have reported, debrief in a class session.

3. Recall a teacher who you believe handled minor disruptions well. Join five of your peers to list and classify effective behaviors for handling minor disruptions. Report to the class. Debrief in a class session.

4. Use Data Collection Form 5.2 (Appendix A) to help you analyze Case Study 5.2. Your instructor may pose specific questions for your response.

SUMMARY

- Appropriate classroom management is a critical part of effective instruction.
- From a student perspective, effective classroom management provides students with opportunities to socialize while learning interesting content.
- From a teacher perspective, effective management involves preventive discipline, and interesting instruction.
- Approaches to classroom management range from those involving the highest level of teacher control (intimidation and authoritarianism) to those involving extreme permissiveness. The most productive approach avoids the extremes and combines elements of the others as circumstances suggest.
- Classroom-management skills that support productive student behavior include professional awareness, "overlapping," efficient movement management, and fostering group focus.
- Classroom-management skills that support effective instruction include building positive student–teacher relationships, organizing group and individual work effectively, and monitoring classroom activity.
- Control of classroom behavior and learning activities should vary on a continuum that ranges from teacher to student control as students mature and develop the capability to be responsible for their own learning.
- Effective classroom-behavior management depends largely on student motivation and problem prevention, and involves training students to exercise positive self-discipline.
- Minor disruptions will occur, even in the well-managed classroom, and can be ignored (if they are likely not to be repeated) or dealt with promptly and quietly by signaling the student to focus on the assigned task.
- In dealing with a major disruption, the primary consideration is the safety of students and staff. A support system involving Guidance and/or administrative staff, as well as parents, School Board, and community resources should be available and used as necessary.

KEY WORDS

basic management
   skills
      professional
         awareness
      "overlapping"
      managing
         movement
      fostering
         group focus

classroom
   management
      effective
         management
      preventive
         discipline
      interesting
         instruction
   control
   disruptions
   eclectic management
      style

individual choice and
      accountability
management
      approaches
organization
penalties
reality therapy
responsive discipline
rewards
student/teacher
      control
teacher intervention

RECOMMENDED READING

Bauer, A., & Sapona, R. (1991). *Managing classrooms to facilitate learning.* Englewood Cliffs, NJ: Prentice-Hall.

Bowd, A., McDougall, D., & Yewchuk, C. (1994). *Educational psychology for Canadian teachers.* Toronto: Harcourt Brace & Company.

Curwin, R., & Mendler, A. (1988). *Discipline with dignity.* Alexandria, VA: Association for Supervision and Curriculum Development.

Sanford, J., & Emmer, E. (1988). *Understanding classroom management: An observation guide.* Englewood Cliffs, NJ: Prentice-Hall.

Travers, J., Elliott, S., & Kratchowill, T. (1993). *Educational psychology: Effective teaching and learning.* Madison, WI: Brown & Benchmark.

CHAPTER 6

THE "COSMIC CLASSROOM": MEETING LEARNERS' NEEDS

■ ■ ■ ■ ■

If students do not learn the way we teach them, then we must teach them the way they learn!

(MARSHALL, 1991, P. 226)

■ ■ ■ ■ ■

OVERVIEW

Students' cultural backgrounds affect their learning strengths and preferences, and influence their achievement in school. Cultures are a compound of geographic, social, economic, religious, and political elements that influence personal and group thought and behavior. Teachers must recognize how culture affects themselves, their community, and their students. They must be sensitive to and respect differences, recognize bias in instructional materials, and become proficient in cross-cultural instruction. Every teacher has a duty to combat racism and help all learners achieve their potential by promoting change that involves a multicultural approach to learning.

"Mainstreaming," or accommodating students of different abilities in regular classrooms, is becoming more and more common. Every classroom has at least some special-needs or exceptional learners who may have learning problems or physical disabilities or who may be gifted, bilingual, socio-economically advantaged/disadvantaged, or recent immigrants. This diversity contributes to the complexity of teaching. It demands special training, use of human and professional resources, and the reflective practice of professional development techniques.

■ ■ ■ ■ ■

LEARNER DIVERSITY: MEETING THE NEEDS

Professional teachers know that classrooms are microcosms of the broad ranges of human diversity (see Chapter 4). They recognize that, in reality, an "average" learner is an abnormality, for classrooms, like communities, contain a cross-section of diverse persons with distinctive characteristics. Three dimensions contribute to the diversity of learners in classrooms: learning-style preferences, cultural background, and exceptionality. Learners vary in the following ways:

◆ natural abilities (developmentally or physically challenged, gifted);
◆ innate tendency to approach learning through the left *or* right brain hemisphere;

♦ preferred learning style (see Chapters 1 and 4);
♦ cultural, social, and economic background.

In every classroom, therefore, as in every community, diversity should be expected and valued.

Instruction and Cultural Perspective

All around the world, individuals' upbringing, the behaviors and value systems of their peers, and the social systems to which they belong affect their cultural perspectives, the way they see the world. Cultural background, too, affects students' academic strengths and learning-style preferences.

Culture, the unique lifestyle of a particular group of people, derives from the combined circumstances of **ethnic group**, geographic location, regional beliefs and customs, religion, social class, occupation, and outside influences. Although culture grows out of the past, it functions in the present and, thus, is constantly changing, influencing language, patterns of communication, and styles of behavior. All persons acquire and belong to a dominant culture and a number of subcultures.

CULTURAL COMPONENTS

A culture may be considered to have five components: "personality," which is reflected in attitudes, values, and beliefs; language, which includes basic communications, symbolism, and jargon; social structures based on family and community groups, customs, religion, technology, and education; occupations, which involve resource gathering, service, agriculture, manufacturing, and government; and environment, which includes land forms, climate, vegetation, and wildlife (Brown, 1963).

Other factors that derive from and influence culture include

♦ **social stratification**, the hierarchical structuring of society according to a person's or group's political, economic, and social power;
♦ **the dominant group** composed of those members of society who exercise the greatest degree of political, economic, and social power;
♦ **subordinate groups** whose members hold less social, economic, and/or political power than do the members of the dominant group;
♦ **ethnic groups** composed of people who share a common race, language, and history.

We can analyze culture according to various categories, including communication and language, mental processes and learning, beliefs and attitudes, values and norms, sense of self and space, time and time consciousness, relationships, rewards and recognition, dress and appearance, and food and feeding habits, as well as the processes by which a group organizes itself: kinship, religion, education, business and social association, economics, politics, health, and recreation.

The Culture of Poverty

As well as belonging to the culture of certain ethnic groups, many students are also subjected to a "culture of poverty" that cuts across those groups. Many of these children achieve little in schools, where

- they often lack opportunities to interact with peers who have learned the behavior patterns that help people get ahead in the dominant culture;
- they experience discrimination; and
- their needs are not met.

All these factors can reduce students' self-concept and help to make them underachievers in school.

One way to help replace this negative process with one productive of positive outcomes is to provide all learners with education that has strong multicultural components. To implement such a target will take commitment, steady effort, time, an open mind, organizational skills, tact, and training, but the results can amply justify the investment.

■ ■ ■ ■ ■

MULTICULTURAL EDUCATION

"Multicultural education is built on human relations" (Colangelo, Foxely, & Dustin, 1979, p. 4). It has two components: training in human relations and ethnic studies, which show people as unique members of identifiable cultural groups. North American societies are multicultural. Sometimes skin color or other physical traits make the diverse cultural mix in schools easily observable; at other times diversity, while just as deep, is less obvious. Differences include ethnic background, geographic location, cultural heritage, income, family organization, and exceptionality. The home setting and personal characteristics of the child—his or her abilities and disabilities—affect the school experience. In view of this,

> Multicultural education deserves more than ... lip service ... schools can play vital roles in teaching their students to recognize, accept, and respect cultural differences. Developmental changes in ... learners occur constantly; concepts of one's self and of one's culture can fluctuate daily. Schools can [help students] ... understand cultural and ethnic stereotypes, myths about cultural differences, racism, and the effects of all three on one's ability to function in an increasingly multicultural world. (Manning, 1991, p. 218)

Becoming a Multicultural Teacher

Practicing multiculturalism in the classroom requires positive intent, practical action, cooperation, and patience. Begin by considering the following aspects of fostering a "cosmic" classroom.

IDENTIFY YOUR PERSONAL PERCEPTIONS

To become a truly multicultural teacher, you must recognize that your own cultural background affects your behavior and expectations. People perceive things according to what their cultural background has taught them: "good" food, for instance, may be a slice of beef or a candied ant; "lawful marriage" may unite two persons or several; children may be trained to show respect by looking at the elders speaking to them or by keeping their eyes lowered. Like everyone else, you react to situations and the persons in them according to your culturally conditioned perceptions of them. Initially, therefore, a mix of cultures in the classroom may complicate communication and cause confusion.

To clarify your personal perceptions, identify the chief qualities of your family culture, and examine how they determine your perception of the world. You will soon see that some of your perceptions may differ from those of your students. You can act with more patience and wisdom if you realize *why* you act in certain ways, and why some students may act differently.

If, for instance, your family belongs to North America's majority culture, you may value planning and saving, enjoy competition, and view education as promoting individual freedom, autonomy, and achievement; you may believe that people should be "workers," using technology to control nature. By contrast, if your family culture is more group-oriented, you may value ancestral traditions and beliefs, and put loyalty to the group before individual autonomy and group cooperation before personal achievement. You may focus on the present in the expectation that the group will provide for your future; you may value relaxation, meditation, and method; and you may believe that people should respect and become one with nature rather than exploiting its resources. In either case, your classroom behavior and expectations can dramatically affect your students.

LEARN ABOUT THE COMMUNITY

To model and teach positive multicultural behavior and attitudes, you must recognize that children learn much in their homes and community before they come to school. Learn as much as you can about your students' backgrounds in order to be sensitive to their cultures and needs. Compare cultural heritage and contemporary life styles, taking into account cultural and historical developments and the influence of contemporary values, social and political activities, issues and leaders as they affect education. Remembering that individual instances differ in all cultures, inform yourself about general home and family relations as shown by patterns of family structure, role definitions, and effects of child-rearing practices on behavior and learning style. Consider community cultures as they relate to **group structures** and roles, and to functions of schools and other institutions. Use your personal development and interpersonal skills to relate your own culture to the cultures of others, and to deal with any conflicts that arise.

Interviews can help you to inform yourself and your students about the ethnic composition of your community. Ask parents about their educational goals for their children, the school subjects they consider important, and the extracurricular activities they value. Note any factors that may not fit school expectations. Try to learn about areas that might create conflict between teaching given at home and instruction given in school, the sort of behavior parents consider polite and impolite, the ways in which they show friendship or respect, and the sorts of actions that embarrass them. Their suggestions for change may make your classroom more comfortable and enjoyable for your students.

Adopt Multicultural Objectives

As a multicultural teacher, you will target a number of professional characteristics (see Chapter 1): an open mind, flexibility, self-confidence, genuine respect for and interest in the values and traditions of others, and a sense of humor. Try to see actions common to your own culture through the eyes of your students, thus showing respect for their cultures. Adapt the curriculum to acknowledge and honor the cultural mix in your classroom, and provide hands-on multicultural experiences.

Learn to live with ambiguity and to cope with stress, for trying to communicate and teach interculturally *is* stressful, particularly if the other cultures represented in your classroom are very different from your own. Communication failures can cause guilt, anger, and sometimes fear, but in learning to cope with these feelings and develop positive human relations, you will be helping your students to do so as well. The key to resolving stress caused by disconcerting differences is likely to be empathy, developed through clear communication.

Plan Multicultural Components

Humanistic approaches to teaching are all the more important when your cultural background differs from that of some of your students. Building trust is harder in situations in which people have little in common, and you may face the challenges of learned distrust, disguised feelings, and even ridicule of those who are different. Though you may need to put extra effort into planning and providing trust-building activities to help minority students bridge the gap of significant cultural differences, this effort is worthwhile, for the classroom may be the only place where students of different backgrounds can learn to understand and trust one another.

Train yourself to recognize stereotypical language and perceptions that hurt people or limit potential, and to avoid racist terms and labels. Pay particular attention to modeling and teaching positive communication, interpersonal, and group skills. Avoid **biased** texts and teaching materials, and emphasize that differences in race, sex, or social group do not limit an individual's potential. Teach your students standard English usage, but try to ensure that they do not feel "stupid" or consider their "home" language wrong or inferior. Whenever possible, let your students approach their tasks in their own ways to encourage different learning styles and to show that you cherish and celebrate the traditions and values of the cultures represented in your classroom. The pay-off is higher rates of student motivation, achievement, and satisfaction.

To help your students value their cultural heritage and build positive self-concepts, you will need to use a variety of teaching styles, instructional methods, and grouping patterns. Select teaching methods and classroom activities that help overcome prejudice, stereotyping, and **ethnocentrism**. Effective teaching methods include role playing, simulations, and small-group strategies, particularly those stressing cooperative learning (see Chapter 15).

MODEL MULTICULTURALISM

If you are aware that your beliefs and practices are the products of your experience, and if you make an effort to become more knowledgeable about the value systems and beliefs of other cultures, you can become a good **cross-cultural** teacher. The classroom climate that you establish and your approach to instruction will be truly pluralistic and bias-free if you help *all* your students to develop a positive self-concept. Realizing that cultures are always changing, accept the validity of each child's learning and living environment, and build upon it by showing that you value racial, cultural, and linguistic differences in your class. Know where bias can occur and what you can do to make assessment less biased (see Chapter 17). Guard yourself from reacting negatively to children of another culture because of their verbal or nonverbal ways of communicating. Since language has developed differently in different parts of the world and even in different parts of most countries, consider national and regional differences neither good nor bad, but valid and interesting.

Remember that your nonverbal behavior shows your expectations and attitudes about your students. Be aware that teachers tend to reciprocate the nonverbal behaviors—positive and negative—of their students. Guard yourself against modeling any form of behavior that you do not wish to encourage in your students. Consider, too, that your placement of students in the classroom may reflect your evaluation of their contributions: teachers tend to stand farther away from "low ability" and "rejected" students, making it harder for them to see, hear, and feel part of what is going on (H. Smith, 1984, pp. 185–189). Students placed close to their teacher participate more actively in class proceedings and behave more positively. Do all you can to give *all* children in your classes a positive self-image and pride in their cultural heritage, and to provide equal educational opportunities on which each child can build.

INCORPORATE MULTICULTURAL CONTENT

As you target and monitor your progress in becoming an effective multicultural teacher, you will develop ways of introducing multiculturalism into your classroom climate, teaching methods, and nonverbal behavior. You will, for instance,

- without preaching or showing anger, model appropriate behavior and language, and initiate discussion of questionable language or practices;
- help your students to recognize universal behaviors and needs, and to identify aspects of society common to various peoples, but to understand, as well, that group and individual differences are normal;
- teach your students to appreciate and respect diversity, and to value various cultural groups' contributions to today's society;
- involve children from minority groups in the dominant group's activities by integrating the standards and priorities of the former groups into class activities;
- encourage your students to use critical-thinking processes (see Chapter 10) to identify and reject prejudice, discrimination, and racism in their own thinking and that of others.

TEACH THE "HIDDEN CURRICULUM"

If schools are to become truly multicultural, teachers must not focus on one culture and ignore the positive resources, vitality, and creativity of others; nor should they assume that the Anglo-Celtic culture is "correct," while other cultures are handicaps to be overcome. In teaching history, geography, art, literature, science, and so on, you can and should give attention to *all* cultures represented in your classroom. Multicultural material is, in fact, a "hidden curriculum" that you can and should emphasize. Strategies for teaching this hidden curriculum might include noting significant events in the histories of various ethnic groups to point out our society's multi-ethnic heritage, displaying a multi-ethnic calendar, and celebrating birthdays of significant persons of other cultures.

Promote Positive Self-Concept and Integration

Stress integration and participation of students from other cultures in contrast to **assimilation** into mainstream culture. Assimilation, which involves denying and downgrading minority cultures, is likely to damage the self-concept of students from nondominant cultures. Encourage positive self-concepts and attitudes toward others by providing opportunities for positive participation and productive interactions in the teaching and learning process. Use cooperative learning techniques that place children in racially and ethnically mixed groups where interpersonal contact is maximized, and success depends on everyone's effort.

Table 6.1 summarizes some of the special knowledge and competencies that you will need to teach multicultural class groups.

PRACTICE *and Projects*

1. a. Working in a small subject-specific group, prepare a list of at least six suggestions for applying multicultural teaching to course content in your subject.
    b. Post your list on a classroom bulletin board, and choose two or three of the most interesting or controversial suggestions for class discussion.

2. a. Working with a partner, plan a lesson based on the use of a minority-group community resource.
    b. Form subject-specific groups, outline your lesson plan, and ask for feedback.

3. Working with a partner, analyze Case Study 6.1 and construct a plan of procedure for Ms. Gregory and her colleagues.

TABLE 6.1

Preparing to Teach Multicultural Classes

Learn about Dominant and Subordinate Cultural Groups
- Examine the structure and values of your own culture and other cultures to learn how your society's dominant culture affects your behavior toward people from other cultures.
- Discover the feelings of the general community toward minority groups.
- Learn how members of minority groups feel toward the general community and other minorities.
- Learn all you can about the present culture, history, and cultural heritage of minority groups in your community.
- Try to discover the social, economic, and political forces within the dominant community that affect the behavior of minority groups.
- Learn what you can about the politics within minority groups.

Reflect On and Adopt Professional Attitudes
- Be committed to the principles of democracy, and accept the worth and dignity of each individual.
- View teaching as a "helping profession."
- Commit yourself to using empathy, flexibility, willingness to change, trust, and openness.
- In preparing lessons, consider and involve students, parents, community leaders, paraprofessionals, teachers, administrators, and school boards.
- Try to counteract any cultural bias shown by students and/or community members.
- Intervene positively as necessary, using conflict-resolution skills.

Acquire Competencies in Multicultural Education
- Use teaching methods that build tolerance, understanding, and a sense of community.
- Discover the backgrounds and value structures of your students. Set goals for helping each child to achieve positive self-concept and to recognize the contributions of each culture.
- Model and teach communication, interpersonal, and group skills.
- Work with community agencies and resource persons who have worked with minority groups, paraprofessionals, and parents to plan, implement, maintain or adapt, and evaluate multicultural education programs.
- Learn about, practice, receive feedback and reflect on the use of cross-cultural teaching methods and procedures.

CASE
STUDY **6.1**

CROSS-CULTURAL TEACHING

Ms. Gregory teaches in a high school in which just over half the students belong to recent immigrant families from China, India, Japan, and Jamaica. Racial tensions are escalating. The school is rapidly developing a reputation among city teachers as a tough place to teach. The teachers, a committed and capable group of professionals, are not experienced in multicultural teaching, and they realize that they must take some action as soon as possible.

Ms. Gregory, who has experienced discrimination and self-doubt, believes that students need to see themselves as competent and worthy human beings who can succeed at the tasks they undertake. She wants to have the children from each ethnic group develop positive self-concepts. Secure people, she believes, do not fear or scorn things that are different. Children, she knows, need to learn to value diversity, particularly cultural and linguistic diversity. They need school experiences that will teach them to think of themselves as worthwhile human beings, to see their origin and cultural background as strengths; to respect and value others' origins and cultural backgrounds; to interact with peers in positive and productive ways; and to succeed at meaningful school tasks.

What suggestions will you give Ms. Gregory and the rest of the staff to help promote these goals?

■ ■ ■ ■ ■

RACISM IN SCHOOLS

Cultural differences can easily lead to misunderstanding and prejudice that result in an unequal division of power, and **racism**. Although, in theory, all ethnic groups should be able to preserve their cultures and live out their lives "with respect and without penalty," not all such groups have equal social, economic, and political power. Some people are denied equal opportunity and equal access to education and jobs. These restrictions rob them of self-respect and limit their opportunity to earn a living, to gain the respect of the community, and to be heard. This comes about because in North America, as in other parts of the world, "Different cultures"—seen primarily in terms of ethnic heritage—"are not afforded the same value" (Thomas, 1984, p. 21).

Causes and Results of Racism

The problems of racism and unequal power are reflected in every institution of North American society, including schools. To analyze these problems, we should examine their causes and results, and reflect on the means that might be used to resolve them.

CAUSES OF RACISM

Ignorance, prejudice, and stereotyping cause racism; discrimination, in a destructive cycle, both feeds prejudices and is nourished by them. Injured people who fight against prejudice may be labeled extremist, hard line, radical, or leftist. To fight racism effectively, fair-minded people must determine how it is rationalized and perpetuated, and then set an example and provide education to bring about change.

RESULTS OF RACISM

One of the results of racism is that Native, Métis, Afro-American, and Hispanic children, among others, are often "dead-ended" in North American schools. School drop-out rates in Canada for the first two groups currently stand at about 95 percent. English, French, and Spanish are treated as more valuable languages than Cree, Punjabi, or Jamaican English. Children from Britain or other European or North American countries are considered to "fit in" better than Native children or children from developing countries (Saskatchewan Teachers' Federation, 1988). The problems are all the more severe because they are often hard to prove; indeed, they remain prevalent and persistent.

Of course, you, like most teachers, will not knowingly discriminate against any student, but things you say and do with the best of intentions may be interpreted as discrimination. You can learn to avoid unintended discrimination by respecting human rights and differences, and by becoming proficient in cross-cultural teaching procedures. A first step is to learn the basic concepts associated with human rights, discrimination, and racism.

Social Attitudes and Beliefs

A social **attitude** is a "readiness to respond favorably or unfavorably to a person, object, situation, or event. It is a person's mental set; the feelings an individual has toward various problems that determine the way he or she will act. It is a readiness to verbalize or behave." A **belief**, by contrast, is "something that is thought to be true" (Alberta Human Rights Commission, 1978, p. 5). For Example 6.1 illustrates attitudes and beliefs. In each example, the first statement reflects an attitude and the second a belief. Obviously, beliefs can be incorrect, and attitudes may be based on wrong beliefs. The result is prejudice.

FOR EXAMPLE 6.1

Social Attitudes and Beliefs

EXAMPLE 1. "I would never let my daughter marry a Martian."
"Nor I! Martians always treat their wives as servants."

EXAMPLE 2. "I don't want somebody who is on welfare living next to me."
"You're right! People are on welfare because they're lazy and don't really want jobs."

Prejudice and Discrimination

Prejudice is "an attitude or belief formed or held without really considering the facts. It is for or against something or someone" (Alberta Human Rights Commission, 1978, p. 6). Prejudice usually results from faulty or incomplete information interpreted on the basis of preconceived notions and resulting in prejudgments (see For Example 6.2).

Prejudice may be positive as well as negative: to anticipate, for instance, that every Japanese person you meet will be unfailingly polite is a form of prejudice. Both forms are undesirable because they impose one's preconceived notions on other people, and prevent one from seeing those people as they really are.

Discrimination is "prejudice transmitted into actions [on the basis of] ... attitude or belief" (Alberta Human Rights Commission, 1978, p. 6). When students reject fellow students because of skin color or language differences, they are practicing discrimination. Discrimination creates two categories of people: the privileged and the unprivileged. Factors on which discrimination is often based are skin color, race, national origin, religion, social class, sex, and age.

Stereotyping

Stereotyping is the application of a "fixed set of ideas, often exaggerated and distorted ... [in regarding] all members of a group as being the same" (Alberta Human Rights Commission, 1978, p. 8). It is a generalization that denies members

FOR EXAMPLE 6.2

Prejudice

John Doe and Mary Buck are about to meet Harry Brit, who just stepped off the boat from England. John says to Mary, "I'm not looking forward to this. I'm sure he'll be a pushy know-it-all like your cousin who went to Oxford."

Mary replies, "I suppose so—and what's worse, I expect he'll be a real sissy. He's an artist, you know!"

of a given group individual differences: for example, "Women are not good at math." Stereotyping may occur in textbooks or in teaching methods, as well as in conversation, and it may be positive or negative. Wherever and however it occurs, it should be regarded as dangerous and replaced by a more open attitude.

Self-Fulfilling Prophecies and "Scapegoating"

"Prejudiced people try to prove their invalid stereotypes and faulty generalizations by seeing in the world only what they want to see" (Alberta Human Rights Commission, 1978, p. 7). Stereotypes, used as an excuse for neglect, cruelty, or attack, may become a self-fulfilling prophecy. This occurs when a member of a targeted group "acts or is a certain way because he or she is *expected* to act or be a certain way" (Alberta Human Rights Commission, 1978, p. 9).

Some people seem to need scapegoats in order to deal with personal problems, mistakes, or inadequacies. "Scapegoating" is the "process of singling out an individual [or] group ... upon whom blame for the mistakes or crimes of others is thrust" (Alberta Human Rights Commission, 1978, p. 16). Hitler, for example, used Jews as scapegoats for Germany's economic problems. Even today, some people try to scapegoat certain groups—for example, welfare recipients—for the country's economic and social problems.

Approaches to Change

Cross-cultural, antiracist, and antidiscrimination education seeks to change the attitudes of prejudiced people toward one another. Acquiring information about different cultures is not usually enough, however, to increase students' tolerance; indeed, those who are prejudiced may simply use new information about different groups as further grounds for dislike. To address the root of the problem, you might begin by deepening your working relationships with other teachers who face similar problems. Talk frankly with them about issues; share ideas and materials; and, where possible, cooperate in providing heritage and alternative-language programs; arrange for professional development, and collaborate with parents or others in the community who can extend your own and your students' positive experiences of different groups.

At the same time, use classroom experiences to help students of both dominant and minority (subordinate) groups to learn the skills they need for living and working in the dominant community: that is, teach them how to

◆ communicate effectively;
◆ work cooperatively;
◆ seek complete information;
◆ think critically;
◆ make unbiased decisions.

Teach your students attitudes of respect, cooperation, "fair play," and commitment to remedying injustices. Teach them to identify stereotypes, scrutinize them critically, and explore and evaluate any reasons given for retaining unequal power, opportunity, and social status among different social groups. Help them learn, too, how to respond effectively when they encounter prejudice and discrimination. Explain why some people will resist efforts for change:

> There are some who will resist such [involvement] because of fear, or because they are doing just fine in their current situation. People who have power, or who benefit from current power relations are not likely to be in the forefront of changing those power relations ... The fight against racism has been led by those who suffer most [from] its effects. It is difficult for those who are hurting from racism, to put racism "in a positive light" so as not to offend ... those who do not want to see it. (Thomas, 1984, p. 23)

Bring community and world events into your classroom for students to examine and discuss. Confront any student who tells a joke or makes a remark based on prejudice.

USING PRINT RESOURCES

Do not assume that all "educational" print resources are free of bias. For Example 6.3 identifies some of the types of bias to look out for when selecting textbooks. It is also important to read carefully the resources that you plan to use to ensure that they are suitable for your students' levels of maturity.

If you are teaching young children, you should avoid books that show bias; with more mature students, you will find it productive to have them read more widely and to discuss with them any observable biases. History and literature, for instance, will bring to students' attention realities that should be discussed with the positive intent of creating or promoting change. There are now many excellent sources of multicultural and cross-cultural activities. Text resources and other materials, many free, are available from commercial and public sources. Contact government and human-rights agencies for lists of materials available to classroom teachers and others involved in multicultural or antiracist education.

ENCOURAGING ANTIRACISM

The Council on Interracial Books for Children (Childcare, 1983) suggests activities to help students recognize and deal with racism. Obviously, activities should vary with the age, experience, and maturity of your students.

FOR EXAMPLE 6.3

Bias in Print Resources

The Manitoba Indian Brotherhood (at Goulet, Manitoba, 1987) identified several types of bias and distortion in the treatment of Native groups in some textbooks. The same categories apply, by extension, to bias against other ethnic groups.

◆ *Omission.* Failing to mention all relevant facts.
◆ *Defamation.* Attacking the reputation of a group.
◆ *Invalidity.* Using out-of-date or inaccurate information.
◆ *Disparagement.* Belittling or denying the contributions of a group.
◆ *Cumulative implication.* Selecting information that reflects positively on one group and negatively on another.
◆ *Obliteration.* Ignoring significant aspects of history.
◆ *Disembodiment.* Using terms such as *menace* and *annihilation* in a casual or depersonalized manner.

Promote Respect for Other Cultures

Be alert to ideas that you can use to promote respect for "other" cultures. Depending on the age and interests of your students, you might, for instance,

◆ create a class book with a chapter on the family of each child;
◆ use songs and play music of various cultures, in various languages;
◆ take students to concerts, performances, and displays that reflect various cultures;
◆ invite musicians, artists, and actors of different races and cultures to talk to or perform for staff and students;
◆ use special days in various cultures as opportunities to teach and discuss the achievements of celebrated people in those cultures;
◆ teach about the achievements of antiracist leaders.

Promote Community Respect

Display pictures and hangings that show people of all cultures, ages, walks of life, and colors. Show "positive" pictures of scenes in all parts of your community. Invite local community leaders to talk about how racism affects the community. Ask teachers and parents to help build class files on various cultural, racial, or national groups.

Show interest in children who speak or learn other languages. Learn and encourage your students to learn common words (e.g., greetings, numbers from one to ten) in languages spoken in the homes of classmates.

Deal Openly with Racially Determined Physical Features

Discuss skin color openly. Use books and puzzles depicting people of different skin colors and features. Have children make dolls representing people of different skin colors.

Make a photo collage of people with different hair styles, colors, and textures. Use books and pictures that show different hair colors and styles.

Build positive feelings about the colors black and brown. Use these colors in positive ways, and avoid negative uses.

Confront Racism Directly

Discuss racism and stereotyping openly with your students. Use examples sensitively, and encourage the combating of negative attitudes by means of positive (*not* retaliatory) actions.

The Childcare Council (1993) recommends ways of responding to children's racial or cultural insults. It is not enough to feel discomfort when we hear a racist remark or an "ethnic" joke. We should listen carefully, assess the remark, and respond immediately and appropriately. Responses should include the following elements:

- Acknowledge that you have heard the insulting remark.
- State clearly that such remarks are not acceptable.
- Identify the incorrect element in the remark.
- Offer correct information.
- Offer support to the child who has been insulted.
- If the remark occurred in the course of a larger conflict, help children resolve any part of that conflict that had nothing to do with race or culture.

PRACTICE *and Projects*

1. Join a group of four or five colleagues to discuss racist remarks or behavior that you have witnessed. Suggest ways in which you might deal constructively with such situations.

2. Invite community speakers who represent minorities to speak about racism and its effects.

■ ■ ■ ■ ■

TEACHING SPECIAL-NEEDS LEARNERS

The policy of free public education and the right to attend public schools is universal in North America. "Special education" programs exist within public school systems for learners whose abilities differ from those of their peers. Such students include those with learning problems or physical disabilities, the gifted, bilingual or multilingual students, the socioeconomically disadvantaged, and recent immigrants. Although some of these students may be disadvantaged in some ways, they may have strengths in others. By concentrating on their strengths, you will help these students to reach their potential.

Students with Learning Problems

Children with difficulties that may create learning problems have the right to programs suited to their needs. Various authorities have classified such difficulties in different ways, but we shall briefly consider the following types:

◆ physical or motor disorders;
◆ communication (speech or sensory) disorders;
◆ developmental delays;
◆ behavioral disorders;
◆ specific learning disabilities;
◆ multiple disabilities.

PHYSICALLY OR DEVELOPMENTALLY CHALLENGED LEARNERS

Learners who are physically challenged include those with neurological or glandular abnormalities, orthopedic difficulties, birth-related abnormalities, or problems resulting from infection or disease. They may have difficulty moving all or parts of their body, or have limited vitality, alertness, or strength.

Learners with communication disorders have difficulties of speech (producing sounds) or language (expression), or sensory perception or expression that limit their communication; they may be autistic or have severe speech and language disturbances. Sensory disorders include auditory or visual impairment so severe that even with auditory or optical aids, learners have a critical loss of hearing or sight.

Learners with behavioral disorders may suffer from social maladjustment, psychoses, or emotional disturbances. They have one or more of the following characteristics: inability to learn (unrelated to health or intellectual problems), poor relationships with peers and teachers, unusual responses or overreaction to normal events, and unusual physical symptoms or fears relating to school. Those who are aggressive tend to receive attention, while those who are withdrawn may be overlooked.

Developmentally challenged learners function at a level of intellectual ability that is significantly below average. Their handicap may result in or be accompanied by impairment in adaptive behavior. Slow learners tend to have a limited attention span and deficiencies in basic reading, writing, and mathematics skills. They need many and varied repetitions to learn a task.

Learners with multiple disabilities have two or more of the above conditions. How best to recognize, place, and work with learners in this category are matters under debate.

Learners with unspecified learning disabilities are a group, fairly recently identified, who puzzle educators. They raise the vexed question: "What's wrong when nothing is wrong? ... How do you explain what is wrong with a student who is not mentally retarded, emotionally disturbed, educationally deprived, or culturally different, who has normal vision, hearing, and language capabilities and still cannot learn to read, write, or compute?" (Woolfolk, 1990, p. 472)

■ ■ ■ ■ ■

WORKING WITH SPECIAL-NEEDS LEARNERS

Classifying and grouping learners raises problems. One learner may be both gifted and hearing handicapped; another may be both slow and hearing handicapped; and still another may be physically handicapped, slow, and bilingual. Some learners are gifted in one subject but slow in another. The range of combinations seems endless—and each situation requires its own thoughtful and patient approach.

Teachers' Concerns

Many teachers have concerns—or even fears—about working with special-needs learners. Some are concerned about the adequacy of their own level of training, the level of support offered by the education system's administration or special consultants, the time and energy needed, and the limits these needs impose on attention to other duties, especially in a mainstream class.

Teachers who work well with special students recognize the challenges, but deal with them matter-of-factly and emphasize the characteristics these students share with other students. These teachers plan carefully, establish a positive classroom climate with smooth management procedures and routines (see Chapter 4), and prepare other students to interact constructively with special students. They match their questions to the individual student's level of ability, are encouraging and supportive, and provide positive feedback (see Chapter 7). They manage behavior quietly, and organize individual success experiences as they model, teach, and expect general respect, courtesy, and social acceptance in the classroom (see Chapter 5).

To help students with learning difficulties,

- be aware that each student is likely to have a unique problem;
- determine whether the student is on medication; if so, ask the parents about its effects. If those effects create a problem, check with parents to see if the dosage can be adjusted or the medication changed;
- observe carefully to determine each student's preferred learning modality (see Chapter 4);
- start at each student's readiness level, and provide direct, hands-on experience whenever possible;
- when questioning, allow ample time for response. Wait rather than rephrasing a question, as this may only confuse the student;
- assign tasks that allow immediate success;
- make assignments brief, and check often for understanding;
- review often.

WORKING WITH GIFTED LEARNERS

The needs of gifted learners are sometimes overlooked simply because they often learn academic material easily and quickly, and score high on intelligence tests. Gifted learners usually have above-average powers of concentration, are often more emotionally stable than their peers, and are usually larger, stronger, and healthier, as well. It is a mistake, however, to think that every gifted student has these characteristics. Although schools sometimes recognize only facility with words as giftedness, this is only one kind of proficiency, and teachers should nurture other special abilities, as well.

Not all teachers are initially comfortable working with gifted learners. Some may feel less secure because gifted students tend to surprise them with correct answers that they did not anticipate. Moreover, a gifted child may be "turned off" by content that is too simple or by a slow pace of teaching, and may consequently underachieve. Insistence on conformity to precise directions, unnecessary repetition or drill, and a lack of opportunity to take creative "short cuts" or to pursue individual interests may create boredom among gifted learners. Not all gifted students are socially adept; some may need opportunities to interact productively with peers, without being cast constantly in the role of a "little teacher."

By contrast, a teacher may find it so rewarding to work with gifted learners that he or she neglects the rest of the class; this extreme, too, must be avoided. Educators disagree on how to teach the gifted, but adaptations can and should be made. Some support "acceleration" (rapid progress through the grades), while others prefer "enrichment" (keeping gifted students with their age group, but giving them more challenging tasks). Full mainstreaming and complete segregation have both been suggested. Mainstreamed students may be grouped and given attention before and/or after class, may be tutored during regular classes, or may be assigned independent study. Segregation may involve special summer schools, evening or weekend programs, or enrollment in special classes or schools. Students may be enrolled in limited courses, assigned to resource rooms or clinical centers, or invited to take part in limited-participation trips or events.

TEACHING BILINGUAL OR ESL LEARNERS

Bilingual instruction is given in a mix of two languages, with the goal of making students proficient in both. In Canada, the most common mix is English and French; in the United States, it is English and Spanish. Bilingual programs may help students to make the transition from their mother tongue to another language, or to maintain or even retrieve an ancestral language and culture.

English-as-a-second-language (ESL) programs are similar to bilingual programs, except that instruction takes place in English. These programs are usually provided for recent immigrants. Teachers of ESL will find many opportunities to help students become familiar with the customs and culture of their adopted country, relating them, where possible, to those of their country of origin.

In schools with a large minority-language population, instructing children in their first language in the early grades may help them to adjust. Try from the beginning to make the children aware of the benefits of speaking two (or more) languages, and do all you can to ensure that they maintain their self-esteem and pride in being heirs of two cultures. This is particularly important when students are economically disadvantaged or are subject to racist discrimination.

Problems of school adjustment may be compounded when children must move often. Frequent moves can make it difficult for schools to keep track of a student's progress, and for the child to form trusting student–teacher relationships and peer friendships. It becomes doubly important for you to give such children as much support as you can in achieving positive self-concepts and pride in their language and culture of origin. The same principle applies, of course, for immigrant children who have experienced the traumas of economic struggles, racism, violence, or wars.

MAINSTREAMING SPECIAL LEARNERS

Although there is a variety of placement or grouping patterns in schools, special learners are increasingly being "mainstreamed," or "integrated" (placed in regular classrooms rather than in "special resource" facilities). Students are considered to be mainstreamed if they spend any part of the school day with regular-class peers.

Although research findings on the effects of mainstreaming are far from conclusive, it is plain that the current use of mainstreaming places additional demands on classroom teachers. Research suggests that programs that place students with learning problems in special rooms seem to have fewer positive effects than those that accommodate them in regular classrooms; that the quality of instruction for the mildly disabled often remains low; and that too many students are still labeled "special education students" and assigned to pull-out programs (Good & Brophy, 1990, p. 658).

Practical problems remain: How can you and your colleagues cope with the perplexing mix of backgrounds, states of health, abilities, dispositions, and behaviors of all learners in a typical school system? In particular, how can you provide quality instruction for students who are economically disadvantaged, physically or developmentally challenged, or socially and educationally deprived? Since special students range from severely challenged to gifted and well adjusted, should they be homogeneously grouped in special classrooms, special schools, or residential schools? Should they be placed in regular classrooms but be involved in pull-out programs, integrated but receiving special attention or tasks? Or should they be "educationally integrated" in regular classrooms?

It is doubtful whether there is any single right answer to these complex questions, though many educators agree that less able learners, regardless of their disability, should have opportunities to observe and interact with more able learners in a process and environment that some call "normalization." Whatever system is used, preservice and in-service teachers will need and should receive training in procedures for working with special students. Opportunities for consultation and collaboration with resource teachers, specialists, parents, and perhaps students themselves should also be provided. In addition, the following methods have been identified as "promising mainstreaming practices":

- continuously assessing student achievement;
- varying instructional methods and materials;
- preparing explicit individual instruction plans;
- using self-management as appropriate;
- using student peer assistance;
- teaming teachers and other staff;
- using consulting teachers (Good & Brophy, 1990, p. 661).

PRACTICE *and Projects*

1. Debate one of the following issues:
   a. Resolved that students with disabilities be taught separately from the more able students.
   b. Resolved that the gifted should be allowed to progress through the academic grades at their own pace.

2. Visit an elementary, a junior secondary, and a secondary school. Interview the principal or a counselor about arrangements for special-needs learners and, if possible, view facilities and speak with teachers who work with special learners. If classrooms are mainstreamed, ask a teacher to describe how he or she works with special-needs students.

3. Get in touch with your local, state or provincial, or national Council for Exceptional Children and your regional Department of Education to discover and report the services available to teachers of special-needs learners.

4. Seek permission to observe an exceptional learner in either a mainstreamed or an accelerated classroom. Record everything the student says and does for half a day. Report what you observed to a group of five peers. With them, form a tentative interpretation.

5. Working with a partner or small group, analyze Case Study 6.2, and decide what you might do, if it were your classroom, to help each of the students described.

CASE STUDY 6.2

SPECIAL-NEEDS LEARNERS

Ms. Chavez, beginning her first year of teaching, has a diverse group of students in her Grade 4 class. She is particularly concerned about the following students:

Donald is a highly capable learner and a good athlete, with a broad range of interests. He reads at the Grade 10 level. In class, Donald always seems to have the right answers, which he blurts out, even before Ms. Chavez can complete her questions, excitedly providing detailed and interesting explanations far beyond the understanding of his classmates. Ms. Chavez finds herself

(continued)

(continued)

giving more and more attention to Donald, even turning a lesson, at times, into a two-person discussion. Realizing the danger to other students, she has begun to cut Donald off before he can launch into lengthy details. Donald is now trying only halfheartedly or failing to complete his assignments. He often sulks or tries to disturb the students near him.

Leora, as her classmates and former teachers know, though very polite, is rather slow. She also seems to be a "loner." She is overweight and has thick glasses but rarely wears them. At a recent PTA meeting, Ms. Chavez met Leora's mother, who immediately volunteered that Leora's slowness was an embarrassment to the rest of the family. Leora clearly is having trouble with her school work: she finds the simplest math difficult, reads poorly, and is always the last to finish seatwork, if she completes it at all. Leora never acts up in class. In fact, she sits near the back and is so quiet that, as Ms. Chavez has just realized, she sometime does not ask Leora a question for days. She would like to involve Leora more.

Brigit uses a motorized wheelchair. She was born with severe physical handicaps, and her body is short and twisted. She has minimum use of her limbs, but can write well and has normal sight and hearing. She resents attempts to help her, testily remarking, "Leave me alone! I can do it myself." When her classmates first saw her, they did not know what to make of her. Most have been giving her a wide berth, but some are now whispering about her, and one loud and boorish boy is starting to tease her. Her records indicate that she has been a good student, but she is not living up to her earlier achievements.

Miguel just arrived at school four days late, without lunch money or school supplies, or any record of his previous academic performance or behavior. His parents are migrant crop workers who recently arrived to work the crops, and he has four older sisters and a younger brother. A group of boys has made fun of his ill-fitting clothes, unkempt appearance, and foreign accent, and some of them have also made racial slurs. This has prompted Miguel to fight. Ms. Chavez has been checking Miguel's work and has found that he is far behind the rest of the class in basic skills. Instead of completing written assignments, he constantly doodles, but his doodling often hinges on the work assigned.

SUMMARY

- Classrooms show the broad ranges of human diversity.
- Cultures represent the unique lifestyles of particular groups of people.
- A "culture of poverty" that cuts across ethnic groups affects many children.
- Multicultural education has a vital function in teaching students to recognize, accept, and respect cultural differences.
- To become a multicultural teacher, identify your personal perceptions, learn about your community, adopt multicultural objectives, plan and practice multicultural lesson components, and promote students' positive self-concept and integration.
- Examine the causes and results of racism in North American schools, and reflect on the means that might be used to resolve these problems; confer with colleagues; teach students the skills and attitudes they need to live productively in the dominant community; help them to deal with prejudice and to develop fair-mindedness and self-esteem; promote respect for other cultures and encourage antiracism.
- Children with learning problems have the right to educational programs suited to their needs.
- Teachers who work well with special students recognize the challenges involved, but deal with them matter-of-factly and emphasize the things these students have in common with their peers, rather than their differences.
- The current practice of "mainstreaming" places additional demands on classroom teachers, who should receive training in procedures for working with special students.

KEY WORDS

bias
community
cross-cultural
   education
culture components
   personality
   language
   social structures
   occupations
   environment
discrimination
ESL

ethnic groups
gifted learners
   acceleration
   enrichment
hidden curriculum
integration
learner diversity
   learning-style
      preferences
   cultural
      background
   exceptionality

learning problems
mainstreaming
multiculturalism
"normalization"
positive self-concept
prejudice
racism
special needs
stereotyping
unspecified learning
   disabilities

RECOMMENDED READING

Multicultural Education

Baruth, L., & Manning, M.L. (1992). *Multicultural education of children and adolescents*. Boston: Allyn & Bacon.

Cushner, K., McClelland, A., & Safford, P. (1992). *Human diversity in education: An integrative approach*. New York: McGraw-Hill.

Kierstead, F. & Wagner, P., Jr. (1993). *The ethical, legal, and multicultural foundations of teaching*. Madison, WI: Brown & Benchmark.

Sleeter, C., & Grant, C. (1993). *Making choices for multicultural education: Five approaches to race, class, and gender*. New York: Merrill.

Special-Needs Learners

Andrews, J., & Lupart, J. (1993). *The inclusive classroom: Educating exceptional children*. Scarborough, ON: Nelson Canada.

Bloom, B. (1985). *Developing talent in young people*. New York: McGraw-Hill.

Lewis, R., & Doorlag, D. (1991). *Teaching special students in the mainstream*. New York: Merrill.

PART 3

Mastering the Basics

■ ■ ■ ■ ■

Part 3 of *Teaching: Strategies and Methods for Student-Centered Instruction* focuses on the basic processes and procedures for planning and presenting lessons. You will reach peak professional performance as a teacher only by mastering these basic skills of classroom instruction: asking and answering questions; teaching and demonstrating skills and explaining information; and teaching concepts and critical-thinking procedures.

Chapter 7 deals with framing and delivering questions and handling students' responses in ways that encourage and optimize the inquiry process and train students to participate productively in it. Students, too, should ask questions, both of their teachers and of one another, and teachers should stimulate this process. Responding appropriately to your students' questions may often involve clearly explaining information or procedures to help your students understand any unfamiliar procedure, process, concept, generalization, or principle.

Chapter 8 discusses a systematic approach to the teaching of concepts (generalizations) through a process of perception, definition, analysis, and provision of examples and nonexamples. Examples should illustrate critical attributes, and students should learn to distinguish critical and noncritical attributes.

Chapter 9 describes the principles and practice of teaching skills: cognitive, psychomotor, and affective procedures that can be learned and performed to demonstrate learning. Before teaching a skill, it is useful to make a task analysis that identifies and links the components (subskills), following a step-by-step procedure that includes orientation, demonstration, monitoring of student practice, evaluation of performance, provision of prompt and pertinent feedback, and periodic review. This plan, modified "on the spot" as necessary, will promote effective lesson delivery. Skills teaching usually includes the processes of demonstrating and explaining. Suggestions are made for effective delivery of these processes.

Chapter 10 outlines the classification of thinking skills and suggests approaches to teaching them. By teaching thinking skills and processes, and training your students in task analysis, you can help them to achieve the more general goals of education. Students need to understand a variety of problem-solving procedures, practice them, receive feedback on their practice, revise them, and apply them so that at some stage, they will be able to conceptualize them.

CHAPTER 7

ASKING AND ANSWERING QUESTIONS

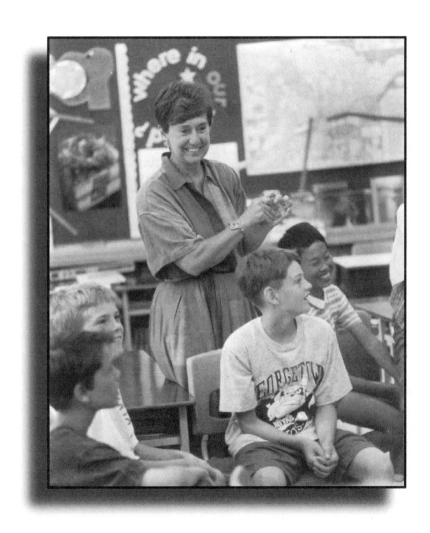

■ ■ ■ ■ ■

*What's in a question, you ask: Everything. It is the way of evoking stimu-
lating responses or stultifying inquiry. It is, in essence, the very core of
teaching.*

(Dewey, 1933, p. 266)

■ ■ ■ ■ ■

OVERVIEW

Posing productive questions and handling students' questions and responses is
an important part of every teacher's day. Effective questioning involves a step-by-
step process of gaining attention, directing a question to your whole class, allowing wait time, asking an individual to respond, listening to the response, and
again waiting briefly before acknowledging the answer in one of many ways.

The wording of questions and the manner of directing them make a considerable difference in the way students respond. In framing and asking questions,
consider your students' ability and developmental levels. Distribute questions
widely, and handle students' responses positively, to encourage them to "risk"
answering and to ask questions of their own, both of you and of their peers.

Responding to your students' questions often involves explaining information or procedures. Explanations are needed to clarify any unfamiliar procedure,
process, concept, generalization, or principle. Effective explanations must be
planned carefully, in a process that involves analysis, logical organization, definition, finding examples, and summarizing. Delivering explanations effectively
includes keeping to essentials appropriate to your students' level of development,
providing relevant examples, and monitoring and checking your students' understanding of the material presented.

■ ■ ■ ■ ■

ASKING USEFUL QUESTIONS

Since the age of Socrates, most famous of the citizens of ancient Athens, questions
have been considered essential to effective teaching. You might, for instance, use
questions as a pretest to discover what your students already know about a topic,
or what aspects of the topic interest them most. You might begin a new lesson
by asking a challenging or thought-provoking question to motivate your students.
During the course of your lesson, you might use questions to stimulate and direct

thinking, emphasize key points, keep your students alert and on task, and help them consider a topic in greater depth, or personalize the information you are presenting. After your presentation, you might ask questions to determine whether your students have achieved the learning goals set, to check their recall or understanding of new information presented, or to help them process and interpret that information. At other times, you might use review questions to increase students' retention of information, or step-by-step questions to guide their comprehension of concepts and their development of skills.

Questioning Procedures

Although questions vary widely in their content and form of delivery, there are certain commonly used steps in the classroom question-and-answer process. Figure 7.1 illustrates these steps. The suggestions below can help you frame and use questions productively.

- ◆ *Secure attention.* Before you ask a single question, secure the undivided attention of your whole class. By so doing, you will reinforce your students' sense that they are part of the classroom teaching/learning process, and that you are addressing each one of them personally. You can use eye contact, gestures, and changes of position to secure and hold your students' attention.

- ◆ *Distribute questions widely.* Distribute your questions widely, selecting students from among both volunteers and nonvolunteers to give answers. Avoid choosing responders according to any set pattern (e.g., by rows): if participation is predictable, students will be encouraged to let their attention wander, and management problems are likely to ensue. Recording question-distribution patterns on Data Collection Form 7.1 (Appendix A) will help you to keep all your students actively involved.

- ◆ *Distribute questions realistically.* Encourage active participation in lesson development by matching the difficulty of the question to the capability of the student. Do this tactfully, however, to avoid sending negative messages about certain students' abilities. Treat incorrect responses as "deferred successes" rather than as failures.

- ◆ *Pause productively.* When you have asked a question, pause for three to five seconds before you call on a particular student to respond. This practice provides students with "think time," during which you can look about the room as a signal that you may choose any student to answer, and that no one is "off the hook."

- ◆ *Use "wait time."* Once you have named a responder, allow three to five seconds for a response. Learning to use **wait time** effectively takes courage and perseverance: at first, you may fear that if you wait three or more seconds after asking

TEST

FIGURE 7.1

Basic Steps in Asking Questions

Basic Steps

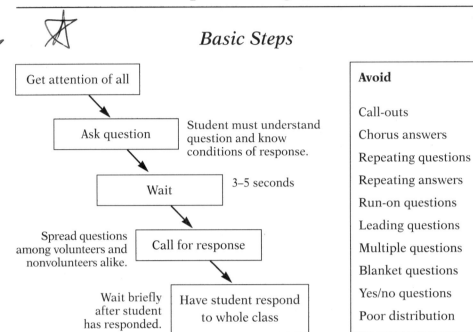

Get attention of all	
Ask question	Student must understand question and know conditions of response.
Wait	3–5 seconds
Spread questions among volunteers and nonvolunteers alike. → Call for response	
Wait briefly after student has responded. → Have student respond to whole class	

Avoid

Call-outs

Chorus answers

Repeating questions

Repeating answers

Run-on questions

Leading questions

Multiple questions

Blanket questions

Yes/no questions

Poor distribution

After Call for a Response

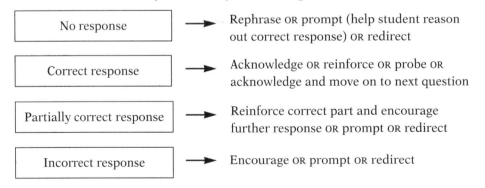

No response	→ Rephrase OR prompt (help student reason out correct response) OR redirect
Correct response	→ Acknowledge OR reinforce OR probe OR acknowledge and move on to next question
Partially correct response	→ Reinforce correct part and encourage further response OR prompt OR redirect
Incorrect response	→ Encourage OR prompt OR redirect

Source: Derived from "Reflectivity: The Edsel of Education?" by J. Moore, S. Mintz, and M. Berriman, in H. Waxman, H. Frieberg, J. Vaughen, and M. Weil (Eds.), *Images of Reflection in Teacher Education*, Reston, VA: Association of Teacher Educators.

a question, your lesson will drag. In fact, while that wait time may seem long to you, it seldom does to students. To encourage your students (in a nonblaming, nonthreatening way) to frame their replies in complete, well-worded, and well-constructed statements, you must give them time to think their answers through. You will find that slowing down the learning process may actually be a way of speeding it up!

The benefits of a wait time of at least three seconds are impressive:

- More students volunteer to respond and show more confidence in responding.
- Students give longer answers (by as much as 700 percent).
- The proportion of logical, well-supported, and higher-order responses increases.
- Failures to respond are reduced.
- Students, including those rated "slow" by teachers, respond more often and ask more questions.
- Student–student exchanges increase.
- The number of speculative responses increases, since students have more time to think an answer through, rehearse it, and "screw up their courage" to express it.
- The need to discipline students decreases and, consequently, classroom climate improves (Tobin, 1980).

You, too, will benefit from increased wait time. Your questioning techniques will improve because you will be carefully considering who should respond, and how best to handle responses. Increasing wait time will make you seem more flexible; you will make fewer errors and show more continuity in developing ideas. Extending wait time will reduce the number of your questions, but extending your thinking time will allow you to make better use of student responses by requesting more clarification or elaboration. As your students participate more, and more effectively, you will find your classroom climate and your opinions of some groups improving (Tobin & Capie, 1982).

- ***Require courteous group behavior.*** Train your students to raise a hand if they wish to volunteer an answer. This courteous behavior, which gives the floor to one person at a time, allows you to acknowledge correct responses and use them more productively: a student's answer may lead to your next question or to a redirect (passing the question along to another student to obtain clarification or comment) and, thus, become part of a topic's development. Also train your students to direct their answers to the whole class and not just to you, to emphasize that answering questions is part of a cooperative—not just an individual—

learning experience, and that all students share responsibility for a lesson's development.

Framing Questions

The way in which you frame your questions will relate closely to their effectiveness. Question-and-answer sessions should help students to progress well beyond the level of a "trivial pursuit" that relies heavily on the recall of isolated facts. Teachers must therefore vary the **level of questions** asked. Whereas simple (low-level) questions may be useful for drilling basic facts, questions that are **open-ended**, requiring analysis, synthesis, or the forming or support of opinion, will stimulate students to move beyond recall into higher **levels of thinking**. Plan your questions to meet the following objectives:

◆ *Keep questions brief.*   Long questions can tax anyone's memory. A lengthy or complex question can easily make students forget what you are asking them and, thus, embarrass them. Avoid **run-on questions**: it is better to put a series of questions to a number of students than to ask a single complex question that will keep one student struggling for minutes while others lose interest and cease to pay attention.

◆ *Sequence questions logically.*   In presenting a topic, use your early questions to elicit answers that will provide background material. Follow with questions that increase students' information or understanding about the topic, and then move on to ask them to use that information or understanding to solve related problems.

◆ *Adapt questions to students' abilities.*   It is pointless to ask students questions that are beyond their experience and capabilities. Plan your questions on the basis of the information and skills that students either have or are capable of deducing or attempting without risking their confidence or self-esteem. Use language that is clear and straightforward to specify how students should respond. If you must use new or complex words, define them clearly before you ask your question.

◆ *Promote thinking.*   Ask questions that require thought as well as memory. Introduce questions with "why" and "how" rather than stopping at "what, where, and when." Build from simpler to higher-order questions. Use **convergent questions** (i.e., questions that require the student to bring concepts together to get a "right" answer), **divergent questions** (i.e., questions that lead students to a new perspective, or help them to synthesize or be creative, but have no "right" answer), and **evaluative questions** (i.e., those that require students to make carefully considered and clearly substantiated judgments). The questions with which you conclude a lesson might prompt evaluation or lead the class to new insights. Checking for understanding calls for questions that elicit a review of topical and background information, and allow you or members of the class to give more critical feedback.

+ ***Promote general participation.*** Direct questions to your entire class rather than to a specific student. Each student should feel that he or she might be asked to respond. Use eye contact and body language to emphasize this message. Keep the class involved cooperatively by asking students to supplement one another's answers. Promote constructive criticism among students, teaching and training them to challenge ideas, but never permit personal attacks.

Table 7.1 lists some key words, phrases, and concepts that will help you to frame questions appropriate to each of six different levels of thinking: knowledge, comprehension, application, analysis, synthesis and evaluation.

TABLE 7.1

"Question" Words by Level of Thinking

Knowledge
(requires recalling or recognizing information)

Recall	List	Define	Who?
What?	Where?	When?	How many?

Comprehension
(requires describing, paraphrasing, giving examples)

Describe	Summarize	Interpret	Explain
Paraphrase	Give an example	Identify main idea	

Application
(requires applying information to a new context; using a concept to solve a problem)

Classify	Operate	Demonstrate	Select
Solve	Relate	Prepare	Use

Analysis
(requires discovering or subdividing into parts; finding structure)

Determine causes	Analyze	Subdivide	Organize
Diagram	Infer	Outline	State reasons

Synthesis
(requires organizing in a new way or into a new whole)

Plan	Produce	Devise	Construct
Design	Combine	Create	Rewrite

Evaluation
(requires judgment based on criteria, rationale, or standards)

Decide	Determine	Criticize	Appraise
Compare	Justify	Support	Debate
Conclude	Agree?/Disagree?		

ASKING THE "WRONG" QUESTIONS

Although you will be focusing your attention on asking the "right" questions, it is also helpful to know how to avoid asking the "wrong" ones. Avoid **"yes/no" questions** that encourage guessing rather than recalling or reasoning; **leading questions** that suggest or contain a portion of the answer, encouraging your students to depend on you rather than themselves; run-on or interrupted questions that may confuse students with unnecessary detail; **multiple questions** that leave students uncertain as to which part to answer; and **blanket questions**, general questions that have little or no learning value and encourage students to talk out of turn. Repeating questions may encourage inattention, interrupt the flow of discussion, and center interchanges on you rather than the class. (Of course, if your original question was too complex, you may need to subdivide and reword it, but careful lesson planning and your own professional development will soon help you to frame questions effectively.)

Some other types of questions have limited value, but may be useful in particular circumstances. Short-answer questions, for instance, are useful for drill or practice, but their general use tends to restrict students to exercising recall and does little to improve thinking skills. Questions inviting choral responses have the same limitations, except when used to review or drill facts, or to practice foreign language pronunciation. **Rhetorical question**s (i.e., questions asked to emphasize or dramatize a point rather than to elicit an answer) may be useful for focusing attention, but their overuse makes students inattentive.

Specific questions are teacher-centered: teachers can use them to control the learning process by eliciting specific information. Such questions often begin with "what," "where," "when," and "how." They tend to be convergent (have a single "right" answer) and to require simplistic (or low cognitive level) responses. Use specific questions with discretion, since they may encourage guessing at answers and discourage insightful responses and creativity. Specific questions can be useful, however, for assessing levels of student recall and comprehension of information or skills (i.e., to determine the extent to which you and your students have achieved lesson objectives and goals), and as a means of reviewing earlier learning or of drilling students to promote retention of information or skills. You can increase the effectiveness of specific questions by the frequent use of "why" and the occasional use of "what if."

PRACTICE *and Projects*

1. Use Data Collection Form 7.2 (Appendix A) to record your observations as your instructor teaches a brief model lesson to demonstrate questioning techniques. Debrief, in class or small groups, commenting on the techniques used and the sequencing of the questions asked.

2. a. Recall a teacher who made effective use of questions and answers. Note briefly how this teacher handled questions.
   b. Join four or five peers to frame at least four principles for handling classroom questions and answers effectively.

3. Use Data Collection Form 7.3 (Appendix A) to analyze Case Study 7.1. Your instructor may pose specific questions for your response.

4. Microteach a lesson with the professional target of distributing questions widely. Use Data Collection Form 7.1 (Appendix A) to help you achieve your target.

CASE STUDY 7.1

QUESTIONING

Ms. Lepage's Grade 2 class has been working on a farm theme for several days. Today, Ms. Lepage has her students gather at the back of the room and sit on the carpeted area. "Today," she says, "I'm going to ask you some questions to help you think."

Ms. Lepage pauses until everyone seems ready and then explains, "I want everyone to have a turn to answer today, and so I'm going to ask you to put up your hands instead of calling out an answer. I'll give you time to think before I ask anyone a question, to help us get some very good answers. When I ask one of you to answer, the person I ask will answer loudly and clearly so that all of us in the room can hear and keep up with what is going on. Listen carefully because there isn't time to repeat all the answers. Now put your hand up if you heard me speaking loudly and clearly." (All the hands go up.)

Ms. Lepage continues, "This afternoon, we're going to make haystacks. What do you think we'll need?" Children's hands begin to go up. She acknowledges volunteers by smiling, but waits for more hands before she

(continued)

(continued)

begins to call on students by name. Answers include "Hay" and "Straw."

"Think about what haystacks look like," Ms. Lepage prompts. "What else could we use?"

Again a few hands go up, then more, until most hands are up. Ms. Lepage calls on students by name for their answers: "Grass," "Weeds," "Corey's hair"—all laugh, including Corey—"String," "Twine," "Bulrushes," "Cat-tails."

"Good answers!" Ms. Lepage says. "You really do remember what haystacks look like! Now I'm going to give you another clue that will change your answers quite a bit. We're going to be able to *eat* the haystacks. What do you think we'll use to make them?"

The children wave their hands. Again Ms. Lepage waits until many hands are raised. The students are very eager to be chosen, and one blurts out an answer. Ms. Lepage looks at her and smilingly shakes her head while putting an index finger to her lips.

When Ms. Lepage begins to call on students by name, their answers include "Spaghetti," "Fettuccini," "Linguine," "Cotton candy," and "Noodles."

"Oh, that's close," says Ms. Lepage. "What kind of noodles?"

The children guess several kinds of noodles, but since no one guesses chow mein noodles, Ms. Lepage holds up a box. "Have you ever seen this kind of noodles?" she asks. She then shows the children the recipe written on chart paper, and the class prepares to cook the noodles.

■ ■ ■ ■ ■

PROMOTING STUDENTS' RESPONSES

Your handling of students' responses can make an important difference to their learning experience. Ensuring that students achieve a high success rate (from 70 percent to 80 percent) in their responses is perhaps the most effective way to encourage them to respond (Wilen & Clegg, 1986, p. 157). Beyond acknowledging this principle, different circumstances make different responses appropriate.

When a student answers a question correctly and confidently, it may be appropriate simply to accept it with a nod or a smile and move on. If the student responds correctly but hesitantly, you might explain why the answer is right, using the opportunity to explain the content again to students who may need the review. Reinforcing answers will sometimes encourage more students to contribute. Vary the form of your reinforcement: an endless stream of "OK's" or "Right's" soon becomes meaningless. Building on a student's response, immediately or later, provides strong reinforcement. Give praise judiciously when effort and/or achievement merit it, but do not allow your praise to become repetitious and meaningless.

If you find that an initial question is too difficult, or if you wish to encourage a student to extend or clarify a response, you might use **prompts** (clues) and/or **probes** (a series of step-by-step questions to encourage students to move just beyond the point they have reached with their initial answers). **Cueing** (reminding students of information that will help them take a further step in framing a response) is another skill that you can use to guide pupils to the right answer without giving it to them.

Acknowledge any correct element in an incorrect or incomplete answer. Be sure to interpret to the student's advantage any sincere attempt to respond. Make it plain that you value such attempts as contributions to the progress of the class in solving problems (i.e., in proceeding from the "known" to clarify the "unknown"). If a student's response is unclear, ask him or her to rephrase it, or redirect the question. Move on to the next question only when you think that the class is ready. Try to return later with a similar question to a student who has given a hesitant or incorrect answer. If necessary, you might use a probe to elicit clarification or a higher-level response, or a prompt to help the student build on the correct element; or you might reword or redirect the question to elicit a correct or complete answer. Do not insist that every responder work out a totally complete and correct answer, as this would only turn a potential learning experience into an inquisition and embarrass some students. Instead, use answers to earlier questions as a basis for subsequent questioning.

If a student does not respond to a question, you might encourage and prompt him or her or redirect the question to someone else. Be patient, however, in letting students complete their answers: pause for three seconds after you receive a response to allow the responder to expand or emend it. (By jumping in too quickly, you might prevent some students from giving a fuller answer.)

Students' responses should sometimes take the form of class or group discussion. You can support discussion in several ways. You might, for instance, build on student's responses, immediately or later, to show that you consider these contributions important. If you want to keep discussion moving about the classroom, you might invite comment from several students in succession or redirect a question to another student to confirm a response. In a free-flowing discussion, it is usual to permit unsolicited responses. Polite dissent should be permitted on all matters of opinion.

Encouraging Students' Questions

Classroom questioning should not be a "one-way street." Encourage your students to direct questions to you and to their peers, and answer as promptly as you can without interrupting the flow of your lesson. Encourage students to ask constructive and higher-level questions that motivate them and encourage them to take more responsibility for their own learning, but make it plain that questions of almost any sort can be of use. Explain to your class that all questions should be treated respectfully because they can open up new trains of thought that may lead to investigation and solutions. Increase student-initiated questions by providing wait time before and after students respond, by creating a positive climate, partly through the use of positive reinforcement, and by simply asking students to put more questions and complimenting them when they do.

When a student asks a question that indicates that he or she has not been paying attention, it is generally unnecessary to take any action other than to answer briefly and pleasantly. The other students will usually send sufficient signals to inform the questioner that the answer has already been given. If such incidents often involve a particular student, they might indicate a hearing difficulty.

When a student asks you a question to which you do not know the answer, never pretend that you do, and never panic. Reply pleasantly and calmly that you do not know, and promise that you will try to find out. Follow up on your promise as promptly as possible, and report back to your class, explaining briefly, if appropriate, how and where you found the information.

PRACTICE *and Projects*

1. a. Recall a teacher who handled students' responses effectively.
    b. Describe one such recollection to your teaching partner or other members of a small group.

2. a. Working with your teaching partner or a small group, prepare a skit in which a teacher handles an awkward question from a student.
    b. Perform your skit for your class, and ask for feedback.

3. Microteach a lesson with the professional target of encouraging students to ask questions. Use Data Collection Form 7.3 (Appendix A) to obtain feedback.

■ ■ ■ ■ ■

EXPLAINING

You may know from your own experience how important clear explanations are to students! If you have encountered teachers or professors who lacked the ability to explain clearly, you may remember some frustrating incidents: when, for example, these instructors discovered that you did not understand a piece of information, they may merely have repeated it more loudly or told you that you should have listened more closely in the first place. Responding appropriately to your students' questions may often involve explaining information or procedures.

The Purpose of Explaining

The purpose of explaining is to help students understand any unfamiliar procedure, process, concept, generalization, or principle. As a teacher, you may use explanation to clarify

- ◆ cause-and-effect relationships (e.g., the effect of adding an acid to a base, or the causes and results of the Industrial Revolution in England);
- ◆ the application of a rule or law to a particular circumstance, event, or activity (e.g., the use of the question mark in written English, or reasons why persons in a moving automobile should wear seat belts);
- ◆ a procedure or process (e.g., the operation of an internal combustion engine, or the steps used to solve an algebra problem); or
- ◆ the purpose of an action or process (e.g., the use of color in a painting to create a mood, or the wearing of a uniform by some members of police forces).

Planning Explanations

To plan an effective explanation, you may need to make a careful analysis of the matter you wish to explain (see Data Collection Form 7.2, Appendix A, and Table 7.2). Obviously, you are unlikely to explain successfully any information or process with which you yourself are not thoroughly familiar.

Once you have made your analysis and are sure that you understand the material you wish to explain, you should proceed with your planning by taking five steps:

- ◆ Think through the purpose of the explanation.
- ◆ Organize your explanation logically, beginning with information known to your students and moving into new areas by small sequential steps.
- ◆ Prepare an easy-to-understand definition or outline that contains the key ideas.
- ◆ Select clear examples, or plan a demonstration.

TABLE 7.2

Some Inquiry Stems

You may use the following inquiry stems to stimulate students engaged in conducting an experiment, collecting data, examining cause-and-effect relationships, or analyzing events.

Stems Relating to Activities and Events
- What is happening? What took place before this happened?
- What has happened? Where have you already seen something like this happen? When have you already seen something like this happen? What do you think will happen now?
- How did this happen? How could you make this happen?
- What caused this to happen? How does this compare with what you have already seen or done?
- Why did this happen? How can we do this more easily or more quickly?

Stems Relating to Situations or Objects
- What kind of object is it? What can you do with it?
- What is it called? What other names has it?
- What is it made of? How was it made?
- Where is it found?
- What does it look like? What is its purpose?
- Have you ever seen anything like it? Where? When? How is it like other things?
- How does it work or operate?
- How can you recognize or identify it? How is it different from other things?

- Plan to conclude your explanation with a summary, presented by you or your students.

Since these are planning steps, not teaching steps, and since planning is not always linear, you may take these steps in a different order, but you should take them all. Their use is illustrated in For Example 7.1.

Delivering Explanations

Clear explanations may develop new content or respond to students' questions. A good explanation is "more interactive than a presentation" (Bellon, Bellon, & Blank, 1992, p. 248). Begin an explanation only when *all* your students are attending. To maintain their attention, keep your explanations brief and to the point: they should be just long enough to cover the essentials without launching students on

FOR EXAMPLE 7.1

Explaining the Use of a Colon to a Language Arts Class

PURPOSE: To teach the rule that governs the use of a colon (:) in written English.

DEFINITION: The colon is a symbol used after a formal introductory statement to direct attention to what follows: an appositive after a sentence, a formal list or explanation, or a long quotation.

EXAMPLES: Illustrate on the chalkboard or overhead projector examples of sentences in which colons should be used. Prepare a handout that contains examples of sentences that call for the use of a colon and others in which a colon would be inappropriate.

SUMMARY: Ask students to give an oral or written summary of the rule for use of the colon as a punctuation mark in written English.

a flood of unnecessary and confusing detail. Vary the stimuli of voice, gestures, and pauses for "think time." If attention wanders, rekindle it with an interesting example or illustration, or by asking a question to remind your students that they are accountable for their own learning processes.

Emphasize the fundamentals. Restrict an initial explanation, especially, to "critical attributes," or essential features: that is, stick to what your students need to know, and leave what is nice to know till later. Stress key ideas, and show how they are linked, keeping "noncritical attributes," or unessential information, in the background (see Chapter 8).

Frame your explanations to match your students' levels of understanding. Use language in keeping with their interests. Your students should not have to struggle with the vocabulary you use to explain new information. Train your students to listen for such components of your explanations as the main points, supporting facts or information, essential features, and advantages and disadvantages. Stress these elements as you explain.

Few learners master new material unless the instructor provides clear relevant examples to illustrate his or her explanations. (Several types of examples will be discussed in Chapter 8.) Good examples will help your students to relate new learning to what they already know, provide specific detail, add interest, and make difficult ideas easier to understand.

Monitor the effectiveness of your explanations, and be sensitive to feedback. Watch for signals such as blank or puzzled looks or wandering attention. If you sense that your students seem not to be following your explanation, alter your speed of delivery, or move from abstract to concrete information, asking more questions or introducing more and simpler examples.

Check your students' interpretation and comprehension of your explanation by asking them to paraphrase or demonstrate its content. Provide reinforcement as appropriate, and reteach as necessary.

PRACTICE *and Projects*

1. a. Join a subject-interest group. Brainstorm a list of classroom scenarios where it would be appropriate for you to give an explanation.

    b. Using the suggestions for planning outlined on page 165–166, help a member of your group prepare an explanation to present to the rest of your class. Ask the class to provide feedback, using Data Collection Form 7.4 (Appendix A).

2. Use Data Collection Form 7.4 to analyze Case Study 7.2. Your instructor may pose specific questions for your response.

3. Using Data Collection Form 7.4, plan and teach a microlesson that targets explaining.

CASE STUDY 7.2

EXPLAINING

Mr. Parisien planned to introduce "brainstorming" to his Grade 7 class. He knew his students would benefit from practicing the technique and could apply it to many future situations. He began to explain brainstorming.

"Most of us haven't much practice letting our ideas flow and our minds be creative. Often we're afraid someone will say 'No, that's not right,' or 'It's time to be quiet.' Brainstorming is a way of collecting many ideas about almost anything. It's also a way of 'hitchhiking' on one another's ideas. We accept all the ideas that surface while we're brainstorming, and we don't stop to make judgments about them right then: we just let the ideas come.

"Brainstorming can be exciting and lots of fun. When people let themselves think of different ideas and build on others' ideas without judging them, they pile up a whole range of ideas to choose from later on, some of

(continued)

(continued)

them, perhaps, quite new. Industry uses this technique to solve problems, make decisions, and find new products or ways of working."

Brett volunteered, "Last year, whenever anyone did something really good, our teacher called it a 'brainstorm.' " Several others agreed, remembering the incidents.

Mr. Parisien explained, "People may use the word in different ways, but the technique I'm going to show you today has certain rules. This is how it goes. I'm going to tell you about a problem that needs solving. When I point to you, I want you to call out whatever solution comes to your mind, and I'll record it on the chalkboard. No matter how unusual an idea sounds, we'll accept it. Even if it makes us all laugh, we'll record it. Some very creative ideas sound funny at first, but that doesn't matter because we want to record as many ideas as we can. If someone else's idea makes you think of something, that's fine because it gives us another idea.

"I've prepared a chart that I'll set up here where you can all see it. It shows the basic steps for brainstorming. We'll all use it as a reminder while we're brainstorming a solution to the problem I'm going to give you."

Mr. Parisien posts the chart, which reads, in large letters,

RULES FOR BRAINSTORMING
1. Listen to the problem.
2. Think for a minute.
3. Tell your idea briefly.
4. Hitchhike on others' ideas as much as you can.
5. No editing, judging, storytelling, or eliminating is allowed.

Mr. Parisien asks students to explain each step. "Have you any questions about the procedure?" [He pauses.] "Are you ready to begin?" [Students nod.]

"You are a member of the Board of Directors of a company that manufactures toothbrushes. The Board is responsible for making marketing decisions. One morning, the chairperson calls an emergency board meeting to announce that the plant mistakenly kept producing toothbrushes over a holiday long weekend. The company now has 30 million toothbrushes in stock that cannot be recycled. To avoid suffering a bad loss, the Board must find new uses for toothbrushes (besides brushing teeth) so that it can sell its surplus stock.

(continued)

(continued)

"To help the Board out, we're going to brainstorm as many ideas as we can. I'll give you one minute to check the chart again and review the rules. ... Ready? Let's begin!"

Ideas begin to pour out, and Mr. Parisien writes rapidly. "Jewelry cleaners, fingernail cleaners, cleaning grips on runners, scrubbing carrots ... " The list grows to about fifty items.

"Let's stop a minute and look at the ideas we've thought of so far," Mr. Parisien suggests. The students express surprise at the number of ideas they have produced. Jarrett says, "I think the one about brushing the cat's whiskers is really funny."

"Sure," responds Summer, "but it made Aniko think of the mustache brush idea, and that's a good one. So yours was a good one, too."

"That's how hitchhiking works," agrees Mr. Parisien. "There are many good ideas here. Now, in your work groups, I'd like you to spend time choosing the most useful ideas for selling the extra toothbrushes. Tomorrow, we'll brainstorm ways to reuse the paper that lands in the wastebasket in the photocopy room."

SUMMARY

- Questions are essential to effective teaching to stimulate student thinking, help them to personalize new information, and check their understanding.
- To ask questions productively, secure attention, pause to allow students time to formulate responses, direct questions widely but realistically, model and require courteous group behavior, focus on correct elements in answers, and treat errors as deferred successes.
- To encourage students to answer, keep questions brief and straightforward, and word them logically; focus on questions that require reasoning rather than simple recall; use convergent and divergent questions.
- Avoid "yes/no" questions, leading questions, multiple or confusing questions, and blanket or general questions.
- Avoid repeating questions and/or answers.
- Classify questions according to the thinking level they require, in order to prepare a proper "mix" of questions for your students.

- ◆ Use prompts, probes, or cues, as appropriate, to guide or develop pupils' answers.
- ◆ Respond positively, either verbally or nonverbally, to students' answers as appropriate.
- ◆ Encourage students to ask questions, and insist that they treat all questions respectfully.
- ◆ Model expected student responses in your own responses to students.
- ◆ Responding appropriately to your students' questions may often involve planning and delivering explanations.
- ◆ Planning an explanation often involves making a careful analysis by thinking through the purpose of the explanation, organizing its points logically, framing a definition or outline of key ideas, providing clear examples or a demonstration, and arranging to conclude with a summary.
- ◆ To deliver an explanation effectively, secure *all* students' attention, emphasize fundamentals briefly, provide relevant examples, be sensitive to student feedback, check for comprehension, and provide reinforcement as required.

KEY WORDS

cue	prompt	"think time"
distribution of	redirect	"wait time"
questions	reinforcement	"wrong" questions
encourage	response	yes/no
explain	questions	leading
framing questions	convergent	run-on
levels of thinking	divergent	multiple
participation	evaluative	blanket or general
probe		repetitive

RECOMMENDED READING

Dillon, J. (1984). Research on questioning and discussion. *Educational Leadership, 42*(4), 50–56.

Gall, M. (1984). Synthesis of research on teaching questioning. *Educational Leadership, 42*(4), 40–49.

Sadker, M., & Sadker, D. (1986). Questioning skills. In J. Cooper (Ed.), *Classroom teaching skills* (3rd ed.) pp. 143–184. Lexington, MA: Heath.

Sanders, N. (1966). *Classroom questions: What kinds?* New York: Harper & Row.

CHAPTER 8

TEACHING CONCEPTS

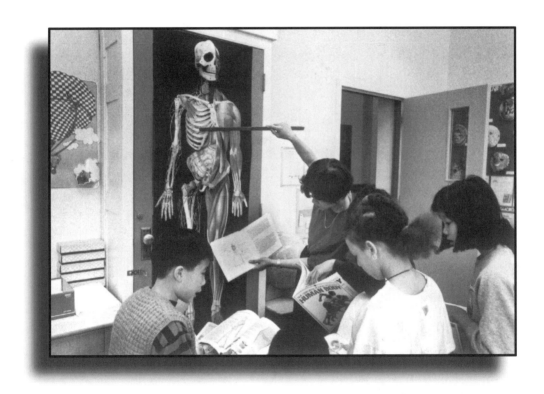

■ ■ ■ ■ ■

Man, unlike any other thing organic or inorganic in the universe, grows beyond his work, walks up the stairs of his concepts, emerges ahead of his accomplishments.

(JOHN STEINBECK, THE GRAPES OF WRATH, 1939)

■ ■ ■ ■ ■

OVERVIEW

A concept is a personal perception of a category or set of similar items represented by a word, symbol, or image. People cannot think, function, or communicate without these mental constructs or images. Acquiring concepts is fundamental to effective schooling. Using a systematic approach to planning and teaching, you should determine, define, and analyze a concept's critical attributes, providing examples and nonexamples (i.e., negative or inapplicable examples) suited to your students' levels of learning.

Concepts can be classified as concrete or abstract; formal or informal; conjunctive, disjunctive, or relational; and superordinate, coordinate, or subordinate. They can be explained in terms of their purposes: to show a cause-and-effect relationship; to show that an action is governed by a general rule or law; to illustrate a procedure or process; or to disclose the intent of an action or process.

■ ■ ■ ■ ■

THE NATURE OF CONCEPTS

A concept can be defined as a mental construct or a personal perception of a category or class of objects, conditions, events, or processes that can be grouped together on the basis of their similarities and represented by some word, symbol, or image. It is simple enough to form concepts of items or attributes (e.g., wheels, words, red, fragrant) that we perceive directly through one or more of our five senses. We can quite easily frame a concept of an event or an entity (e.g., the Summer Olympics, the Métis nation, or a college) that we perceive through general experience. We learn last to form concepts of abstracts (e.g., democracy, beauty, truth) that we acquire through association of ideas or inference. We can frame all these concepts because they represent, through a word, symbol, or mental picture, our perception of a class of objects, ideas, events, or people.

The Importance of Concepts

Conceptualizing, or framing concepts, is fundamental to thought and learning, for most of what we know about our world is based on concepts and their relationships. We can neither think nor function without these mental constructs, or images, that are the basic building blocks of thinking, particularly at higher levels. Concepts promote recall and simplify our learning efforts. They help us cope with living and learning.

Although concepts are often shared, they are essentially *personal* understandings of a symbol, an individual's unique way of acquiring meaning from experience. Concepts develop slowly from experience and information, moving from the specific to the abstract. They are living, growing constructs, constantly open to change through new experiences and insights. Each person acquires concepts differently and at different rates, and experiences them differently at the deepest levels of meaning, though people share similar concepts.

Shared concepts assist the transfer of learning: they are functional shortcuts to efficient communication. Society needs generally accepted meanings of words and labels of concepts so that when A speaks to B about an object of which they both have a concept—for example, "my desk"—both recognize that object's key characteristics or attributes, although that particular desk may differ in some ways from any desk that B has ever seen or heard about before. Both A and B know that a desk is a piece of furniture one sits at, to study or write, in school or at home. The particular color, dimensions, or material of the desk are not important because A and B have both classified the concept "desk" according to common characteristics that apply to a range of different items in that category.

CLASSIFYING CONCEPTS

It is much easier for learners to acquire concepts if they are taught to classify (i.e., mentally group or organize under the same label) all items that have the same essential characteristics. By extending this process, students can learn to classify new concepts as well as familiar ones. Concepts can be classified in several ways. Figure 8.1 illustrates some of these ways.

FORMAL AND INFORMAL LEARNING CONTEXTS

Some concepts are acquired in what are called "formal contexts," referring to systematic instruction given at home (e.g., taking a telephone message, rules of right and wrong), in school (e.g., English spelling, osmosis), or on the job (e.g., oiling an internal combustion engine, using a cash register). "Informal contexts," in

FIGURE 8.1

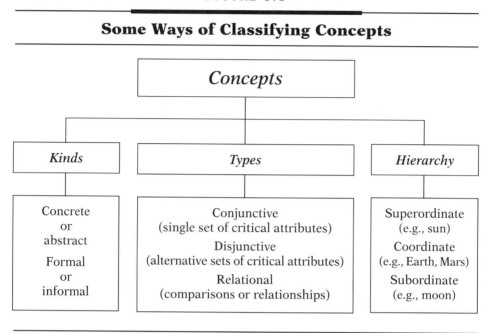

Some Ways of Classifying Concepts

which other concepts are acquired, generally include informal life experiences (e.g., listening to a radio, making an introduction, reading a road map).

■ ■ ■ ■ ■

PLANNING TO TEACH CONCEPTS

To teach a concept well, you must understand it thoroughly yourself. As a starting point, you might construct a mind (concept) map (as shown in Figure 8.3, on page 183), and go on from there. Plan to use as many learning modalities as possible (see Chapter 4).

Points to ponder . . .

❏   When planning a lesson, reflect on the important concept(s) that you wish your students to learn. Ask yourself, "How can I relate these concepts to my students' previous experience?"

Analyzing Concepts

You can help learners to acquire concepts by analyzing those concepts yourself before you teach them and by incorporating your analyses into your lesson plans. Figure 8.2 shows one way of handling concept analysis, but there are many other ways, as well, for the planning and process of concept analysis need not always be linear.

FIGURE 8.2

Analysis of the Concept *Noun*

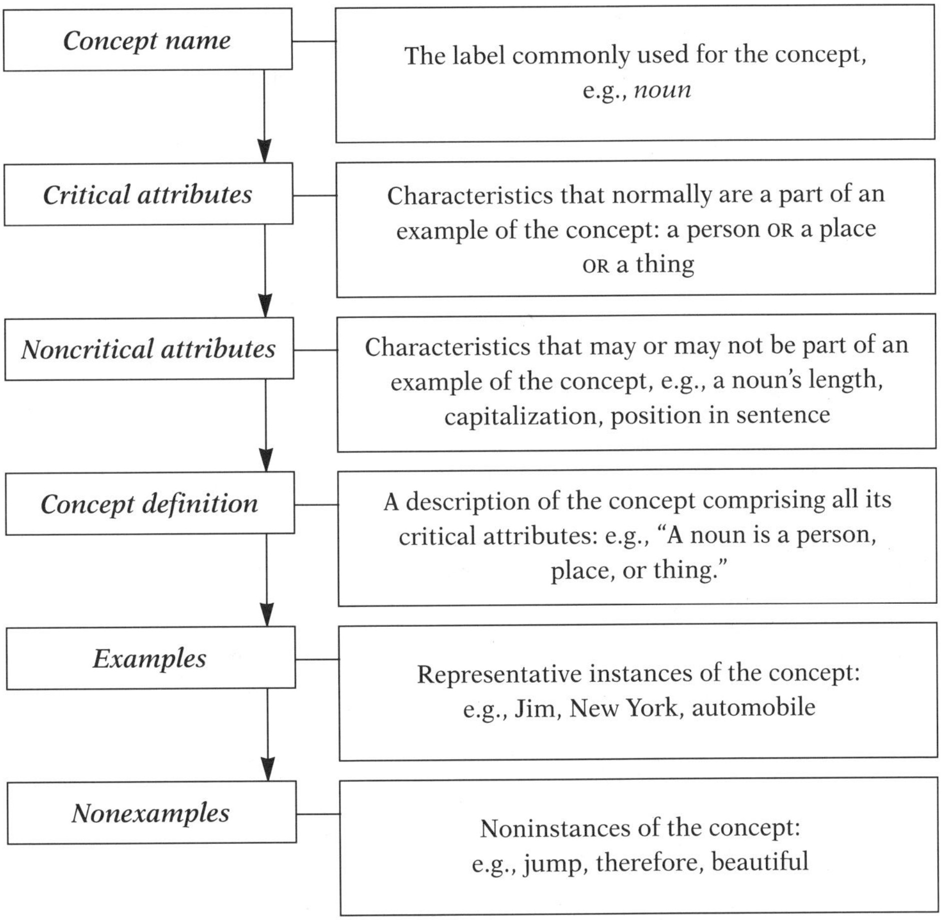

Concept name	The label commonly used for the concept, e.g., *noun*
Critical attributes	Characteristics that normally are a part of an example of the concept: a person OR a place OR a thing
Noncritical attributes	Characteristics that may or may not be part of an example of the concept, e.g., a noun's length, capitalization, position in sentence
Concept definition	A description of the concept comprising all its critical attributes: e.g., "A noun is a person, place, or thing."
Examples	Representative instances of the concept: e.g., Jim, New York, automobile
Nonexamples	Noninstances of the concept: e.g., jump, therefore, beautiful

Generally speaking, concept analysis entails

- naming or labeling a concept;
- identifying its critical attributes (essential features);
- identifying its noncritical attributes (incidental features);
- finding examples of the concept;
- finding nonexamples of the concept;
- defining the concept;
- distinguishing concepts;
- recognizing hierarchies (groups of items arranged in order of importance).

Naming or Labeling Concepts

Most concepts can be named or labeled, and the **concept name** or label is the symbol by which all its particular instances are grouped or classified. We use names to identify and communicate such concepts as "lake" or "jump." A first step to acquiring a concept, therefore, is naming or labeling it.

IDENTIFYING PROTOTYPES OF CONCEPTS

Concepts are often best acquired from examples that illustrate what they are. Examples are inclusive: that is, they specify what the concept *is*. The first examples of a concept should be very "pure," with few noncritical attributes. "Pure" examples, usually called **prototypes** or **exemplars**, are the "first and best" examples of a category or class of items because they are the original or basic forms. You may find it useful to introduce learners first to prototypes of concepts because the prototypes may have stronger and clearer characteristics than examples derived from them, which may have been changed or "watered down."

PROVIDING FURTHER EXAMPLES OF CONCEPTS

Students should first deal with concepts at a very simple level. For Example 8.1 illustrates some simple examples of concepts. Most learners need at least three to five examples of a concept, presented in sequence from most to least obvious, to help them identify the critical attributes, or essential characteristics, of a concept. Young or slow learners may need more examples, and so will students who must acquire complicated concepts and be able to generalize their attributes in order to recognize new instances.

In introducing concepts, choose examples that match the learners' language skills and developmental levels, and that reflect some part of their experience. Examples are more effective when they differ widely in a number of noncritical attributes. Make sure that early examples clearly represent the concept, focusing

FOR EXAMPLE 8.1

Examples of Concepts

CONCEPT	EXAMPLES
lake	Lake Superior, Cayuga Lake, Lac LaRonge
nation	Chinese, Canadians, Americans
dream	fantasy, nightmare, ambition

on no more than four or five of its critical attributes. When students have grasped the critical attributes of a concept, prevent **undergeneralization** (i.e., making the concept too narrow, by choosing more complex examples with more detailed and varied noncritical attributes.

PROVIDING NONEXAMPLES OF CONCEPTS

Nonexamples (negative examples) of a concept are exclusive: that is, they specify what the concept *is not*. It is important to have students consider nonexamples as well as examples, because neither examples nor nonexamples, by themselves, can convey a complete picture (see For Example 8.2). Select appropriate nonexamples, and present them in a logical order.

Like the first examples you present, the first nonexamples should be obvious and should contain few critical attributes. To prevent **overgeneralization** (i.e., making the concept too broad), later nonexamples should apply closely to the definition, differing, perhaps, in only one attribute. With very young learners, you should place less emphasis on nonexamples and more on examples.

Help learners to identify both examples and nonexamples of a concept by distinguishing the concept's critical and noncritical attributes, and by giving reasons for the distinctions. Nonexamples are more effective—initially, at least—when they differ in only one or a few critical attributes, to help students avoid making overgeneralizations. Students should also learn to avoid undergeneralizing—that is, forming concepts that are too narrow.

FOR EXAMPLE 8.2

Nonexamples of Concepts

CONCEPT	NONEXAMPLES
lake	Amazon River, Pacific Ocean, Juan de Fuca Strait
nation	P.E. Islanders, New Yorkers, Asians
dream	hope, fear, expectation

DISTINGUISHING EXAMPLES AND NONEXAMPLES

To identify examples and nonexamples suggested or used to illustrate the concept you are teaching, you should always ask yourself, "Why is this an example/nonexample (or a positive/negative example)?" Since most students recall concepts through examples and not through definitions, you *must* ensure that your students understand how the examples used relate to the concept. The first three or four examples you offer should be as "pure" as possible. When you judge that your students understand the concept you are teaching, introduce a few nonexamples; then ask learners to distinguish between examples and nonexamples, and explain their distinctions. The value of having students memorize definitions, however, is questionable.

IDENTIFYING CRITICAL ATTRIBUTES OF CONCEPTS

The essential, nonvariable, common characteristics of a concept are its defining attributes or **critical attributes** (see For Example 8.3). A good dictionary and the textbook for the course you are teaching will help you determine what these attributes are so that you can decide how to present them to foster learning. Remember, however, that these sources are just starting points! They may not identify all of a concept's critical attributes; they may even be misleading or present information of an inappropriate level for your class, and you may need to consult other sources or devise your own definitions.

IDENTIFYING NONCRITICAL ATTRIBUTES OF CONCEPTS

Noncritical attributes—attributes that are variable—are found in some, but not all, instances of a particular class of items. They may belong, but do not need to belong, to a particular instance of a concept, and so are not normally part of that concept's definition (see For Example 8.4).

EX. 8.2

Clearly identifying noncritical attributes helps ensure that learners clearly understand a concept, for much of the confusion that some students experience in trying to acquire concepts occurs because of associated noncritical attributes.

FOR EXAMPLE 8.3

Critical Attributes of Concepts

CONCEPT	CRITICAL ATTRIBUTES
lake	standing body of water; surrounded by land
nation	group of people; common political allegiance
dream	imaginary experience; lack of distinction between reality and unreality

A young child, for instance, may first associate the term *chair* with yellow kitchen chairs. To this child, all chairs must look like those kitchen chairs. Chairs of a different color and shape are not yet "chairs" to the child because he or she has not yet learned to distinguish noncritical attributes of the concept "chair" (e.g., color and shape) from critical attributes—a piece of furniture with a back, seat, and legs, designed to accommodate someone in a sitting position.

Some noncritical attributes are particularly befuddling to learners and should be discussed specifically. For example, children who believe that all birds fly may be confused when they encounter examples of birds that cannot do so.

Defining Concepts

Once you have reviewed examples and clearly identified critical and noncritical attributes, select or compose a suitable definition for the concept you are teaching. **Concept definitions** should cover all the essential, or critical, attributes and express the relationship of those attributes to one another (see For Example 8.5). Noncritical attributes should be avoided, however, because they can produce a "muddy" definition that confuses students and interferes with learning and transfer. Move from simple to more complex and more specific definitions as learners develop higher-level skills.

DISTINGUISHING CONCEPTS

Part of the processes of analyzing and defining concepts is distinguishing various types. Concepts are distinguished on the basis of various criteria, which may or may not be present simultaneously.

- A **concrete concept** is one that can be acquired directly through one or more of our five senses.
- An **abstract concept** is one that can be acquired only <u>indirectly</u> or through <u>inference</u>.
- A **conjunctive concept** is one that has a single set of two or more characteristics, or critical attributes, that are always present (e.g., a lake is always a body

(2 Critical attributes always present)

FOR EXAMPLE 8.4

Noncritical Attributes of Concepts

CONCEPT	NONCRITICAL ATTRIBUTES
music	tempo, range of notes, instrumental, vocal
surgeon	gender, race, height
cow	size, color, length of tail, habitat

FOR EXAMPLE 8.5

Definitions of Concepts

CONCEPT	DEFINITION
wheel	a circular frame of hard material that can turn on an axle
applaud	strike one's hands together to produce a series of sharp sounds that signify approval
nation	a group of people with a common political allegiance

of standing water surrounded by land, and a square is always a quadrilateral with four equal sides).

◆ A **disjunctive concept** is one that has two or more sets of critical attributes, each of which is sufficient, by itself, to define the concept (e.g., a "strike" occurs in baseball when the batter swings and misses _or_ when the batter hits a foul ball _or_ when the umpire judges that the ball has passed through the strike zone; a "noun" is the name of a person _or_ a place _or_ a thing).

◆ A **relational concept** is based not on distinctive attributes of its two or more parts, but on a fixed relationship of those parts (e.g., a line cannot be "parallel" _unless_ it has a fixed relationship with another line; a woman is not an "aunt" _unless_ she has a niece or nephew).

Concepts may fit more than one of the above criteria (see For Example 8.6).

Although this classification system is useful in a general way, some concepts cannot be defined according to a specific set of features. Many concepts, such as social class, justice, alienation, and poverty, have no clear boundary, and no one can state with certainty what is or is not an instance of them.

Relating Concepts

Since learners acquire new concepts more easily if they can relate them to similar concepts, organizing related concepts can be a very useful part of concept

FOR EXAMPLE 8.6

Distinguishing Types of Concepts

CONCEPT	DEFINITION
copper	concrete conjunctive concept
citizenship	abstract disjunctive concept (because citizenship can relate to a city, a state or province, or a country, and it can be conferred by birth or by law)
moon (a satellite)	relational concept (because a moon is a moon only because of its relation to a specific planet)

FIGURE 8.3

A Concept Map: Hierarchy of Minerals

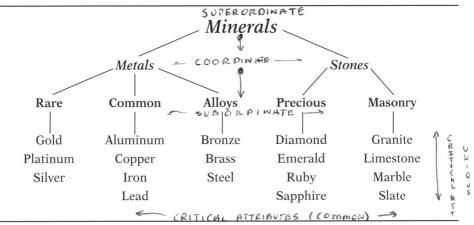

analysis. Figure 8.3 illustrates a group of related concepts in what is known as a **concept map**.

RECOGNIZING HIERARCHIES

Related concepts can sometimes be organized as parts (components) of a hierarchy, occupying superordinate, coordinate, and/or subordinate positions.

- ◆ **Superordinate concepts** are broad generalizations that include a number of narrower and more specific concepts with varying critical attributes. In Figure 8.3, "minerals" is a superordinate concept, and the more particular concepts— such as "metals" and "stones"—that it broadly covers are subordinate to it or included in it.

- ◆ **Coordinate concepts** share some critical attributes, but have one or more unique critical attributes that distinguish them from one another; they also have an equivalent relationship to the same superordinate concept. "Metals" and "stones," for example, are coordinate concepts in that they have some common attributes and share equivalent relations to the superordinate concept "minerals."

- ◆ **Subordinate concepts** are those that are covered by (or included in) a broader classification. "Metals" and "stones" are subordinate to "minerals"; "rare" and "common" metals and "alloys" are subordinate to "metals"; and so on. Subordinate concepts share some common critical attributes, but each also has one or more unique critical attributes.

Presenting concepts that are part of a hierarchy in a hit-and-miss fashion makes little sense. To help your students learn and retain information, plan to teach concepts in logical sequence, recognizing and taking advantage of groupings and relationships, vertical (i.e.; hierarchical) or horizontal (i.e., coordinating). You might prepare or obtain an advance organizer that presents the hierarchy in the form of a chart or table so that as you introduce each concept, you can point out its relation. As students' developmental levels rise, plan to present hierarchies that are more inclusive.

Not all concepts, however, lend themselves easily to placement in a hierarchy. There are unclear cases, since it is difficult to identify and define critical attributes for many concepts: Is a tomato, for instance, a fruit or a vegetable?

PRACTICE *and Projects*

1. Select several concepts that are common to a school subject of your choice. Analyze each in terms of examples, nonexamples, critical attributes, noncritical attributes, and definition. Use Data Collection Form 8.1 (Appendix A) for this purpose.

2. In a text relating to a subject you plan to teach, find examples of the following types of concepts:
    a. concrete and abstract
    b. formal and informal
    c. conjunctive, disjunctive, and relational

3. a. Select a concept relating to a subject of your choice; list all the examples of that concept that you can think of.
    b. Arrange the examples in order from pure and easily recognized to more complex.

■ ■ ■ ■ ■

TEACHING CONCEPTS

Because concepts underlie the basic units of school curricula, most of a teacher's instruction time is spent introducing them or enriching learners' understanding of them. Helping learners, whether in kindergarten or graduate school, to master concepts is one of the greatest challenges that you will face.

Teaching Abstract Concepts

Abstract concepts are harder to grasp than concrete concepts. Helping your students to understand the two kinds of concepts may call for different instructional approaches. Some concepts are learned informally, while others may need to be learned formally; many concepts are learned through a combination of formal and informal experiences.

One approach to teaching an abstract concept is to use analogies (comparisons). It is best not to stop with one analogy, but to use several, identifying various attributes of the concept until your students can distinguish the critical ones and frame a definition. You might start to teach the concept of "clan," for instance, by comparing some of its critical attributes to those of the concept of "family": families, like clans, are groups of people who have common ancestors and common attributes. You might then ask your students to consider examples of clan tradition, and, from their responses, have them infer other attributes of clans. Next, you might describe instances and noninstances of acts and consequences or causes and effects of clan allegiances. This process should continue until your students can form a definition of the concept.

A Teaching Cycle

Helping learners acquire concepts involves a teaching cycle that includes the following elements:

- preparing and motivating learners;
- presenting advance organizers;
- delivering the body of the lesson in an efficient, well organized, and interesting way by using a variety of media;
- providing for transfer, reviewing, and arranging meaningful practice.

The teaching model presented below will take you through the steps required to teach a concept effectively. It is *not*, however, intended to suggest a rigidly sequential approach to either planning or teaching concepts.

PLAN TO TEACH A CONCEPT

Effective teaching of concepts cannot be left to chance: it requires careful planning and sensitive methodical instruction to help learners master concepts. Mastery involves the ability to

- find or create examples of a concept and explain what makes them examples;
- modify nonexamples to make them examples of a concept and justify the changes;
- correctly name or label concept examples and justify choices by citing critical attributes.

Because of their cultural and educational background or level of development, students find some concepts harder to acquire than others. A rule-of-thumb guide for teaching concepts suggests relating your approach to learner development as follows:

Age/Developmental Stage	Approach to Concept Teaching
Up to 7 years	Enactive (i.e., hands-on)
Up to 11 years	Enactive moving to iconic (i.e., pictorial)
Eleven years and beyond	Iconic moving to symbolic (e.g., verbal, numeric)

Students with rudimentary language skills will learn best from hands-on experience. As language and other learning skills develop, pictures become a useful means of enlarging learners' basic concepts. At a still higher level, verbal or numeric symbols may be appropriate teaching tools, though it always helps, even with mature learners, to have "real things" (or at least pictures) available for handling or viewing. Abstract concepts that relate to such matters as algebra or sentence structure are learned indirectly through the senses and inference. Methods for teaching them may have to be heavily verbal or symbolic.

As you plan the specifics of your lesson, therefore, consider your students' learner readiness.

◆ How old are your students?
◆ What are their developmental levels?
◆ What are their preferred learning styles?
◆ What background or previous experience have they in relation to the concept?

Review the textbook your students will be using and other appropriate reference materials, and choose lesson content in keeping with the curriculum. The kind of concept to be learned should influence the medium you choose for teaching.

For Example 8.7 provides a sample lesson plan for concept teaching.

FOR EXAMPLE 8.7

A Lesson Plan for Teaching the Concept "Planet"

I. *Topic*: Planet
II. *Content Identification*: The topic "planets" in a unit titled "Our Solar System"
III. *Objectives*:
    1. Given a diagram of examples and nonexamples of a planet, each student will correctly identify each planet.
    2. Given the above items, each student will be able to write a suitable justification for the selections made.

(continued)

(continued)

IV. *Materials and Aids*: Large chart of solar system; three-dimensional model of the planets, sun, and moons; short film on solar system; one-page diagram of solar system.

V. *Prerequisite Student Learnings*: Awareness of solar system concepts, and exposure to concept hierarchies. Familiarity with the concepts of critical and noncritical attributes and superordinate, subordinate, and coordinate concepts.

VI. *Presentation Activities*:

1. *Introductory*
   - Questions to discover students' knowledge of the solar system, gained through watching the television series or movie *Star Trek* or other sources.
   - Using a large unlabeled chart of the solar system, provide an advance organizer and state the lesson objectives.

2. *Developmental*
   - Show a short film on the solar system, asking students to pay particular attention to the planets.
   - Ask students to name the planets mentioned in the film.
   - Using a large three-dimensional model of the planets, sun, and moons, demonstrate how planets orbit the sun.
   - Have students form groups of five to select critical attributes of planets; have groups report to the class to achieve consensus.
   - Have same groups select and report on noncritical attributes.
   - Using questions and discussion, draw the concept definition from the class.
   - Using the unlabeled chart of the solar system, randomly point to stars, planets, satellites. Ask students to identify items as examples or nonexamples of planets, and to justify their responses.

3. *Closing*
   - Using questions and answers, review critical and noncritical attributes and the concept definition.
   - Have students classify concepts relating to "planet" as super- and subordinate, and coordinate.
   - Ask students how their learnings about planets can be useful.
   - Relate "planet" to the topic of the next lesson.
   - Distribute unlabeled diagrams of the solar system. As homework, students will label the planets and explain, in writing, their decisions.

VII. *Evaluation Methods*
   - Questioning; reports by groups; homework assignment; unit test.

Note: This example is based on Data Collection Form 8.2 (Appendix A).

EXAMINE THE CONCEPT HIERARCHY

Before you make definite lesson plans, study the **concept hierarchy** to which the concept you will teach relates. Concepts are often part of a hierarchy that suggests a logical sequence in which to present components. When you have determined the concept's place in that hierarchy, you will be ready to make a logical sequencing decision that will help learners to understand and recall the concepts to be taught in the unit and their relationship to one another.

Select an appropriate instructional approach and suitable learning activities, and plan an appropriate advance organizer. You may find that a concept hierarchy can serve as an advance organizer and as part of the set for a teaching unit. The complexity of a hierarchy you prepare for this purpose should, of course, depend on the experience, age, and learning stage of your students.

CLASSIFY THE CONCEPT

Once you have selected a concept, you must determine what kind it is by classifying it according to the information given on page 181–182.

ESTABLISH SET

Find motivating ways to introduce and develop concepts. Concept learning need not consist of plodding through steps in a dull-as-dishwater fashion. It can be both productive and enjoyable when it touches the personal lives and needs of students. At the outset, you should usually explain the lesson objectives and, as appropriate, show how the content relates to what the students have studied before and what they will study later. If students ask, "Why do we have to learn this?" be prepared to provide a good answer that takes their point of view into account. Statements such as "You may need this later in life," "Astronauts need to know this," or "It's going to be on the exam," are not likely to motivate your students. At this point, you might share your advance organizer with your class. Showing your enthusiasm and your high, but achievable, expectations will strengthen your students' motivation (see Chapter 4).

DEVELOP YOUR LESSON

Be aware of your students' interests, and try to lead them through exciting learning adventures. Recognize their developmental level, and vary your modes of instruction as appropriate. Consider students' learning styles and cultural background; strive to challenge every learner but still be an "organizer of success experiences." Encourage interaction, and involve as many senses and as much direct participation as possible. Include examples and nonexamples of the concept chosen, to help learners recognize and define it, and understand its critical and noncritical attributes. Your clear explanations, your use of a variety of appropriate media, and your skillful handling of questions and answers, and class discussion will help your students learn. If learners are to transfer (or apply) their learnings to new or related examples, or use new information in higher-level operations, teach for transfer.

During your lesson, learner participation should be as active as possible, in keeping with the instructional approach and teaching methods that you have planned. Provide your students with opportunities to

- gather or retrieve data;
- identify and report examples;
- compare new with familiar information to discover differences and similarities;
- summarize information to define the concept; and
- classify items to decide whether they are examples or nonexamples.

CONSOLIDATE YOUR LESSON

To help your students remember the new concept you have taught, provide them with opportunities to use it: have them practice differentiating both examples and nonexamples, giving reasons for their decisions. Close with a review of the concept definition, asking your students to state the concept's critical attributes and their relationships rather than reciting them yourself. Frame questions to check that students can identify related superordinate, coordinate, and subordinate concepts.

CHECK COMPREHENSION

This final step in the cycle lets you and your students know how effective your planning and instruction have been, and how well your students have mastered the concept. Checking might be informal, consisting of observing students' consolidation activities or conducting a question-and-answer session. Alternatively, it might be formal, consisting of a test or written assignment to be done at once or later. In either case, you should use this phase to determine whether any part of the lesson should be retaught or retested.

Inferring Concepts

Examples and prototypes can help learners to acquire concepts, but only when those concepts are part of the learners' background. Since it is not always possible, however, to show learners examples or prototypes of a concept, you must give your students opportunities to infer some concepts.

No one can actually show a learner an atom or an amp, ohm or erg, even with a microscope. Similarly, nationalism can be described, and its effects may be plain, but it cannot be seen. For such concepts, or hypothetical constructs, "connection with the observable level of experience is made only through a chain of inference" (B.O. Smith, 1985, p. 688). Teachers often use models and diagrams to help students make the necessary inferences to acquire concepts; analogies or instances of acts and events and their consequences might also be used.

Making Generalizations

Generalizations are based on concepts expressed in a relationship, but they are more complicated than their component concepts. Generalizations include rules, regulations, principles, laws, conclusions, inferences, axioms, proverbs, mottoes, propositions, and hypotheses. They express relationships of broad applicability: the proverb "A stitch in time saves nine," for instance, is a generalization composed of several concepts (stitch, time, saves, nine) that suggests that it is more efficient or easier in the long run to take time do a small task promptly or properly, in order to save the time needed for doing a larger task later.

To understand a generalization, students must understand its component concepts. For example, to grasp the rule that "Water freezes at 32° Fahrenheit," students must understand the concepts "water," "freeze," "degree," and "Fahrenheit," or they will not understand the generalization, and learning will be reduced to a process of memorizing a fact. True learning requires connecting concepts.

PRACTICE *and Projects*

1. Join a subject-interest group. Brainstorm examples of concrete and abstract concepts. Select three examples of each type, and try to reach consensus on the critical attributes, noncritical attributes, and concept definitions of each.

2. Working in the same group, brainstorm, agree upon, and justify the selection of examples of conjunctive, disjunctive, and relational concepts.

3. Working in the same group, use Data Collection Form 8.2 (Appendix A) to analyze an example of a concrete and an abstract concept.

4. Using Data Collection Form 8.1, analyze Case Study 8.1. Your instructor may pose specific questions for your response.

CASE STUDY 8.1

TEACHING A CONCEPT

Ms. Yanski's Grade 11 Law class is studying the law of contracts. She has told her class that there are five elements in a binding contract. One of these elements is "consideration."

"A valid contract," Ms. Yanski says, "must include a 'consideration.' Do you know what that is?"

After a long pause, Damon volunteers, "Well, before you sign anything you should consider things carefully."

Ms. Yanski replies, "That's certainly true, Damon, but the legal definition of 'consideration' is a bit different. Let me give an example. When you buy a camera for a friend that has a price tag of $210, the camera is consideration and so is the $210. If the person who had the camera agreed to take a pair of car wheel mags for the camera, the mags would also be consideration. You could even promise to paint the car in exchange for the camera. The service you promise to provide is consideration, too. Does this suggest some other ideas about what consideration might be?"

Freda responds, "I've heard of cases where people bought something really valuable, like a house, for one dollar. I think that would be consideration, but would it be legal?"

Ms. Yanski replies, "Yes. Consideration doesn't have to be of equal value to make a contract legal. One dollar is a consideration."

Ms. Yanski draws the essential features of consideration from the class. Students discover that consideration need not be adequate, that both parties need not benefit personally: for instance, a consideration might be a promise to make a donation to a charity or to stop cutting a lawn at five in the morning.

After considering all the examples, the students define "consideration." Their definition states that consideration is money or money value given or promised in return for benefit received. The courts will not enforce a promise to do or give something unless the person benefiting does or gives something in exchange, or promises to do so.

Ms. Yanski distributes a handout outlining ten cases. She asks her students to decide whether consideration is present in each case and to justify their answers. She works out the first case with the class and assigns the rest as seatwork. The next day, she takes up the cases, using probing questions to determine whether students understand the definition and the critical and noncritical attributes of consideration.

SUMMARY

- A concept is a mental construct, or personal perception, of a category or class of similar objects, conditions, events, or processes represented by a word, symbol, or mental picture.

- Concepts are fundamental to thought and learning, for people cannot function without these personal mental symbols, and shared concepts are functional shortcuts to efficient communication.

- Before you can teach a concept successfully, you must thoroughly understand it yourself, preferably through personal analysis.

- The name or label of a concept is the symbol by which all its particular instances are grouped or classified.

- Concepts are often best acquired from "pure" examples (prototypes or exemplars) that illustrate what they are.

- Most learners need at least three to five examples (illustrations of what a concept *is*), presented sequentially from most to least obvious, to help them identify a concept's critical attributes (essential characteristics).

- Learners also need nonexamples (illustrations of what a concept *is not*) to clarify a concept because neither examples nor nonexamples, by themselves, can convey a complete picture.

- Awareness of a concept's critical (nonvariable) and noncritical (variable) attributes is also necessary for complete understanding.

- Concept definitions should cover all the critical attributes and express the relationship of these attributes to one another.

- Concepts are classified as concrete, abstract, conjunctive, disjunctive, and relational. Concepts are distinguished on the basis of these criteria, which may or may not be present simultaneously.

- Related concepts can sometimes be organized as parts of a hierarchy, occupying superordinate, coordinate, and/or subordinate positions.

- Students learn some concepts informally, but may need formal instruction in others.

- Effective teaching of concepts requires careful planning and sensitive, methodical instruction that should vary according to students' age, level of experience, and learner readiness.

- Active learner participation is important to successful learning of concepts.

- Some concepts cannot be demonstrated, but must be inferred.

- Generalizations are based on concepts and express relationships of broad applicability. To grasp a generalization, students must understand its components.

KEY WORDS

analogy

concept

   concrete

   abstract

   conjunctive

   disjunctive

   relational

critical attribute

definition

exemplar

example

formal learning

   context

generalization

hierarchy

   superordinate

   coordinate

   subordinate

infer

informal learning

   context

mental construct

noncritical attribute

nonexample

overgeneralization

prototype

pure example

undergeneralization

RECOMMENDED READING

Hyde, A., & Bizar, M. (1989). *Thinking in context: Teaching cognitive processes across the elementary school curriculum.* New York: Longman.

Marzano R., Brandt, R., Hughes, C., Jones, B., Presseisen, B., Rankin, S., & Suhor, C. (1988). *Dimensions of thinking: A framework for curriculum and instruction.* Alexandria, VA: Association for Supervision and Curriculum Development.

McKinney, C., Gilmore, H., Peddicord, H. & McCallum, S. (1987). Effects of a best example and critical attributes on prototype formation in the acquisition of a concept. *Theory and Research in Social Education, 15,* 189–202.

CHAPTER 9

TEACHING AND DEMONSTRATING SKILLS

■ ■ ■ ■ ■

[The mastery of a skill] depends on the ability to perform it unconsciously with speed and accuracy while carrying on other brain functions.

(BLOOM, 1986, P. 70)

■ ■ ■ ■ ■

OVERVIEW

Skills may be classified as cognitive, affective, or psychomotor procedures that can be learned and performed. To plan a skills lesson you must make a procedural, hierarchical, or combination task analysis by identifying the sequence of parts (or subskills) that constitute the skill, or the relationships that link the subskills, or both. You must also decide whether to teach the "whole" skill (as one entire process) or its "parts" (i.e., a sequence of subskills to be practiced and performed separately).

Teaching a skill involves the following stages: orientation; presentation; structured, guided, and independent practice sessions, each followed by prompt feedback; and periodic reviews.

Most skills need to be demonstrated clearly and explained lucidly before they are practiced, tested, and put to use in real situations. Demonstration is a multistep procedure that involves planning, preparing, delivering, providing practice, testing, encouraging transfer, and providing review.

■ ■ ■ ■ ■

PRINCIPLES OF SKILLS TEACHING

The principles that apply to teaching in general apply also to teaching **procedures** and skills. As you read the following sections, relate them to the principles and practices with which you have already become familiar.

Concepts and Skills

Education neither starts nor stops with acquiring concepts (**conceptual** or **declarative knowledge**), since putting concepts to use requires a wide variety of **skills** (**procedural knowledge**, or "how to," knowledge), and every skill relates to a concept. Perceptive teachers know how to integrate concepts and skills in their lessons by teaching a combination of declarative and procedural knowledge.

Skills, acquired by practice, translate knowledge into expert action, but only when learners clearly understand that action and the principles that underlie it.

Just as understanding concepts does not, of itself, confer the corresponding skills needed to put those concepts to practical use, so the ability to perform a skill does not, of itself, ensure understanding of the concepts involved. A child may know what swimming is but be unable to swim. A student may have the conceptual knowledge to define the term *verb*, but lack the procedural skills to use verbs correctly. It is only when learners integrate concepts and skills that they can truly be said to have grasped an area of knowledge.

Though in practice, knowledge of concepts and ability to perform skills are often closely related, it is important to distinguish the types of instructional skills that each requires. The wise teacher knows how skills and concepts are interrelated, and when and how to apply the appropriate teaching principles to promote procedural or declarative knowledge.

Classifying Skills

Since teaching skills and promoting their development are important parts of education, it is helpful to classify the chief categories of skills through which knowledge is translated into performance. Many people think of skills as requiring only physical dexterity, but there are other types of skills, as well. Skills are generally classified as procedural knowledge—that is, knowledge of how to do something—in contrast to declarative (informational) knowledge. Educators often find it useful to subdivide skills into three categories: cognitive, affective, or psychomotor procedures. It is seldom possible to classify skills in this way with complete precision, since each type of skill usually includes elements of the others, but practical distinctions can be made according to the type of skill that is *mainly* involved in a given activity. Thus, the types of skills that appear below relate to a general rather than a precise classification system:

♦ **Cognitive skills** relate to perceiving, learning, and knowing. Thinking, problem solving, and decision making are important cognitive skills.
♦ **Affective skills** relate to forming and determining attitudes and values. Interpersonal skills such as perception checking and behavior description, and group skills such as consensus seeking and conflict resolution have affective (emotion- and/or value-related) elements.
♦ **Psychomotor skills** are those used to direct or control motion resulting from mental activity. Physical activities such as playing tennis or typing require the use of psychomotor skills.

CHARACTERISTICS OF SKILLED PERFORMANCE

Have you ever watched a seemingly flawless musical performance by a solo guitarist, pianist, or singer? a tennis match between top-ranking players? a teacher quickly solving a complex algebra problem on the chalkboard? Each of these is an example of "expert" performance, or **skilled performance**. While elements of these activities will vary, each performer is likely to exhibit appropriate selection, economy of effort, and performance **automaticity**.

Appropriate Selection

An expert performer rapidly selects and initiates an appropriate response to a given situation. As a golfer walks toward her ball on the fairway, for instance, she plans her next shot, considering slope of the fairway and green, distance to the green, wind and grass conditions, placement of the flag, and club and swing selection. By the time she reaches her ball, she knows exactly what she is going to do.

Economy of Effort

An expert performs a skill accurately, with great economy of effort, movement, and time. When an expert musician plays his instrument, he performs each subskill unhesitatingly and smoothly, in the appropriate sequence, with just the right amount of effort, and without a single unnecessary movement.

Performance Automaticity

Experts seem to perform their special skills consistently, without having to think about them and with minimum effort because they have "automatized" many aspects of their performance. One substep "cues" (i.e., triggers) or flows into the next, without pause or conscious attention. Automatic skill performance is efficient, consistent, and habitual. A highly skilled touch typist, for instance, can perform a cognitive skill (e.g., preparing an outline for an assignment) while using a psychomotor skill (keyboarding), without having to think about what hands and fingers are doing.

■ ■ ■ ■ ■

PREPARING FOR SKILLS TEACHING

Teaching skills effectively requires a thorough understanding of a wide variety of basic procedures, competence in their performance, and appreciation of their value in life situations. You can best gain this understanding by learning to make a **task analysis** of the skills you will target and teach—that is, identifying their component tasks to discover the chain of subskills involved.

Task Analysis

To prepare an effective skills lesson, you will need to analyze the targeted skill by identifying *either* the sequence of procedures (or steps) *or* the hierarchy of skills involved in performing it, *or* a combination of these two factors (see For Example 9.1). All three kinds of task analysis may be needed to identify the subskills required to perform the tasks involved and their relationships to the skill you will teach.

PROCEDURAL TASK ANALYSIS

Procedural task analysis involves identifying a particular sequence of subtasks to achieve a learning goal. This type of analysis is useful for identifying a chain of elements and the points at which those elements must be linked to achieve smooth performance (Siedentop, 1983, p. 157). It will provide clues to guide you in framing an approach to teaching a chosen skill or subskill, demonstrating each component task, directing and monitoring student practice, selecting evaluation criteria, and providing feedback.

A procedural task analysis starts with determining the final product, then "walking through" the process, recording the nature and sequence of each step, as well as its input (or prerequisites), procedure, and output (results). An analysis of a procedure for folding and inserting a business letter into a standard business envelope is illustrated in Figure 9.1.

Each step of the process involves stages: the input of one step initiates a process that results in an output. This output, in turn, becomes the input for the next step. Although each step is independent and could be taught independently, the steps

---

FOR EXAMPLE 9.1

Task Analysis

SEQUENCE OF PROCEDURES OR STEPS
To find a location on a city map, students must be able to follow such steps as
- reading the index;
- using the vertical and horizontal block systems.

HIERARCHY OF SKILLS
The hierarchy of skills involved in learning to ride a bicycle might include
- mounting the bicycle;
- dismounting the bicycle;
- keeping one's balance while pedaling;
- operating the gears while in motion.

FIGURE 9.1

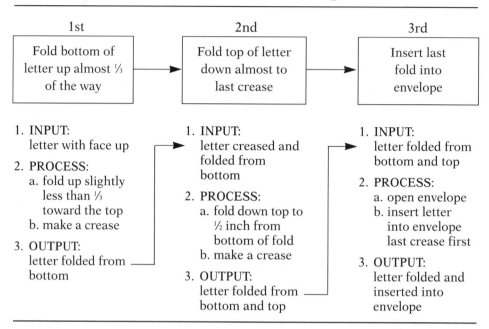

Procedural Task Analysis: Folding and Inserting a Letter into an Envelope

follow a particular sequence (Dick & Carey, 1978, p. 27). Procedural analysis is often particularly appropriate for preparing to teach psychomotor skills.

HIERARCHICAL TASK ANALYSIS

Although making a **hierarchical task analysis** is usually more complex than making a procedural analysis, the former is a useful way of discovering the kinds

FOR EXAMPLE 9.2

Enabling Skills

Writing sentences is an enabling skill that students need in order to write paragraphs successfully.

- ◆ To write sentences, students must know how to write in script.
- ◆ To write in script, students must know how to form each letter of the alphabet.
- ◆ To form each letter of the alphabet, students must be able to control a pen or pencil.

and sequence of subskills—often called "enabling" skills—that students must acquire in order to perform a higher-level, or "terminal," skill objective (see For Example 9.2). Figure 9.2 illustrates a fairly complex hierarchical analysis. You may find that you need to revise such an analysis a number of times before you are satisfied, but persistence will pay off by providing you with practice that will help you learn to perform this skill efficiently.

Figure 9.2 shows that an effective hierarchical task analysis requires background knowledge of the ultimate skill objective, and the ability to identify and arrange the subskills in a logical order. Teaching complex skills, particularly cognitive skills, usually requires making a hierarchical analysis.

FIGURE 9.2

Hierarchical Task Analysis: Job Interview

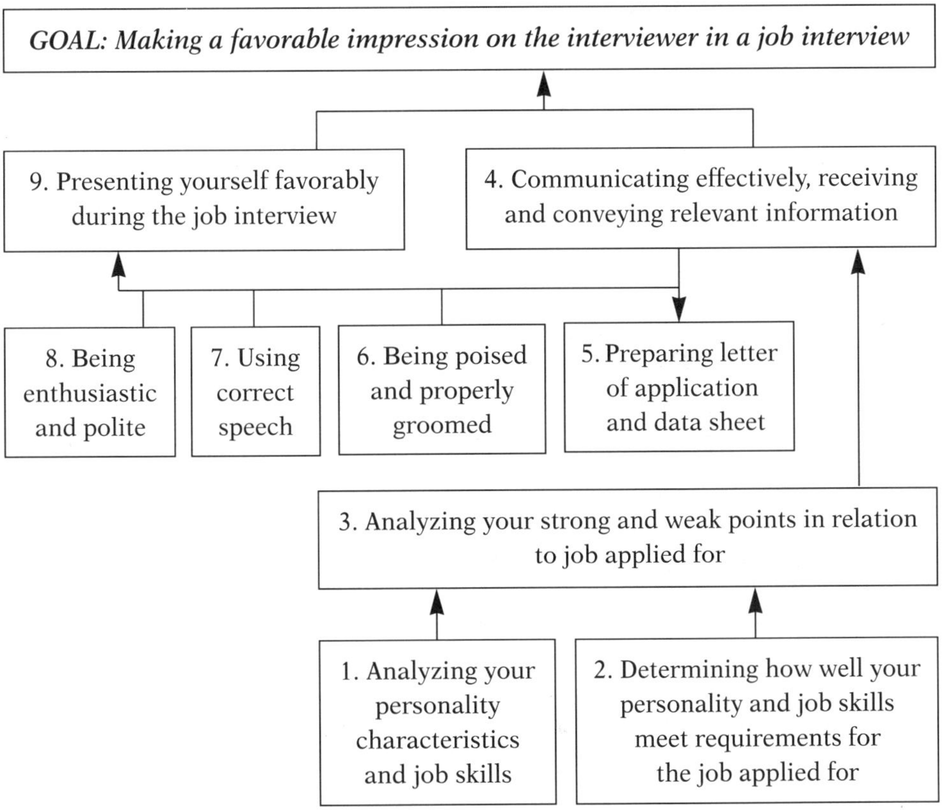

GOAL: *Making a favorable impression on the interviewer in a job interview*

9. Presenting yourself favorably during the job interview

4. Communicating effectively, receiving and conveying relevant information

8. Being enthusiastic and polite

7. Using correct speech

6. Being poised and properly groomed

5. Preparing letter of application and data sheet

3. Analyzing your strong and weak points in relation to job applied for

1. Analyzing your personality characteristics and job skills

2. Determining how well your personality and job skills meet requirements for the job applied for

COMBINATION TASK ANALYSIS

Preparing to teach a complex skill often requires a combination of procedural and hierarchical analysis. You should use the combination approach to analyze a relatively complex psychomotor skill or linear chain of cognitive tasks. Figure 9.3 illustrates the task of finding a word in a dictionary as outlined by a **combination task analysis**. Making a procedural analysis (shown horizontally in Figure 9.3) consists of examining each step in terms of input, process, and output. The output of the first step is the input for the process of the second step, while the output of the second step becomes the input for the third. Selecting and ordering the prerequisite subskills requires making a hierarchical analysis (shown vertically).

FIGURE 9.3

Combination Task Analysis: Finding a Word in a Dictionary

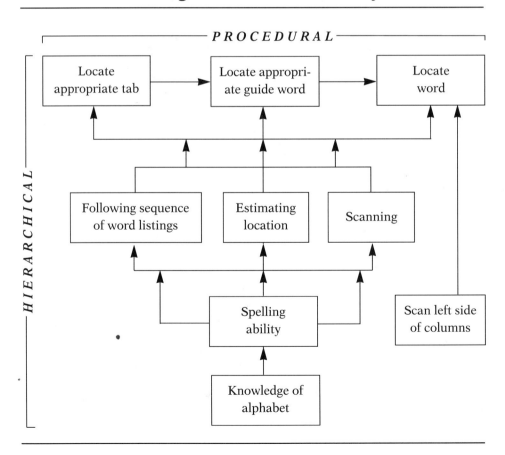

Approaches to Skills Teaching: Whole or Part

The **"whole approach"** to skills teaching involves teaching or demonstrating a complete skill as a single unit. This approach is appropriate when skills are relatively simple and their subskills are closely knit. It has the advantage of presenting an overview of the entire skill and the relation of its parts to one another. For some skills, practice of individual parts (or subskills) takes place while performing the whole. For example, a student may concentrate on punctuation while writing sentences.

Skills with many subskills should likely be broken into parts. In using the **"parts" approach**, a rule for efficient learning is to "work with the smallest amounts possible without sacrificing maximum meaning or wasting time" (Hunter, 1969, p. 53). You must also choose the order in which to introduce the component subskills, basing your selection on their nature and their dependence on one another. One approach is to move from the simplest subskill to the most complex. Probably the most common method is to follow the sequence in which the subskills occur in the total process.

If successful performance of one subskill depends on proficiency in another, you should teach the foundational skill first. (For example, beginning players usually learn how to grip a baseball bat before they learn how to swing it.) Sometimes the individual elements of a skill chain can be learned independently and then put together. Sometimes skills must be learned in a certain order; sometimes they need not. In any case, students must eventually learn to integrate the components of a skill into a single smooth sequence of responses.

PRACTICE *and Projects*

1. Examine a can of pudding that has a pop-top opening. Make a procedural analysis of opening the can.

2. Obtain a city map. Prepare a hierarchical analysis of the skills involved in finding a given address.

3. a. Join a subject-interest group, and brainstorm examples of procedural skills, hierarchical skills, and skills that are a combination of procedural and hierarchical.

   b. Working with a partner, prepare a task analysis for one of the examples listed.

▪■■■

TEACHING A SKILL LESSON

Teaching a skill lesson involves applying principles you have learned in more general situations. As usual, you will begin with planning.

Planning For Skills Teaching

Effective skills teaching requires careful planning, since skills learned only to basic performance level and practiced without understanding are likely to bore the learner and be quickly forgotten. Before you begin to teach any skill, therefore, you will need to consider a number of critical questions.

Points to ponder . . .

- ❑ What kind of skill do I intend to teach?
- ❑ What place has it in the chain of skills to which it belongs?
- ❑ What subskills are involved? In what order are my students likely to use them?
- ❑ What level of these subskills do my students already possess?
- ❑ What stage of learner readiness have my students reached?
- ❑ How much time can I afford to allocate to teaching the new skill?
- ❑ How shall I present the lesson?
- ❑ What degree of learning or overlearning is my objective? How much practice is necessary? What kind of practice? How much guidance is needed?
- ❑ How much feedback should I give, and of what kind? What kind of reinforcement is desirable?
- ❑ How can I foster transfer?

To answer these questions, you will need to assess carefully the content of your lesson and your students' learning levels. You may find it helpful to break the planning process into the components outlined below, and summarized in Figure 9.4.

◆ *Identify the skill.* Focus on skills that are part of the course curriculum. You may wish to refer to a "curriculum guide," a textbook, or other reference materials to ensure that you clearly understand the context of the skill relative to the unit of instruction.

FIGURE 9.4

A Seven-Step Planning Model for Teaching a Skill

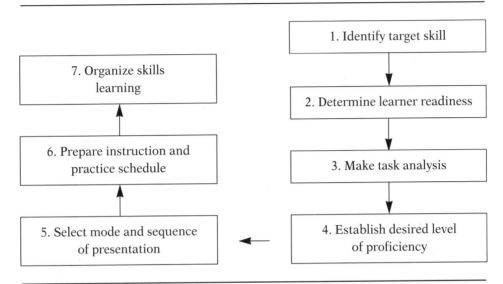

- *Determine learner readiness.* To teach a skill efficiently, you must know what subskills your students already possess, for effective instruction must be given at the learners' level of ability and insight. Consider the learners' age, degree of mental maturity and physical readiness, and intellectual, affective, and moral developmental levels. Determine, too, their previous experiences with the skill you plan to teach or a related one so that you can use those experiences to make new learning meaningful.
- *Make a task analysis.* Depending on the skill you have targeted, choose a procedural, hierarchical, or combination method of task analysis. Each kind of task analysis involves identifying subskills and their relationships, and determining the sequence in which you will teach them.
- *Determine the desired level of proficiency.* Learners tend to progress along a five-phase skill-development continuum that includes the elements shown in Figure 9.5. When you plan to teach a skill, you must first determine your students' position on the skills-development continuum and then decide what level or degree of proficiency you wish them to achieve. Take into account the time for skills development that the curriculum affords and the benefit to learners of acquiring the skill. If you decide that your students need only to become familiar with a skill, you might plan to teach it during part of a lesson, but if they will be expected to perform the skill automatically, they may need to practice it over a period of several weeks or longer.

FIGURE 9.5

Continuum of Skill Development

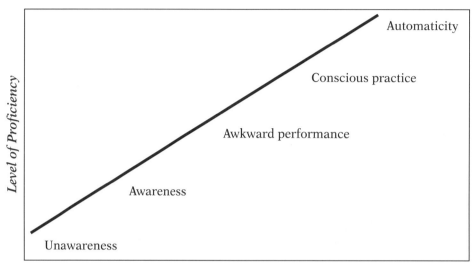

Skill Practice

- *Unawareness*. A learner may begin in a state of unawareness of the particulars involved in the performance of a new skill, and, perhaps, of where, when, and how the skill is to be used.
- *Awareness*. The learner must be made aware of the skill, discover its purpose, and understand why he or she should learn it.
- *Awkwardness*. The learner is aware of the skill and its components, and is able to practice it awkwardly. First efforts are often inefficient and incorrect.
- *Conscious practice*. Conscious **practice** of a skill develops as a result of numerous tries, **guidance**, and feedback. The learner gradually becomes proficient but must think consciously about what he or she is doing. Because the learner lacks complete spontaneity, the performance is still somewhat mechanical.
- *Automaticity*. The final stage of skill learning is automaticity, the point at which the skill is fully integrated into the learner's repertoire. Eventually, as a result of practice, the learner makes the skill habitual and uses it appropriately, correctly, spontaneously, comfortably, and creatively.
- ◆ **Select mode and sequence of presentation.** Depending on the skill to be taught, you may find it more efficient to teach it as a whole or to break it up into its component subskills and teach each one separately. In making your decision, you should consider the age and experience of the learners, their learning-style

preferences (see Chapter 4), and the complexity and importance of the skill. Whatever approach you decide to take, you should plan to teach the subskills in their logical order of use.

◆ ***Prepare an instruction and practice schedule***.   If your students are to learn and retain a skill, and to transfer it to new contexts, you must set a suitable schedule for instruction and practice. The usual approach to teaching a new skill is to review applicable knowledge, establish set (see Chapter 3), demonstrate and explain, and check for comprehension; provide guided practice and check proficiency; provide independent practice and check proficiency; test.

Your target in providing some practice experiences may be to help students **overlearn** in order to retain a skill that they can use later on in different contexts. Students should usually overlearn basic skills to the level of automaticity. To achieve this, you must plan intermittent practice sessions that include drills, reviews, and performance tests. As you plan, you will have to make a number of decisions:

 ◆ How many practice sessions are necessary?
 ◆ How long should each one be?
 ◆ Should practice sessions be massed or distributed?

It is very difficult to generalize about these matters. Decisions depend on the nature of the skill to be learned, and the developmental levels and learning strengths of your students. In general, it is better to distribute practice, unless breaking it up interferes with the flow or level of learning. In the latter case, **massed practice**—practice concentrated in one or a few longer sessions—is preferable. Motor skills are often best learned in **distributed practice** sessions with rest intervals in between, unless time is limited and your students are able to perform efficiently without rest intervals.

◆ ***Organize skills learning.***   The way you organize skills-learning experiences will help or hinder your students' acquisition and retention of skills. You can help learners to discover the uses of organization by presenting elements of skills in logical ways so that each part is clearly seen to fit the whole.

PRACTICE *and Projects*

1. Using Figure 9.5 as an example, construct a diagram of a skill-development continuum for a skill relating to a subject that you plan to teach. Add details to specify the steps suggested in the sample figure.

2. Form subject-specialization groups of six. Select a skill relating to your subject, and prepare a lesson plan to teach that skill. Use Data Collection Form 9.1 (Appendix A) to record your lesson plan.

Procedures for Skills Teaching

Essential procedures involved in the direct teaching of skills are orientation (establishing set), presentation, "structured" or guided practice, and independent practice (Klausmeier, 1985; Rosenshine, 1987; Woolfolk, 1987, 1990). Figure 9.6 illustrates the method for skills teaching described below.

◆ *Provide a positive classroom climate.* Since learning skills involves direct risk taking, it is important for you to make sure that your classroom climate during these lessons encourages risk taking and stresses learning from "deferred successes." Errors should never be considered failures, but opportunities for advancing learning.

FIGURE 9.6

Procedures for Skills Teaching

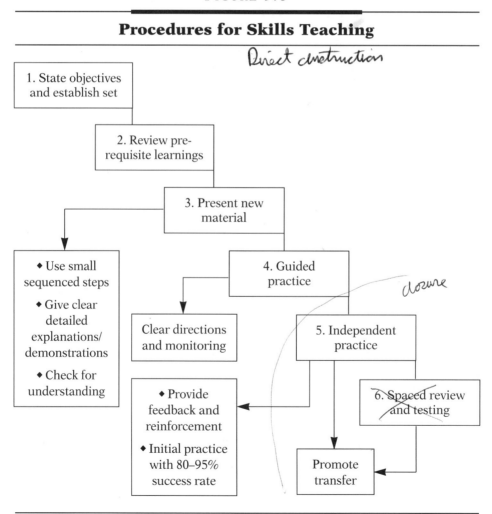

Direct instruction

1. State objectives and establish set

2. Review prerequisite learnings

3. Present new material

◆ Use small sequenced steps
◆ Give clear detailed explanations/ demonstrations
◆ Check for understanding

4. Guided practice

Clear directions and monitoring

5. Independent practice

closure

◆ Provide feedback and reinforcement
◆ Initial practice with 80–95% success rate

6. Spaced review and testing

Promote transfer

- *State objectives and provide set.* You should begin a skills lesson by explaining the lesson objectives and establishing a learning set. For a skill lesson, set may often include providing an overview of what your students will accomplish. It is essential at this stage to ensure that your students understand clearly why it is important to each of them to meet the skill objective.

- *Review and check the previous day's work.* Plan a daily review of material that your students will need to retain for subsequent learning. The processes of daily review and checking assignments emphasize the connections between lessons; they also ensure that students will retain prerequisite knowledge and skills applicable to new lessons, and see new material as extensions of content they have already mastered.

- *Present new material in small steps.* Spend enough time presenting new material and providing guided practice to ensure that your students will grasp the main points. To promote understanding, make the purposes of the skills procedures clear, providing step-by-step directions and opportunities to practice them. (Giving directions is discussed in detail in the last section of this chapter.) Start with a generous number of clear simple examples and demonstrations, and move gradually to more complex ones. Show your students that you believe it is important for all of them to understand the information and directions you are providing.

- *Use appropriate teaching strategies.* Appropriate teaching strategies include individualizing teaching and learning procedures, providing guidance and positive reinforcement, encouraging active learner participation, promoting learner success, giving feedback, and facilitating skills transfer.

  Skillful, carefully planned modeling and demonstration are important, since these practices encourage imitation. When you model and demonstrate a skill, make sure that your performance is accurate, and explain exactly what you are doing and why. (Demonstrating skills is discussed in detail in the following section.) Ensure that all your students can see your actions and hear your explanations. Discussing the skills and their uses helps learners' later performance.

- *Provide active practice.* Providing sufficient overt (observable) active practice when students are learning a new skill promotes successful learning. Indeed, some skills can be learned only through participation and practice, and while it is possible for students to participate covertly (or unobservably) in skill learning (e.g., by silently thinking through the steps of solving an algebra problem as you demonstrate), they are far more likely to lose their train of thought or become bored and unobservant when their participation is not active.

  Start by having your students practice a skill with you, step by step, as you demonstrate. In the early stages of skill learning, practice should focus on correct techniques rather than on obtaining a correct result. Observe learners carefully to ensure that they are performing skills correctly, since it is important for them not to practice incorrect procedures that they might later have to "unlearn."

Decide on the nature and quantity of further skill practice, which should lead as soon as possible to actual use; it should also emphasize process and provide a high rate of success. Whereas simple or isolated behaviors may require little practice, practice becomes more important as learning becomes more complex: prolonged practice is needed, for instance, to polish skills such as touch keyboarding, reading, writing, and driving.

◆ *Consider individual needs.* Successful skill teaching recognizes individual differences. Each learner has different areas of strength and weakness, and so some students will need more skills practice than others, and the focus of practice may vary for each person. Take account of this, and initially, at any rate, do not impose the same expectations of speed, dexterity, and accuracy on your whole class; to try to do so would only lead to confusion and frustration!

Cooperative group strategies or peer teaching may be useful for **individualizing** objectives, instruction, and the practice of many cognitive and affective skills. You can also help students to individualize their practice as you circulate during seatwork sessions.

◆ *Check for understanding.* To learn a skill, students must do more than memorize steps or operations. They must understand how and why the steps connect. Check after each step to make sure your students have understood its function and mastered it before you go on to the next step. Avoid asking one student to perform the last step of a procedure and then assuming that everyone else can do so too. Instead, evaluate and record *each* student's progress. Remember that poor skill development may result from a failure to assess the progress of individuals.

◆ *Provide guidance.* The kind and amount of guidance you give should depend, in part, on the individual student and his or her developmental level and previous experience. Match your guidance to cues gleaned from the learners. Make it positive, concise, and focused on the skill you are teaching. Wise guidance in the initial stages of skill learning can greatly increase your students' success rate. As your students' skills levels rise, you should help them learn to function independently by gradually withdrawing your guidance.

◆ *Provide positive reinforcement.* Approving or rewarding correct or desirable behavior gives students the positive reinforcement they need. Reinforcement is particularly effective in promoting skills learning when it is immediate, earned, details the aspects of performance and explains their success. Vague approval is not helpful, nor is merely telling a learner what not to do, especially if it makes him or her feel negative about practicing a skill.

Ideally, every correct performance of a skill or subskill should be reinforced positively and immediately until it becomes habitual. Since this ideal is obviously impractical in teaching a class, you should give reinforcement intermittently, not regularly. Studies indicate that, whereas regular reinforcement speeds learning, intermittent reinforcement improves retention (Woolfolk, 1990). Reinforcement can actually have a ripple effect, encouraging both the learner who receives it and the other students who observe it. Nevertheless, it is wise to remember that, to be effective, reinforcement must be individualized.

* ***Organize success experiences.*** To maintain task involvement, give clear and concise explanations and directions, and check to ensure that all your students understand them. When tasks involve understanding content, allow time for students to discuss and debrief, showing that they have accomplished transfer by linking the new to familiar content. Since learners need tasks at which they can succeed after reasonable effort in order to maintain their self-esteem and interest (see Chapter 4), it makes sense to organize success experiences. Students should achieve a success rate between 80 percent and 95 percent in initial practice sessions; it is, after all, pointless to allow them to practice incorrect procedures (Woolfolk, 1990).

* ***Monitor seatwork.*** When you have given your students clear directions for performing a skill and have checked to ensure that they all understand how to perform it, they are ready to begin monitored individual practice. Monitoring practice will give you opportunities to assess your own and your students' success in dealing with the lesson, and to ensure that your assignments are not too difficult or complex.

    Students should be well prepared and able to perform a skill successfully before you expect them to practice it independently. When you are confident that they can practice capably on their own, you might assign further practice to be done as homework for the following day. Always check assigned work, ensuring that your students finish tasks that involve product.

* ***Provide feedback.*** Circulate to give feedback on each student's seatwork or homework practice. Effective feedback focuses on process and tells learners early in a learning experience what they are doing correctly, and what needs modification. Provide specific and descriptive feedback, telling students precisely what they have done well, and why. Give correction when needed, and suggest tips for improvement in a supportive way.

    A learner who receives such descriptive, specific, and prompt feedback will succeed in mastering a skill much more rapidly than one left in doubt about his or her performance. **Knowledge of results** is essential for speedy and efficient learning.

* ***Promote transfer.*** Transfer is a central tool for problem solving and other higher-order mental processes, for innovation, and for artistic achievement.

Encourage your students to transfer skills learned in one context to other situations in school and in life, for the more examples of transfer learners recognize, the more likely they are to make transfers for themselves.

Since transfer seldom occurs spontaneously, you must teach for it. Because highly overlearned skills are transferred more readily than those that are half learned, you should deliberately point out how transfers can be made and provide opportunities for students to make them. There are several ways to facilitate transfer. A perceptive teacher is aware of the power and transferability of *associations*, and will

- point out similarities and differences between familiar and new information and skills;
- use associations that students have made between things that are not directly related (e.g., a science teacher might use students' knowledge of a television series on space adventure to stimulate learning in a lesson on astronomy);
- promote overlearning of transferable skills, knowing that the greater the degree of original learning, the greater the likelihood of transfer;
- stress the essential unvarying elements of concepts (i.e., the main concepts and processes and their organization), and help learners to realize how they apply to new contexts (Hunter, 1971).

◆ *Review and test.* If students are to consolidate and retain a skill, they must learn it very well initially and then review it intermittently. Testing should disclose current performance capability, levels of understanding, and ability to transfer (see Chapter 17). Test often to identify skills that need to be retaught or practiced further.

PRACTICE *and Projects*

1. Watch your instructor model a short skill lesson to illustrate its steps. Analyze the components of the lesson.

2. Use Data Collection Form 9.2 (Appendix A) to help you analyze Case Study 9.1. Your instructor may pose specific questions for your response.

Demonstrating Skills

Direct skills teaching makes extensive use of demonstration, since we learn many of the skills we acquire through watching others. A **demonstration**, which often involves performance of actions, skills, or processes, can provide a critical observed-

CASE STUDY 9.1

TEACHING DICTIONARY SKILLS

Mr. Aftahi plans to teach his Grade 2 class how to put words into alphabetical order and organize information alphabetically. Though the children read at various levels, and several have been using primary dictionaries and other reference books, dictionary skills have not yet been formally taught.

Mr. Aftahi has collected several dictionaries, telephone directories, encyclopedias, reference books, and enlarged copies of index pages. When the children enter the classroom after recess, Mr. Aftahi has the books displayed so that everyone can see them. The children look with interest at these materials, and Jaya asks, "What are we going to do with all those books and papers, Mr. Aftahi?"

Mr. Aftahi looks around to make sure that he has everyone's attention. "Let's see if we can answer Jaya's question," he says. "Tell me what you see on these tables." The children respond with, "Books," "Dictionaries," "Encyclopedias," "Papers," and "Telephone books."

"What is in these books?" asks Mr. Aftahi. The students respond, "Names," "Words," "Sentences," "Stories," "You can find out stuff you want to know," "I saw maps in one of those books," and "My mom looks up telephone numbers in the telephone book."

"So there are words, names, sentences, stories, maps, and telephone numbers in these books? Can you think why people would use these kinds of books?"

After several suggestions, the children agree that people would use these books to find things out. "If I wanted to find a telephone number in this book, what would I do?" Mr. Aftahi gestures toward the telephone directory.

"You would look it up," says Danny.

"OK, what does that mean?" asks Mr. Aftahi.

Danny explains, "Find the name of the person you want to phone, and the right number is beside his name."

"All right, let's look up Mr. Jessop's number. You say I look for his name, and his number will be right there?" Danny nods vigorously, and Mr. Aftahi begins at the first page and reads the first few names. "Danny, can you help me here?" Danny studies the page, looks at the name on the board and back at the page. "I don't see it yet," he remarks.

"Do you notice anything about the names here?" asks Mr. Aftahi. Students begin to wave their hands. "These names all start with A," Danny says.

(continued)

(continued)

"Is the whole book like that?" asks Mr. Aftahi. Danny looks at various pages. "No," he announces. "There are lots of other letters at the start on other pages."

"What else has A at the start?" "My name," says Andrea. "Yes, it does, but I'm thinking of something bigger than a name," responds Mr. Aftahi "The ABCs," answers Tuan.

"Right. The ABCs, or the alphabet, starts with A. I wonder if the rest of the book is anything like the alphabet. Tuan, come and work with Danny to see if the telephone book is like the ABCs." Tuan and Danny pore over the book, turning pages, and saying the names of the letters as they come to them. "Yes," they report. "First come the 'A' names, then the 'B' names, and the 'C' names, and so on. The 'Z' names are at the end."

"So where will we look for Mr. Jessop's name?" asks Mr. Aftahi. "In the 'J' names," answer several children. Danny and Tuan turn to the 'J' section and find Mr. Jessop's name and number.

"See how easy that was once we knew how the names were organized? What is it that tells us what comes first or last, or helps us to know where to look for names?"

"We can look at the alphabet on the wall, or we can just say the ABCs," says Yvette.

"Right! The alphabet can be our guide." Mr. Aftahi then assigns three or four children to each resource to see if the information is organized in the same way. The students are excited to discover the same pattern in all the resources they examine. Some say, "I knew it all the time!"

"Putting things like words or names in ABC order, or alphabetical order, is an important thing to be able to do. It's easy to understand, and it helps many people find information more quickly. Today we'll practice arranging some word cards in alphabetical order. What shall we use as our guide?"

"The alphabet," the children respond.

"That's right. Now look at these three words and decide which would come first, second and third if we put them in alphabetical order." He shows the words *cat*, *apple*, and *ball*, and the children easily put them in order. "How did you do it? What did you do first?" he asks.

Tara explains, "I just thought of A, B, C and matched up the words." Matt says that he looked at the letters on the wall to help him put the words in order.

(continued)

> *(continued)*
> "Both ways are good," says Mr. Aftahi. "Let's try these." He shows word cards saying "Candice," "Ewen," and "Dominique."
>
> The students arrange these words and two other examples that Mr. Aftahi presents. Finally, he gives each child a set of three words and asks the children to arrange the words in alphabetical order. "When you have finished, look around for someone else who is finished, and check each other's. Look at the alphabet on the wall if you're not sure. Then trade your cards with someone else whose cards have been checked, and do the same thing again. Try to put three sets of cards in order, and check three other sets of cards. Don't do the same set twice."
>
> The children work busily at their desks, on the floor, and at a large table as Mr. Aftahi walks about the room, checking their progress.

action experience that transcends verbal explanation, linking knowledge about a skill with ability to perform it.

EFFECTIVE DEMONSTRATIONS

Every subject taught sometimes requires effective demonstrations. To give your students a clear idea of the performance you expect of them, you will often need to model or demonstrate a skill as you explain it. Figure 9.7 illustrates the procedural steps for making effective demonstrations.

Steps in Demonstrating a Skill

◆ *Analyze.* Before you begin a demonstration, make a procedural, hierarchical, or combination skill analysis. Ask yourself, "What are the key steps to be followed? What words should I use in my explanation? What steps will students find most difficult?"

◆ *Practice.* Rehearse your demonstration to ensure that it is effective.

◆ *Set up.* Set up demonstration materials before your students arrive to avoid wasting class time. Plan for quick distribution of materials that students will need, or have these materials in place at classroom work stations.

Ensure that all your students can see and hear you clearly. Remember that when you face your students, they see your right and left in reverse. If possible, therefore, conduct your demonstration so that your students will not have to make a right/left transfer.

FIGURE 9.7

Steps in Demonstrating

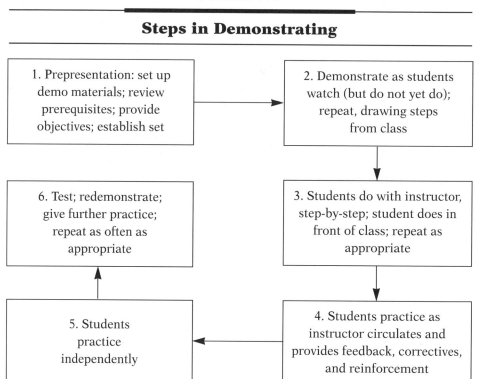

- ◆ *Establish set.* State the objectives of your demonstration, and establish set. If necessary, review prerequisite knowledge or skills. Provide an overview that lets students know why it is important for them to learn the skill you plan to demonstrate and motivates them to do so. If appropriate, highlight points that students should watch for.
- ◆ *Secure and maintain attention.* Secure undivided attention before you begin a demonstration. To maintain students' attention, keep your demonstration moving, while watching for nonverbal clues of inattention or lack of understanding, and checking for comprehension as necessary.
- ◆ *Demonstrate.* Be sure to make your actions and the sequence of skills and subskills very plain. Do not move too quickly. It is sometimes helpful to perform an act at normal speed and then repeat it in "slow motion." If a procedure is complex, break it into steps that you can demonstrate separately.
- ◆ *Describe and explain.* As you perform your demonstration, describe each step clearly and concisely. Stress key aspects, making your explanations as

interesting, complete, and relevant as you can, for students need to see how skills relate to what they have already studied and what they will study later. Do not include too many details in a single explanation or give more directions than a beginner can possibly assimilate at one time.

◆ *Record key aspects.*   You may find it useful to record important steps or points for review on the chalkboard, or on a transparency or handout.

◆ *Redemonstrate.*   To ensure that your students understand, repeat the steps as necessary, checking to see that students know "how" and "why" to perform the process, and whether they are ready to advance to practice.

◆ *Provide practice.*   Students should begin their practice of a new skill or subskill by performing it with you, step-by-step, as often as necessary. When you are satisfied with their performance, you should have them go on to carefully monitored, individual, guided practice that has a success rate of 80 percent to 95 percent. Assign independent practice only after you are sure that your students can perform the skill well enough to do it correctly and without frustration. At each stage of practice, it is important for you to provide prompt, descriptive feedback, correcting and reinforcing as necessary.

PRACTICE *and Projects*

1. Working in a small group, analyze Case Study 9.2, and prepare a list of recommendations for M. L'Heureux.

2. a. Working with a subject-interest group, brainstorm examples of demonstrations that the subject might require.
   b. Classify these examples as skills, processes, procedures, or illustrations.
   c. Help your group to prepare a demonstration and present it to the class. Class members will provide feedback using Data Collection Form 9.3 (Appendix A).
   d. Debrief.

Giving Directions

Direction giving is a critical skill that you will use many times each day to arrange distribution of materials and supplies, completion of assignments or activities, relocation of individuals or groups, and transition from one activity to another. It is also a skill essential to implementing rules and procedures that create and maintain a classroom climate that supports learning.

M. L'Heureux has talked with his Grade 6 class about making macramé plant holders as Christmas gifts. Though none of the students know any knot-tying techniques, M. L'Heureux, who was in charge of a crafts program at a children's camp one summer, feels sure that he can quickly teach students to tie a half-hitch. He plans to demonstrate tying this knot first and then teach some others.

After recess, M. L'Heureux begins to explain how to tie a half-hitch. Though several students are not attending, he describes the procedure in detail. He soon realizes, however, that some students are having trouble following his directions. He looks in his desk drawer for cord and finds a length of string. He explains the procedure again from the front of the room, inadvertently omitting a step in his explanation. When he realizes his omission, he points out the change in procedure. Some students look anxious; others seem confused.

The string that M. L'Heureux is using is rather fine, and the students are soon fidgeting and muttering that they cannot see. M. L'Heureux tells them to pay closer attention, remarking that if they had been watching in the first place, they would now know how to tie the knot. "I'll show you once more," he says, "and then you'll have to tie it yourselves."

M. L'Heureux goes through the procedure again and then leaves the classroom to fetch the macramé cord stored in the art supply room. When he returns with two colors of cord, the students are arguing noisily about the correct procedure. He calls for attention and asks each student to choose a color and cut off an arm's length of cord. The students cannot follow these directions because no one can find a pair of scissors. M. L'Heureux remembers that since the last budget cuts, scissors are kept in the principal's office; he sends a student to get a set.

The frustrated students are quickly losing interest in the project, and begin to make negative comments about it. When the scissors arrive, only a few children seem interested. Some others have to be encouraged and a few ordered to begin the task. In the general confusion, many students call out questions, and the noise level in the classroom rises dramatically.

M. L'Heureux begins to circulate, showing one student at a time how to tie a half-hitch. Most of the students have given up working on their own and sit waiting for help. There is a hum of complaints and demands for help or a change of activity. One boy, who has been doggedly working by himself, suddenly throws down his materials and sits glowering. A girl behind him

(continued)

> *(continued)*
> laughs and points at him, and he leaps up , overturning his desk, and rushes from the room. M. L'Heureux looking up, asks the class, "What's up with Mark? Doesn't he like doing macramé?

VERBAL DIRECTIONS

Verbal directions relating to instruction may have different purposes: to alert students that there will soon be a change of activity, to secure full attention, to clarify information, or to anticipate and prevent potential problems. To avoid the uproar and anger that misguided directions can cause, try to make your directions explicit, concise, clear, and positive in tone, stressing what students should do rather than what they should not do. When planning directions, test their tone by saying them aloud to yourself. Use directions for the following purposes:

♦ *Alert students.* A sudden request for attention may interrupt students' activities. To respect your students' concentration on a task, you can notify them that they should finish their task or at least prepare for an interruption. For example, you might say, "In five minutes, I shall give you directions for completing your graphs."

♦ *Secure attention.* Begin to give verbal directions only when you have secured the attention of *all* students to whom you wish to speak. Repeating information because some students were inattentive wastes time and can annoy attentive students. Most students will respond cheerfully to a designated signal that clearly requests their immediate attention. Signals useful for alerting students include saying clearly, "May I have everyone's attention, please?" clapping hands, or ringing a bell. Once you have sent a clear signal, you might check for attention by looking around the room to make eye contact with any nonattending individual.

♦ *Make your meaning clear.* Learning to give clear verbal directions requires careful planning and practice, but it is a skill that you can and should acquire, for student achievement and satisfaction are closely related to clear instruction. Students judge teachers largely by the clarity of their instruction (Cruickshank, 1985).

When you are giving directions for an assignment, be sure to state clearly all its features and requirements, including standards for form, neatness, accuracy, and legibility. Specify the due dates for submissions and the penalties for late submission or noncompletion.

♦ *Anticipate.* Effective direction giving anticipates potential difficulties. When planning directions, identify the language or procedures that your students may find difficult. Simplify the language, choosing synonyms or giving examples, and explain the procedures sequentially. Plan ahead to eliminate frustration:

your students should not have to ask, "Where do I put this assignment now?" or "What do I do now that I've finished?"

◆ *Check up.* Never take for granted that your students have understood your directions. Be alert for such signs of uncertainty as a barrage of questions, nudges, talking, or misbehavior. To check for understanding, you might ask one or more students to review the directions for the class. Avoid such questions as, "Does everybody understand … Has anyone a question?" Instead, address questions to individuals, taking care not to embarrass special-case students who may need individual help (see Chapter 6).

When your students begin to work, circulate about the room to check that they are "getting off on the right foot." After they have been working for a time, circulate again to see that they are continuing to follow directions and are progressing satisfactorily.

PRACTICE *and Projects*

1. a. Sit back-to-back with a partner while one of you directs the other in tying a shoe. The other must follow the directions precisely. Meanwhile another pair of partners will observe you and your partner, and then report what they saw and describe their perceptions of your feelings and your partner's during the activity.

    b. Debrief as a class.

2. a. You are about to begin a teaching unit on gymnastics with a Grade 8/9 class of 24 students. You wish to train your students to assist you, as a matter of routine, to place the mats and then line up quickly for instruction. Working with a small group, consider the steps needed, and plan in detail the initial directions you will give. Choose a spokesperson to report your group's plans to the class and ask for comments.

    b. Rejoin your group, and revise your plans in light of what you have heard. Debrief as a class.

3. a. Join a subject-interest group. Select a lesson topic in your field of interest, and choose an activity to follow the lesson. Plan the directions that you will give as you introduce the activity.

    b. Choose a group member to give directions to a second group, for no more than five minutes, on the activity selected. The members of the second group should use Data Collection Form 9.4 (Appendix A) to collect data on the exercise. Debrief jointly.

4. Use Data Collection Form 9.4 to help you analyze Case Study 9.3. Your instructor may pose specific questions for your response.

CASE STUDY 9.3

GIVING DIRECTIONS

Ms. Hersch wants to ensure, at the very start of term, that her students will make productive use of each of her Grade 10 Keyboarding classes. She plans to have students begin their work the moment they enter the room rather than waiting for her to provide directions or begin a presentation.

Ms. Hersch walks into the classroom and begins, "When you enter this room, place your books neatly under your chair. Uncover your typewriter; fold the cover neatly, and place it on top of your books. Look at the upper left-hand corner of the front chalkboard. Your warm-up and review assignments will be written there. Open your text to the page number shown, and begin your work. When I ring the timer bell, stop typing immediately. Don't finish the word or sentence. You won't need to correct or hand in what you have been working on. Now take out a sheet of paper." Ms. Hersch then begins to demonstrate how to insert paper into a typewriter.

The next day, the class trickles into the room. About half the students follow the directions given the previous day. Of the rest, five students chat together; the others sit silently, waiting for instructions. Ms. Hersch moves toward the five students who are chatting and says, "Get to your seats and do as I told you yesterday." The students move uncertainly to their desks. Ms. Hersch then turns to the students who are waiting quietly, and says, "Get to work! You can't learn if you aren't practicing!"

Gillian, one of the five, shyly asks, "What are we supposed to be doing?"

SUMMARY

- Skills are coherent units of specific procedural knowledge acquired by practice; skills translate declarative knowledge into expert action when learners clearly understand that action and the principles that underlie it.
- To put concepts to use requires the possession and practice of many skills.
- Educators often subdivide skills into three categories: affective, cognitive, and psychomotor.
- "Expert" performance of skills is usually marked by appropriate selection, economy of effort, and automaticity of performance.
- To achieve competence in the performance of a variety of basic skills and to appreciate their value in life situations, learn to make task analyses of skills by identifying their component tasks to discover the chain of subskills required.

- A task analysis may be procedural (i.e., recording the nature and sequence of each step) or hierarchical (i.e., discovering the kinds and sequence of "enabling" skills that students must acquire to perform a higher-level skill objective) or a combination of the two.
- Skills may be taught through a "whole" approach (i.e., in their entirety) or a "part" approach (i.e., as a series of subskills).
- Planning for skills teaching requires that you identify the skill, determine learner readiness, make a task analysis, determine desired level of student proficiency, select your teaching approach and your mode and sequence of delivery, and prepare an instruction and practice schedule.
- Following the teaching principles that you have already learned, you will establish set, deliver your lesson, provide guided and independent practice, check for understanding and performance, encourage transfer, and arrange review.
- To demonstrate a skill effectively, you will analyze and practice it, set up any apparatus needed, secure attention, perform the skill, describe and explain it, point out its key aspects, redemonstrate, and provide practice.

KEY WORDS

declarative knowledge
demonstration
enabling skills
  (subskills)
"expert" performance
  selection
  economy
  automaticity
intermittent
  reinforcement

learner readiness
level of proficiency
overlearning
planning
practice
  active
  guided
  monitored
  independent
procedural knowledge

regular reinforcement
skill-development
  continuum
skills
  cognitive
  affective
  psychomotor
task analysis
  procedural
  hierarchical

RECOMMENDED READING

Dick, W. & Carey, L. (1978). *The systemic design of instruction*. Glenview, IL: Scott Foresman.

Kemp, J. (1985). *The instructional design process*. New York: Harper & Row.

Marzano, R. (1992). *A different kind of classroom: Teaching with dimensions for learning*. Alexandria, VA: Association for Supervision and Curriculum Development.

West, C., Farmer, J., & Wolff, P. (1991). *Instructional design: Implications from cognitive science*. Englewood Cliffs, NJ: Prentice-Hall.

CHAPTER 10

TEACHING
CRITICAL THINKING

■ ■ ■ ■ ■

Model students ... have well-structured knowledge of content and a repertoire of cognitive and metacognitive strategies ... access information and execute strategies flexibly; strive to conceptualize [clearly] what they learn ... enjoy being productive, solving problems and making decisions; and ... can evaluate information critically and creatively.

(Marzano et al., 1988, p. 134)

■ ■ ■ ■ ■

OVERVIEW

Humans, by their very nature, are thinkers, and the field of study about thinking is enormous. A number of researchers have developed classification systems to help educators comprehend and promote discussion of the teaching of thinking skills.

Teaching for thinking—that is, for promoting critical thinking skills and creativity—requires significant school time to ensure integration of thinking skills across the K–12 curriculum. Thinking skills such as critical thinking, creative thinking, decision making, and problem solving, and their transfer to new contexts require direct classroom instruction and practice. Teachers should plan carefully for the teaching of these skills, use a variety of approaches, and encourage their students to use them. They should also model and teach the important processes of deductive and inductive reasoning, particularly in relation to the identification and analysis of concepts, encouraging transfer of these and other thinking skills into daily life situations.

■ ■ ■ ■ ■

TEACHING FOR THINKING

Teaching for thinking—that is, instructing learners in developing and using **thinking skills** (Resnick, 1987)—is a fundamental component of instruction. A group of researchers who prepared a report for the National Research Council of the United States of America came to the same conclusion, adding that, "if we can find effective ways to teach [thinking skills], we can imagine an important increase in educational efficiency" (p. 16). This same point of view was stressed by Jones, Palincsar, Ogle, and Carr (1987), who advised teachers to "improve educational opportunities for all [your] students" (p. 4) by helping them to acquire integrated thinking skills. As a teacher, you will wish to help your students learn to think better, regardless of their stage of development. "It is a new challenge to develop educational programs that assume all individuals, not just an élite, can become better thinkers" (Resnick, as cited in Nickerson, 1989, p. 7).

These researchers believe that **intelligence** can be modified through appropriate instruction and an individual's own efforts to learn and apply productive thinking skills. Such skills include the strategies that students need to acquire knowledge: declarative (informational), procedural (pertaining to the performance of skills or processes), and conditional (determining when and where to apply the other two types). Although such skills can never be taught or learned apart from content, once learned, they can be applied to all school subjects and used in daily life, as well (De Bono, 1983).

Approaches to Teaching for Thinking

As a teacher who plans to help your students acquire these important skills, you must know what processes they will need in order to think and to link previous experience to new information. A number of researchers have developed approaches to teaching for thinking.

BLOOM'S TAXONOMY

In 1956, Benjamin Bloom et. al, at the University of Chicago, introduced a **taxonomy**, or classification system, which many educators today still consider a valuable tool for guiding instruction and evaluating learning.

The Domains of Learning
Bloom's system divided learning and its content into three major domains, or fields:

- the **cognitive domain** (i.e., the informational/intellectual field);
- the **psychomotor domain** (i.e., the field of conscious performance of physical actions);   I M P A N
- the **affective domain** (i.e., the field of emotions, values, and attitudes).
   R R V O C

Cognitive Learning Skills
Bloom went on to subdivide cognitive skills (i.e., thinking/learning) into six categories:

- *knowing*, or possessing, information or content (i.e., recalling it just as presented);
- *comprehending*, or understanding, information or content (i.e., grasping its basic meaning and being able to paraphrase it);
- *applying*, or transferring information or content to use in a new situation;

◆ *analyzing*, or subdividing, content by identifying and relating its components;

◆ *synthesizing*, or organizing, content components in ways new to the organizer (e.g., creating, inventing, composing, or designing);

◆ *evaluating*, or applying criteria, a rationale, or standards to content or information, to determine its value as demonstrated by skills performance.

Psychomotor Learning Skills

Psychomotor skills relate to motion or action that proceeds directly from mental activity. Psychomotor skills develop on a continuum, governing

◆ *basic voluntary movements* resulting from combining reflex movements, such grasping, crawling, pulling, or pushing;

◆ *perceptual responses*, or reactions to stimuli received through the senses, such as balancing, dodging or catching a ball, or following spoken instructions;

◆ *complex voluntary movements* that depend on muscular endurance, strength, agility, and precision (e.g., walking, running, swimming, lifting, writing, or typing);

◆ *skilled movements* that require efficiency (e.g., participating in sports, dancing, or playing a musical instrument);

◆ *body language*, or sending messages by means of facial or body movements that express thoughts or emotions.

Affective Skills

Affective skills relate to the development and/or adjustment of feelings, emotions, values, and attitudes. An individual adds or changes components of the affective domain through a five-step sequential process by

◆ *receiving*, or becoming aware that a message is being sent and choosing to accept its transmission;

◆ *responding*, or signaling that the message has been received;

◆ *valuing*, or accepting, ascribing worth to, or committing to (i.e., personalizing or internalizing) the message;

◆ *organizing*, or classifying (ordering), understanding, and applying the content of the message;

◆ *internalizing* (i.e., self-monitoring in order to behave in ways consistent with the message received and accepted).

WASSERMAN'S THINKING OPERATIONS

In 1967, Raths, Wasserman, Jonas and Rothstein framed a system of thinking skills applicable to any school subject at any level of learning. These educators did not distinguish between skills and processes at that time, but a decade later, Wasserman reported on some of the skills they had classified.

Wasserman (1978) applied the earlier research of Raths and his colleagues to teaching basic thinking operations by analyzing a number of learning processes and skills. He came to the following conclusions:

- *Observing* involves looking and sometimes listening, touching or smelling, as well. Accurate observers check the evidence of all their senses. To encourage your students to observe perceptively, carefully, and accurately, you should show them that errors stemming from inaccurate observation can lead to misinterpretations and false inferences. In order to check the validity of your students' observations, you will need to teach them reporting skills. Observation should produce greater understanding and more accurate data on which to base conclusions.

- *Collecting and organizing data* are processes that require several skills: identifying appropriate sources; locating and assembling; examining and selecting; and organizing systematically, logically, and coherently. Students may organize data in the form of essays, reports, research proposals, menus, almanacs, bibliographies, charts, maps, solutions to mathematical problems, and so on.

- *Comparing* involves looking for similarities and differences between two or more (sets of) items that may be closely related (e.g., violins and violas), or more distantly or subtly related (e.g., trains and steamships). Comparing requires the following steps:
  - observing details;
  - seeking and sorting similarities;
  - seeking and sorting differences;
  - summarizing (listing) information.

By making comparisons, students gain awareness and insights. After much experience of this process, students learn to observe and compare before drawing conclusions.

- *Classifying* involves examining an assortment of items, sorting them systematically, either mentally or in writing, into related groups, and giving each group a name. This process, which helps bring order into life, requires the following three steps:
  - examining data;
  - creating categories;
  - classifying items by category.

Encouraging students to create their own categories allows them to maximize the learning potential of this operation.

Classifying, like comparing, involves the discovery of similarities and differences. Students should discover that although they may classify items in a number of different ways, each category must be internally consistent. Normally, they should classify items on the basis of one factor—e.g., color, use, cost—at a time.

◆ *Imagining* requires letting the mind exercise its powers freely and creatively, unrestricted by time, place, or known "facts." Imagining should release the thinker from rules, regulations, and restrictive data, and promote divergent thinking. This rich inner resource leads to creativity and invention, and brings humor, joy, spontaneity, and beauty into life. It can provide a sense of accomplishment and enlarge self-concept.

◆ *Hypothesizing* encourages students to frame a variety of possible explanations to resolve a question, problem, or situation. After identifying various possibilities, students determine which are most credible. High school students may be asked to find ways of testing their hypotheses, which makes the process more complex. Steps might be as follows:
  ◆ present the problem;
  ◆ ask students to hypothesize solutions;
  ◆ have students consider solutions;
  ◆ have students anticipate outcomes;
  ◆ have students select most appropriate hypothetical solution.

Hypothesizing reduces dogmatic assertions and "black or white" judgments that reflect a single perspective on life. It is a creative process that gives students a means of dealing constructively with problems in school and beyond.

◆ *Criticizing* encourages students to offer opinions, make judgments, and evaluate, thereby practicing discrimination. Train your students to specify the criteria (standards) and identify the evidence they use in making judgments.

◆ *Identifying assumptions* requires recognizing an instance of taking something for granted. To draw a conclusion or make a decision on grounds that are possible or probable rather than established is to make an assumption. Learning to discriminate between what is assumed to be true and what is observable fact stands at the heart of logical reasoning. As students become skilled at scrutinizing and identifying assumptions, they become less susceptible to propaganda and seductive advertising; less willing to accept experimental data as proof and conclusions based on probability as "right"; less likely to leap to conclusions based on limited data; and, gradually, less impulsive in their actions.

◆ *Coding* is a sort of "shorthand" system for pointing out thought patterns or expressions in the writings or speech of others. The code X, for example, can be used to identify extreme words and phrases (e.g., always, everybody, the worst, the only). Q might signify qualifying expressions, and V might designate value statements. As students use coding to analyze the words of others, they become more aware of their own statements, learning to "put their minds in gear" before they put their tongues to work.

♦ *Summarizing* requires condensing data to frame a concise but coherent and reasonably comprehensive statement that expresses the core message or main ideas of a work. To prepare such a statement, one must learn to distinguish relevant and consequential content from irrelevant and trivial content.

♦ *Interpreting* is the process of "reading the message" and explaining the meaning that an experience (e.g., story, event, picture, film, poem, graph, chart, joke, body language) has for an individual. This process puts meaning into a body of data and extracts meaning from it. Misinterpreting the message, of course, reduces the meaning; generalizing on the basis of insufficient evidence distorts the interpreter's conclusions. Skillful interpretation, on the other hand, deepens meaning and understanding, as well as the satisfaction derived from the experience.

Wasserman's system provides a good place for student teachers to start to analyze thinking skills. By planning and teaching lessons that include a procedural (thinking skill or process) objective, you can modify your teaching to incorporate the skills discussed above. Students must practice these skills, like any others, in order to use them proficiently.

OTHER VIEWS ON THINKING

Marc Belth (1977), a professor of education at Queen's College, City University of New York, stated:

> The forms or models and metaphors that enter into the character and direction of thinking are the same in every field. And thus, however distinctive each field becomes in its special vocabulary, in methods unique to their material and specific purposes, in special instruments of inquiry, or in specific findings, what is common to them is the singular, generic process of thinking.(pp. 83–84)

Nickerson (1989) holds that "Informal reasoning is reasoning that involves attempting to resolve the truth or falsity of claims ... [which is] the most common type of reasoning that people do in everyday life and in academic life" (p. 5). Though not all educators agree that learners can apply thinking skills to a wide range of learning domains, many hold that they can. Nickerson states, for instance, that "the more prevalent [view] is that, while there are indeed domain-specific aspects of thinking, there are also certain processes, skills, strategies, principles, attitudes, dispositions and beliefs that are applicable to thinking in many domains" (p. 29).

Provost (1991) describes three promising and popular models for teaching thinking: "stand-alone"; "embedding"; and "immersion." Both the embedding model and the immersion model build thinking skills into regular school subjects, though only the former, which is the more commonly used model, teaches thinking skills explicitly—a necessary approach for most students, especially when you decide that your students should practice a specific skill to the point of automaticity (see Chapter 9). Students appear to understand and transfer skills better when they are taught and studied both separately and in context.

■ ■ ■ ■ ■

PLANNING TO TEACH THINKING SKILLS

In preparing to teach a thinking skill, you should deliberately plan ways to go about the process. Figure 10.1 illustrates steps in planning to teach a thinking skill. Although the planning process should be a careful one, it should not be rigid or always linear.

FIGURE 10.1

Steps in Planning to Teach a Thinking Skill

1. Determine skill label and definition	→	2. Determine rules or steps in using the skill

| 8. Identify areas for and methods of nonschool-related transfer | | 3. Determine students' use of skill in current context |

| 7. Identify areas for and methods of school-related transfer | | 4. Decide how you will model, explain, and demonstrate the skill |

| 6. Choose method of performance evaluation | ← | 5. Decide on form of guided and independent practice |

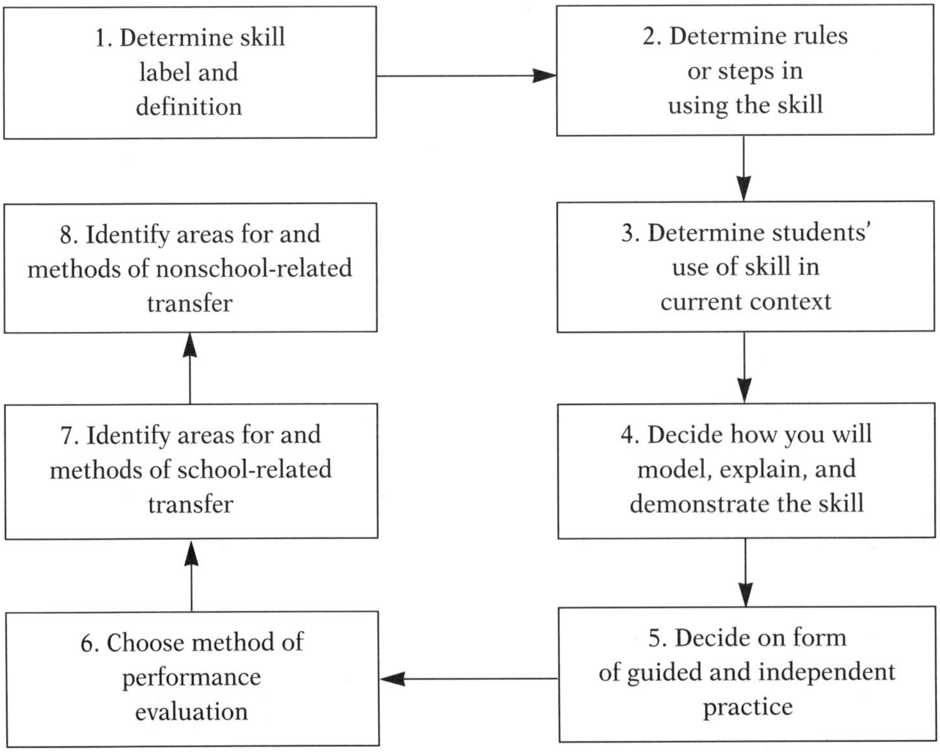

Consider Modes of Thinking

The broad range of thinking modes (patterns) includes some that are particularly useful for promoting learning.

CRITICAL THINKING

Critical thinking begins with an attitude of inquiry: willingness to consider, in a thoughtful and perceptive way, a comprehensive variety of subjects and problems. All teachers should consider, model, emphasize, and encourage this attitude. The process of critical thinking involves fair-minded interpretation, analysis, and evaluation of information, arguments, or experiences; it also involves the use of a set of reflective attitudes, skills, and abilities that guide thoughts, beliefs, and actions. Specific inquiry skills indispensable to effective critical thinking, as suggested, in part, by Orlich et al. (1985), are as follows:

- observing
- classifying
- using numbers
- measuring
- relating space and time
- predicting
- inferring
- defining provisionally
- forming hypotheses
- interpreting data
- controlling variables
- experimenting
- communicating

Critical thinking skills should be taught through curricula that provide a variety of content areas and in ways that are "true to the way problems appear in our everyday lives" (Sternberg, 1985, p. 278). Through practicing these skills, students should learn to distinguish between verifiable facts and value claims; determine the reliability of a claim or source; determine the accuracy of a statement; distinguish between warranted and unwarranted claims; distinguish between relevant and irrelevant information, claims, or arguments; detect biases; identify stated and unstated assumptions; identify ambiguous or equivocal claims or arguments; recognize illogicalities in a line of reasoning; and determine the strength of an argument.

Critical thinking also requires development of a set of attitudes that need to be taught. Intellectual curiosity, for example, stimulates critical thinking by motivating students to seek answers to various kinds of questions and problems through investigating the causes and explanations of events. Lead questions should often begin with the interrogative words *why, who, what, when,* and *where.*

Critical thinkers avoid holding inflexibly to dogmatic attitudes and rigid views. They show respect for others' viewpoints by listening carefully and responding accurately to their words. They are willing to admit that they may be wrong and that others may be right. They are intellectually honest, accepting statements as true when there is sufficient evidence, even though such statements may negate cherished beliefs, and not slanting facts to support a particular position. They are constructively skeptical, reasoning systematically and consistently to form a conclusion only when it is supported by adequate evidence; they are open to new answers and willing to change points of view or methods of inquiry.

Critical thinking requires objective decision makers to rely on empirical (experiential) evidence and objective factors, and not to form decisions solely on the basis of emotive and subjective factors. They must consider all facets of a situation with an open mind, supporting certain points of view but continuing to seek evidence and arguments. They must take into account the possibility that any of a wide variety of beliefs may be true, and consider the evidence without bias or prejudice, while avoiding irrelevancies that would obscure issues. They must avoid unnecessarily lengthy arguments, on the one hand, and snap judgments, on the other, persisting in seeking ways of resolving disputes, but reaching a conclusion as soon as evidence warrants.

Students are unlikely to transfer critical thinking skills to everyday life or even to other subjects unless you deliberately point out transfer possibilities and encourage them to seek transfer of past critical thinking procedures to new situations. Students need to practice this skill, as well as to learn to discover problems for themselves.

DIALECTICAL THINKING

Dialectical thinking has been defined as the ability to critically examine one's own thinking and to sympathetically use a style of reasoning from a perspective that is different from, or even opposed to, one's own (Rudinow & Paul, 1987). This type of thinking might also be termed *reflective self-criticism*.

Rudinow suggests that teachers begin to train their students in dialectical thinking by posing a question for team discussion, without suggesting a position that responders might take. When the teacher has introduced and clarified the topic, the students take positions and prepare to defend them clearly and concisely. They pose questions for those supporting other positions to answer, and prepare answers in support of their own position. Then each team prepares to defend a position to which it was initially opposed.

Though such an exercise might be more appropriate for Grades 10 and 11, you might also adapt it for elementary students. You might, for instance, record early discussions to help your students review and critique their own performances.

DECISION MAKING

Decision making involves choosing among options, a process that requires the use of several thinking skills. This process usually involves the following operations (Beyer, 1984):

♦ identify the desired goal;
♦ identify obstacles to reaching that goal;
♦ identify options for overcoming each obstacle;
♦ examine the options in terms of time, resources, costs, and constraints on their use;
♦ rank options in terms of likely results;
♦ choose the best option or combination of options

CREATIVE THINKING

Creativity has long been recognized as the highest form of mental functioning. **Creative thinking** has been defined as "the ability to form new combinations of ideas to fulfill a need" (Halpern, 1984, p. 324) and as "thinking patterned in a way … [that produces] original and otherwise appropriate results" (Perkins, 1984, pp. 18–19). Individual creativity has been linked to divergent and/or original thought or execution; it need not be original to all humankind. Good and Brophy (1990) observe that "There is little point in searching for a single creativity score [comparable] to an IQ score" because creativity is not a single process (pp. 617–618).

Creativity is not limited to geniuses or the highly talented, or to specific subject matter such as "the arts," but is found in all areas of life. Every student has creative potential, and you can foster that potential in your students by valuing creativity even though it may mean adjusting some established rules and procedures. Students who have not yet learned to channel their creativity positively may sometimes be irritating, disruptive, or contradictory. Indeed, when you promote creativity, you can expect a mixture of novel, imaginative, and valuable answers, as well as answers that may seem silly or bizarre.

You can either encourage or discourage creativity in your classroom. To teach for creativity, provide an atmosphere in which students can explore original ideas without fear of criticism or ridicule. Model creative thinking by using divergent questions. Present open-ended challenges across the curriculum, and help your students to seek different ways of performing tasks, to use divergent ideas to solve problems, and to express themselves in an open-ended manner through small-group activities. Any barriers to creative thinking often lie in students' own minds, and even students who are intelligent may hesitate to use their imagination because they lack confidence or fear being wrong. Help your students to believe that they can become more creative. Let them know that few inventors, scientists, or artists succeeded on their first tries.

Teach students what is involved in creativity. Help them to explore their environment, using all their senses to discover and describe things that interest them. Encourage them to acquire information and use it creatively by framing alternatives or making inferences. Train them to use specific thinking skills, and inquiry and problem-solving processes, but show them that they can become more creative by using a greater variety of options and transferring their knowledge to new contexts. Teach them how to disagree constructively, challenging ideas and procedures without attacking people and personalities. Promote diversity of interests by varying activities with field trips, guest speakers, and media experiences. Let them see that being creative is fun! (Rothstein, 1990, pp. 274–275).

Select Appropriate Activities and Materials

You should carefully select teaching activities and materials to promote your students' development of higher-level thinking skills. Thinking activities are inquiry oriented and often open ended, without a specific answer or set of answers. When selecting activities, consider the following criteria.

Points to ponder . . .

- ❑ What are my targets?
- ❑ What performance goals am I setting for my students?
- ❑ Does this activity have significant content?
- ❑ Is it worth thinking about?
- ❑ Will it increase awareness or insight?
- ❑ Does it permit a wide range of responses?

When selecting materials, consider

- ◆ their safety, availability, cost, and the time available for their use;
- ◆ the needs, interests, and developmental levels of your students;
- ◆ the amount of supervision, space, and equipment students will need to use materials appropriately.

PRACTICE *and Projects*

1. a. Working with a partner, negotiate the choice of a subject area, and choose a lesson plan that one of you has already developed in that area.

   b. Analyze the lesson plan to identify the thinking skills it requires students to practice.

2. Plan a lesson to promote *either* critical *or* creative thinking in a subject and at a grade level of your choice. You may find Data Collection Form 10.1 (Appendix A) useful for planning it.

CASE STUDY 10.1

PROMOTING A THINKING SKILL

Ms. Arnott's Grade 2 class has been developing a unit about farming for several days. The students have learned about different kinds of farms, farm animals, and farm machinery. Ms. Arnott wishes to build on the new learning and introduce the thinking skill of comparing. She plans to use consecutive lessons to introduce comparing by having the children compare, first, two farm animals familiar to them; next, two live pet turtles, a snapping turtle and a box turtle; and then, two stories. She hopes to help the children learn to transfer the skill of comparing by using it in different situations.

Ms. Arnott begins the first lesson by saying, "This afternoon we're going to use a special kind of thinking skill called 'comparing.' First we'll practice using it about ourselves, and tomorrow we'll try it with something else.

"Have you ever heard the word 'compare'?" As she asks this question, she writes the word on the chalkboard.

Some of the children have heard the word and offer examples.

"My mom compares prices when she shops."

"I'm tall compared to my baby brother."

"My sisters don't like to be compared."

"Those are good examples of ways to use 'compare,'" Ms. Arnott assures them. "What do you think the word means?"

Trish volunteers, "It means checking to see whether two things are the same."

(continued)

(continued)

Ms. Arnott records the term *Same* on the board, under *Compare*. "Yes," she agrees, "looking for ways in which things are the same is called 'comparing.' And it means something else, too."

"It means standing up to see if you're as tall as your brother," Petra responds.

"If you are small and your brother is tall, are you the same?" Ms. Arnott asks.

"No. We're different."

"Then could comparing also be looking for ways in which things are different?"

"Yes," answers Petra, and Ms. Arnott writes *Different* under *Compare* on the chalkboard, asking, "Now can we add something to our definition of 'compare'?"

Ivan answers, " 'Compare' means looking for ways in which things are the same *and* ways in which they're different."

"That's right!" Ms. Arnott replies, "and that's what we're going to do. Now let's see how this would work. Suppose we compare two boys in our class, just to see if you get the idea. Have we any volunteers? … Paul and Jacques, you'd like to volunteer? All right. Come on up, and stand here at the front of the room. We'll make a place for information on the chalkboard."

Ms. Arnott writes on the chalkboard the headings shown below, and notes the similarities and differences that the children identify.

<u>COMPARING</u>

<u>Different</u>		<u>Same</u>
PAUL	JACQUES	PAUL & JACQUES
brown hair	black hair	both are boys
taller	shorter	both are in Grade 2
wearing runners	sock feet	both play soccer at recess
wearing a sweater	wearing a "Turtles" shirt	both are wearing jeans
blue eyes	brown eyes	both have short hair
		both are Montreal
		Canadiens fans

(continued)

(continued)

"That's great," says Ms. Arnott. "Now let's see if you can compare two farm animals we've been learning about. Which ones should we compare?" Many hands wave. After looking over the class, Ms. Arnott chooses Marcus, who suggests goats and sheep.

Ms. Arnott asks the students to work in pairs and then distributes forms, giving one to each pair. The forms are ruled in the same manner as the chart the class has worked out on the chalkboard. Ms. Arnott reviews with the class information about goats and sheep and then asks the pairs to begin discussing this information.

"Decide which things are different, and which are the same, and then record the information on your worksheets," she instructs them. "When everyone is finished, we'll talk about your charts."

When the students have completed their task, Ms. Arnott asks them to share their responses. Following the discussion, through which she discovers that the students have grasped the idea of similarities and differences, she concludes, "You all did a good job of comparing today. Tomorrow we'll do more comparing, but we'll look for things that are the same and different about two different kinds of turtles. I'm going to bring my pet box turtle and my pet snapping turtle. We'll look at them, touch them, see what they eat, and how they act in a new place. Then we'll compare them to see in what ways they are the same, and in what ways they differ."

■ ■ ■ ■ ■

TEACHING THINKING SKILLS

The theories and models for teaching thinking skills outlined above suggest a number of components that you will wish to consider in more detail.

Direct Teaching

Beyer (1984, p.558), summarizing a body of opinion, advises that teachers should

◆ define the skill to be learned, its purpose, and the thinking it calls for;
◆ model (demonstrate and explain) the skill;
◆ provide a classroom climate and use teaching methods that enable students to concentrate fully on the skill they are learning;

⬧ provide frequent (not massed) practice sessions that include feedback and correction;
⬧ provide learners with opportunities to talk about their use of the skill;
⬧ provide learners with guidance for achieving a content-related goal;
⬧ provide learners with opportunities to practice learning skills in new contexts.

TEACH PROBLEM SOLVING

All students face problems every day, whether with schoolwork, with peers, or at home. Students approach a problem in one of four ways:

⬧ they ignore the problem and hope it will go away;
⬧ they ignore the problem and don't care whether it goes away;
⬧ they try to solve the problem as best they can, even though they lack training in **problem solving**; or
⬧ having been taught problem-solving skills, they approach the problem in a sound and systematic way.

You can help your students to take the fourth approach.

"A problem exists when a person perceives a need to achieve some goal but does not immediately know how to achieve it" (Good & Brophy, 1990, p. 260). Problem solving requires the transfer and application of knowledge and skills to obtain a solution or to achieve a goal. Problem solving has two aspects:

⬧ recalling or acquiring the information needed to solve a problem;
⬧ following an effective problem-solving procedure.

Expert problem solvers do not begin by suggesting a large number of hypotheses and then testing each one. They first narrow a problem down by identifying its key features and relating those features to information they have memorized or can look up. They then select one or a few hypotheses for testing. This approach, which prevents their spending time investigating low-probability hypotheses, requires rapid and accurate problem definition and pattern recognition. Thus, you should teach students, as soon as they are ready, how to seek patterns, select strategies, and use appropriate thinking skills for problem solving.

One organized approach to problem solving is outlined in Data Collection Form 10.2 (Appendix A). You might use the approach suggested there to help your students to analyze problems by taking the following steps:

⬧ Identify the problem.
⬧ Determine the causes of the problem.
⬧ Focus on the most serious cause.

◆ Brainstorm possible solutions.
◆ Choose the most promising solution.
◆ Identify action needed to apply solution.
◆ Apply action.
◆ Observe results.
◆ Use your observation as necessary to deal with other problems by repeating the steps.

In following these steps, students will discover their learning-style preferences (see Chapter 4): some will identify the problem's key features mentally, while others will need to write them down, and still others will need a picture, chart, or symbol to represent those features. Encourage your students to use a variety of approaches, to look at problems creatively, and to take risks in seeking solutions. Help them to take a step-by-step approach (Rothstein 1990, pp.268–270) as follows:

◆ Explain that a well-defined problem is half solved, and show students how to go about defining a problem by analyzing its features and identifying those that are "essential" (see Chapter 8).
◆ Train them to ask themselves what materials they have to work with, and how they can use these materials to solve the problem.
◆ Show them how to use analogies by identifying similar problems and considering the solutions already applied to them. (This process should reduce errors and shorten the time needed to solve a new problem.)
◆ Teach them not to jump to conclusions, but to generate and evaluate hypotheses, recording the implications or consequences of several before they select or combine the best.
◆ Provide "incubation time," since a solution can suddenly seem to suggest itself when a problem has been set aside to "warm" for a while.

Academic problems are usually more structured than life problems, which rarely have a single solution. Data Collection Form 10.1 (Appendix A) is useful for identifying problems and for hypothesizing and choosing possible solutions. Although students should not expect to work out a "perfect answer" to every life problem, those who have been taught how to solve problems by using appropriate thinking skills should be able to apply those skills constructively to personal problems.

TEACH PROCESSES

Thinking and problem solving are thinking **processes**, that normally include two or more thinking skills. Processes involve skills that can be learned (Vallet, 1986).

TABLE 10.1

Thinking Processes and Skills

Processes	*Skills*
Desired outcome: development of student flexibility and process adaptability	Desired outcome: automaticity in performance
Steps may be indefinite and sequence varied	Specific techniques in fixed sequence
Often difficult to analyze	Can be analyzed in fine detail
Examples: ◆ problem solving ◆ decision making ◆ estimating ◆ summarizing information	*Examples*: ◆ adding numbers ◆ serving a tennis ball ◆ writing letters of the alphabet ◆ using a compass

Processes and skills are compared in Table 10.1.

Teaching a process is somewhat similar to teaching a skill (see Chapter 9): you must teach both explicitly so that your students can understand, practice, and evaluate them. You will also need to learn how to assess process learning as you did skills learning. Process assessment requires a student to apply a process in a new context to ensure that transfer has taken place. Table 10.2 relates a number of processes to specific academic subjects to illustrate relationships that you will need to recognize. Figure 10.2 charts a complete process-teaching cycle.

PROMOTE THINKING IN YOUR CLASSROOM

What you do in your classroom promotes or limits your students' learning and use of thinking skills. Raths, Wasserman, Jonas, and Rothstein (1967) pointed out that the way teachers organize their classrooms, the climate they provide, and the strategies they use lie at the core of teaching for thinking. The teacher who shows willingness to listen and provides opportunities for students to be heard creates a positive climate for acquiring thinking skills. Students need to discuss their thinking processes, points of view, and attempts at analysis. They need to make decisions, examine alternatives, and act on their decisions. They need to think of ways of organizing and using the learning skills they are acquiring. They need a degree of autonomy to promote this development and exercise of thinking skills, rather than a limiting degree of dependency.

TABLE 10.2

Process Classification

General	Thinking	Revising	Science	English	Mathematics	History
Problem solving	Recalling	Adapting	Observing	Paraphrasing	Measuring	Investigating
Decision making	Comprehending	Improvising	Measuring	Summarizing	Estimating	Analyzing
Creating	Analyzing	Patterning	Classifying	Describing	Verifying	Classifying
Generalizing	Synthesizing	Varying	Verifying	Debating	Checking	Comparing
Differentiating	Evaluating	Comparing	Recording		Problem solving	Recording
	Communicating					

FIGURE 10.2

Teaching a Process

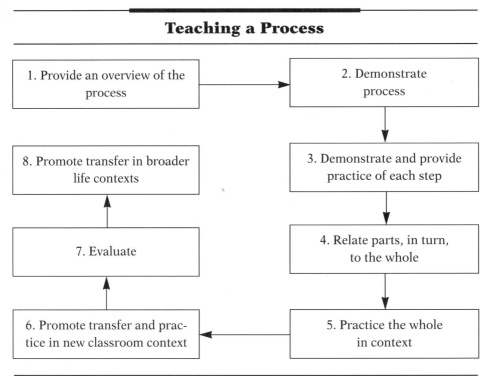

1. Provide an overview of the process

2. Demonstrate process

3. Demonstrate and provide practice of each step

4. Relate parts, in turn, to the whole

5. Practice the whole in context

6. Promote transfer and practice in new classroom context

7. Evaluate

8. Promote transfer in broader life contexts

TEACH TRANSFER

One of the most commonly debated issues in the teaching of thinking is transfer. Baron and Sternberg (1991) point out that "One must teach for transfer, rather than merely hoping … that it will occur" (p. 258). Perkins and Salomon (1989) observe that "when general principles of reasoning are taught together with self-mentoring practices and potential applications in varied contexts, transfer often is obtained … [but] only under specific conditions, which often are not met [in life]" (p. 22).

To accustom your students to observe and implement opportunities for practicing transfer, you should emphasize, in both the set and the closure of your lessons, the connections that will enable them to transfer familiar skills and knowledge to new contexts. Give your students opportunities to observe and to use such opportunities in broader contexts until they become accustomed to doing so on their own initiative.

OBSERVE AND MONITOR STUDENTS' USE OF THINKING SKILLS

In classrooms in which students receive little encouragement to practice thinking skills, student behaviors tend to exhibit the following characteristics:

◆ extreme impulsiveness, with an emphasis on doing, unsupported by much thinking;

◆ overdependency on the teacher's instructions;

◆ dogmatic assertions that indicate unwillingness to consider new approaches to learning;

◆ an inability to apply learned principles to new situations;

◆ an unwillingness to accept personal responsibility for implementing learning strategies.

Learning that emphasizes thinking relates to students' emotions, the pressures they perceive, their self-concept, the dynamics of the class group, and the teacher's attitudes. Involving learners in the process of acquiring knowledge promotes thinking skills, as do acceptance, support, probes, and encouragement.

EVALUATE STUDENTS' USE OF THINKING SKILLS

Not only should thinking skills be directly taught, but they should also be evaluated and rewarded. Reward students who show evidence of creativity, and reward improvements, for students who have been encouraged to use their creative talents will likely use them well throughout their lives. Allocate some marks in each subject to reflect students' progress in their use of thinking skills. Thinking skills must be practiced in both broad and narrow frameworks, in many different contexts (e.g., through written and oral descriptions, record keeping, and problem solving), and in both supervised and self-monitored situations. The use of a thinking skill in its simplest form and in a familiar context should be acknowledged at the lowest level of reward. The level should be advanced as the learner uses a skill in increasingly divergent contexts.

PRACTICE *and Projects*

1. Working in a subject-interest group, choose a process, analyze it, and plan the steps to teach it.

2. Use Data Collection Form 10.1 (Appendix A) to help you analyze Case Study 10.1. Your instructor may pose specific questions for your response.

■ ■ ■ ■ ■

DEDUCTIVE AND INDUCTIVE REASONING

Sherlock Holmes, the mastermind of detective fiction, continually dazzled his friend Watson with his brilliant solutions: "Elementary, my dear Watson! ... " The mystified Watson never became aware, until Holmes explained all, how the great detective used both **deductive** and **inductive reasoning** to analyze a mystery and reach the only logical conclusion. Wiser than Watson, we can diagram the deductive and inductive reasoning processes.

As Figure 10.3 shows, the terms *deductive* and *inductive* refer to the direction in which thoughts flow during close logical-reasoning processes. The deductive and inductive methods of reasoning are particularly useful for teaching students to identify and frame concepts (see Chapter 8), processes that often call for these methods of reasoning.

Deductive Reasoning

The deductive reasoning process begins with a thinker's identifying a concept or generalization, defining it, and then classifying particular related examples and nonexamples (see Chapter 8) on the basis of the definition framed. In other words, the deductive process or sequence involves framing a concept or generalization and then identifying a number of examples and nonexamples to verify and support it.

PROMOTING DEDUCTIVE REASONING

To encourage students to form a concept by using deductive reasoning (i.e., by reasoning from a general situation to particular instances), you might use the following steps:

FIGURE 10.3

Deductive and Inductive Reasoning

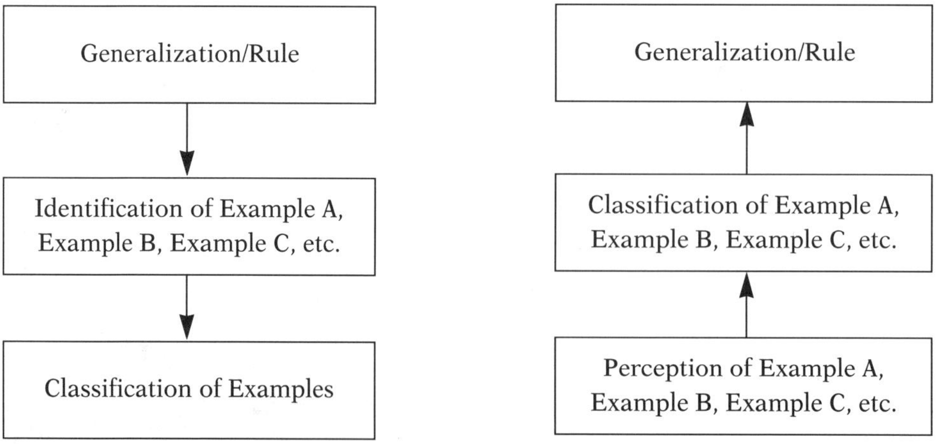

Deductive Reasoning Process — Generalization/Rule → Identification of Example A, Example B, Example C, etc. → Classification of Examples

Inductive Reasoning Process — Perception of Example A, Example B, Example C, etc. → Classification of Example A, Example B, Example C, etc. → Generalization/Rule

- Establish set for determining what constitutes, say, a fish.
- Have students list on the chalkboard examples of creatures that live in aquatic habitats.
- Have students subdivide their list into groups by identifying critical and noncritical attributes of the creatures listed (see Chapter 8).
- Ask for other examples of each group.
- Ask for nonexamples of each group.
- Have students name the groups identified.
- Help students define the term *fish*, including and relating the attributes.
- Provide a list of examples and nonexamples of fish for students to distinguish; have them explain their choices.
- Check for understanding by asking questions or testing.

Inductive Reasoning

The inductive reasoning process begins with identifying a number of particular examples and nonexamples, analyzing and classifying them, and then framing a concept or generalization based on them.

PROMOTING INDUCTIVE REASONING

To encourage students to form a concept through inductive reasoning (i.e., by reasoning from particular instances to a general conclusion), you might use the following steps:

- Establish set for determining what constitutes, say, a mammal.
- Ask for one example of a mammal, and write a correct response on the chalkboard.
- Ask for attributes of the mammal selected, and list correct responses below the mammal's name.
- Repeat the last two steps several times to provide a number of examples.
- Ask for names of creatures that are not mammals, and list correct responses.
- Ask for attributes of creatures that are not mammals, and list correct responses.
- Using the material recorded on the chalkboard, have students compare and relate attributes to distinguish the critical attributes from the noncritical (incidental) attributes.
- Ask students to define the term *mammals*.
- Provide a list of creatures for several small groups, and ask groups to use research sources to determine which creatures are mammals by applying the definition framed by the class.
- Debrief your class when the research is complete, and have them confirm or reframe their definition, drawing attention to examples and their relation to one another.

Deductive or Inductive Reasoning?
—That Is the Question

In planning to teach a topic that calls for close logical reasoning, you will have to decide whether to approach your lesson through deductive or inductive reasoning. Your choices will help you to determine what strategies you will use. Direct and explicit instruction, lecture, inquiry, and small-group problem solving are methods often used in teaching deductive and inductive reasoning. You may find that some methods seem particularly applicable to teaching one or the other approach, whereas others may lend themselves equally to both processes.

Both deductive and inductive reasoning provide valuable approaches to teaching concepts, generalizations, and skills. A deductive approach takes less instruction time and can provide more predictable learning outcomes, since it can involve closer teacher control. An inductive approach may waste time if it results in unplanned and unsuitable examples, or if students are not mature or confident enough to be comfortable working on their own; on the other hand, since the inductive approach requires less teacher involvement, students who are capable of using the approach independently may better understand and remember what they learn.

It is wise to choose your approach according to the learning objectives you have set, and the developmental and skill levels of your class. To facilitate your choice, consider the following points.

Points to ponder . . .

- ❑   How much time is available to teach the material?
- ❑   How well prepared are these students for individual/group-oriented work?
- ❑   Should learning outcomes be predictable and therefore "safe"?
- ❑   What depth of understanding and rate of retention are needed?
     Should my students learn this material for use later in this course? in more advanced courses? in other life contexts?

Doubtless you will sometimes decide to take a deductive approach and sometimes an inductive approach. As your students become more experienced in using these forms of reasoning, you may often have to decide, too, whether to encourage them to approach a topic deductively or inductively. It is important to have them vary the methods they use so that they will become comfortable with both.

PRACTICE *and Projects*

1. Your instructor may model two short lessons on the same topic to illustrate the deductive and inductive approaches to teaching a concept. Using Data Collection Form 8.2 (Appendix A), record the components of each lesson. Debrief in class or in small groups.

2. Working with a partner or a small group, select a concept and prepare two lesson plans, one illustrating a deductive and the other an inductive approach to teaching the concept you have chosen.

3. Using Data Collection Form 8.2, microteach a lesson with the professional target of teaching a concept inductively or deductively. Attach a completed copy of Data Collection Form 8.1, Concept Analysis, to your lesson plan.

SUMMARY

- "Teaching for thinking," for which a number of systems have been developed, is a fundamental component of instruction that requires a positive classroom climate and high student self-concept.
- Deliberate planning, a prerequisite for successful teaching of thinking skills, includes considering various modes of thinking (e.g., creative, critical, dialectical, and decision making) and selecting methods of instruction, activities, and materials.
- Direct teaching of thinking skills includes integrating new and familiar information, organizing process or content, delivering instruction, promoting and monitoring practice, rewarding effort and achievement, and reflecting and evaluating.
- The teaching, modeling, and provision of opportunities for the use of deductive and inductive reasoning are important means of promoting students' development of thinking skills.
- Deductive reasoning involves identifying a concept or generalization, defining it, and then classifying particular related examples and nonexamples on the basis of the general definition.
- Inductive reasoning involves identifying a number of particular examples and nonexamples, and framing a concept or generalization based on them.

KEY WORDS

analysis	procedural	planning
creativity	conditional	problem solving
domains of learning	linking	process
cognitive	modes of thinking	reasoning
affective	critical	deductive
psychomotor	dialectical	inductive
intelligence	decision making	thinking skills
learning strategies	creative	transfer
declarative	organizing	

RECOMMENDED READING

Costa, A. (1985). *Developing minds: A resource book for teaching thinking.* Alexandria, VA: Association for Supervision and Curriculum Development.

Kaplan, M. (1992). *Thinking in education.* Cambridge, U.K.: Cambridge University Press.

Nickerson, R. (1989). On improving thinking through instruction. *Review of Research in Education, 15*, 3–37. (Edited by E. Rathkoph)

Paul, R. (1990). *Critical thinking: What every person needs to survive in a rapidly changing world.* Rohnert Park, CA: Sonoma State University.

Resnick, L., & Kloper, L. (Eds.). (1989). *Toward the thinking curriculum: Current cognitive research.* Alexandria, VA: Association for Supervision and Curriculum Development.

Sternberg, R. (1990b). Thinking styles: Keys to understanding student performance. *Phi Delta Kappan, 71*, 366–371.

CHAPTER 11

TEACHING
ATTITUDES AND VALUES

■ ■ ■ ■ ■

The notion of "value-free education," popular in some circles from about mid-century until fairly recently, harbors a contradiction in terms ... What we consider "good" or "bad," "right" or "wrong," "important" or "unimportant" constantly guides our practice ... there is simply no denying the vital and influential presence of values in every facet of educational practice.

(CARBONE, 1991, P. 290)

■ ■ ■ ■ ■

OVERVIEW

Since values and attitudes underlie all societies, schools have a duty to help students grow in their ability to acquire constructive ones. Affective learning relates to the emotions, values, and attitudes that students develop in and out of school. Steps in teaching for affective growth are discovery of students' existing values and attitudes; preparation and delivery of pertinent information and experiences; provision of opportunities for understanding and reflection; checking for commitment; and checking for change and action. Effective teaching of values and attitudes should result in "integrated" persons.

■ ■ ■ ■ ■

AFFECTIVE INSTRUCTION

Educators generally apply the term *affect* to emotions, values, and attitudes. Affective instruction focuses on mental health as evident in self-concept and self-esteem, human relationships and experiences, feelings and emotions, character, personality, personal philosophies, and personal and social adjustment. It does *not* consist of playing psychologist, invading privacy, adopting permissiveness as a substitute for efficient classroom management, trying to make everyone conform to an educator's ideal, sensitivity training, a novel way to teach listening skills, or an attempt to make teachers "buddies."

 Teaching for affective growth combines instruction and training to make students aware of, and help them to deal with, feelings, values and attitudes that shape their behavior, their relationships, and their lives. Children need to experience affective growth if they are to function well in cooperative situations, learn to understand and like themselves and others, make decisions, set goals, cope with normal problems, clarify values, exercise their rights, and carry out their duties as human beings and citizens. To achieve these ends, they must deal positively with their feelings and emotions, and form healthy and constructive values and attitudes. As a teacher, you will need to be aware of, and teach directly for, affective outcomes as you simultaneously concern yourself with the other domains of learning (see, especially Chapters 3, 8, 9, and 10).

Affective Goals and School Curricula

School curricula can and should be framed to include appropriate affective content: while promoting students' cognitive development, educational programs should help students to become more aware of themselves and to clarify who they are, what they want in life, and how they can achieve their goals without hurting others. Courses should include activities to help students develop self-esteem and to acquire communication and problem-solving skills through which they will be able to take a constructive part in society and cope with life in general. Teachers should learn to identify affective content, judge its difficulty, present it in appropriate sequence, relate it to learners' experience, and construct suitable means of evaluation.

Affect and promotion of social behavior are built into curricula through direct study or integration into other subject matter to promote students' growth toward moral maturity, a state in which they will base their attitudes, judgments, and actions on principles of equality, fairness, and justice. Students, like all other persons, go through different stages of values development; they can be taught, at all levels, to distinguish between facts and values, and to reason more clearly about value and attitudinal issues.

It is important to remember that no "value-free" curriculum or teaching exists or can exist. Attitudes and value assumptions exist in varying degrees of explicitness throughout all education systems and all human societies (West & Foster, 1976, pp. 274–275). The important thing is to keep these realities as open as possible, to allow for maximum freedom of thought and opinion without causing harm to individuals or society.

SETTING AFFECTIVE GOALS

Teaching and learning for affect should not be a hoped-for byproduct of academic curricula. The administrative goal statements of North American education systems typically include, along with acquisition of basic skills, the affective goals of interest in lifelong learning, understanding and relating to others, developing a positive self-concept and life style, spiritual growth, learning to make realistic career and consumer decisions, and becoming productive members of society. The ways in which you plan and deliver lessons and evaluate instruction should reflect this emphasis of curricula on affective growth, for affective education promotes general educational goals, given the following premises (Coombs, 1982):

- learning is fundamentally a discovery of personal meanings;
- learning is an emotional affective experience;
- to learn, students must see course content as significant to their needs;
- self-concept is the most important set for behavior and learning;
- feelings of belonging and being cared for promote learning;
- personal feedback is important to learning.

Integrating General and Affective Teaching Skills

Although, for instructional purposes, *Teaching* examines affective education as a distinct topic, the development of feelings, values, and attitudes is an integral part of learning. *All* teaching and learning have cognitive and affective aspects, for they relate to cognition, and produce feelings and emotions (i.e., have affective outcomes). At times, affective outcomes are incidental to cognitive learning; at other times, curriculum objectives will require direct teaching of values or attitudes to promote affective growth.

To promote your students' affective development, you will need to acquire and use a broad repertoire of teaching skills. The general teaching skills that you are already targeting and practicing will help you to teach for affective growth. You will, for instance, sometimes use a lecture method to give information rapidly or to bridge other teaching techniques. You should also make ample use, when opportunities serve, of methods that actively involve your students in using cooperative learning strategies such as games, simulations, and exercises to teach and practice communication, interpersonal, and group skills (see Chapter 2).

TARGETING AFFECTIVE INSTRUCTION

To promote your students' affective development, you will need to set and support the following professional targets:

- Help your students to take responsibility. Students must learn to be accountable for their behavior. Explain that rules are guides to protect the well-being of students and staff, and not idle inventions of malicious adults. Inform your students of the consequences of their behavioral choices (e.g., they may work quietly or continue to provoke their neighbors and take the consequences).
- Give students opportunities to change specific disruptive behaviors. Your message should be, "I don't like your behavior at this time, but I still like you." Avoid

extracting promises or pledges of good conduct that students cannot keep. If you ask a student to make a commitment, set a specific time to review progress, but leave responsibility for change with the student; you might suggest areas for change and ways of adapting, but the onus of changing belongs with the student.

◆ Control students' behavior unobtrusively. If students misbehave, try to control their behavior through proximity and nonverbal feedback. Use overlapping (see Chapter 5) to deter misbehavior without interrupting instruction: students may be devastated if you humiliate them in front of peers. If you must reprimand a student, do it privately or in a whisper to avoid causing a ripple effect in the classroom. Avoid punishing, rejecting, or giving absolute responses: *never* tell students that they will *never* change, or that you *never* want to see them in your class again. Remember that you are reacting to *current* behavior, no matter how often it has occurred before.

◆ Apply logical consequences of undesirable student behaviors as needed to help students learn new behaviors. Experience may turn out to be the best teacher: many have learned that fire is hot by getting too close, and one such experience can have more impact than a dozen verbal warnings. When the effects of punishment are unpredictable and experience is not a reasonable consequence, allow students to suggest alternative consequences. Thinking through logical consequences can help students to recommend fair and relevant options. You may find it more productive, however, to motivate your students to pursue more positive consequences.

◆ Be aware of your limitations. No one is perfect! Recognize your areas of intolerance and ineffectiveness, and admit your need of help. To recognize these realities is fundamental to your professional growth.

PRACTICE *and Projects*

1. a. Working with your partner, prepare a lesson plan for a lesson that targets affective growth.
    b. Teach your lesson in a microteaching-lab or classroom setting.

Teaching for Affective Growth

Among the skills particularly useful for integrating general and affective instruction to produce affective growth are classroom management, modeling, identifying students' values, motivating, being sensitive to feelings, soliciting responses, reacting, and resolving conflict.

CLASSROOM MANAGEMENT FOR AFFECTIVE GROWTH

Effective classroom management skills (see Chapter 5) give you the freedom to teach and your students the freedom to learn. Principles that you have already learned will become even more important as you stimulate affective growth.

◆ Structure classroom arrangements and activities to facilitate group learning. Be flexible in arranging furniture and materials as various student groupings require.

◆ As far as possible, use questions rather than direct instructions to remind students of limits and invite cooperation. This approach leads learners to make sense of and take responsibility for their actions. If your goal is to help students learn self-control, give them opportunities to monitor their own behavior.

◆ Avoid personal comments such as "You are not supposed to be doing that!" Instead, state rules in as impersonal a way as possible, such as "Littering is not allowed in class." Except in unusual circumstances, rules should apply to *all*.

IDENTIFYING STUDENTS' VALUES AND ATTITUDES

Discovering the current values and attitudes of your students is the first step in promoting needed changes. Only by identifying your students' learning needs can you choose wisely the affective goals on which they should focus. When you have established those goals, you should analyze them to determine the most effective teaching methods for promoting their achievement. To teach for affective growth, analyze values and attitudes that govern affect (i.e., feelings, emotion, and desire—especially those that result in action). By being genuine and empathetic and by showing respect for others, you will help your students to identify affective learning goals for themselves.

To identify your students' values and attitudes, observe their actions, collect data on their behavior, analyze the data you have collected, and draw inferences from it. You can infer values and attitudes from their behavior or find evidence through testing techniques such as asking students to choose between competing value statements or to justify actual or hypothetical behavior. (Be very careful in using such techniques, however, for any process, whether concrete or hypothetical, that imposes competition or calls students' self-worth into question can intimidate and even be traumatic for those who lack self-assurance.)

MODELING AFFECTIVE BEHAVIOR

The most effective way of teaching and promoting affect and values is to be an exemplary role model. This includes creating a positive environment for students' affective growth, and facilitating affective goals and their transfer. If you wish your students to develop trust, openness, and genuineness, be trusting, open, and genuine. If you wish them to develop tolerance, respect, and acceptance of others, be tolerant, respectful, and accepting of them. If it is important for your class members to listen, listen to them. When necessary, admit your mistakes. Showing that you can handle and correct a mistake positively will provide a valuable model for your students and enhance your credibility.

Being Sensitive to Feelings

Your reactions to students or classroom incidents make a difference in the way your students respond: they can be strong motivators (see Chapter 4) or serious disincentives. To establish positive relationships with your students, you will need to be sensitive to their feelings and they to yours. Reflection is a technique used to "mirror" another's behavior by focusing on feelings and reflecting them accurately without expressing a positive or negative judgment. This technique can cause students to consider and reprocess the information you are sending about themselves. You might introduce reflective statements with such words as "You look ... You sound ... You seem ... "

Use "I" messages, or self-disclosure, to convey feelings: be open, honest, and real. Although it would be inappropriate for you to reveal everything about your personal life, you can sometimes build class morale by letting students know some of your interests and preferences (e.g., your favorite season, color, or sport), your views on some important issues (e.g., the importance of voting, but not your political affiliation), or how their behavior makes you feel (e.g., "I'm concerned about your being off task now because I know you don't like staying after school to finish your work").

PRACTICE *and Projects*

1. a. View a film or read a story that shows the influence of a teacher on his or her class.
    b. In a small group, discuss the following questions:
    - What ideas does the film or story contain that would help you teach values?
    - Should students have some choice about the values they are taught? If so, how can they be involved in that choice?

TEACHING COMMUNICATION, INTERPERSONAL, AND GROUP SKILLS

Teaching appropriate communication, interpersonal, and group skills (see Chapter 2) is particularly important to affective development because these skills are basic to understanding oneself and others, developing a realistic positive self-concept, and promoting social behavior. Students should learn these as cross-curricular skills, and practice them reflectively.

PROVIDING INFORMATIVE EXPERIENCES

Your students, too, will need to "discover"—that is, become conscious of and examine—their existing values and attitudes before they can modify them or acquire new ones. Your role is to provide information and structure experiences that will help them to "discover" and reflect on their feelings and the ways in which they show them, discuss possible changes, and plan revisions.

Do not take it for granted that your students already know or accept the values and attitudes that make for a good learning environment. Teach these elements to help your students acquire a positive, growth-promoting, value system that stimulates productive attitudes. Beneficial changes in attitude might include students' learning to

◆ like certain subjects or topics, their teacher, and their classmates;
◆ work well alone and with others;
◆ take care of their own and others' property;
◆ start work on time, stay on task, and complete tasks assigned.

Students learn from direct experiences with persons and ideas, concrete examples, and media resources. Your students may discover their own attitudes and the problems they can cause for others through such means. New situations and experiences in the classroom or on a field trip may also help them to examine old values and attitudes and develop new ones. By encouraging and praising your students for trying, and by ensuring that they achieve a high rate of success in learning, you can predispose them to risk changes and new experiences.

PROMOTING PERSONAL INTEGRATION

Affective education should help students to become "whole" (i.e., "integrated") persons. Evidence of this process appears as a range of changes that include awareness, concern, **values clarification**, commitment, and internalization, or a relatively permanent change in behavior.

Helping students to set realistic goals and achieve success at an appropriate level fosters their interest in learning and contributes to their forming a positive self-concept. Your expectations for individual students should be challenging but attainable. You help students attain the goals set when you encourage them and recognize the progress they are making.

Promoting Positive Self-Concept

Students need to feel good about themselves generally, and to believe that they are worthy and capable of achieving learning goals. To develop these feelings, they need to receive recognition and approval in the form of "acceptance," interest, and constructive feedback. Your modeling of this behavior will help your students to develop self-esteem, and to accept you and one another. Students who lack this sense of acceptance may not perceive themselves positively.

Promoting Self-Control

Depending on their age, developmental level, temperament, and social conditioning, some students will find it harder than others to develop self-control. Your humane and consistent matching of behaviors and consequences can help students to achieve this goal.

Encouraging Positive Social Behaviors

Two variables contribute to the adoption and habitual use of positive social behaviors: development and enhancement of the students' self-esteem, and development of productive interpersonal relationships. Students achieve productive relationships when they reject prejudices and learn to like others and to see matters from others' perspectives. Following a model and joining in small group activities that teach cooperation, role playing, and observing can help students develop positive social behaviours and even **altruistic behaviors**.

ALLOWING TIME FOR COMPREHENSION AND REFLECTION

Since adopting values and attitudes is a highly personal process, your students will need time to grasp and reflect on new information and experiences that will initiate change. Small group activities provide a useful way of allowing students the time they need for comprehension and reflection. Talking and working with persons who have desirable attitudes, as occurs in small group cooperative projects, promotes learning about one's attitudes and their effects on self and others. You might, for instance,

- organize students into awareness/discussion groups. Groups of this sort work particularly well if most of their members are interested in the topic discussed, and if the discussion is positive and well structured;
- arrange for group decision making, which fosters acceptance and ownership;
- stress cooperation within groups;
- use role play, which allows "safer" expressions of feeling and experiments with different attitudes.

Soliciting Affective Responses

To solicit affective responses from your students, give clear, simple instructions (see Chapter 9). Check for understanding: posting instructions or using a handout can be helpful. State your expectations briefly to avoid confusion caused by multiple commands or wordiness. Show your students that you are open, nonjudgmental, fair, caring, and willing to help, but, apart from an occasional nudge in the right direction, do not do things for them, for this denies them the chance to succeed. Initiate dialog with students who resist contact in such a way as to invite, but not force, communication. Offer to meet with students to discuss concepts, talk about test scores, or resolve difficulties, but do not demand interviews on these topics.

Resolving Conflict Situations

Conflict is an inevitable part of growth from childhood to adulthood. When conflict arises in the classroom, try to resolve it or use it as an opportunity for growth. Control your impulse to react, and choose the most effective response to defuse the situation. Keep your professional "cool," and take time to think the situation out calmly. Adopt a problem-solving approach to a positive goal by seeking a solution that identifies other options or imposes consequences.

You can promote growth in conflict situations by modeling an effective alternative. Your students will watch to see how you respond to provocation, and your real influence will lie more in what you do than in what you say. If you wish your students to control their impulsive behaviors, control your impulsive reactions. Convey calm confidence: be shockproof during conflicts, and do not lay blame. Detach yourself from arguments, and avoid power struggles in which one person tries to satisfy a desire to gain control, mastery, superiority, or security. Avoid such "games" by

- simply withdrawing from the argument (e.g., "I'm not going to argue with you about this now. We can talk it over later, if you wish.");
- by not "playing" (e.g., "I'm not going to get into this. I have work to do, and so have you.").

When a student repeatedly promotes conflict, you can help him or her gain insight into the dynamics and consequences of the type of behavior he or she is using. Once a conflict has subsided, "touch base" with the student(s) involved. After a student–teacher conflict, residual feelings of anger, shame, or fear may remain. It is helpful to clear the air by showing that you can be pleasant or even use humor to neutralize stressful situations. Tension and stress hamper learning and increase anxiety; laughter relaxes.

ENCOURAGING DELIBERATE CHANGES OF ATTITUDE

When your students discover a current value or attitude, they can begin to analyze it by noting its effects on themselves and others. If they see those effects as undesirable, you may be able to encourage them to change. It is important to encourage students to be open to justifiable changes of values and attitudes, and to accept them as part of the learning process.

ASSESSING DESIRED CHANGES

As your students progress through changes of values and attitudes, you will wish to assess their progress and commitment. Look for changes in action and behavior that indicate the adoption of new values and attitudes. Repeat this sequence as required, providing more information or experiences and more time for comprehension and reflection; check again for comprehension and commitment. In assessing affective progress, record evidence of appreciation of learning in specific subject areas, of appreciation of cultural and individual differences, of valuing trustworthiness and free and open inquiry into problems, and of awareness of personal abilities and characteristics helpful to others.

PRACTICE *and Projects*

1. a. Working with other members of a small group and using Data Collection Form 11.1, analyze Case Study 11.1.
    b. Debrief as a class.

Affective Growth Experience

Affective growth evolves through experiences that enlarge or modify values and attitudes. Values are personal assessments of worth attributed to all concepts, experiences, relationships, and material things. They affect what we are willing to do and what we avoid doing because they influence our evaluations of, or our attitudes toward, the desirability of behaviors or events. Attitudes are personal predispositions (feelings and urges), generally based on values, that evolve from experience and influence individuals to behave in certain ways toward themselves and other persons and things. Through acquiring and enlarging values and attitudes, people grow affectively, becoming "whole" (i.e., "integrated") persons in the process. A major shift in attitude usually requires a change in all one's values (i.e., one's value system).

Mr. Enrico has just begun a unit on "Prejudice and Discrimination" with his Grade 10 social studies class. He has prepared a one-page handout that contains two sets of questions, one on each side of the page. "Page one contains questions that you must answer with a yes or no," he explains. "Underline the answer you choose. Pick the answer that is closest to your view, even though your yes or no may not be absolute. Wait until we're all ready before you turn the page. I'll let you know."

The questions read:

1. Do you like dogs?   Yes No
2. Do you like raw oysters?   Yes No
3. Do you like bagpipe music?   Yes No
4. Do you like to waltz?   Yes No
5. Do you like to eat yellow peppers?   Yes No
6. Would you like to live in Eire?   Yes No
7. Do you wrap silverware in newspapers before you store it?   Yes No

"Now that you have all completed page one," Mr. Enrico continues, "turn the page over, and answer the questions on the second side by underlining either yes or no."

These questions read:

1. Have you ever owned a dog for more than two months?   Yes No
2. Have you ever eaten raw oysters?   Yes No
3. Do you or any members of your family listen to bagpipe music? Yes No
4. Do you know how to waltz?   Yes No
5. Have you eaten yellow peppers fairly often?   Yes No
6. Have you ever been to Eire?   Yes No
7. If you saw a package wrapped in an old newspaper, would you think there was something valuable inside?   Yes No

When the students completed their responses, Mr. Enrico divided the class into groups of six. "Share your answers to each question in turn," he directed. "Then, as a group, decide what this exercise is about."

After students completed their discussion and reported, Mr. Enrico asked the groups to seek consensus and report on the following questions:

(continued)

(continued)

1. Can you really judge something you have had little or no experience with?
2. What risks might there be in jumping to conclusions on hearsay evidence or on the opinion of a friend about something or someone?
3. Is there a difference between jumping to conclusions about something like an oyster or music and jumping to conclusions about a person or a group of people?
4. People are like packages: we can see what they look like on the outside, but we can never be sure of what's inside. What happens when we judge a person by what she wears, eats, or listens to, or by where she lives?

Since values are products of learning experiences, they tend to form slowly. Once "internalized" (i.e., adopted and practiced as one's own), however, values tend to last for relatively long periods and serve as guidelines by which one judges one's own and others' attitudes and behaviors (West & Foster, 1976). New experiences and information can change values and attitudes, sometimes by shifting or reversing them, and sometimes by confirming and strengthening them.

Teachers undoubtedly have a powerful effect on students who are experiencing this process of **personality integration**, which requires making an "adjustment to the environment that is characterized by a positive self-concept, self-control, ethical behavior, social responsibility, and other attributes beneficial to the individual and society" (Klausmeier, 1985, p. 420). This "adjustment" is a process of internalization that progresses through the following sequence of steps (Klausmeier, 1985, pp. 394–403):

♦ *receiving*, or becoming aware of, current values and attitudes; acquiring new information and/or further experiences;
♦ *responding to*, or assuming or participating actively in practicing, a new value or attitude;
♦ *valuing*, or attaching worth to, the new value or attitude, and demonstrating this in behavior;
♦ *organizing*, or bringing together different values and attitudes, thereby beginning to build a consistent value system;
♦ *internalizing*, or adopting and applying, a new value system that shows itself in consistent, stable, behavior patterns.

PRACTICE *and Projects*

1. Discuss the following questions:
   a. How are attitudes developed?
   b. What attitudinal objectives are a legitimate concern of teachers?

2. a. Working in a small group, draw up a profile of a hypothetical student and identify a desired attitudinal change for that student.
   b. Prepare a list of performance objectives that would allow you to assess the desired attitudinal change.

SUMMARY

- Affective education combines instruction and training to make students aware of, and help them to deal with, values and attitudes that shape their behavior, their relationships, and their lives.
- To experience affective growth, students must form healthy and constructive values and attitudes, and deal positively with their feelings and emotions.
- Teachers powerfully affect students who are experiencing the process of personality integration through affective growth; modeling and positive acceptance are potent teaching strategies.

KEY WORDS

affect	commitment	internalization
affective education	concern	
affective growth	emotions	
attitudes	feelings	
awareness	integrated person	

RECOMMENDED READING

Civikly, J. (1992). *Classroom communication: Principles and practice*. Dubuque, IA: Wm. C. Brown.

Good, T. (1987). Two decades of research on teacher expectations: Findings and future directions. *Journal of Teacher Education, 38*(4), 32–48.

Kagen, S. (1992). *Cooperative learning*. San Juan Capistrano, CA: Resources for Teachers.

Johnson, D., & Johnson, R. (1994). *Learning together and alone: Cooperative, competitive and individualistic learning* (4th ed.). Boston, MA: Allyn & Bacon.

Leming, J. (1993). In search of character education. *Education Leadership, 51*(3), 63–71.

Nucci, L. (1987). Synthesis of research on moral development. *Education Leadership, 44*(5), 86–92.

PART 4

Instructional Strategies

■ ■ ■ ■ ■

Part 4 of *Teaching* surveys a range of approaches to effective instruction that help teachers to use many different ways of promoting learners' achievement of specific learning goals. It reviews a number of options available in selecting an instructional approach and suggests how these might be classified. It discusses the factors that might affect your choice and advises on ways of ensuring that you will make appropriate choices. The effectiveness of your teaching will depend heavily on the breadth and depth of your repertoire of instructional approaches, for the wider the choices you can exercise, the better you will be able to plan, deliver, and evaluate your teaching.

Chapter 12 presents the contrasting approaches to teaching inherent in direct and indirect instruction. Direct instruction is an efficient means of providing students with basic information and procedural skills, often through lecture, guided practice, and drill. Indirect instruction provides students with opportunities to "discover" information through guided and/or unguided inquiry and discovery learning, effective strategies for promoting metacognitive (higher-level) and affective learning goals.

Chapter 13 surveys interactive instruction, which stresses interpersonal and group work, particularly through discussion and sharing, experiential instruction, which involves learning cycles consisting of action, reflection, and application that stress process rather than product; and individual study. Individual study offers a variety of learning strategies, including the use of seatwork and homework. All these approaches give students direct responsibility for sharing in the experience of using strategies that can help them to establish patterns of life-long self-instruction.

Chapter 14 deals with individual study and instructional technology. The broad selection of items that make up modern instructional technology can be used productively to interest and involve students in their own advancement in learning.

Cooperative instruction is the focus of Chapter 15. Cooperative instruction stresses the key components of cooperative learning: positive interdependence, face-to-face promotive interaction, group processing, and group self-evaluation. Essentials of cooperative learning are individual responsibility and accountability to the group.

CHAPTER 12

DIRECT AND INDIRECT INSTRUCTIONAL STRATEGIES

■ ■ ■ ■ ■

Most teachers are made, not born ... Knowledge of and ability to apply the variety of ways, patterns, or teaching strategies on the current scene is one of the crucial distinguishing differences between the layman and the professional teacher. Within the profession, possession of a repertoire of strategies is a measure of competency that helps to separate the master teacher from his more limited colleagues.

(GILSTRAP AND MARTIN, 1975, P. 4)

■ ■ ■ ■ ■

OVERVIEW

Chapter 12 outlines the processes of direct and indirect instruction and learning. Direct instruction tends to be teacher centered: among its most commonly applied methods are lecture, practice, and drill. To maintain students' interest, lecture should generally be adapted to their developmental levels and mixed with other instructional methods. To benefit from lecture, students must be taught to take notes. Direct instruction promotes the acquisition of information and skills.

Indirect instruction tends to be learner centered: it commonly involves inquiry instruction, which consists of guided and unguided inquiry. Based on effective questioning skills, inquiry instruction encourages students to investigate a range of topics, often introducing case studies, games, and simulations, while the teacher acts as clarifier and learning facilitator. It is an effective strategy for promoting higher-level cognitive or affective outcomes.

No single learning strategy is equally effective for promoting all domains of knowledge. It is important, therefore, for teachers to vary and balance strategic approaches in order to meet all the instructional needs of their students. Learning strategies should relate to the acquisition of cognitive, procedural, and affective knowledge, as appropriate, for presenting academic content to students is of little use unless they are also "learning how to learn."

Direct and indirect instruction both have their place in the repertoires of effective teachers and in the well-managed classroom. The sections that follow examine these **instructional strategies** and their various strengths and uses.

■ ■ ■ ■ ■
DIRECT INSTRUCTION

Direct instruction can draw on largely teacher-centered strategies that are particularly effective for presenting declarative information in a step-by-step way, through lecture (illustrated with examples and often reinforced by visual materials and handouts), explanation, and the provision of guided practice through oral drills or written seatwork. Direct instruction can be used just as effectively to promote procedural learning through a systematic, small-step, success-oriented approach to the acquisition of simple and complex (multistep) action sequences and skills; a high rate of active learner participation; and careful checks for understanding. Direct instructional strategies are indispensable for helping students to overlearn information and procedures for the mastery of content and process. Figure 12.1 shows the chief components of direct instruction.

Although it is sometimes suggested that direct instruction is easy to plan and use, its effective use involves much more than a teacher's monologue: it requires careful planning, the selection of suitable content, and the integration of other strategies. It should not, however, be overused, since it is important for learners

FIGURE 12.1

Applications of Direct Instruction

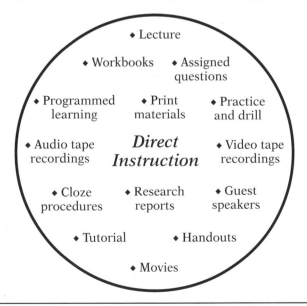

- Lecture
- Workbooks
- Assigned questions
- Programmed learning
- Print materials
- Practice and drill
- Audio tape recordings
- *Direct Instruction*
- Video tape recordings
- Cloze procedures
- Research reports
- Guest speakers
- Tutorial
- Handouts
- Movies

to be comfortable with a broad range of instructional strategies, and to keep the product of cognitive learning in balance with the process of procedural learning. Some of the most common direct instructional strategies are surveyed below.

Lecture

The teaching method most commonly associated with direct instruction is probably lecture, followed by assigned (written) questions. Classroom lectures should not be boring, full-period monologues. Make your lecture sessions as stimulating and challenging as you can, for maintaining a high interest level pays dividends in student learning, as For Example 12.1 illustrates.

A good lecture is like a good speech: the speaker must catch students' interest at the beginning, hold it during the session by delivering pertinent information logically arranged, involve listeners overtly or covertly, and stop before they reach saturation point. Table 12.1 lists a number of suggestions for making lecture an effective teaching strategy.

Straight lecture, delivered well, can be an efficient means of communicating basic facts, concepts, principles, generalizations, points of view, and arguments about a particular area of knowledge. Lecture can also be usefully combined with other techniques, such as discussion, visuals, demonstrations, or question-and-answer sessions. Depending on a variety of circumstances, you might deliver "straight lecture," or combine lecture with other methods of instruction, or use "lecturettes" to prepare your students for seatwork. In whatever form you choose to use lecture, you can personalize your approach by inviting overt, or at least covert, student participation. You will find lecture a valuable part of your instructional repertoire as long as you use it appropriately and selectively, along with other strategies. The proportion of instructional time used for classroom lecture usually increases as the grade level rises.

FOR EXAMPLE 12.1

Dramatic Proof

In one experiment that supports this claim, the researcher arranged for one division of a course to be taught by the usual instructor, while the other was taught by professional actors performing incognito. When term-end examination results were compared, the students taught by the actors proved to have learned and retained "dramatically" more information (Renner, 1983, p. 37).

TABLE 12.1

A Recipe for Effective Lecture

- Plan to begin your lecture-and-assigned-question sessions with stimulating advance organizers or pattern guides to pique your students' interest.
- Adapt the content and your style of presentation to your students' developmental levels by using words and speaking at a rate suitable to those levels. Avoid "talking down."
- Show enthusiasm for the topic you are teaching: your students will not be interested in a topic that does not interest you.
- Reinforce the points of your lecture and provide for transfer by relating key points to your students' experiences, successes, or interests, drawing examples from your class, if possible, but taking care to avoid causing anyone embarrassment.
- Pause to ask for summaries at the beginning of your lesson (past learnings), during the presentation (to check for attention and comprehension and allow for questions), and at the end (to check for comprehension and allow for questions).
- Pause, also, to provide emphasis or give your listeners chances to catch up by summarizing information for themselves.
- Invite covert participation by asking rhetorical questions or suggesting that students note points they may wish to ask about or discuss later on.
- Supplement your lecture by supporting key ideas with a generous number of visuals; use the chalkboard, an overhead projector, charts, or slides.
- Do not read from notes or a text, a procedure that promotes mechanical transfer of information from those sources to your students' notebooks, while leaving the minds and memories of all parties almost undisturbed.
- Do not present too much information at once: two or three major points per half-hour are enough.

SELECTIVE USE OF LECTURE

Selective use of lecture involves remembering that your students' attention span has limits and assessing those limits realistically. It also involves assessing the extent of your students' future need of the information you will deliver: classroom time constraints make it impractical to linger over detailed information that your students are unlikely to need later on and will soon forget.

APPROPRIATE USE OF LECTURE

To use lecture appropriately, you must be sensitive to your students' needs and observe their responses carefully. Take your students' developmental levels and innate learning-style preferences into account (see Chapters 1 & 4), and supplement lecture with other instructional strategies if you observe your students losing interest. Follow up your lecture by checking carefully to ensure that your students understand fully the information you have given them, and by taking time for class discussion that allows for individual differences and provides time for both you and your students to ask questions. Provide opportunities for students to apply newly acquired knowledge, preferably by initiating some activity that involves experiential or hands-on learning.

Lecture can be a useful teaching strategy when

- the subject matter is factual and provides little opportunity for forming opinion or solving problems;
- you need to rouse your students' interest or provide background information before using another method of instruction;
- you are instructing your students in practicing a learning technique; or
- your class is large, teaching time is limited, and critical information must be provided succinctly.

Lecture is not a recommended teaching strategy when

- the content is complex, abstract, or detailed;
- high rates of learning and long-term retention are instructional goals;
- the content deals with feelings and attitudes, or communication, interpersonal or group skills;
- learners must integrate content with previous learning or life experience;
- an experiential approach to learning may be more appropriate; or
- thinking skills or processes and process outcomes are more important than product (informational) outcomes.

TEACHING NOTE TAKING

Before you require your students to take notes during a lecture session, be sure to teach or discuss the process in class, and to provide chalkboard examples and practice. Remember, too, that if students are to take notes effectively, instructors must pace their rate of delivery and pause frequently. If your students are inexperienced in taking notes, monitor their early attempts, and give them plenty of time, feedback, and encouragement. Table 12.2 provides tips for fostering effective note taking.

TABLE 12.2

A Guide to Fostering Effective Note Taking

- ◆ Provide an overview, or outline, of what you intend to present.
- ◆ Present information logically and sequentially, and teach your students to be aware of and listen for structure that will help them to organize their notes.
- ◆ Provide verbal and nonverbal clues, including appropriate pauses and tonal or volume variations, to help your students identify key points and subpoints.
- ◆ Teach your students to paraphrase ideas in order to define concepts for themselves.
- ◆ Encourage your students to ask questions.
- ◆ Avoid dictating notes, unless you must confirm important features such as summaries or definitions.
- ◆ Monitor students' notes to check that they are complete and accurate, or provide time for students to check their notes against the text or other reference materials.
- ◆ Provide or elicit summaries at appropriate points.
- ◆ Have your students practice making point-form notes that they can restructure or "flesh out" later by using reference materials.

USING HANDOUTS

Although it is very important to teach your students note-taking skills and to provide them with opportunities to practice, you may sometimes wish to use handouts instead. Providing handouts has both advantages and disadvantages. On the "plus" side, it conserves time (since you need not pace your lecture to allow students to take notes) and thus allows you to cover more material. It gives both you and your students greater mental freedom: your students are free to think about your presentation and to formulate questions, and you are assured that they will have a correct record of *all* the pertinent material you have covered. On the "minus" side, students' minds have been known to wander without the stimulus of having to concentrate on taking notes. In the end, you will base your decision on handouts versus notes on the ages, developmental stages, and needs of your students; the nature and extent of their learning skills; and whether or not reference materials are available in a text or other readily accessible learning resource.

Practice and Drill

"Practice makes perfect," runs the proverb. Lecture, like some other teaching strategies, is often followed by practice and drill, to promote long-term retention of material learned and/or its instantaneous recall or application. In fact, students may need to overlearn some material to the point of automaticity (see Chapter 9) in order to use it efficiently in new contexts. Practice should stress understanding, and students should learn—and practice—how to transfer a skill or process to another aspect of a subject, other subjects, and extracurricular life.

MAKING PRACTICE AND DRILL EFFECTIVE

The effectiveness of practice and drill in your classroom will depend on the way you conduct them. Well-conducted practice and drill will extend or polish a skill or habit, or help your students to recall and apply information, and generate feelings of accomplishment or success. For practice and drill to be most valuable, original learning must be thorough; in addition, it must be based on students' prior understanding and mastery of information or skills and the provision of sufficient time to overlearn the content to the desired level. Learning must also be a problem-solving process in which each student, with your help or support, explores ways of making connections for him- or herself, linking new content to past and future learnings.

In planning practice and drill, consider whether it is best to review earlier work, provide extensive or intensive practice through short or longer sessions, teach by part or by whole, and practice new skills with the old (see Chapter 9). Determine, too, the point of diminishing returns for effort. Assess your students' levels of skill and recall, and budget time for an appropriate practice schedule. Ensure that materials are sufficient and working conditions appropriate. Before you begin the practice and drill sessions you have planned, make sure that your students clearly understand why they need the skill or information you wish to reinforce, and check that they can perform or recall it correctly so that they are not at risk of learning or practicing errors.

Preface practice sessions with clear demonstrations and directions, and begin with guided (often teacher-led) practice. Space early practice sessions close together, and provide reviews. Drill only a few skills simultaneously; avoid boring your students by using a variety of enjoyable practice situations in which you can provide immediate feedback and positive reinforcement, both verbal and nonverbal. Supervise your students' initial practice sessions closely; supply feedback and corrections, and give generous encouragement. Focus on technique, accuracy, and speed as appropriate, but try to keep your students from becoming unduly product- or error-conscious. Although some pressure is desirable, too much is counterproductive: it is wise to de-emphasize group competition and stress individual performance while recognizing individual differences. To promote transfer, conduct practice under conditions as similar as possible to those that attend the actual use of the skill or information, and provide your students with regular and sufficient opportunities to apply what they have learned.

Practice and drill are not recommended when adequate supervision and immediate feedback are not available to prevent the practice of incorrect responses. Practice and drill are not necessary when procedural skills or recall are not important. Do not select these instructional strategies when the focus of instruction is on creativity, concepts, or values, or on process rather than product ("getting the right answer"). There are times, for instance, when students can easily access information and need not have it at their fingertips. There is no point in taking time away from more important learning to drill trivia of little or no value.

Other Direct Instruction Methods

The direct instruction methods discussed above are not the only means available for varying or individualizing instruction. Other techniques include the use of programmed learning materials: video-, audio-, or slide-tapes: computer-assisted instruction; learning contracts; the development of workbooks; individual or group projects that require information seeking and presentation; group tutorials; panels; debates; **brainstorming** sessions; field trips; and presentations by outside speakers.

EXPLICIT INSTRUCTION

Explicit teaching is a direct instructional strategy for helping students to memorize basic information (e.g., the alphabet) or master well-defined performance skills (e.g., how to add and subtract). This strategy requires setting clear goals for your students, providing enough time to cover teaching of extensive content, using appropriate pacing, ensuring high levels of student time on task, asking many low-level questions that elicit a high level of correct responses, careful monitoring of students' progress, and providing prompt, academically oriented feedback. The most important features of explicit instruction are teaching in small steps, providing guidance during initial practice, having students practice each step of a new process separately, and ensuring a high level of performance success (Rosenshine, 1986, p. 62). For Example 12.2 summarizes the steps involved in explicit teaching. = p. 270-271 + Rp 276

You should *not* take the procedure set out here as a rigid prescription, but adapt it to the needs of your own class. Explain to your students what explicit teaching/learning is, and when and why it is needed. Gradually transfer responsibility for implementing the strategy from yourself to your students by teaching them to observe, access their prior knowledge, construct meaning, monitor their

FOR EXAMPLE 12.2

Steps in Explicit Teaching

1. Motivating students (anticipatory set)
2. Explaining task (purpose and objectives)
3. Presenting new information or skill (input)
4. Modeling (demonstrating)
5. Checking for understanding (observing and questioning)
6. Guided practice (step-by-step, with teacher)
7. Independent practice

Source: Adapted from "Knowing Teaching and Supervising" by M. Hunter, 1984, in P. Hosford (Ed.), *Using What We Know about Teaching*, Alexandria, VA: Association for Supervision and Curriculum Development.

own levels of understanding, organize and relate ideas, and summarize and extend meaning. Educators refer to this process as developing metacognitive (higher-level thinking and organizational) skills. Students need to know about and practice these skills in order to think about what they know, how they learn best, and how to manage their own learning process.

PRACTICE *and Projects*

1. Use Data Collection Form 12.1 (Appendix A) to help you analyze Case Study 12.1. Your instructor may pose specific questions for your response.

2. Plan a lesson on a topic that lends itself to lecture or assigned questions. Share your plan with two peers, and ask for their feedback.

3. Teach a lesson that has effective lecture as a professional target. Provide an observer with Data Collection Form 12.1, and ask for feedback, or complete the form yourself after teaching your lesson.

4. Observe a teacher conducting practice and drill. Use Data Collection Form 12.2 to record your observations.

CASE STUDY **12.1**

LECTURE

Mr. Braun planned to begin a series of lessons on sound and hearing with his Grade 8 class. Although his students had studied the human ear and its structure in Grade 7, Mr. Braun thought he should introduce his lesson series with a review lecture on the nature of sound. The learning goals that he had set were to strengthen research and independent and group study skills through work on individual and group projects.

During recess, Mr. Braun assembled charts and other materials. When the class returned, he began, "I mentioned yesterday that you were going to choose a project about sound and hearing. Can someone tell me why we should all be deeply concerned with this subject?"

Hands were raised all over the classroom. The students Mr. Braun called on responded, "I want to be a musician. I need to hear … We couldn't use the telephone if we couldn't hear … My Dad's a bird watcher, and he learned to imitate lots of birds by listening to their calls … If we couldn't hear cars honking, we wouldn't be as safe on the streets or roads."

"You've got the idea," Mr. Braun encouraged. "Sound and hearing are very important to us in many different ways. You'll find out more about these by working on your projects. First, though, let's review the basic information you need to start work on your projects.

"Your ears are very special equipment. They gather information from every side, and keep you in touch at all times with the world around you." Mr. Braun then explained that sounds are caused by motion, which sends out sound waves in every direction. He took out a metal ruler and held it tight against the edge of the table with about eight inches extending. He twanged the free end, causing the ruler to vibrate and produce a low humming sound.

"What is causing the sound you hear?" Mr. Braun asked.

Jon responded, "The ruler is moving up and down."

"That's right. And why does that make a sound?"

Miriam answered, "I think it has something to do with molecules."

"That's so. Does anyone know how sound is related to molecules?" He paused, but no one volunteered.

Mr. Braun drew a series of diagrams on the chalkboard, showing the effect on air molecules when a ruler moves up, down, and up again. As he

(continued)

(continued)

drew, he explained the diagrams, using the terms *compression* and *expansion*. "While the ruler continues to vibrate and push the air into a pattern of compression and expansion, we hear the disturbance as a humming noise. The air molecules push against one another, transferring the force of the disturbance across the air. The disturbance, which we hear as sound, moves incredibly quickly: 1120 feet (336 m) each second." He drew a wavy line to represent the sound and showed it reaching a human ear.

Next, Mr. Braun demonstrated that plucking a guitar string made it vibrate and cause a sound, though the vibration was harder to observe. The sound was higher pitched as well. When the students noticed this, he explained the differences in compression and expansion between higher-pitched and lower-pitched sounds.

"Remember learning about the human ear?" Mr. Braun put up a large diagram of an ear. "How is it that we 'hear' sounds?" Marc recalled the project he did last year on sound and hearing; and, using the diagram, showed how sound waves are heard. After a discussion, Mr. Braun asked his students to get pen and paper and form their work groups.

When each group was settled in its work area, Mr. Braun gave instructions. "There are many things about sound and hearing that we have not talked about today. There are questions that haven't been answered. Let's have each group prepare a list of the questions that you think need to be answered. We'll pool all our questions to find ideas for each group's research topic. Please record all the questions that your group suggests. When we've put them together, you may choose a topic and start work."

■ ■ ■ ■ ■

INDIRECT INSTRUCTION

Indirect instruction is a learner-centered, "open" approach to education that helps students to practice a range of thinking skills. This approach is based on the premise that, as learners mature, they need to take increasing responsibility for seeking and discovering knowledge for themselves, and to go on to draw conclusions from their learning experience. The basic steps of indirect instruction involve identifying a problem to be investigated by student inquiry until a discovery is made or a solution achieved.

Indirect instruction encourages students to participate in the learning process by taking advantage of their natural interest in making discoveries, suggesting

alternatives and options, and solving problems. It encourages students to expl
many possibilities, and fosters cognitive and affective skills, including problem
solving, decision making, creativity, independent learning, and interpersonal and
social skills. It uses such methods as Socratic questioning (using questions to lead
the responder, by small logical steps, to a particular conclusion) and inductive and
deductive reasoning (see Chapter 10), and stresses personal motivation and involvement, to promote understanding and long-term retention of concepts. Indirect
instruction takes a flexible approach, freeing students to identify basic information
and explore diverse possibilities, and reducing their reluctance to risk giving incorrect answers. Figure 12.2 illustrates the scope of indirect instruction.

Inquiry Instruction: Teaching through Questions

Inquiry instruction, or teaching through skillful questioning, encourages students
to investigate a range of topics, thus taking responsibility for their own learning.
The teacher's role is that of a clarifier and learning facilitator who helps students
to "discover" information and structure its meaning for themselves by making
inferences and generalizations. This strategy consists of two main branches:
guided inquiry and unguided inquiry. The instructional process usually moves

FIGURE 12.2

Applications of Indirect Instruction

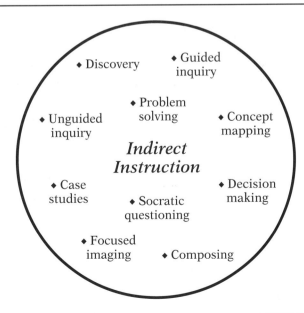

from guided to unguided inquiry as students become more adept at identifying and analyzing problems and structuring solutions. An important aspect of inquiry instruction is the use of assigned (written) questions.

USING INQUIRY INSTRUCTION

Inquiry teaching is a challenging process that requires considerable planning. Before launching your students into an **inquiry**, discover how much experience they have had with inquiry learning. If students' experience is limited, teach and provide practice in inquiry skills and procedures before you have them begin to investigate a topic by inquiry.

Ensure that the topics you select for investigation are curriculum related, and that they are within the scope of your students' developmental levels. Remember that the content of inquiry is its "process" (the experience of working through it), and that achieving a solution may be less important than acquiring procedural skills. Consider, too, that you will be relinquishing some control of the learning process, and that learning outcomes will be less predictable and less "safe." Check that you have adequate facilities, and organize appropriate resources and materials (including data sources) to promote successful learning outcomes (Martin, 1983, p. 62). Figure 12.3 outlines basic steps in using an inquiry model.

In following the steps illustrated in Figure 12.3,

◆ ask open-ended and higher-level questions, solicit and accept divergent responses, and use probes and redirects;

FIGURE 12.3

Basic Steps in Using the Inquiry Model

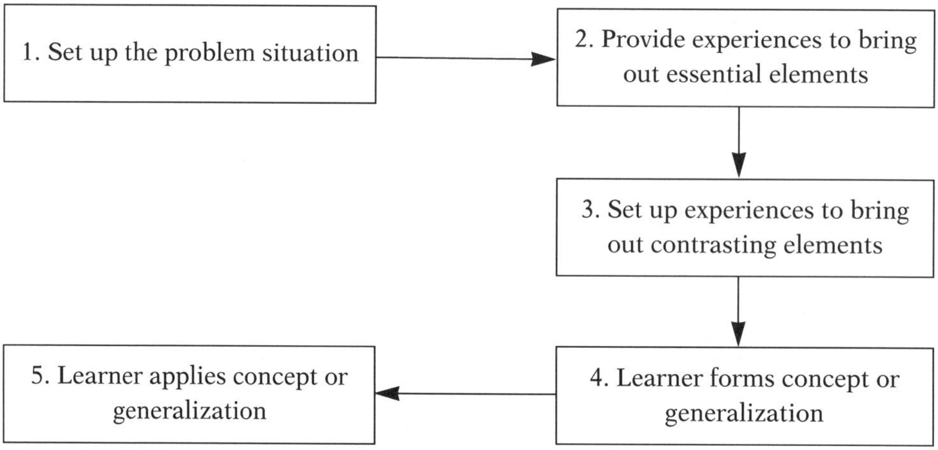

- avoid "telling" answers or suggesting what students must do next; instead, act only as a clarifier or facilitator;
- encourage and reinforce your students in taking more responsibility for making learning discoveries;
- be supportive of their responses, suggestions, and differing views and interpretations, but insist that they back up their comments with logical evidence;
- teach your students how to phrase or write the concepts, principles, or generalizations that they are forming (see Chapter 8);
- encourage them to act on current verified "best answers" (rather than not acting until they find ultimate "truth"), understanding that additional evidence may lead to a new "best answer";
- teach and encourage students to distinguish between "healthy" and "negative" skepticism;
- encourage student–student interaction and sharing by stressing support and cooperation rather than competition;
- point out any errors in logic, misuse of inferences, or generalizations that are too broad, but allow your students to make their own corrections as far as possible, for if you supply corrections, you may defeat the purpose of inquiry;
- be sure to identify errors and verify conclusions and generalizations in nonthreatening ways.

WHEN TO USE INQUIRY MODELS

Inquiry can be part of almost every teaching strategy and method. It is useful when

- you wish to stress cognitive or affective skills or processes;
- procedural learning is more important than content learning;
- students need to "discover" or experience something rather than just hear or read about it;
- learning goals involve decision making or creativity;
- several "right" answers are possible, depending on circumstances.

Inquiry methods are not recommended, however, when learning goals require rapid recall of basic information, or when the emphasis is on memorizing cognitive content or practicing cognitive or affective skills that are to be used later in another context.

Inquiry Processes

The basic processes of inquiry are closely associated with critical thinking skills(see Chapter 10, p. 231). Every student, no matter what his or her aptitude for learning, can and should spend classroom time learning and practicing inquiry processes in a systematic way, in order to open doors to educational realms beyond textbooks.

There are two main branches of inquiry instruction: "guided inquiry" is a process carefully structured to lead students to make a specific discovery or generalization (an informed conclusion about a class or category of matters); "unguided inquiry" (free discovery) is a process that allows students to take responsibility for investigating a topic by formulating questions, choosing the best methods of pursuing answers, and then conducting a study from which they draw conclusions and make generalizations. Figure 12.4 diagrams an overview of guided and unguided inquiry.

GUIDED INQUIRY

Guided inquiry is a useful strategy for moving students gradually from direct to indirect instruction. In teaching through guided inquiry, you will act as a learning

FIGURE 12.4

Overview of Guided and Unguided Inquiry

> *Guided Inquiry*
> Teacher carefully guides students toward a
> discovery or generalization

> *Unguided Inquiry*
> Students are given responsibility for formulating
> questions, selecting methods of inquiry, drawing
> conclusions, and making generalizations

> *Steps for Both*
> 1. Problem identification
> 2. Tentative research hypothesis and objectives
> 3. Data collected; tentative results tested
> 4. Data interpreted
> 5. Tentative conclusions or generalizations
>   formed
> 6. Conclusions applied or retested
> 7. Original conclusions revised

facilitator: you will ask questions and use prompts, cues, and probes to obtain thoughtful responses; make available appropriate educational materials; and structure learning situations and activities, becoming the major organizer of experiences that help your students to achieve learning goals. You will also teach your students to develop systematic learning habits, and to make and record observations from which they will draw inferences and ultimately make generalizations.

Prompting Responses

Your chief function in guided inquiry instruction is to interact with your students, asking them questions and prompting thoughtful responses. Some stems for prompting responses were provided in Table 7.2 (see p. 166) Such prompts can help students to understand all kinds of relationships, which is a goal of inquiry and investigation. You might support the questions suggested in Table 7.2 with pictures, models, or other visuals, particularly when teaching younger children or children who lack firsthand experience of the object of the inquiry.

UNGUIDED INQUIRY

Unguided inquiry is an open-ended teaching strategy that targets raising both students' interest in learning and the degree of personal responsibility they take for the learning process. In using unguided inquiry, you will provide your students with opportunities to interact through making "discoveries" and then questioning and exploring what they have observed; encourage them to plan, conduct, and evaluate their own learning experiences by teaching them to observe and examine occurrences, objects, or data; train them to analyze and evaluate evidence, make inferences, test hypotheses, and discover meaningful structure or patterns that lead them to form virtually unlimited generalizations; and motivate them to exercise creativity. Challenging inquiries can stimulate classroom discussions in every school subject, encouraging students to share their inferences and generalizations so that all class members can benefit from one another's perceptions.

"Discovery" Learning

Indirect instruction promotes **discovery learning** through the skills of observation, investigation, reasoning (see Chapter 10), drawing inferences, or forming hypotheses (see Chapter 8) that go beyond the information at hand.

GUIDED DISCOVERY

Guided discovery encourages students to identify for themselves the principles and processes involved in acquiring a skill by "discovering" its successive steps and their relation. This approach, which can be useful in speeding learning and promoting transfer, often includes asking questions (see Chapter 7) that will help students to discover the processes and summarize the steps or principles involved in a skill before you model or demonstrate them.

As your students practice a skill, you will help individuals by asking them what they think should be done as a next step, and why. When the students have practiced independently, and you are reviewing the skill, you will ask questions that stress both the "how" (methods) and the "why" (reasons) of performance.

The Discovery Process

The following steps (Womack, 1966, p.13) will be useful in helping your students make discoveries (i.e., form generalizations or solve problems) through guided inquiry processes:

* Decide on the information you wish your students to discover from a particular unit of study, the inferences you wish them to draw from that information, and the generalization(s) you wish them to form on the basis of their learning experiences.
* Organize learning materials and activities in ways that will expose to your students the strands or parts of the generalization(s) that you wish them to form.
* Ask your students to write a summary of the unit content.
* Ask them to identify the sequence of the pattern of events comprising the content, omitting references to particular people, places, or times.
* Ask them to synthesize the various parts of the pattern of events into one complete sentence that generalizes the information they have gleaned.
* Ask them to offer proof that the generalization they have formed is valid, by citing examples of its existence and operation in other periods and places, and among other peoples.

Other Indirect Instruction Strategies

Indirect instruction involves the use of a variety of teaching strategies ranging from question-and-answer interludes during a lecture to totally unguided inquiry, in which students work completely on their own and the teacher serves only as a resource person. It may involve students in debates, panels, field studies, research reports, group investigation, brainstorming, and simulations.

Using Indirect Instruction Effectively

Since the fundamental goal of indirect instruction is to help students become self-sufficient learners, teachers must carefully plan and sequence learning activities and experiences that promote growth in procedural and affective skills and processes. Rather than telling, teachers should *ask* for information, using open-ended questions, prompts, and probes, and accept divergent responses (see Chapter 7).

You will need to create a classroom environment that offers opportunities for student involvement; in addition, you must provide prompt descriptive feedback and give help as requested. In this climate, students should engage actively in learning by discovering concepts and principles that make their experiences meaningful to them (see Chapter 8), and in transferring their learning to new situations.

Although indirect instruction is less structured than direct instruction, students are more directly involved and so busy that there is usually less need for teacher control. Your role will likely shift, therefore, from that of lecturer/director to that of facilitator/supporter/resource person who provides little direct information, but creates situations in which students can learn on their own. Of course, since indirect instruction calls for minimal teacher input, it exposes students to content more slowly than does direct instruction, and produces outcomes that are less predictable or "safe." Initially, this element of risk may cause you difficulty and frustration with some aspects of indirect instruction, and you may wish for a more evident structure. If so, remember that direct and indirect approaches can and should be combined as appropriate, for it is neither necessary nor wise to "tell" your students everything you wish them to know or to ask them to rediscover all knowledge for themselves. Some content is taught and learned most efficiently through direct instruction and some through indirect instruction.

Indirect instruction is not recommended when the desired learning outcome is acquisition of information, memorization of content, "finger-tip" recall, or step-by-step skill performance. Nor is it the strategy of choice when appropriate materials or facilities are not available, or when students have not been trained to use inquiry, decision-making, or problem-solving procedures.

PRACTICE *and Projects*

1. Using Data Collection Form 12.3 (Appendix A), analyze Case Study 12.2, above. Your instructor may pose specific questions for your response.

2. In a subject-specialization group, brainstorm topics that you and your peers might teach effectively using indirect instruction strategies.

3. Using Data Collection Form 12.3, plan and microteach a lesson targeting indirect instruction strategy.

CASE STUDY 12.2

INDIRECT INSTRUCTION

Ms. Jacques, a teacher-in-training in a Grade 4 class, has found that the students participate enthusiastically in most activities, but often become highly competitive. Ms. Jacques has tried to use small-group learning, but the children, finding it difficult to follow the instructions and support the structure of group learning, appear to lose interest almost before a task begins. Ms. Jacques, unhappy with the results of trying to enforce her basic expectations, decides to try a less direct instructional approach.

Ms. Jacques explains to the class that they will form three groups to work on a project at three different work stations. She reads out clearly the names of the children assigned to each group and work station, and gives instructions for the task. This time, however, she does not explain how to work together in groups. As the children gather at the work stations, Ms. Jacques' cooperating teacher and teaching partner each attaches herself to one group, leaving Ms. Jacques to work with the third. Both of the other groups receive direction and coaching as they work. They resolve disagreements without fuss and keep on task.

In Ms. Jacques' group, however, work does not go smoothly. The children quarrel over the materials and disagree about their task, and three of them compete strongly for leadership. Difficult as it is, Ms. Jacques keeps to her plan and does not intervene. At the end of the period, her group has not completed its task, whereas the other two groups proudly display finished products. With prompting from their respective learning facilitators, they explain how they worked to complete their tasks.

Ms. Jacques then gathers her group together and asks them how they feel about their group work. They mumble that they wish they had finished their task so that they could have had something to show the other groups.

"I wonder why we didn't finish?" Ms. Jacques says. "Did we understand the task we had to do?" Heads nod as the group agrees that they knew what to do. "Did we have the materials?" she continues.

"We had everything," Jesse volunteers. "We just didn't do our job right."

"That's right," adds Ari. "We should have started working instead of arguing."

"If we'd chosen a leader, she could have made sure that we listened to everyone's ideas, and we could have decided how to do our project sooner," offers Amanda.

(continued)

(continued)

"And better!" Pat breaks in. "I still have a great idea about getting started."

"I wanted to be the one who drew our invention," Kiyo said, "but I should have shared instead of keeping all the markers myself."

"We wasted our time," said Simon.

"I wish we could still do our project," Ari says. "I'd miss recess if we could."

The others agree. "Well, I think that's possible," says Ms. Jacques. "It sounds as if you have good ideas of how to work as a group now. Maybe we didn't waste our time if we've learned ways *not* to work in a group. Let's list the things we want to do as we work on our project. Then we'll decide when we can get together to have another go at it."

Balancing Teaching Strategies

The teaching strategies you choose are meant to help your students learn and use instructional content effectively, and your choice will strongly affect the outcome of your students' learning experiences. "Content," in this sense, includes both subject matter and also cognitive, procedural, affective, communication, interpersonal, and group skills. You will need to balance your use of teaching strategies to help your students become proficient in all these areas of learning and living. Where possible, use interactive approaches, including student–teacher discussion and peer teaching. This last approach, particularly when used to teach higher-order thinking, will lead to higher achievement by students of all achievement levels.

The methods of instruction outlined in this chapter have various uses, strengths, and limitations. Your students and classes will vary greatly, too, and you will need to be constantly alert to group and individual needs in order to combine and apply the most productive "mix" of teaching strategies to achieve a broad range of instructional goals. To succeed, you will need to

- reflect constantly on professional development targets;
- develop a consistently expanding repertoire of effective instructional skills;
- carefully observe individual and group dynamics within your classroom and school.

Above all, you will need to keep an open mind in selecting a variety of teaching strategies that will provide information, skills, and affective development appropriate to students' learning levels, while focusing on the ultimate target of equipping individuals to learn productively and independently throughout their lives.

TABLE 12.3

Criteria for Selecting an Instructional Strategy

◆ Have you prepared yourself, by planning, training, and practice, to use the strategy productively? Does the strategy suit your teaching style?

◆ Does your classroom schedule allow time for productive use of the strategy you have chosen?

◆ Is the cost of using the strategy reasonable in terms of the school's budget? your resources as a teacher?

◆ What kinds of content does the strategy involve? Cognitive? Procedural? Affective? Combination?

◆ Is your classroom adaptable? Has it the necessary equipment?

◆ Is the strategy appropriate to your students' developmental levels? to their cognitive, psychomotor, and moral or emotional levels? Have your students had previous experience with the content, strategy, and teaching methods involved? Is the strategy adaptable to your students' preferred learning styles?

◆ Will the strategy motivate your students? catch their interest? complement their background? Will it be congruent or compatible with their previous experience of success? Will it replace "deferred successes" with successes?

◆ How deeply do your students need to understand the content? Will they need to recall it? Does it call for performance?

◆ Will the strategy you are considering provide the most effective way to meet your instructional objectives?

PRACTICAL CONSIDERATIONS

Table 12.3 outlines a number of practical considerations that you should reflect on before you select a particular instructional strategy.

PRACTICE *and Projects*

1. In a class session, describe and discuss the inquiry approaches used by cooperating teachers that you and your peers have observed. Do not use teachers' names.

2. In a subject-specialization group, brainstorm topics that you and your peers could teach effectively by using guided or unguided inquiry strategies.

(continued)

(continued)

3. a. Join a subject-interest group to design a lesson using guided inquiry.

   b. Using the same lesson topic, design a lesson using unguided inquiry.

   c. Microteach your lessons while the class observes and provides feedback, or compare the two instructional approaches in your subject-interest group.

4. a. Form subject-specialization groups of six. In each group, choose a lesson topic that lends itself to questions and answers.

   b. Compose a series of questions on your chosen topic that will move students through the levels of Bloom's cognitive domain (see Chapter 10, pp. 225).

SUMMARY

- ◆ Plan and promote curriculum-related inquiry instruction to challenge students and help them take increasing responsibility for their own learning.
- ◆ Ensure that you have appropriate facilities, resources, and materials, and that your students are adequately prepared for inquiry instruction.
- ◆ Focus on "process" rather than "product" in implementing inquiry models.
- ◆ Inquiry instruction may be guided (involving teacher direction) or unguided (stressing learners' self-direction). Move students gradually from the former type into the latter.
- ◆ Do not try to use inquiry instruction to promote rapid recall of basic information, memorization of cognitive content, or practice in cognitive or affective skills to be used later in another context.

KEY WORDS

cognitive skills	guided discovery	metacognitive skills
direct instruction	guided inquiry	note taking
lecture	indirect instruction	planning
practice	inquiry	procedural skills
drill	instruction	processes
explicit	discovery learning	unguided inquiry
instruction	instruction strategies	

RECOMMENDED READING

Bellon, J., Bellon, E., & Blank, M. (1992). *Teaching from a research knowledge base: A development and renewal process*. New York: Merrill.

Gall, M., Gall, J., Jacobsen, D., & Bullock, T. (1990). *Tools for learning: A guide to teaching study skills*. Alexandria, VA: Association for Supervision and Curriculum Development.

Hunter, M. (1982). *Mastery teaching*. El Segundo, CA: Cambridge University Press.

Orlich, D., Harder, R., Callahan, R., Kauchak, D., Pendergrass, R. & Jeighm A. (1990). *Teaching strategies*. (3rd ed.). Lexington, MA: Heath.

Resnick, L., & Kloper, L. (Eds.). (1989). *Toward the thinking curriculum: Current cognitive research*. Alexandria, VA: Association for Supervision and Curriculum Development.

Rosenshine, B. (1986). Synthesis of research on explicit teaching. *Educational Leadership*, *43*(7), 60–69.

CHAPTER 13

INTERACTIVE AND EXPERIENTIAL INSTRUCTIONAL STRATEGIES

■ ■ ■ ■ ■

Groups are highly important to people because they satisfy a variety of human needs. Yet in North America, in contrast to … Japan, we have not yet mastered the art of working effectively in groups … Because of the nature of our work, educating, we must make a special effort, and … set an example to other segments of the work force, to learn to make groups work.

(KNOOP, 1986, P. 16)

[Learning is] the process whereby knowledge is created through the transformation of experiences.

(KOLB, 1984, P. 38)

■ ■ ■ ■ ■

OVERVIEW

Interactive instructional strategy promotes active student involvement in the learning process, and emphasizes discussion and sharing. This strategy is useful in groups that range in size from a whole class to small work units, triads, or pairs. Effective group operation depends on the teaching and use of communication and interpersonal skills. The teacher should monitor group activities and intervene as necessary.

Experiential instructional strategies involve students actively in a cycle that begins with action (experiencing), moves through reflection (sharing, analyzing, and inferring), and ends with application. When application is in progress, the cycle can begin again. The content of experiential instruction is process rather than product, and the process often uses multisensory, affective, and reasoning experiences. Many students acquire a more positive attitude to learning when they are invited to share in identifying and selecting learning experiences that take account of their psychological and cultural characteristics and needs.

Experiential instruction methods can be used to teach both subject-specific skills and the common essential learnings that are most likely to be transferred into life experiences.

■ ■ ■ ■ ■

INTERACTIVE INSTRUCTION

The term *interactive* describes a pattern of communication and relations between two or more persons in which the behavior of one directly stimulates the behavior of the other(s) (McNeil & Wiles, 1990, p. 185). By extension, **interactive instr** **tion** is a student-centered approach to teaching/learning that relies heavily on guided or open discussion and sharing, often involving question-and-answer exchanges and cooperative small-group work. It encourages students to react and respond to the knowledge, experience, insights, and ideas of their teachers and peers, as well as to reflect on their own experience (Seaman & Fellenz, 1989, p. 119). In learning from their peers, students gain practice in organizing their own thoughts, framing rational arguments, and developing social skills. Personal reflection teaches them to generate different ways of thinking and feeling, and to state personal viewpoints. Figure 13.1 illustrates interactive instructional strategy and the methods associated with it.

Selecting Interactive Objectives, Content, and Strategies

Like indirect instruction, interactive education increases learner participation and reduces the need for direct teacher intervention. The need for careful teacher planning and preparation still remains, however. To use interactive instruction effectively, you will need well-developed observation, listening, instruction, and

FIGURE 13.1

Components of Interactive Instruction

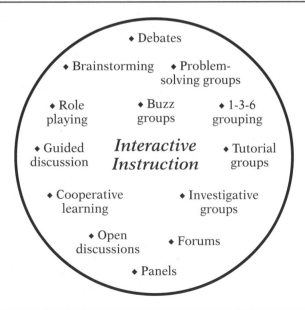

◆ Debates

◆ Brainstorming ◆ Problem-
solving groups

◆ Role
playing ◆ Buzz
groups ◆ 1-3-6
grouping

◆ Guided
discussion *Interactive
Instruction* ◆ Tutorial
groups

◆ Cooperative
learning ◆ Investigative
groups

◆ Open
discussions ◆ Forums

◆ Panels

intervention skills, and your students will need you to teach them good communication, interpersonal, and group skills. Groups of more than twelve students require more structure and leadership than do smaller groups.

In choosing to use interactive instruction, you accept responsibility for selecting appropriate lesson objectives and content, structuring effective interaction patterns, and being flexible in your choice of teaching strategies. If, for instance, you wish to strengthen your students' motivation, increase their active participation, and ensure a high rate of learning retention, you should choose interactive strategies that foster these objectives. If you wish to promote recall of information and performance of step-by-step skills, you might decide to use instructor or peer tutoring. If you wish your students to acquire high-level cognitive, decision-making, or interpersonal skills, you should use strategies that call for investigation and critical or creative thinking. To promote cross-cultural understanding, you might use cooperative learning methods.

Whole-Class Interactive Instruction

You will often teach your class as a whole, particularly when presenting information or step-by-step skills, or when conducting a class discussion. While you will sometimes need to use a highly teacher-centered method of whole-class instruction, you will often find that students learn and retain more by participating interactively in the development of a lesson. To establish a positive learning climate and to increase the productivity of your class and component small groups, you will need to provide training in group participation, for students must be taught how to participate effectively through learning and using group-process and discussion skills.

Your Class as Social System and Work Group

Every class is a social system affected by friendships, power and influence, communication patterns, member roles, and school, peer, and classroom norms. Attraction patterns affect, to some extent, the way individuals interact, and how well the class functions. Positive interaction and participation improve individual self-concept, thus reducing apprehension and making students more comfortable with one another. In the climate of positive peer influence that emerges, students are free to risk attempting a wider range of learning activities, and the class can develop into a mature group that learns more efficiently and interacts more productively.

Whole-Class Discussion

Whole-class or large-group discussion is meant to promote and strengthen students' skills of analysis and interpretation, to shape their attitudes, and to develop their skills of positive interaction. Large-group (class) discussion requires teacher and students to interact verbally; its objective is to help students value their contributions and increase their sense of contributing to their own and others' learning experience.

Class discussion is based on recognition that knowledge is more than the ability to produce correct answers, and that active student participation in creative inquiry can produce good communication skills and knowledge rooted in understanding. Discussion can be adapted to many classroom situations. If, for instance, during a presentation you notice that your students are particularly interested in a topic, and you involve them in a class discussion, a "magic moment" may occur in which teaching and learning combine to produce an unforgettable "instructional event." Such events help to build a positive classroom climate and active student interest in a school subject. Data Collection Form 13.1 (Appendix A) will help you observe and target large-group instruction methods when you are microteaching a lesson.

Guided Discussion

Discussion that is carefully guided, step-by-step, by means of thought-provoking questions and the timely interjection of information is termed **guided discussion**. Its chief purpose is to promote the understanding of important concepts, but it is also useful for helping students review material or for promoting the application of learning.

Your role in guided discussion is to be a leader and a source of authority or, when required, of information. You will seek wide participation and elicit necessary information by making frequent use of convergent questions, prompts, and probes (see Chapter 7). You might wish to review the principles of guided inquiry (see Chapter 12), since they are very similar to those of guided discussion.

Open Discussion

Open discussion makes more demands on the teacher than does guided discussion, but it can be exciting and rewarding, as it flows much more freely. When you choose discussion as a method of instruction, it becomes your responsibility to plan and monitor the degree of openness that you consider most beneficial to your class. Help your students grow by giving them the freedom to take their discussions as far as they can in productive directions. When student-student discussion is flowing freely and on track, you should intervene only to encourage, mediate, broaden participation, provide necessary information, or reinforce conclusions. Avoid overuse of questions, since they might impede students' interaction. Be genuine and businesslike, and treat each student with respect, avoiding and discouraging inappropriate behavior such as judging, blaming, attacking, placating, distracting others' attention, showing off, or rudeness.

There are, of course, degrees of openness: completely open discussion consists largely of interchanges among students. Although such discussion can be an exciting way to involve students in high-level creative thinking, its outcomes are unpredictable. Relatively mature students may be able to sustain and benefit from completely open discussion, but less sophisticated students may have trouble staying on track.

THE TEACHER'S ROLE

Facilitating effective class discussions involves using a range of skills: you will need to plan, motivate, listen constructively, encourage participation, focus contributions, set boundaries, ask for examples, seek and paraphrase additional information, welcome diverse opinions, check for listeners' feelings, probe to discover bases of opinions, promote positive interaction, encourage high-level critical and creative thinking and original expression, keep discussion on track, and elicit summaries, without pushing the class toward predetermined conclusions. Class discussion should resemble a business-like, or focused, conversation that is student centered. Teach, review, and model the rules of common courtesy to be sure that students understand and accept them. Make it plain that students may challenge ideas, but should never attack personalities. Train your students to conclude discussion with consensus, a solution, or a summary, preferably made by themselves. You and your students will enjoy and learn from participation in discussions of this sort.

Choosing a Topic

The topic you choose for classroom discussion might be an issue that has no "correct" answer or a problem to which students wish to discover a solution. It must be one, however, that your students know something about and are interested in, for productive discussions are based on material familiar to the participants: students should never simply "pool ignorance." It is important for you to ensure that the whole class understands the terms and concepts involved, and to stress that opinions offered must be supported by evidence. You may need to set the stage by motivating students to engage in discussion, or the students themselves may ask to discuss a pertinent issue.

Involving All Students

All students in a class should have chances to contribute to their own and their peers' learning experiences. When a few eager or aggressive students dominate discussions, others tend to "tune out" or to participate only passively. If you find that some students are monopolizing class discussions, you can use a simple diagram to record interaction patterns as a first step to moving discussion from one person to another. Figure 13.2 provides an example. To diagram interaction patterns, draw a single short stroke, at five-second intervals, to show where the discussion is centered at that point. Draw arrows to show the interactions that occur. By observing and reflecting on the resulting pattern, you can significantly improve student interaction.

FIGURE 13.2

Teacher–Student and Student–Student Interaction Analysis

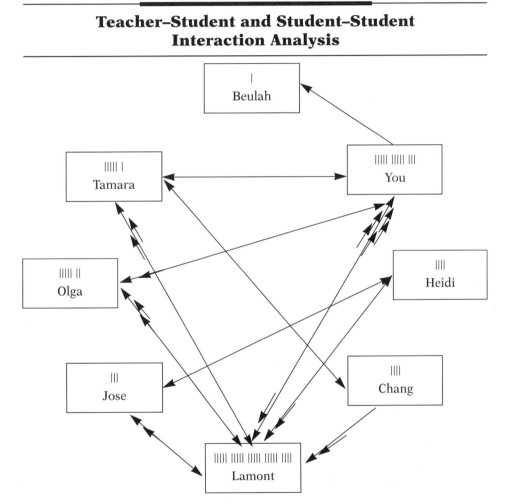

The diagram shows the following:
- ◆ very low teacher control;
- ◆ discussion centered on Lamont (24 tallies);
- ◆ Lamont initiated conversation 15 times;
- ◆ other participants collected 3–7 tallies each;
- ◆ Beulah did not participate.

Encouraging Participation

You can do much to encourage positive and productive participation in class or group discussions by teaching your students to listen attentively and take turns speaking clearly and to the point. You might use the following techniques to help your students interact and participate positively in discussions:

♦ To promote listening skills, have students, during some discussions, paraphrase the previous speaker's words before they may speak.

♦ To achieve more balanced student participation, designate a student to act as participation monitor by passing a note to advise a student that he or she is speaking too long or too often during a discussion.

♦ Use a "limited number of entries" system to allow everyone a turn to speak.

♦ Distribute "time tokens" to equalize participation. Each student receives tokens designating short periods of time (e.g., 10–30 seconds). Students may contribute to the discussion until they have used up all their tokens.

♦ Hand a beach ball to younger students as a sign to start the discussion. Only the person with the ball may speak. Any student who wishes to speak raises a hand, and the holder of the ball passes it to him or her. You might sometimes arrange that students must pass the ball to someone who has not yet spoken. When all have spoken, the procedure can begin again.

Data Collection Form 13.2 (Appendix A) will help you observe and target group participation when you are microteaching a lesson.

PRACTICE *and Projects*

1. a. Working with a partner, list at least three topics that could motivate discussion at the grade level of your choice.

    b. Join three more sets of partners with similar subject and grade-level suggestions. Take turns at choosing one of the suggestions and chairing a five-minute discussion on the subject of your choice.

2. Use Data Collection Form 13.1 (Appendix A) to help you analyze Case Study 13.1. Your instructor may pose specific questions for your response.

3. Use Data Collection Form 13.2 to help you observe and target group participation as you microteach a lesson.

Small-Group Interactive Instruction

Small-group instruction develops students' higher-level cognitive, interactive, and communication skills, and increases their accountability and independence.

CASE
STUDY **13.1**

**LARGE-GROUP
DISCUSSION**

Mr. Shaw and his Grade 8 students begin each day with open discussion. As the students come into class, they pull their desks into a circle, where Mr. Shaw joins them. The topic of discussion varies, but it usually comes from the class; students take turns chairing the discussion. Though it is not compulsory to take a turn, most students do.

Since Mr. Shaw taught interpersonal and communication skills earlier in the year, his students chair the discussions with confidence. The chair's role is to help choose a topic, introduce the topic, keep the discussion on topic, encourage balanced participation, and bring the discussion to conclusion. Mr. Shaw clarifies or summarizes as required, modeling effective group skills.

Today, the students have just heard about a police shooting of a young man in a high-speed chase of a stolen vehicle. The students feel strongly about the "rights and wrongs" of the shooting, and there has been heated discussion on the school grounds and in the corridors.

It is Naomi's turn to chair. She begins, "Can everyone see and hear? Some people want to talk about the police shooting. Do you agree?" Most students agree, but Jason, who is an avid sports fan, suggests that they discuss the nearly completed World Series. There are many moans and several comments in support of discussing the shooting. "Is anyone else interested in discussing the World Series?" Naomi asks.

"I'd be interested another time," Morgan responds, "but I think the shooting story is more important now."

"I think so too," adds Jason. "It's the third shooting this year, and my Dad says that the police need better training."

Naomi looks around the group. "Do you all agree on this story, then?" The students nod. "OK, Jason?"

"Yeah," Jason replies, "but let's not forget to talk about the Series tomorrow. We could each pick the team we favor to win."

"OK," Naomi begins. "Who knows the whole story of what happened with the shooting? We need the facts."

Alyson gives an overview of what she heard on the news, and several classmates add details. Discussion becomes so intense that Naomi has to intervene to prevent some students from interrupting and dominating the group. Some support the police action, pointing out that stealing is wrong

(continued)

(continued)

and that driving at high speeds is very dangerous. Others empathize with the young man, whose crime seems minor compared to the police action. Many of the students state or restate their views. Few seem to listen closely to other participants' arguments or questions. Some become more emotional as they sense that their peers are not listening.

Finally, Mr. Shaw intervenes. "Let's see if we can identify the issues here. I hear some of you saying that because stealing is wrong, people who steal should be punished. I hear others saying that stealing is wrong, but the police should not shoot someone for stealing. You've identified an issue about stealing and an issue about appropriate police action. Are there any other issues?"

"The boy who was shot was Afro-American," responds Hamad. "My parents say that the police treat white people differently from Afro-Americans. Everyone the police have shot this year has been Afro-American." Some students agree, though others argue that people from minority groups are more likely to be shot because they commit more crimes.

Naomi seeks consensus on the issues, and everyone agrees that stealing is wrong. There is disagreement, however, on the fitness of the police action. As the discussion draws to a close, it is evident that the group will not reach consensus. Naomi asks for a summary of positions, and the discussion ends with their review.

Mr. Shaw makes himself a note to think of ways in which he can build on the content of this discussion in other classes. He intends to have his students expand on this topic in both Social Studies and English.

Moreover, good group teaching/learning methods can promote self-discipline and reduce classroom management problems (Stanford, 1977). Think carefully about the way you select and use small-group teaching methods. Ensure that your classroom climate is open, friendly, and nonthreatening so that group members will feel "safe" to contribute to discussion. Data Collection Form 13.3 will help you to plan small-group activities.

SMALL-GROUP DISCUSSION

Effective small-group discussions do not happen by accident. They result from careful nurturing of appropriate communication skills. Complex social conditions make it imperative for schools to teach skills that will equip students to lead useful, responsible, and productive lives.

Your Role as Teacher

Consider the content of the lesson you are planning, the resources needed, and the needs of individual students. Reflect on your choices of group size and membership, and see that your classroom is arranged to serve group work, that appropriate materials are available, and that seating is arranged to encourage face-to-face communication and allow students to work together without violating personal space.

Ensure that students acquire the basic skills for working together by determining their readiness to work in small groups and, if necessary, providing practice through activities that gradually build group-effectiveness skills—verbal and social interaction, group participation, goal setting, consensus seeking, problem solving, decision making, conflict resolution, and monitoring for group effectiveness—before you expect small groups to function effectively on their own. Use practice sessions to help your students deal productively with you and one another, and to promote their use of responsible, self-monitored learning methods. You may train your class as a whole or in small groups as the need arises.

Organize small groups of five to nine members and arrange face-to-face seating to encourage communication. Tell the groups their meeting times and the date on which you expect them to complete a task. Present content clearly, and monitor participation and interaction carefully, applying the general principles discussed here and in Chapter 2. Train your students to begin each meeting by identifying their task and to end by evaluating task completion and group effectiveness. Have groups report on their discussions, orally or in writing. Establish an operational routine, and stress the importance of task accomplishment, but make it clear that consensus is not always possible or required.

Some teachers have used small-group discussion unsuccessfully and have dismissed it, complaining that "The students just sat there like bumps on logs!" or "They just waste their time socializing!" or "I have far too much important material to cover to use small groups." The problem in the first two instances may have been that the students were not fully prepared to participate in small-group discussion, or that the topics suggested did not meet their interests and needs. In the third instance, the teacher may not have understood that small-group methods lend themselves better to some kinds of content than to others.

Students' Role

Small groups function and produce effectively to the extent that students understand the duties of group leaders and participants. All students should be aware that leaders and other members have specific duties, and that all are accountable for group performance.

A group leader's duties are to see that the group's task or problem is clarified; to initiate discussion and keep it on topic and moving; to ensure that all phases of a task or problem are addressed; to encourage full participation by drawing out noncontributors; to be objective; to paraphrase and clarify statements or have others do so; to see that summaries are made and that a conclusion is reached; to see that all members are treated with respect; and to report the group's thoughts fairly or ensure that a reporter does so.

Members' duties are to be present on time for all group sessions; to accept responsibility for their behavior; to be genuine and open; to take an active part in contributing information and ideas; to help maintain a positive group spirit; to respect and interact with other members, listen when they speak, and hear them out; to support others by seeking and being open to their ideas and suggestions; to be sensitive to the feelings and concerns of others; to respect individual differences; to help clarify, mediate, encourage, summarize, and praise; to use problem-solving, decision-making, and conflict-resolution skills; to confine argument to ideas and avoid personal attacks; to act as group leader, recorder, or group-effectiveness monitor, as appropriate; to avoid "showing off" or talking about off-task or off-topic matters; to avoid prejudices; and to reject biases and self-serving, judgmental, blaming behavior.

Students should be taught and expected to share all the following roles during small-group discussion. An *initiator* helps the group organize, gets discussion under way, and keeps it moving toward the goal. A *contributor* offers relevant opinions, facts, anecdotes, or examples. A *clarifier* ensures that all group members understand the task, terms, and contributions offered. If necessary, he or she suggests seeking more information. A *summarizer* sums up what has been discussed or learned to a particular point, ensuring that all members understand the group's positions. An *evaluator* keeps track of the group's progress and tactfully points out any problems the group may be having in working together. A *recorder* notes the main points and conclusions reached in discussion, sometimes reading back information to help the group recall or verify data. An *encourager* invites participation, listens carefully, is friendly, and compliments members on appropriate contributions. A *peace keeper* pours oil on troubled waters by relieving tension, sometimes through humor, suggesting and promoting compromises, and settling disputes (Stanford & Roark, 1974, p. 103).

OTHER SMALL-GROUP METHODS

At least one effective method of small-group instruction is applicable to almost any content. The first three methods discussed below are particularly useful for building students' confidence and encouraging their participation. Data Collection Form 13.4 (Appendix A) will help you observe and target small-group instruction methods when you are microteaching a lesson.

"Think, Pair, Share"

In using the **think, pair, share** method (Lyman, 1985), begin with a short presentation, and then ask your students to spend a minute or two thinking, on their own, about an issue or generalization that you have raised. Next, pair students, and have them share their thinking. You might ask partners to take turns making and paraphrasing statements until both agree on the meaning. At that point, have each pair report to two or three other pairs, or some pairs report to the whole class. The process is complete when all major ideas have surfaced.

"Brainstorming"

Small groups or individuals may use **brainstorming** in almost any teaching/learning situation to initiate active participation and provide a refreshing change of pace. "Team" brainstorming can resemble a game that promotes friendly and enjoyable competition. The process works as follows:

- Assign four to nine participants to a particular problem.
- Give the group five to ten minutes to suggest and record as many solutions to the problem as possible.

The chief objective of brainstorming is to generate a large number of ideas without stopping to judge their value or implications, with the understanding that one or some of them will later be explored, improved, or combined. By providing a nonthreatening climate, brainstorming can relieve any pressure to produce an immediate "right" answer, release students' creative potential, promote freedom of expression, and lead to solutions for seemingly insoluble problems. Because students find the process fun, it motivates their thinking and encourages them to speak out.

Like other teaching methods, brainstorming has its limitations. Some people find it hard to adjust to a freewheeling mental process that dispenses, temporarily, with reasoned ideas. Time is spent in listening to and recording many ideas or suggestions that cannot be pursued. Some participants may find it difficult to have their pet ideas discarded.

"Buzzing"

To **"buzz"** a solution to a problem, present an issue, and then have a group consider the pros and cons of a number of possible solutions, and reach consensus about one. The process includes the choice—by appointment or election—of a leader and a recorder for each group. The leader's role is to ensure that all group members participate; the recorder's is to note contributions. Give groups five to ten (or more) minutes to discuss a problem and reach consensus on a solution. Have the leader report the points and rationale of consensus or, failing that, of an alternative solution.

Most lessons provide frequent opportunities for using buzz groups. Buzzing, in groups of four to seven participants, might succeed brainstorming and involve all class members in discussion. Teachers who use this activity sometimes call the process a "Buzz 36" (i.e., groups of three discuss a topic for six minutes) or a "Heinz 57" (i.e., groups of five discuss a topic for seven minutes).

Buzzing can be an interesting instructional method that actively involves students and elicits fresh ideas. Interaction and individual participation in discussion tend to be higher in a small group. Successful buzzing requires, of course, that participants be well trained in interpersonal and group skills.

Buzzing, too, has its limitations: you may need to monitor groups to keep them on task and to prevent an individual from dominating the group. Moreover, if all groups in a class deal with the same topic, contributions may be contradictory or hard to combine.

Panel, Symposium, Forum, Dialogue, and Round Table

These methods are largely spinoffs of small-group discussion that you can use to involve your students directly in the teaching process. Successful use requires providing your students with training and practice so that, as their skills develop, you can gradually give them more responsibility and independence.

A panel consists of a group of students, chaired by teacher or student, that discusses a topic before the class. A committee may be appointed or elected to investigate a topic and report to the class. A symposium requires that several students become "experts" on a topic and make brief presentations about it to the class. A forum involves class discussion, guided by a chairperson, to explore a problem through questions and answers and short statements. Participants in a dialog (involving two students) and a round table discussion (involving a group), examine a topic before the class. All these types of discussion should conclude with a summary to ensure that speakers have organized their material and linked it to the topic under study, and that listeners have correctly understood it.

Problem Solving

When **problem solving** becomes a group process, members seek solutions in a systematic way, according to the so-called scientific method. Participants in this process define a problem, brainstorm its probable causes, focus on the most likely principal cause, brainstorm possible solutions, determine pros and cons of a number of options, select the most likely option, and decide when and how to implement it.

Providing Tutorials

Teachers set up **tutorial groups** to help students who need remediation or additional practice, or who can benefit from enrichment. A teacher or student may lead a tutorial group (see Chapter 15). These groups can increase the amount of attention given to individual needs and the degree of active student participation.

Laboratory Practice

An experiment, project, or practice may be conducted by a **laboratory group** formed to investigate or complete a presentation that requires solving or consolidation.

Role Playing

Role playing requires that each member of a group be assigned a role to illustrate or explore a topic of interest. Whether students agree or disagree with the position of the character whom they are representing, this activity can help them to consider all sides of an issue and to understand the ideas or feelings of others.

One-Three-Six Consensus Group

In using the **one-three-six consensus group** method, your students first record their personal opinion on an issue. When this is done, the students form groups of three to achieve consensus on their opinion. Two groups of three then form a group of six to seek consensus and report their view to the class. This method can be used at almost any point in a lesson.

STRENGTHS AND LIMITATIONS OF SMALL-GROUP METHODS

Predictably, small-group methods have their strengths and limitations. On the positive side, group involvement increases motivation, personal and social growth, learning retention, and commitment to a goal. Group work extends learning resources, since groups have access to more information and broader backgrounds than any individual has. Since group members are often stimulated by the presence of others to create ideas, groups are likely to experience more insights than are individuals. "Ideas beget ideas," and "mental hitchhiking" often occurs. Because ideas generated in a group can be clarified, refined, combined, and evaluated through the interaction of group members, groups often produce better decisions than do individual students. Group members may have a strong commitment to group success because they wish for social approval, or because their active participation in a process motivates them strongly to accept the result and build on their work. The experience may increase their understanding of self, others, and group processes; improve their interpersonal and social skills; and enlarge their self-concept. It may also reduce prejudices, for students who gain insights into the attitudes, reactions, and sensitivities of others may examine and modify their own behavior. Small-group members are more likely to understand the thinking skills or processes involved in a learning process, and therefore to transfer their learnings to new situations.

On the other hand, groups may sometimes be indecisive: since no one is solely responsible for its procedures, talk may be substituted for action, and "visiting" may take precedence over productivity. One or two individuals may do all the work, and the other members may merely go along for the ride. Less aggressive students may suppress their personal convictions if they are not given a chance to present their ideas or if they want to avoid confrontation or censure. Some students prefer to work alone, either because they think that they can learn better on their own or because they are shy, lack social skills, or believe that others will not accept them. Most of these limitations can be overcome, however, by careful planning, group-skills instruction, and monitoring.

There remains the time factor: group planning and decision making take longer than do corresponding individual activities, since all members' views must be heard, and disagreements may arise that take time to resolve. There is no doubt that more material can be covered in less time by direct instruction methods. You may choose, therefore, to plan for individual performance of routine or simple tasks, or the acquisition of information. In effect, it is important to keep a balance in selecting instructional methods, and to teach and accustom your students to use a very wide range of learning skills comfortably and efficiently.

Small-Group Functioning
Small-group learning works best in a warm, supportive classroom climate that is open, friendly, and nonthreatening (see Chapter 4). Group members need acceptance, trust, and security to contribute freely, and to speak their minds safe from teacher and peer censure and pressure.

Teach groups how to monitor their own effectiveness, both directly and by following your example, for without able guidance or the efficient use of group skills, discussion can wander, be misled or hindered or concerned with trivia, or reach no significant conclusions. Such discussions waste time.

Assessing Small-Group Functioning

When a small group is functioning well, all members are involved and at task, and seem to be enjoying themselves. Discussion flows. Assess how well a group is functioning by observing its activities carefully, and by asking yourself key questions as follows. Your answers can serve as a basis for improving group effectiveness.

- Is the group happy? tense? apathetic?
- Is the group staying on task or on topic?
- Is it trying to include and respect all?
- Who talks to whom? for how long?
- Whom do members look at as they talk?
- Does someone dominate?
- Are there subgroups (cliques)?
- Does anyone seem to be excluded?
- Are decisions being made by consensus? by vote?
- How do members react to group decisions?
- Why does pattern X or behavior Y occur?
- What can I do to promote or change pattern X or behavior Y?

Data Collection Form 13.5 will help you assess small-group functioning.

P RACTICE *and Projects*

1. View a film on small-group teaching methods, and then answer the following questions:
   a. What parts did the teacher play in the operation of small groups?
   b. What parts did the group participants play?
   c. What kinds of groups did the film present? What were the purposes of each kind?
   d. What kinds of learning were taking place in the groups?
   e. What are the strengths and limitations of small-group teaching methods?
   f. What skills does a teacher need in order to use small-group methods effectively?
   g. What kinds of skills should participants have to benefit most from group instruction methods?

2. a. Discuss in class the strengths and limitations of small-group learning. Suggest how the limitations might be overcome.
   b. Using Data Collection Form 13.5, discuss and record suggestions as to how Ms. Treblioni might solve her current group-functioning problems.

3. a. Join a subject-interest group. Brainstorm for five minutes all the topics in that subject area that you could teach by using small-group methods.

(continued)

(continued)

    b. Classify the topics you have listed, according to the small-group methods you have studied, along with any other small-group methods you might suggest.

4. Join a subject-interest group to consider what special classroom management and control considerations this subject might present, and how they could best be handled. Choose one or two group-effectiveness evaluators to collect data and report. They might use Data Collection Form 13.6 to record their observations.

■ ■ ■ ■ ■

EXPERIENTIAL INSTRUCTION

Experiential instruction facilitates the acquisition of knowledge through experiences and reflection; it is a self-paced and personalized action strategy, focusing on process rather than product, and involving students in self-directed, hands-on experiences that involve the "real world" of people and things, and affective experiences that shape feelings, attitudes, and values (see Chapter 14). Hands-on experiences may take the form of projects, games, work situations, field trips, field interviews, simulations, role playing, skits, dramatizations, and building models. These experiences move students beyond "knowing about" to "knowing how" and "being able to do," and help them benefit from other forms of instruction as well.

CASE STUDY 13.2

SMALL-GROUP FUNCTIONING

Ms. Treblioni, a Grade 11 Social Studies teacher reputed to be one of the best in the system, often uses small-group methods. Rarely is she dissatisfied with the results. Until recently, most of her students have enjoyed group work, but lately their enthusiasm seems to be waning. Ms. Treblioni suspects that the problem lies mainly with a few students. Three concerns have emerged. Trenton and Teresa, both very pleasant and sociable young people, seem to let the others in their groups do all the work. Hazel always demands her own way and dominates every group she is in. No one now seems willing to work with her. Whenever Fred and Austin are in the same group, they try to outclown each other. Although their competition is sometimes amusing, it leaves the other group members disgruntled and Ms. Treblioni frustrated.

In the past, Ms. Treblioni has always solved problems by gently teasing or privately encouraging the students involved. Currently, these methods are not working, and Ms. Treblioni realizes that she will have to try others.

Experiential education shares some of the characteristics of indirect instruction: it is learner-centered, integrated, less structured than direct instruction, and promotes inductive and deductive reasoning. It takes account of individual learning needs and styles, and can accommodate different cultural interests and values. Learners often work cooperatively, combining cooperative experiences with reflection, which encourages them to construct personal meanings and apply their learnings in new contexts (transfer).

The experiential learning process—a sort of internal "creation" of knowledge—requires more of the learner than just "being there." Personal reflection on experience and planning to apply learnings in other contexts are integral parts of the process. In fact, this type of learning occurs only when learners "participate in an activity ... critically look back on the activity to figure out learnings and feelings ... draw useful insight from analysis, and ... put learnings to work in new situations" (Pfeiffer & Goodstein, 1982). To do this, experiential learners must develop the flexibility to work cooperatively, helping to make curriculum decisions with varying degrees of teacher direction. Moreover, they must learn to adapt in a holistic way to their social and physical environment. Figure 13.3 illustrates components of experiential learning.

FIGURE 13.3

Components of Experiential Learning

FIGURE 13.4

The Experiential Learning Cycle

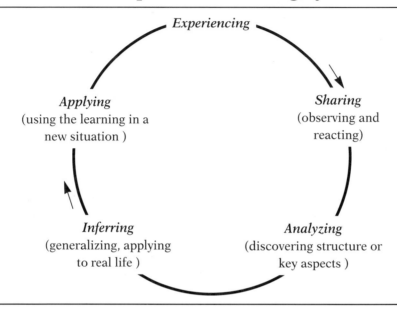

Source: Based on "Role Playing" by J. Jones and W. Pfeiffer, 1979, *The 1979 Annual Handbook for Group Facilitators (The Eighth Annual), San Diego, CA: University Associates.*

The Experiential Learning Cycle

The experiential learning cycle consists of five phases illustrated in Figure 13.4.

Experiencing

The experiential learning cycle begins with an instructional experience initiated by means of any individual or group activity that involves interaction with the environment and/or with others, and that generates information and leads to responses or feelings. Students usually find this phase of experiential learning fun or like a game. Examples of such experiences include

Playing a game	Simulation
Manipulating symbolic objects	Skit
Conducting an experiment	Improvisation
Making a model	Role playing
Creating an art object	Field project
Making a product	Field interview
Writing	Field observation
Making a case study	Work experience
Fantasy	

The purpose of this phase is to have students use whatever happens to develop a common data base for subsequent discussion and reflection. The process experienced is the desired product.

Sharing

Sharing is the second phase of the cycle: students recall their experiences and report the personal perceptions and feelings generated, sharing this information with members of their group or class. In this way, they provide a data base for later analysis. Students may share their observations and reactions through oral reports, free discussion, interviews, or written reports, or by posting points on a bulletin board or chalkboard.

Analyzing

Analyzing is the process of determining patterns and dynamics. This key phase involves processing data by systematically "talking through" the shared, or "published," experiences and feelings. Strategies include classifying experiences, seeking common themes, completing a questionnaire, discovering key terms or skills, and identifying patterns of events or behavior. Students do *not* make interpretations or form inferences during analysis, but rather seek structure, patterns, or key aspects of their experience. The focus of analysis should be on dynamics rather than "meaning."

Inferring

Inferring is a process of making logical assumptions or drawing logical conclusions based on experience. These assumptions or conclusions may be expressed as principles, rules, or generalizations that respond to the questions, "What am I beginning to learn?" or "What have I learned?" Valid inferences depend on systematic and thorough analysis and careful reflection.

Applying

Applying is the final phase of the experiential learning cycle. It includes planning and learning to use, in the present and future, the experience-based inferences formed in a preceding phase. Ideally, learners will transfer the principles, rules, or generalizations inferred into new academic contexts and into life. Strategies that can help students to integrate their experiential learning include group planning for application, individual or group contracting to apply learnings, and practicing applications. Written or publicly made statements of intent increase the likelihood of follow-through.

Experiential Instructional Strategies

Experiential instructional strategies can strengthen motivation, heighten students' levels of social and personal responsibility, increase their self-esteem, and contribute to creativity and the use of higher-level mental processes. Capitalize on the stronger motivation induced by experiential teaching strategies by using them to teach both subject-specific content and also the knowledge, values, skills, and abilities related to common essential learnings such as communication, critical and creative thinking, and personal and social values.

Experiential instruction can be effectively combined with direct instruction. You might begin by explaining terms and concepts, and then assign an individual or group experiential learning project. Such a project requires that you transfer at least partial control of the instructional process to your students, depending on their developmental levels and experience in independent learning (see Chapter 14). Your students' capacity to learn independently and manage their own productivity will increase as you teach and provide practice in the use of interpersonal and group skills.

Assess your students' readiness before you plan specific experiential learning projects. You might begin by using highly structured experiential methods (e.g., a game with set rules) and gradually work toward completely unstructured methods (e.g., improvised role play). Your evaluation will become less structured as the structure of your students' learning experiences decreases. Although you may initially find it difficult to assess both process and product, your evaluation skills will increase with your experience in using experiential instruction.

THE KOLB MODEL OF EXPERIENTIAL LEARNING

The Kolb theory of experiential learning (1984) suggests that "ideas are not fixed and immutable elements of thought but are formed and reformed through experiences" (p. 4). Thus, learning is a process in which concepts are constantly modified by experience. The learning process involves conflicts between opposing ways of dealing with the world that may set concrete experience against abstract concepts and generalizations, or action against observation.

To deal with these conflicts productively, learners must

- participate actively in new experiences;
- use reflective observation to relate their previous experiences, both personal and vicarious (acquired indirectly from listening, reading, viewing films, etc.), to new observations;
- form abstract concepts through which they can create theories and generalizations that are logically sound;
- use these new theories in making decisions and solving problems.

This four-phase cycle can be described as the interaction of two "dimensions," or two areas of conflict. To achieve the highest level of creativity and growth, the experiential learner must resolve the two areas of conflict by integrating the four types of activities. This "involves the integrated functioning of the total organism—thinking, feeling, perceiving, and behaving" (Kolb, 1984, p. 30). The first area of conflict, the concrete versus the abstract, reflects two ways of "taking hold" of experiences: first, through "comprehension," the process of interpreting concepts by relating them to symbols; and secondly through "apprehension," or relying on the feelings produced by immediate experience.

By moving from action to reflection, people transform experience to create knowledge either through manipulating the external world (i.e., circumstances) or through their own thought processes. The former activity is called "extension"; the latter is called "intension."

STRENGTHS AND LIMITATIONS OF EXPERIENTIAL LEARNING

For many students, exercising some personal control over their educational experiences is a critical concern. These students feel better about themselves and the value of their educational experiences if they have a hand in identifying and selecting learning experiences that affect their growth, development, and progress toward self-integration. They may need to perceive their educational experiences as "real" in order to find them meaningful. Experiential education may satisfy such students, for by providing direct involvement in content and encouraging reflection on their experience, it can enlarge learners' understanding and skills, and change their attitudes.

Though experiential education has become quite popular, not all educators agree that it works constructively. One team of researchers argues that to stress "being there," "seeing for oneself," "getting into the action," and "using common sense" as valuable means of learning may conceal problems and lead to incomplete understanding or error. The team claims that firsthand experience tends to emphasize only the senses, and that those who believe in the superiority of such experience as an instructional method visualize the "mind ... as a container to be filled by whatever comes from the various sense organs" (Buchmann & Schwille, 1982, pp. 1, 4).

Sight, sound, and touch can convey misinformation; samples may not provide an adequate basis for drawing inferences and forming generalizations. Firsthand experience may limit learning to established practices and standards, whereas learning often requires imagination and awareness that realities other than current circumstances may exist. To "realize" this, learners must conceive abstract categories (see Chapter 8) based on collective experience that may be vicarious: you may never climb Mount Everest, for example, but by reading about a successful Everest expedition, you may develop concepts that will help you enjoy the experience vicariously. Students can learn without direct experience by using print, visual, and human resources.

> Unlike firsthand experience, secondhand information … lends itself to a consideration of what is typical, what is generalizable, and what can be found that is different from what is already known. It enlarges the number of cases that can be considered, can include rare occurrences of high value for learning, and represents more adequately than firsthand experience the distribution of events in the real world. (Buchmann and Schwille, 1982, p. 22)

Conversely, by limiting learning to direct experience, one can close avenues to new knowledge and social change.

You must decide when experiential instruction is appropriate for your students. Experiential instruction may be a highly effective means, for instance, of motivating students or clarifying concepts before using visual (iconic) or conceptual (symbolic) instructional methods. Experiential education "personalizes" learning, greatly increases learning retention, and helps to make learning a life-enriching process. Of course, indirect instruction, which must be part of a well-rounded educational process, should be combined with experiential instruction.

Although the limitations of experiential instruction must be recognized, there are things that people can understand or appreciate better through "doing," when that is practical, than through reading, hearing, or viewing. The limitations of some firsthand experiential learning can largely be overcome through careful planning of suitable experiences, realistic anticipation of what those experiences have to offer, and systematic selection of a variety of types. "Given a choice between two methods," one educator advises, "choose the one that involves students in the most active participation" (Knowles, 1970, p. 294).

PRACTICE *and Projects*

1. Debate or discuss in small groups or as a class the claim, "The only way you can really learn something is to do it. Reading or hearing about it is not as effective."

2. Form pairs, and stand facing your partner. Spread out with arms outstretched so that you and your partner are not touching the pairs on either side of you.

    Agree with your partner to take the role of "leader" or "follower." The leader holds her hands up in front of her body. The follower positions her hands to present a mirror image of her partner's hands.

    STAGE 1. As the leader moves her arms and hands, the follower mirrors the

    (continued)

(continued)

movements. Keep up the movements for fifteen seconds, and then describe your feelings and what you perceived your partner's feelings to be (perception-checking).

STAGE 2. Exchange roles, and repeat the exercise.

STAGE 3. Agree nonverbally with your partner as to who will lead and who will follow as you repeat the exercise for the last time.

STAGE 4. Discuss with your partner your thoughts about leading and following.

STAGE 5. Discuss as a class what this exercise has taught you about experiential learning.

3. a. Participate in an off-campus, outdoor educational experience or an extended field trip.

b. Referring to the five phases of the experiential learning cycle, analyze the experience.

4. Using Data Collection Form 13.6, analyze Case Study 13.3. Your instructor may pose specific questions for your response.

CASE STUDY 13.3

TARGETING EXPERIENTIAL LEARNING

Mr. Chang's Grade 3–4 class is about to begin a unit on the topic "Air." Mr. Chang, plans to introduce the topic through experiential learning. He has prepared six science experiment stations about the classroom. Two of these demonstrate that air occupies space, two that air has weight, and two that air exerts pressure.

Mr. Chang begins, "What if I told you, 'There's no such thing as air?' How many agree? No one? Well, you're all right, but how do we know that there is such a thing as air? Can we see it? Feel it? Hear it?"

When Mr. Chang has asked for and received a few examples to prove the students' contentions, he continues, "Today we're going to do some scientific experiments to find out other things about air. There are six experiment stations in our room, and at each, you'll find a card that gives its number. I have listed the members of six experiment teams on this chart, and have numbered the teams. Each team will work at the experiment station with the matching number. You will find instructions on the back of the number card at your station.

(continued)

(continued)

"You'll all be helping to find answers to the questions, 'How do we know that air exists? What is air like?' Please follow your instructions carefully, and carry out each experiment twice to be sure of your results. Record what happens on the sheet you'll find under the number card. You'll have a chance to share your results afterward."

A group of four students works at each experiment station. The students follow the directions for their experiment and record the results on their data sheet. They discuss their activity animatedly as they work. When all the groups have done their experiment twice and recorded the results, Mr. Chang asks them to bring their data sheets to the large-group discussion area. A member of each group reports its results. The data sheets are gathered, and the students help to record notes of the results on large pieces of chart paper.

"Let's look at the six reports," Mr. Chang says. "What patterns or similarities do you see? Are there similarities between 1 and 2? 3 and 4? 5 and 6? Is there something that always happens? Is there anything that never happens?" The children discuss and compare results enthusiastically.

After five minutes, Mr. Chang probes, "Well, what did we learn about air? Have we proof that air exists? Do we know more about what air is like?" As the children respond, he lists on the chalkboard the points they make: air takes up space; air has weight; air pushes or has pressure. The children make new charts, outlining and illustrating what they have learned, and attaching data sheets to the charts.

Mr. Chang concludes with the following requests, "Give me an example of air taking up space … exerting pressure … having weight." Students generate examples, mentioning vehicle tires, airplane floats, dinghies and rafts, decorative balloons that move when the owners let go of their strings, and bubble packing.

SUMMARY

◆ Interactive instruction is a student-centered approach to teaching/learning that relies heavily on discussion, inquiry strategies, and large- and small-group work.

◆ To use interactive instruction effectively, teachers and students need well-developed observation, communication, interpersonal, and intervention skills.

◆ Large-group discussion in a positive climate should help students to value their contributions and increase their sense of contributing to the general learning experience.

◆ Guided discussion promotes students' understanding of important concepts, and helps them review material and transfer learning.

◆ Open discussion, especially in small groups, involves less teacher intervention, but requires careful planning and training of students to enable them to monitor group use of productive inquiry and discussion strategies.

◆ Experiential instruction, which focuses on process, facilitates learning through self-directed hands-on experiences that involve the "real world" of people and things and that are followed by reflection.

◆ Since every instructional strategy has strengths and limitations, it is best to choose a combination of strategies, ensuring that students participate in all learning experiences as actively as is practical.

KEY WORDS

conflict resolution
consensus seeking
decision making
discussion
   guided
   open
   small-group
   large-group
experiential
  instruction

experiential learning
  cycle
   experiencing
   sharing
   analyzing
   inferring
   applying
group effectiveness
interaction patterns
interactive instruction

paraphrasing
participation
process
problem solving
role playing
self-monitored
  learning
summarizing

RECOMMENDED READING

Bowd, A., McDougall, D., & Yewchuk, C. (1994). *Educational psychology for Canadian Teachers*. Toronto: Harcourt Brace & Company.

Cazden, C. (1988). *Classroom discourse*. Portsmouth, NH: Heinemann.

Kagan, S. (1992). *Cooperative learning*. San Juan Capistrano, CA: Resources for Teachers.

Katz, L., & Chard, S. (1992). *Engaging children's minds: The project approach*. Norwood, NJ: Ablex Publishing.

Kolb, D. (1984). *Experiential learning: Experience as the source of learning and development*. Englewood Cliffs, NJ: Prentice-Hall.

McGowan, M. (1988). Problem-solving initiatives. *Journal of Experiential Education*, *11*(3), 15–17.

Seaman, D., & Fellenz, R. (1989). *Effective strategies for teaching adults*. Columbus, OH: Merrill.

CHAPTER 14

INDIVIDUAL STUDY
AND INSTRUCTIONAL TECHNOLOGY

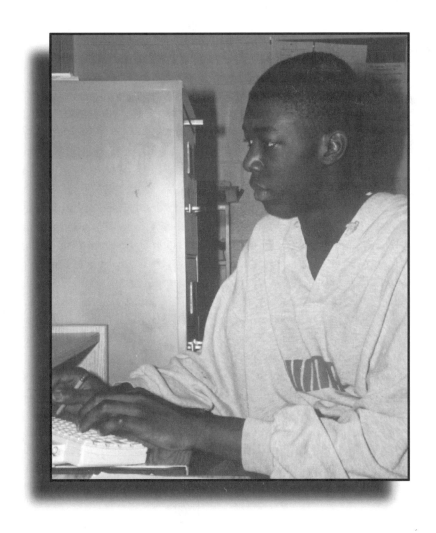

■ ■ ■ ■ ■

To take responsibility for their lives in times of rapid social change,
students need to acquire life-long learning capability. As most aspects of
our daily lives are likely to undergo profound changes, independent learn-
ing will enable individuals to respond to the changing demands of work,
family and society.

(SASKATCHEWAN EDUCATION, 1989, P. 53)

■ ■ ■ ■ ■

OVERVIEW

Individual study requires a mix of learning strategies that may need to be taught
and reinforced with opportunities for practice in the form of seatwork and homework.

Mastery learning, an instructional approach that lends itself to individual use
in traditional settings, offers techniques that can help students reach their maximum potentials of achievement. Though this strategy may be appropriate in many
situations, it requires intense one-on-one interaction between student and teacher.

Seatwork and homework are forms of independent study useful for helping
students to establish patterns of lifelong self-instruction. Learning skills associated with these types of assignments must be taught, practiced, and learned.
Assigned questions are often used as part of these forms of independent study.

A large and growing number of instructional technologies now exists, including those associated with learning centers and computers. Teachers should try to
be aware of these developments, and use technologies, including those relating to
community facilities, when they are available and appropriate. Instructional technologies cannot replace the human element that teachers bring to teaching, but
they can add variety and interest, as well as a broad range of teaching/learning skills,
to the presentation and acquisition of cognitive (intellectual), procedural
(psychomotor), and affective (feelings- and values-related) knowledge.

■ ■ ■ ■ ■

INDIVIDUAL STUDY

Individual study (also known as independent learning, self-directed study, and
self-teaching) relates to any educational pursuit that an individual undertakes to

improve her- or himself. Individual study may range from supervised classroom seatwork to investigating Roman ruins in Italy. The object of individual instruction is self-improvement and the acquisition of lifelong learning skills that include reflection, organizing, problem analysis, and decision making. Like other indirect instruction methods, individual study may produce inappropriate pacing and unintended learning outcomes that are sometimes—but not always—desirable. Acquiring independent study and learning skills is so important a part of becoming a mature learner, however, that the risks involved must be taken.

Although individual study may be self- or teacher-initiated, we shall focus here on planned study done under the supervision of a classroom teacher. This type of individual study requires that you or a student identify a topic, problem, or project based on a course objective; the student must research and analyze, make inferences and generalizations on the basis of the analysis, and evaluate the outcome of the process. Assessment, feedback, and corrections are as important in individual study as they are in the exercise of other learning strategies. You may provide these elements, build them into instructional materials for the learner's use, or combine the two methods. Figure 14.1 illustrates the methods associated with individual instruction.

FIGURE *14.1*

Some Components of Individual Study

Importance of Individual Study

Students who are to become self-sufficient and responsible citizens must be taught and trained to learn and work independently: that is, they must learn how to teach themselves, and how to put their self-teaching into practice. In fact, children should begin to learn and practice individual study skills as early as kindergarten, and should continue the process during their school years and throughout life.

Learning the basics of a school subject does not, however, "automatically lead to increased independent learning" (Blair, 1988, p. 3), and knowledge can easily be lost if students do not continue to use it in new situations. Since "students need to make specific efforts to bridge the gap between mastering basic knowledge and using that knowledge to learn on their own" (p. 4), you should teach individual study skills and provide frequent opportunities for students to learn and practice them. One important benefit of this approach to teaching is that it can provide you with opportunities to "interact individually with [your] students to assess their interests and needs and help them adjust their expectations" (Good & Brophy, 1990, p. 404).

THE TEACHER'S ROLE IN INDIVIDUAL STUDY

Your role in directing individual study is that of helping students to develop independent learning skills and habits. To help your students develop these skills, you must provide a classroom environment that encourages learners' growing independence: that is, you must provide an atmosphere that is supportive, promoting self-confidence, curiosity, and a desire to learn. You will need to organize classroom resources such as learning centers, learning activity packets (LAPs), computer-assisted instruction (CAI), and correspondence study or distance education. You will also need to achieve an appropriate teacher-student relationship, and to teach your students learning techniques and skills that they can use to act more independently in order to benefit from this form of instruction (Saskatchewan Education, 1988). Practice will often take the form of seatwork, homework, creating models, and writing reports and papers. To this end, you will allow your students to take more and more responsibility for their own instructional activities, developing an appropriate teacher–student relationship.

Selecting Individual Study Methods

Individual study methods are adaptable to a range of different situations, from supervised study in a classroom or library to self-directed learning that may or may not follow specific course requirements. You may, for instance, use individual study on a class or group basis as a major instructional strategy, or combine it with other strategies, or use it with one or more individuals while using different strategies with other students. You should base your choices on a number of factors.

Points to ponder ...

❑ What are my students' developmental and field-independence levels? (See Chapters 1 and 5.)

❑ What strategy will be most productive for my class as a whole? For individuals within it?

❑ How adequate are the facilities available for individual study?

❑ How much instructional control am I willing to relinquish by functioning as a resource person rather than a presenter of information?

Once you have chosen to use individual study strategies, your next choice is that of particular activities. Options include preparation of/participation in

reports	brainstorming	independent research
essays	problem solving	acceleration (individual
projects	decision making	progress through
models	learning contracts	text/course)
journals	distance education	learning centers
games	individual assignments	learning activity
fantasies	programmed learning	packets (LAPs)
inquiry	computer-assisted	correspondence courses
interviews	instruction	

Strengths and Limitations of Individual Study

Like other instructional strategies, individual study methods can have strengths and limitations.

STRENGTHS

When teachers have chosen appropriate topics for independent learning, and students are well prepared to exercise the skills required, individual study can

◆ strengthen students' motivation by involving them in selecting topics for study;

◆ maintain students' interest in lesson content by using experiential strategies;

◆ allow students to pursue topics in greater depth and exercise more creativity than is usually possible in group learning situations;

◆ make students see their studies as relevant and important when those studies combine school learning and community reality;

- broaden students' knowledge and skills through the use of community resources;
- emphasize individual student responsibility and accountability;
- contribute to lifelong autonomous learning by developing self-teaching skills;
- allow teachers to supplement and enrich prescribed curricula to match the interests and needs of individual students;
- be adapted to virtually any subject, and allow flexibility of time, place, and other situational elements;
- use many methods that are inexpensive and require only standard classroom equipment.

LIMITATIONS

Some students will find individual study more difficult to practice than other learning strategies. Initially, they may dislike individual study because they

- have not developed the skills needed to direct it;
- lack the confidence to work independently;
- miss the interaction with or social support of peers; or
- prefer an interactive approach.

These are reasons for you to develop expertise in teaching the study skills and learning strategies that your students will need in order to benefit most from independent study; for you to encourage your students to practice these skills and provide supervision; and for you to select topics and projects carefully. These are *not* reasons for neglecting to use this important strategy as appropriate to your students' rising developmental levels.

There are, however, some potential disadvantages and limitations inherent in individual study of which you should be aware. Individual study

- looks deceptively easy, but may actually require more work than direct and indirect instruction strategies, since a low student–teacher ratio is most effective for planning, supervision, feedback and correction, and evaluation;
- provides little social interaction and thus is of little or no use for improving interpersonal and group skills;
- cannot provide wholly predictable learning outcomes;
- is less effective in promoting acquisition of certain content (e.g., step-by-step skills that require rapid feedback and correction to prevent students from practicing errors);
- depends on the availability of adequate supplies of materials and resources (print, nonprint, physical, or human), some of which may be too difficult or too expensive to provide;

♦ may involve some students so deeply that they neglect other work or resent the use of other instructional strategies and develop negative attitudes toward teachers, fellow students, and school.

Independent Study Skills

How well students learn depends on their academic potential, motivation, learning skills, and personal management skills. The term *learning skills* relates to methods of gathering new information and ideas, and connecting them to information and ideas already acquired, organized, understood, remembered, and used. The term *personal management skills* relates to students' methods of managing their time, their emotions, and their relationships with others. Although you cannot change a student's academic potential, you can help your students to extend and improve their learning skills and their personal management skills. In short, you can help your students to acquire effective learning strategies and skills.

PROMOTING INDEPENDENT STUDY SKILLS

To learn efficiently through independent study, students must understand what they have experienced and comprehend what they have read so that they can retain and use "new" information and ideas. Independent study techniques and skills can be classified into two categories:

♦ skills for finding information needed to do an assignment, and
♦ techniques for learning the material found.

By assessing your students' skill levels in these two areas and systematically providing teaching and practice where they are needed, you can help your students to become efficient self-instructors.

To give your students this systematic help, you need to be aware of common study problems. Some students may be deficient in reading and comprehension skills. This is a serious weakness for which there is no "quick fix." Positive motivation, remedial teaching, and individual and/or group practice are the only long-term solutions. Since classroom time for remedial teaching is limited, and since students may be highly sensitive about having attention drawn to their deficiencies, peer teaching may be useful. In some circumstances, family members and/or community volunteers in the school resource center may be able to provide one-on-one encouragement, assistance, and practice.

Weakness in reading may be associated with lack of proficiency in finding material by using references, notes, indexes, or files. If you expect your students to use such sources independently, ensure that they know the alphabet to the point of automaticity, and provide them with practice in using reference sources available in the classroom. They might begin by working in groups or pairs until they are comfortable with the procedures.

Students' skills in note taking, either from print material or classroom presentations, may be weak. Direct assistance in the form of chalkboard examples may be helpful initially. You might also provide short practice sessions by reading a paragraph aloud and then asking a series of students to recall a main point and write it on the chalkboard.

Many students do not budget their time effectively. They do not set up a regular study schedule and cannot estimate how much time they should allow for a particular subject or assignment. Some students are disorganized either because they lack organization skills or because they are not sufficiently motivated. Other students may be distracted by surroundings unsuitable for study: finding a quiet, well-lighted place may be difficult or impossible. Still others may not have learned specific study skills.

Although there may be no perfect solutions for some or all of these problems, it may be helpful to discuss such difficulties with your students in a general way, and to elicit or suggest some steps they might take to make more efficient use of their study time. You can also provide a good example by practicing some of the following suggestions in your classroom (adapted from United States, Department of Education, 1986, p.39):

◆ Adjust study according to the time available, the complexity of the material to be learned, what the learner already knows about the topic, the purpose and importance of the assignment, and the standards set.
◆ Identify the main ideas in new information.
◆ Connect new material to what the learner already knows.
◆ Draw inferences about the significance of new information.
◆ Break learning activities into short sessions, rather than studying one subject or topic continuously for a long time.
◆ Assess how well study methods are working by appraising personal progress often.

MASTERY LEARNING

"The heart of **mastery learning** is the cycle of teaching, testing, reteaching and retesting" (Good & Brophy, 1990, p. 176). Mastery learning is an instructional approach that lends itself to individual use in traditional settings. In theory, at least, students have routinely been expected to achieve success in learning—that is, to "master" the educational objectives prescribed by their curriculum. Advocates of mastery learning believe that differences in achievement result, at least partly, from differences in the length of time that individuals need to learn a given assignment, the degree to which an assignment is appropriate for a learner, and the type of instruction chosen. Other important factors are clear directions, active learner participation, reinforcement of earlier success, feedback, and correction. If all these factors are carefully matched with a learner's developmental level, it is suggested, a success rate of 80 percent or higher in the achievement of well-defined goals may be a realistic expectation (Bloom, 1968).

Mastery learning programs can be arranged for an entire class, a small group, or an individual. Such programs have several common requirements: as teacher, you should determine objectives, divide into small units of knowledge and skills the curriculum to be mastered, and pre-assess students' skills; you should then give your students all the active learning time they need, followed by prompt and full feedback, and correction or remediation as often as required. (Flexible learning time, feedback, and correction are key factors in mastery learning.) Establish definite criteria for evaluation, and make progress checks daily or weekly, in the form of tests that are not part of the grading system.

Because it takes account of the reality that students learn at different rates (Carroll, 1963; Bloom, 1968) and need different materials, mastery learning can result in a higher level of performance and achievement than traditional instructional methods. Some educators contend, however, that all students are not equally capable, and that mastery learning holds back gifted students in order to advance less able students.

PRACTICE *and Projects*

1. a. Working with a partner, research and write a two-page report on a method for teaching independent study that has not been described above. Include answers to the following questions: What is [name the method]? How does it work? What are its advantages? What are its limitations? How can its limitations be overcome? To what kind of subject(s) or content is it particularly suited?

    b. In a subject-area or grade-level interest group, discuss how you might incorporate instruction in learning strategies into teaching the subject(s) you have chosen. Report your conclusions to the whole class.

2. Working in groups of six, obtain a mastery learning package and examine the way that it is set up. Analyze the packet to determine the characteristics of mastery learning.

3. a. Working with a partner, analyze Case Study 14.1, and suggest what Mr. Wang could do to help his students make good use of independent learning strategies.

    b. How could he transfer control to his students in such a way that they would rise to the challenge of becoming independent learners?

In the staff room after school one day, Mr. Wang and three of his fellow English teachers at Beacon High School were discussing students' attitudes to their work. Ms. Traut, a long-time member of the English Department, said regretfully, "Students nowadays appear to want to be spoon fed. Their attitude seems to be 'Tell me what to memorize, and then don't bother me.'" The others agreed that their experience was similar.

Reflecting on the discussion later, Mr. Wang pondered, "Perhaps there are two things the matter. Perhaps we teachers haven't taught our students how to use effective learning strategies. And perhaps we don't encourage them to become independent learners ... If that's so, I ought to see what I can do to change my students' attitudes by giving them some tools to work with.

"I've read that teachers can teach specific study skills and learning strategies and have their students practice them individually. There was that article not long ago arguing that students at almost all levels can learn reading comprehension skills and transfer them to other subjects. I'll have to think out some possibilities. Maybe I could start by ...?"

■ ■ ■ ■ ■

SEATWORK AND HOMEWORK

Seatwork (in-class assignments or study) and homework (out-of-class assignments or study) can provide individuals with opportunities for practice, enrichment, or remediation, as needed. Although seatwork and homework are particularly important elements of individual study, they often form part of other teaching strategies, such as skills instruction, where independent practice provides the repetitions needed to facilitate automaticity in the use of skills, to integrate new and previous knowledge or skills, and to overlearn content (see Chapter 9). Students are unlikely to retain some content, particularly in mathematics and elementary reading, unless they overlearn (Rosenshine & Stevens, 1986, p. 386).

Seatwork

The school activity that elementary students engage in most—close to 60 percent of the time (Doyle & Carter, 1987)—is seatwork, or supervised individual study. Seatwork is common, in fact, even in junior and senior high school. Seatwork most commonly takes the form of whole-class supervised study, but it can also be a useful means of keeping one group of students working independently while you work directly with another.

THE PURPOSE OF SEATWORK

The overall purpose of seatwork should be "to extend or deepen knowledge rather than merely keep students busy" (Good & Brophy, 1990, p. 348). Most seatwork consists of "exercises that are designed for students to perform independently as a form of practice after [they] have learned the work" (Kaplan, 1990, p. 390). Properly conducted practice provides opportunities for you and your students to discover what the latter know and do not know. It also develops students' inquiry skills, deepens their understanding of new content or process, and helps them to retain it, and to gain speed and accuracy in recall and performance (Kaplan, 1990). Time spent at seatwork can also provide you with opportunities to "interact individually with students to assess their interests and needs and help them adjust their expectations" (Good & Brophy, 1990, p. 404).

Assigning Seatwork

You may prepare seatwork assignments yourself or use material from a text or workbook. In either case, choose seatwork assignments carefully, tailoring them to meet individual needs and interests. Sequence seatwork assignments logically, tell your students their purpose and relevance, and give them some choice, if practical. Before you ask your students to begin working, make sure that they understand the concepts and skills involved, and know how to go about the work assigned. Giving clear directions—part by part, if they are long or complex—will increase at-task behavior and avoid the misbehavior that can occur when students do not understand or cannot do an assignment. The time you spend giving initial directions reduces the time you may otherwise have to spend later, providing explanations to individuals at their seats.

Beginning Seatwork

You will find it useful to begin seatwork as a cooperative assignment involving your whole class. If you have assigned your students questions, do the first one or two, step by step, with your whole class, asking individuals to tell you and their classmates what each step is to be. After this guided practice, ask your students to continue their work independently.

Monitoring Seatwork

As your students continue with an assignment, move about the classroom to monitor their work and react to it. Students should be able to do at least 80 percent of a seatwork assignment correctly. Commenting on work that is being done well is at least as important as providing prompt and specific feedback, and making tactful corrections.

When you discover that a student is doing an assignment incorrectly, ask "how" and "why" questions to help him or her discover the right procedure. This will promote understanding much more effectively than simply telling the student what to do next or even having her or him tell you. If you discover that many students are experiencing the same problem, halt the seatwork, and reteach the troublesome material.

COMBINING SEATWORK AND INSTRUCTION

If you anticipate having one group of students working independently at seatwork while you are teaching another, be sure that you and your students' seats are positioned so that you can observe both groups. Set up, in advance, a routine for all students to follow during seatwork. If students need help with their seatwork, for example, instruct them to write their names in a certain place on the chalkboard and to work on another question or some other material until you can help them.

At least initially, provide signals to help students who are doing seatwork to pace their progress. You might say, for instance, "You should have about half of the questions done now," and later, "You have five minutes left." Remember, however, that you are training students to work independently, and gradually allow them to take on themselves the responsibility for pacing.

Make sure that your students know what to do when they have completed an assignment: where they should turn it in, and what you expect them to do next (e.g., work on other assignments, read material of their own choice, or check their work with designated peers).

USING SEATWORK TO DEVELOP INQUIRY SKILLS

Seatwork used to develop inquiry skills has a different purpose from that relating to direct instruction and must be handled in a different way. Its purpose is to provide "varied and interesting opportunities for students to develop their thinking skills" (Blair, 1988, p. 87). In this instance, students should focus on practicing the inquiry process and its specific subskills, while you must allocate sufficient time, allow for a higher degree of flexibility, and allow students to take more control of the process, particularly when they are practicing higher-level cognitive skills. You should still monitor your students' practice, but you should do so unobtrusively.

Evidence suggests that teachers should devote less time to individual seatwork and more to other practice techniques such as teacher-led whole-class practice through question-and-answer sessions and drills (Rosenshine & Stevens,

1986, p. 388). Other effective practice techniques include having students work in pairs, or initiating cooperative group activities.

Assigned Questions

Teachers, particularly those in multigrade classrooms, often assign questions as seatwork or homework. Usually they "take up" these questions (i.e., discuss and correct answers) during the next class period. Such assignments relate to a teacher-centered method of instruction, since the teacher sets the questions and structures their discussion and correction. You may write the questions you assign on the chalkboard, dictate them, provide them in a handout, or assign them from a text or workbook.

Encourage your students to take such assignments seriously by checking that they have learned—or by teaching them—independent study and research skills, and by setting thought-provoking questions. Assigning questions as seatwork will provide you with opportunities to circulate among your students, encouraging some by reinforcing good answers and others by helping them to improve poor ones. Before you assign homework questions, have your students work out samples in class so that you can monitor their work and ensure a minimum success rate of 80 percent for seatwork and 95 percent for homework. Unless students have a high rate of confidence and success in doing such assignments, they soon experience frustration and may resort to "cribbing" or neglecting assignments.

Using Assigned Questions Effectively

Assigned questions are an effective instructional method when they are logically worded, and when answering them involves more than searching out and copying information from a text or other reference source. Such questions can be an efficient means of introducing facts, concepts, generalizations, principles, arguments, and points of view. They can move beyond information acquisition, and promote comprehension and reasoning skills and processes. They can also stimulate higher-level thinking, extend problem-solving skills, provide practice in decision making, and promote affective outcomes. To foster comprehension, students, in framing their answers, should paraphrase information obtained from print or other sources.

Effective use of assigned questions begins well in advance of giving the assignment. To prepare your students for written work, check their research skills, and teach them what they need to know to make effective use of school and community learning resources. Check their reporting and summarizing skills, as well, and help them to upgrade as necessary by teaching and/or providing them with practice. Circulate during seatwork practice sessions, to help with difficulties and provide positive reinforcement and encouragement.

Students who see the worth of questions you assign are more likely to do them well. To motivate your students, use advance organizers, and introduce the questions in ways that will establish positive set for learning. Frame or select questions to ensure that you are directing your students to focus on important information or thinking skills by asking them to apply, combine, or evaluate information in new ways; discern relationships and implications; and use criteria to make judgments and generalizations. Use a mix of convergent and divergent questions (see Chapter 7). When taking up questions with your class, apply the questioning skills described above, challenging students to stretch their minds.

Reinforce your students' learnings from assigned questions by applying methods relating to conceptual, procedural, and affective learning domains. Encourage your students to transfer learnings from past to present and from subject to subject, and to integrate lesson content with life experiences. Data Collection Form 14.1 (Appendix A) will help you to focus your reflection and planning about lessons that target assigned questions and seatwork.

Assigned questions do not generally support instructional goals relating to a high degree of understanding and long-term retention, or to affect, communication, or interpersonal and group skills. Avoid assigned questions when students' motivation is low or the temptation to copy from a text or another student's work is high. Add other instructional methods when experiential learning is required; when educational material is complex, abstract, or highly detailed; or when integration of domains is a goal.

Homework: To Use or Not to Use?

A long-standing and current issue among students, teachers, and parents is whether teachers should assign homework and, if so, how much. The use of homework varies from district to district and from school to school. You may find that it is not always realistic to assign homework or expect parents to check it. To some extent, community norms will govern your policies in these matters.

FUNCTIONS OF HOMEWORK

Teachers assign homework to extend students' learning time beyond the regular classroom hours so that students will have adequate practice time or opportunity to preview material that they will shortly study in school. Homework also supplements in-class instruction time, for secondary-school students, at least. Homework has been found to affect substantially the achievement of high school students and to affect positively that of junior high school students, but to have negligible effects on the achievement of elementary school students (H. Cooper, 1989).

CASE STUDY 14.2

ASSIGNED SEATWORK

Ms. Perez has a split Grade 6-7 class. Nineteen of her students are in Grade 6, and eight are in Grade 7. She plans to begin a study of Paraguay with her Grade 7 students. She must also finish teaching her Grade 6 students the map-reading skills they need for their group projects. Ms. Perez decides to give her Grade 7 students a seatwork assignment to do while she spends the first part of the period with the Grade 6s. She hopes that besides keeping the Grade 7s busy, the seatwork will provide them with valuable background information and help them to think more deeply about Paraguay.

Ms. Perez assembles copies of maps showing Paraguay's physical features, population distribution, and annual rainfall. She also provides world maps and two globes, and writes on the chalkboard the assignment she has planned, as follows:

Postcards from Paraguay

You are touring Paraguay. Write postcard messages to several friends at home, telling each one something different about what you are observing. Use the questions listed below as the starting point for your messages.
1. What are Paraguay's physical features?
2. What might the climate be like? (Give reasons.)
3. Which areas are dry, and which have heavy rainfall?
4. Where are the areas of dense population?
5. Suggest reasons for the way the population is distributed.
6. Judging from the names of cities, towns, and rivers, what language might the people of Paraguay speak?
7. What ways might citizens of Paraguay earn a living?
8. Can Paraguay easily ship and trade with other countries? Explain.

At the beginning of the period, Ms. Perez asks her Grade 6 students to get their materials ready while she gives instructions to the Grade 7s.

"Today we're going to begin the study of some South American countries that we've spoken of. Perhaps you will travel there some day, and so we're going to start by making some preparations for a trip. Wise travelers study maps of a country to find out all they can before they visit them. I have maps of Paraguay that show its physical features and population distribution, and the annual rainfall in different areas. *(continued)*

(continued)

"Remember how, when we studied African countries, we learned that climate, the amount of rainfall, and transportation routes to cities influence the way people earn their living. I want you to build on what you've learned earlier and gather all the information you can from these maps. You're welcome to guess, but have good reasons for your guesses. We'll check your findings later. You may work quietly in pairs or threes so that you can talk over your ideas before you write your postcard messages."

Ms. Perez has the students read the questions, makes sure they understand them, and leaves to work with the Grade 6 students. The Grade 7s move to tables at the back of the room where the maps have been placed and begin to work at their assignment.

"Effective homework assignments do not just supplement the classroom lesson; they also teach students to be independent learners" (Good & Brophy, 1990, p. 42). When homework is used effectively, students gain experience in "following directions, making judgments and comparisons, raising additional questions for study, and developing responsibility and self-discipline" (p. 42).

ATTITUDES TO HOMEWORK

The most important attitude to homework in your classroom may be your own. If you expect your students to take homework assignments seriously, you must do so, too. "Homework is most useful when teachers carefully prepare the assignment, thoroughly explain it, and give prompt comments and criticism when the work is complete" (United States, Department of Education, 1986, p. 42).

Most students think that homework is valuable, even if some are reluctant to do it. Most parents also consider homework valuable and expect teachers to assign it. Inform parents of your homework policy, and let them know when their daughters and sons do their homework well, and when they fail to do it. Depending on circumstances, you might ask parents to check students' homework, even though some of it may have been done at school.

HANDLING HOMEWORK ASSIGNMENTS

Much of the information relating to effective seatwork, given above, also applies to homework that is used to provide practice. Students need instruction and training in organizing homework assignments, and you should plan to provide these helps before making an assignment. Ideally, you should tailor homework assigned for practice to individual needs, but this may be difficult to do if classes are large. In either event, homework should be of reasonable length and difficulty—it works best if it is neither too complex nor completely unfamiliar—and should match your students' ability to work independently.

Establish an accountability system to ensure that homework is done on time. Always check your students' homework, and mark it if appropriate. Provide time for your students to correct their mistakes and, if you consider it advisable, have them resubmit their work. If you find that a homework assignment has defeated many students, you should reteach the material on which it was based. Never use homework—or any school work, for that matter—as punishment. Such a practice can lead students to dislike a subject, the teacher, and school in general.

You may need to teach specific methods of previewing material before you assign students homework that requires independent reading and comprehension. Many individual teaching and learning strategies require students to read, understand, and remember what they have read. This is not a process that occurs automatically. It requires skillful readers to skim, scan, reread, integrate information, take notes, and make inferences or generalizations. Your students may need step-by-step instruction and supervised practice in these procedures before they are ready for independent practice. Step-by-step practice in classes or groups should include

- clarifying the task;
- reading for meaning;
- concentrating on important content;
- checking for comprehension while reading;
- reviewing and self-testing for attainment of objectives;
- drawing inferences (by interpreting, predicting, concluding);
- recovering quickly from distractions.

PRACTICE *and Projects*

1. Review the sections on explaining (Chapter 7, pages 165–168), and on demonstrations and giving directions (Chapter 9, pages 212–217 and 217–220, respectively).

2. a. When an appropriate opportunity offers, ask one or more classroom teachers whether their school has a policy relating to seatwork and homework; which independent study methods they use; and how they handle these activities.

   b. Hold a full-class discussion to consider the information you have obtained.

3. Using Data Collection Form 14.1, plan and microteach a lesson, targeting the use of assigned seatwork.

■ ■ ■ ■ ■

TECHNOLOGY-RELATED INSTRUCTION

A vast, sometimes bewildering, array of teaching/learning resources now exists to supplement the traditional teaching and learning format in which teachers talk and explain, and students ask questions, read, and write. These resources may be human or technological, print or nonprint, teaching aids or primary media of instruction. They are to be found both inside and outside the walls of classrooms and schools. Their range includes any persons, facilities, or instructional technology or media that carry information, stimulate thinking, and broaden and extend the experience of learners.

Technology-related instruction has been defined as "a complex integrated process involving people, procedures, ideas, devices, and organization for analyzing problems, and devising, implementing, evaluating and managing solutions to those problems, involved in all aspects of human learning" (Association for Educational Communications and Technology, 1986, p. 17).

Technology: Support to Instruction

Some people may still believe that technology can be a substitute for teachers, and that teachers and technology should compete in order to make schooling more efficient. Computer-assisted instruction, it has been suggested, could eliminate the need for teachers, and distance education could reduce the amount of time students and teachers need to be in contact. These changes would significantly reduce the costs of providing education.

Professional educators know, however, that while technology is useful in some instructional situations, it is unsuitable in others. Technology in itself does not increase learning: it merely offers options to teacher presentations or student reading. "It is what the teacher does—the teaching—that influences learning" (Clark, 1989, p. 240). Truly professional teachers use technology as an aid to teaching, not a substitute for it.

Much of the value of technology lies in the use that teachers can make of it to motivate learners, structure learning experiences for underachievers, and tailor learning materials to the needs of individuals, each of whom has a preferred way of learning (see Chapters 1, 4, & 16): some students are good listeners, others need to see things to learn best, and still others need hands-on experiences. Advances in instruction technology are constantly increasing the range and sophistication of teaching options. Media alternatives to teacher presentations are available. Many are of high quality and easy to access. Review available technology often, and use it to support your presentations or provide practice for your students.

At times, technology-based information and presentations may be broader and better than yours. Do not hesitate to use them, but remember that, in your presentations, you can not only provide new information quickly and effectively, but you can also add the critical human dimension, responding directly to your students with sensitivity and precision. Teaching is, first of all, a "people business," but technology can be an invaluable aid in a multimedia approach to teaching.

CLASSIFYING TECHNOLOGY RESOURCES

Instructional technology resources can be classified in different ways. One system (McNeil & Wiles, 1990) classifies the types of technology commonly used in today's schools as

- nonprojected (graphic) visuals
- projected visuals;
- audio media; and
- multimedia (or combination audio-visuals).

Figure 14.2 illustrates a range of instructional technology resources.

Print Resources

Textbooks and workbooks are still the most common print resources for classroom use. Many of these resources are very good, but they can be a danger if teachers adhere to them in an inflexible and slavish manner. Truly professional teachers realize that print resources are teaching aids, not teaching substitutes.

Community Resources

Community resources may be public—for example, departments of education, school-district media centers, government agencies, or public corporations; alternatively, they may be private—for example, private citizens, service clubs, nonprofit organizations, professional associations, commercial publishers, or other business firms. Teachers—and sometimes students—can access these resources through personal contact, the mail, or electronic devices such as telephones, fax machines, or computer networks.

Learning Centers

A classroom learning center or station is a self-contained, learning environment for self-directed learning where students work with hands-on materials, independently, in pairs, or in small groups. These centers make it possible for teachers to individualize parts of the curriculum and provide students with choices in keeping with their interests. Such centers provide constructive ways for students to learn when they have finished assigned tasks, especially when the centers can be arranged to provide immediate feedback.

FIGURE 14.2

Instructional Technology for Today's Schools

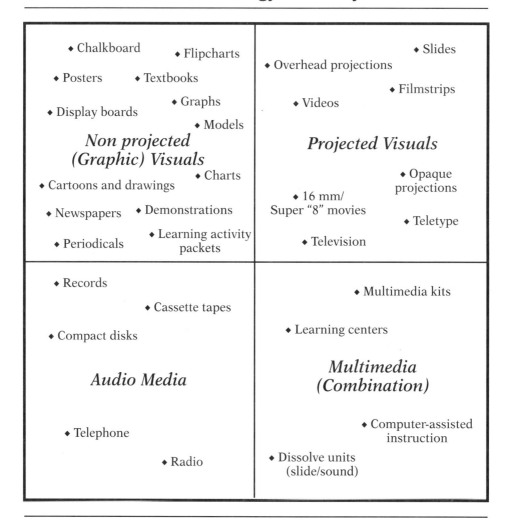

Source: Adapted from *The Essentials of Teaching: Decisions, Plans and Methods* by J. McNeil and J. Wiles, 1990, New York: Macmillan.

Learning centers can be used for all subjects at all grade levels for a broad range of subject-specific or multidisciplinary assignments. Tasks can last for five minutes or several weeks. The centers can be simple and inexpensive to set up, requiring minimum materials and space, or they may be much more elaborate and expensive to provide.

Effective centers are carefully planned to require minimum teacher supervision. They should be set up only after you have assessed your students' knowledge, skills, and maturity levels, and are convinced that they can use the centers appropriately and safely. Your students should enjoy the activities provided so that they will stay on task, and monitoring and feedback should be provided, ideally through a nonthreatening system for recording student progress (see Chapter 17).

Computer Instruction

Computer instruction, which is particularly adaptable to individual instruction, brings novelty and variety to learning, and can provide more fun than the usual seatwork. Three levels of involvement are possible: drill and practice sessions, in which the computer poses questions, scores answers, and provides immediate feedback; tutorial sessions, in which tutorial functions range from requiring simple recall or basic knowledge to advanced problem solving; and simulations that involve users in gamelike or near-real situations. Computers may or may not reduce learning time, but students generally react positively to using them, and their attitude toward instruction may improve. Computer instruction, like all other teaching/learning strategies, has its advantages and limitations.

STRENGTHS AND LIMITATIONS OF COMPUTER INSTRUCTION

Like other technology, computers, as adapted to instruction, have strengths and limitations. As with other methods and technologies, you should keep a balance between computer instruction and other forms of instruction. If computers are available to your students, use them rationally, as opportunity serves, to broaden your students' range of learning.

Strengths of Computer Instruction

Strengths relating to computer instruction include the following points (some of which are from Good & Brophy, 1990, pp. 178–179):

◆ Computers provide additional or different ways of presenting information through sophisticated instructional techniques such as animation, time-lapse photos, and step-by-step demonstration of complex processes; they can also offer unlimited practice and drill, as well as unlimited opportunities for problem solving through the use of case studies and simulations.

◆ Computers provide means of individualizing instruction by omitting unnecessary instruction or practice, or offering needed remediation.

◆ Using computers can improve students' research and writing skills, and extend their creativity. Graphics and gamelike programs, as well as the impression that computers are "fair" because they are impersonal, may induce some learners to take more responsibility for self-teaching.

♦ Students can interact with computers directly and in varied ways, and receive instant feedback on their responses.

♦ Computers can provide compact storage and rapid retrieval of large amounts of information.

♦ Computers can record individual students' responses to help you monitor their progress and provide remediation as needed.

Limitations of Computer Instruction

Interesting and innovative as computer instruction can be, it has several limitations and raises several concerns of which you should be aware:

♦ Computers may encourage an emphasis on facts and the overuse of drill and practice at the expense of higher-level learning skills and instructional strategies that focus on drawing inferences and forming generalizations.

♦ Computer instruction does little to promote affective outcomes; some people, in fact, believe that it is a dehumanizing form of instruction.

♦ Computer instruction gives students little opportunity for oral expression. (Henson, 1988, p. 250)

Technology-Related Skills

Resource- or technology-related skills may involve the use of community or school facilities, various media such as films or publications, or instructional equipment such as the chalkboard, gymnasium or shop facilities, or an overhead projector. Choose instructional technology that supports the activities you plan to help your students achieve learning objectives. In making your choices, consider the size of your class or group; the nature of the lesson content; the instructional strategies that are appropriate; the availability and accessibility (or portability) of the technology, your ability to use it correctly; and the learners' experience with and ability to use the technology.

You should make yourself familiar with any technology that you plan to use before you operate it in your classroom: you may have to practice using equipment or procedures, and you should usually preview presentations (see Chapter 2). Prepare "standby" plans for alternative activities in case of a mechanical breakdown. If possible, set up equipment and materials before your class begins. After your lesson, evaluate the effectiveness of the instruction.

PRACTICE *and Projects*

1. a. Tour the audio-visual or instructional technology area of your university or college.
   b. Select a school subject and join others who have a similar interest to discuss how and where you might use the various aids and technology available.

SUMMARY

- Individual study relates to any educational pursuit that one person undertakes to improve him- or herself.
- To become self-sufficient and responsible citizens, students must learn how to teach themselves, and how to put their self-teaching into practice.
- The teacher's role in arranging and directing individual study is that of helping students to develop independent learning skills and habits.
- Individual study has both advantages and disadvantages, and must be used with discretion. It should not be neglected because students must learn to take responsibility for their own lifelong learning experience.
- Seatwork and homework are important components of individual instruction.
- Technology-related instruction includes any persons, facilities, or instructional devices or media that carry information, stimulate thinking, and broaden and extend the experience of learners.
- Technology is largely a valuable instructional tool because of the use that teachers can make of it to motivate learners, structure learning experiences for underachievers, and tailor learning materials to the needs of individuals.
- Computers, if available, should be used with discretion, to take advantage of their potential benefits and minimize their potentially undesirable effects.

KEY WORDS

assigned questions
audio media
community resources
computer instruction
homework
independent study
   skills
individual study

inquiry skills
instructional technology
learning centers
learning resources
learning skills
mastery learning
multimedia aids
nonprojected visuals

personal management
   skills
practice
projected visuals
remedial teaching
seatwork
technology skills

RECOMMENDED READING

Bellon, J., Bellon, E., & Blank, M. (1992). *Teaching from a research knowledge base: A development and renewal process*. New York: Merrill.

Kulik, J. (1983). Synthesis of research on computer-based instruction. *Educational Leadership, 41*(1), 19–21.

Wang, M., & Walberg, H. (Eds.). (1985). *Adapting instruction to individual differences*. Berkeley, CA: McCutchan.

CHAPTER 15

COOPERATIVE LEARNING

■ ■ ■ ■ ■

Cooperative learning usually supplements the teacher's instruction by giving students an opportunity to discuss information or practice skills originally presented by the teacher; sometimes cooperative methods require students to find or discover information on their own.

(SLAVIN, 1991, PP. 71–72)

■ ■ ■ ■ ■

OVERVIEW

Cooperative instruction stresses the key components of cooperative learning: individual responsibility, accountability to the group, positive interdependence, group processing, and group self-evaluation. Cooperative instruction involves dividing a class into heterogeneous groups that perform assigned or self-selected tasks. Students acquire and use communication, interpersonal, and group skills, applying them to situations in which they learn through cooperative games, peer tutoring, and/or group investigation. The teacher observes and monitors group tasks. Rewards are generally group oriented. Although student responses to cooperative learning are generally positive, training and adjustment may be necessary to help some individuals derive maximum benefit from the experience. Through cooperative learning, students achieve academic and social gains and experience affective growth in overcoming prejudice against "different" classmates.

■ ■ ■ ■ ■

ESSENTIALS OF COOPERATIVE LEARNING

Dominant cultures in North America have tended to stress independence and individual achievement. Although these are important elements in education, students also need to learn how to work cooperatively, for no skills are more important to human beings than those of cooperative interaction: interpersonal, group, and organizational skills (Johnson & Johnson, 1975). According to Manning and Lucking (1991), "The increasing need for all people to work together during the 1990s and beyond indicates that cooperative learning is an educational practice that contemporary educators must consider for their schools" (p. 156).

Particularly important are skills relating to communication, building and maintaining trust, and conflict resolution.

The key principles of **cooperative learning** are individual responsibility and accountability to the task and the group (Johnson & Johnson, 1989). Ideally, these principles combine in relationships of **positive interdependence** within which students perform tasks that cannot be completed by a single student. Thus, cooperative learning can improve students' social skills, increase self-esteem, promote social values, and provide positive motivation (Slavin, 1987). By contrast, when instruction stresses only individual achievement and undue stress is placed on competition, some students may lose self-esteem, as well as the motivation to do their best.

Positive Interdependence

As class or group members develop positive interdependence, a cooperative classroom structure develops. To foster positive interdependence, make your students responsible for individual aspects of group tasks. To learn cooperatively, students must recognize their interdependence: that is, they must know that they are responsible not only for their own learning but also for that of everyone else in their group. To discharge this responsibility and achieve the group's goal, each group member must complete the task(s) assigned to him or her.

Promoting Interdependence

Most curricula stress student interaction with the teacher, instructional materials, and one another; cooperative instruction goes further by promoting, in addition, student interdependence. To promote interdependence within groups of mixed ability, encourage your students to help one another, as needs arise, by explaining content or process to one another as they are learning, making constructive suggestions, helping one another analyze and do assignments, and giving feedback. Good communication, interpersonal, and group skills are important to this process.

Individual Accountability

You promote **individual accountability** when you make each group member responsible to the group for completing a particular part of a cooperative learning task. To discharge his or her role or task, each student will have to demonstrate mastery of the content or process studied and of the interpersonal or group skills that he or she needs in order to share that learning with the group.

■ ■ ■ ■ ■

COOPERATIVE INSTRUCTION

Instruction that stresses cooperative learning offers students the benefits of working together in groups and supporting one another in the interactive process of learning through doing cooperative tasks.

Planning for Cooperative Instruction

Plan cooperative learning procedures, as you plan others, to fit available resources and your students' current levels of cooperative learning skills. These factors will affect the size of the learning groups that you plan to organize: groups of two or three are suitable for young students.

PREPARING FOR COOPERATIVE INSTRUCTION

Arrange your classroom to reflect your choice of cooperative learning goals. Consider movement patterns, separation of groups, and access to materials. Make sure that suitable materials are available, whether all groups need the same materials or different ones.

Organizing Learning Groups

Always name the members of each group. Specify clearly the task assigned, the learning goals involved, and the outcome (product or process) expected.

Building a Climate of Trust

The best way to prepare your students to acquire cooperative learning skills is to build a classroom climate of trust (see Chapter 4). By gradually introducing cooperative learning activities and games, you will help your students to acquire communication and cooperation skills, and practice the basics of small-group organization and operation, helping to maintain the necessary climate for cooperative learning. Your target is to find cooperative ways for your students to acquire, analyze, or synthesize information or skills relating to course content.

To maintain such a climate, you should

- ensure that your students have the skills to express acceptance, support, and the desire to cooperate;
- encourage your students to
  - contribute openly information, ideas, thoughts, feelings, intuitions, hunches, and reactions;
  - share materials and resources;
  - express cooperative intentions, acceptance, and support of one another as they work together;

- discourage rejecting and nonsupportive behaviors (e.g., silence, ridicule, and superficial acknowledgment of an idea) that shut off future cooperation;
- periodically ask cooperative groups to evaluate their behavior, checking that it is trusting and trustworthy, and determining how they might strengthen their cooperation (Johnson & Johnson, 1975, pp. 105–106).

Teaching Cooperative Learning Skills

To teach cooperative learning skills successfully, you must recognize their importance. Ideally, your students will already have learned and used interpersonal and group skills (see Chapter 2), but if not, you can teach these as part of the cooperative learning process.

TEACHING COOPERATIVE PLANNING SKILLS

You should introduce cooperative planning skills gradually, and have your students practice them in a variety of situations before they begin a cooperative learning project. You might, for example, hold whole-class or small-group discussions to stimulate ideas for carrying out an activity that lends itself to cooperative planning (e.g., creating a display or making a class trip).

EXPLAINING COOPERATIVE PROCEDURES

Explain to each group the procedures required for task completion, role expectations, and evaluation criteria. Check members' perception of their task before you ask them to begin work.

IMPLEMENTING COOPERATIVE LEARNING

A number of strategies for implementing cooperative or team learning apply broadly across the curriculum. They all promote direct interaction and cooperation among members of small teams. Some approaches are discussed on pages 350–354.

OBSERVING AND MONITORING

Cooperative learning provides opportunities to observe, reflect, and intervene supportively, even in a large class. Observation may be either global or systematic. **Global observation**, which is informal, is a good way to begin. It may lead naturally to systematic observation, which provides or confirms information on which to base interventions.

During global observation, record what you see and hear. Ask yourself the following questions:

◆ Are all students busily engaged in their tasks?
◆ Are any students uninvolved?
◆ Is the tone of the group friendly, relaxed, animated, or confrontational?
◆ Is there evidence of boredom, frustration, or restlessness?
◆ Are there any "free riders," "isolates," or bullies?

Systematic observation is more formal. It involves using checklists, either commercial or devised by the teacher, that specify essential behaviors for task achievement and group-maintenance interaction.

Monitor members' displays of interest and feelings, and their interaction; observe who is learning, and who needs help. Be a consultant, or intervene as needed to help members solve problems through cooperative behaviors. Remind your students that they are accountable to their group, and teach them to set and use their own group-effectiveness goals. (You will need to monitor group choices and their use carefully to ensure that they are positive in tone and effect.)

INTERVENING SUPPORTIVELY

When you must intervene, do so in a supportive way. Your interventions should encourage, show patience, and provide your students with opportunities for reflection so that they can work together more effectively. It may be tempting to provide answers and solve problems for a group, but to take such action defeats a major purpose of cooperative learning and denies students the opportunity to learn how to practice problem-solving skills (see Chapter 2). Instead, show confidence, whenever possible, in the group's ability to help itself. Occasionally, you will suggest alternative approaches or sources for consideration.

PROMOTING GROUP SELF-EVALUATION

To promote cooperative goal achievement, train groups to evaluate their effectiveness often—perhaps at the end of each group work session. Members should assess the processes they use to achieve their tasks and determine how they can improve their performance. To this end, train

◆ individuals to evaluate themselves;
◆ team members to evaluate constructively one another's use of processes;
◆ groups to evaluate their own use of processes; and
◆ yourself and your students to evaluate group presentations.

OBTAINING FEEDBACK

Obtain feedback on your use of cooperative instruction methods, using Data Collection Form 15.1 (Appendix A). Use feedback to do the following:

- Evaluate group products or processes, using the criteria set. Consider how well students accomplished their task, and how well they helped one another. Assess academic progress in the usual ways, through homework, classroom assignments, projects, papers, or tests.
- Prepare a summative profile of individual progress that records each student's mastery of cognitive knowledge and skills, communication skills, cooperative social skills, problem-solving techniques, and success in working independently. To assess your students' behavior, and to describe and record related data objectively, you might use an observation sheet. Table 15.1 summarizes behavior appropriate to cooperative learning.

TABLE 15.1

Behaviors Appropriate to Cooperative Learning

Leadership: Achieving a Task
- Seeking information
- Sharing information and opinions
- Clarifying or elaborating

- Summarizing
- Checking progress toward the group goal
- Testing for, or facilitating, consensus

Leadership: Maintaining a Group
- Setting or applying standards
- Including/encouraging/ listening to others

- Relieving tension and harmonizing
- Expressing group feelings
- Compromising

Communication
- Listening
- Paraphrasing
- Perception checking
- Describing behavior accurately

- Describing feelings
- Seeking feedback
- Providing solicited feedback

Displaying Trust
- Accepting others and their ideas
- Expressing support/intention to cooperate

- Discharging promises/responsibilities

Conflict Resolution
- Managing personal feelings/ showing empathy
- Defining problem
- Discovering sources of problem

- Proposing potential solutions
- Selecting best potential solution
- Trying proposed solution
- Evaluating attempted solution

USING COOPERATIVE REWARDS

To encourage cooperation, clearly identify the individual responsibility and accountability of each group member and relate these to group rewards given on the basis of individual members' performance. Such rewards do much to foster positive interdependence and direct group efforts. By contrast, students who do not relate their achievements to those of the group may tend to focus on their own experience, since they will be receiving no incentive either to cooperate or to compete.

REFLECTING ON COOPERATIVE INSTRUCTION

On the basis of your observations and evaluations, reflect on your use of cooperative instruction in

+ teaching group skills;
+ promoting positive interdependence;
+ monitoring, facilitating, and evaluating students' use of cooperative learning skills. (Johnson & Johnson, 1978, pp. 12–13).

Figure 15.1 summarizes your role in using cooperative instruction. The two key elements are observation and supportive intervention.

Cooperative Learning Strategies

Once you have taught your students the following cooperative learning strategies, they should progress gradually toward using them on their own, without need of your mediation.

JIGSAW

The **Jigsaw** method of cooperative learning (Aronson, Blaney, Stephan, Sikes, & Snapp, 1978) was developed to encourage peer cooperation and tutoring. It is chiefly used in subjects in which students must learn from texts (e.g., social studies). In Jigsaw, students are assigned to one of five heterogeneous "home" groups (i.e. groups composed of male and female students of different ability levels and different ethnic backgrounds). Material to be learned is assigned to each member by topic, and each student studies his or her assignment and then helps form a "topic group," composed of students from the various home groups, to discuss the findings. Members of each topic group pool information to become the "experts" in their field.

Experts return to their home groups to teach their particular topic to home-team members. Since each of the experts in the home group has unique

FIGURE *15.1*

Role of Teacher in Cooperative Learning

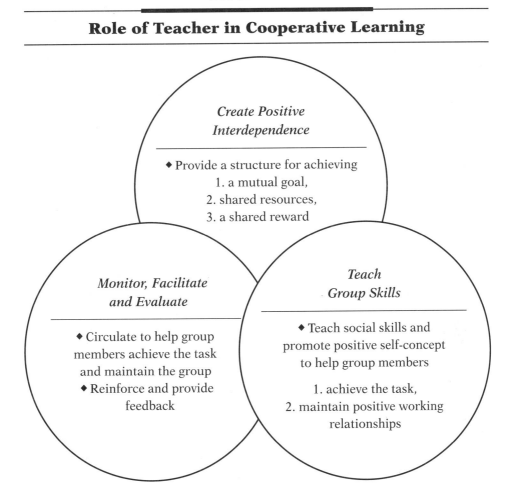

Create Positive
Interdependence

◆ Provide a structure for achieving
1. a mutual goal,
2. shared resources,
3. a shared reward

Monitor, Facilitate
and Evaluate

◆ Circulate to help group
members achieve the task
and maintain the group
◆ Reinforce and provide
feedback

Teach
Group Skills

◆ Teach social skills and
promote positive self-concept
to help group members

1. achieve the task,
2. maintain positive working
relationships

information, and other team members must depend on the tutoring of each expert for instruction, the teams value and pay attention to the experts' contributions.

When all team members have shared their expert knowledge, students are tested on the entire lesson content and graded individually. (There is no team score.)

JIGSAW II

Jigsaw II (Slavin, 1980) promotes an even greater degree of student interdependence than does the basic version. The process of Jigsaw II is the same as that of the earlier version, but test scores, based on individual improvement, are totaled to form team scores. High-scoring teams are recognized in some way, such as through publication of members' names in a school bulletin.

STUDENT TEAMS AND ACHIEVEMENT DIVISIONS (STAD)

The **Student Teams and Achievement Divisions (STAD)** approach, developed by Robert Slavin and his colleagues (Slavin, Sharan, Kagan, Lazarowitz, Webb & Schmuck, 1985), uses cooperative competition by assigning students to heterogeneous teams of four or five members that compete with one another. With peer assistance, students review teacher-taught content, studying for fifteen-minute weekly tests. Teachers translate individual test scores into team scores by using "achievement divisions." The highest six scorers form the top division, and their scores are compared to allocate points: the top scorer receives eight points, the second six points, and so on. Students earning the next six highest scores form the second achievement division, and the same points are allocated. Thus, students are compared only with peers of similar ability, and not with their whole class. This accounting system avoids direct student competition and rewards teams by recognizing their performance.

GROUP INVESTIGATION (GI)

The **group investigation (GI)** approach to cooperative learning (Sharan & Lazarowitz, 1980) can be particularly effective in promoting higher-order thinking skills, especially in high school classes. In GI, students gather data, then discuss, interpret, and synthesize individual contributions to achieve a group product. GI's emphasis on investigation and reporting, rather than on peer tutoring, distinguishes it from STAD.

In the GI approach, a teacher presents a general topic to a class. He or she then divides the class into heterogeneous task-oriented groups of two to six members. Each group investigates and reports on a subtopic. Students are often allowed to choose the topic they wish to investigate, thus determining their team membership.

Each group meets with the teacher to clarify its goals and plan its investigation. The groups identify sub-subtopics and then assign the investigation to particular subgroups, which may use resources both in and outside the school. Members analyze and evaluate data, and frame interesting ways of reporting or displaying their findings to the rest of the class. The teacher acts as facilitator and resource person, monitoring progress and offering assistance as needed. After the presentations, teacher and students collaborate to frame methods of assessing individual or group work, or both.

Comparing Team Learning Strategies

Cooperative learning strategies fall into two categories: one type (e.g., Jigsaw and STAD) emphasizes **peer tutoring**, and the other, group investigation. Critical differences lie in the variety and sources of information, the organization of the classroom, the nature of the learning tasks, the nature of interpersonal relations and communications, and the evaluation of rewards for the academic product (Sharan, 1980, pp. 263–264). Table 15.2 outlines the two sorts.

Peer tutoring. Peer tutoring provides instruction and drill through interaction among peers. This strategy fosters cooperation and interdependence in pursuing learning tasks, though it is generally used to explain or acquire information or skills that a teacher has initially presented or to investigate sources that a teacher has identified. It may involve two students or a small group, and each "team," rather than the class as a whole, becomes the social unit for learning. The same goals may be set for one, some, or all teams.

Given practice and reinforcement, most children become rather good instructors and benefit greatly from teaching fellow students. Moreover, many students learn better from their peers than from adults. Academic goals and evaluation (test scores) relate largely to individual students, and rewards tend to be extrinsic.

Group investigation. Group investigation encourages students to generate ideas, gather broad and varied information, make decisions, and seek consensus. The interdependent process stresses analysis, interpretation, inter-team coordination and reporting, problem solving, content application, and integration of

TABLE 15.2

Peer Tutoring and Group Investigation

Peer Tutoring	*Group Investigation*
Source: Teacher provides the information	*Source:* Students gather the information
Use: information/skill acquisition	*Use:* for problem-solving, content analyzing, interpreting, applying
Method: Peer tutoring (instruction and drill) to explain; acquire information/skills	*Method:* Exchange of ideas/information, planning, coordination
Evaluation: usually individual or done with group, done by teacher	*Evaluation:* individual and/or group; product is interdependent; done by teacher and/or students
Rewards: extrinsic; group recognition	*Rewards:* mainly intrinsic
Organization: a number of teams, each assigned the same task	*Organization:* a "group of groups," with inter-group coordination

achievements. Both individual and group performances are evaluated; rewards, which are often based on self-directed interest in a topic, tend to be intrinsic.

COOPERATIVE GAMES

Classroom games are a highly versatile and adaptable mode of learning that can provide a break in the academic schedule or reward good behavior. All teachers can and should use **cooperative games**, for play is a natural, active, and highly motivating means of promoting social skills. Games can break the ice in new situations; provide practice in communication, interpersonal, or group skills; create a change of pace to stimulate classroom activities; and promote the achievement of cognitive, psychomotor, or affective curriculum objectives. They are useful for introducing small-group teaching strategies and inducing a positive mind-set for cooperation. Many books on cooperative games are available in school and local libraries; they describe hundreds of games, with a vast range of requirements for resources or materials.

Cooperative games, which are usually self-paced and fun, are powerful tools for improving students' feelings about themselves and others. They provide opportunities for maximum participation and active involvement, reducing the likelihood of students' feeling anxious, self-conscious, isolated, or unworthy, and enlarging self-concept, creativity, and the ability to get along with others; they are "sharing" experiences, teaching players that the more they help others, the more they and their team can achieve.

In cooperative games, players are not graded or assessed by winning or losing; in fact, every player wins, for all participants play *with* rather than *against* one another, and their goals are participation, fun, and cooperation. Such experiences help students to learn desirable social values and to become more considerate and caring.

Students' Responses to Cooperative Learning

Students benefit most from cooperative learning when all perform their responsibilities to help others in the group, and each contributes to achieving the group goal. To achieve this degree of cooperation, students need to practice interpersonal and group skills, either independently or as group members. Thus, when conflict within a group must be resolved in order to achieve a goal, the group may have to put aside its assigned task to concentrate temporarily on group maintenance.

POSITIVE OUTCOMES

Cooperative strategies that include group goals and individual accountability consistently increase learning and promote achievement to about the same degree for high, average, and low achievers at all grade levels, in all major subjects, in rural or urban schools (Slavin, 1991, p. 71). Positive outcomes for individuals, as well as groups, may include the following (pp. 75–81):

◆ consistently higher self-esteem and improved perceptions of/greater liking for classmates;

◆ more positive attitudes toward school and better cooperative skills;

◆ personal and social development that produces more supportive, friendlier, and more prosocial behavior; better conflict-resolution skills; and stronger support of democratic values;

◆ greater self-confidence strengthens intergroup relations and promotes more positive interactions among students of different races and abilities, including students with special needs (see Chapter 6);

◆ academic gains, including deeper understanding and increased transfer from short- to long-term memory, especially for minority-group and low-achieving students;

◆ a sense of control of one's school experience, and a stronger desire to do well;

◆ greater willingness to cooperate, more concern for others, and more productive time on task;

◆ better attendance and behavior among economically disadvantaged students, and fewer brushes with the police.

PRACTICE *and Projects*

1. Working with a group of your peers, prepare and present a topic of your choice, using the Jigsaw method. Follow the steps outlined below:

   STEP 1. Introduce and give an overview of your topic.

   STEP 2. Form heterogeneous "home" groups, each consisting of five or six members.

   STEP 3. Review group functions; decide which functions you will practice, and arrange to monitor and evaluate them.

   STEP 4. Form "expert" groups that will include a member of each home group.

   STEP 5. 5. With other members of your expert group, use the special materials available to investigate your topic.

   STEP 6. Prepare the procedure you will use for tutoring your home groups.

   STEP 7. Take your turn with the other experts in your home group to tutor (explain and drill) members on your topic.

   STEP 8. Check progress of your home group and, with other members, prepare for testing.

(continued)

(continued)

STEP 9. With other members of the groups, evaluate the approaches you have used.

STEP 10. Post the results for your group.

STEP 11. With the rest of your class, analyze the Jigsaw process.

2. With your class, view a video that presents specific cooperative models of instruction and learning. Discuss variations, advantages, and disadvantages.

3. a. View the video entitled "Together We Learn," available from the Metropolitan Toronto Board of Education or another video that illustrates cooperative learning.

   b. Later, as you watch the use of cooperative learning methods in elementary and secondary classrooms, consider the following questions and note your observations:

   ◆ How are cooperative learning essentials demonstrated in these class-rooms?

   ◆ What problems arise?

   ◆ How can these problems be overcome?

   c. Discuss your observations in class.

4. Use Data Collection Form 15.1 (Appendix A) to analyze Case Study 15.1. Your instructor may pose specific questions for your response.

CASE STUDY 15.1

COOPERATIVE LEARNING

In one group, five children sit facing one another. Jason is the "Writer" (recorder) and has a pencil and paper on which to record the group's answers. Samantha is the "Teller" (facilitator or chairperson); Arthur, the "Happy Talker" (encourager); Angie, the "Reader"; and Jeannine, the "Checker." The group is working through three problems assigned to them. Jason finishes recording the group's answer, and as he does so, Samantha says, "We're ready for the next problem. What's next?"

Angie looks at the card in her hand and reads, "Nathan and Roger, three-year-old twins, woke up from their nap at Sunnyside Daycare. A staff
(continued)

(continued)

member was preparing an apple for each of them. Roger said, 'Cut my apple in lots of pieces. I want to have more apple than Nathan.' The staff member cut Nathan's apple into six pieces and Roger's into twelve pieces. Who had more apple?"

"It's the same," Jason claims. "They both get the same."

"But twelve is more than six," Arthur objects. "Everybody knows that!"

"Wait a minute," interjects Samantha. "They each get one apple, right? So how could one of them get more? The pieces get smaller when you cut more of them."

"What do you think, Angie?" asks Jeannine.

"Samantha's right," Angie responds. "They only have one apple each. The pieces are different, that's all. Do you get that, Arthur? The twelve pieces and the six pieces are still just one apple. Both kids have one apple apiece."

"OK. Right. I see how that works," agrees Arthur.

"Does everybody agree that the twins both get the same?" asks Jeannine. The group members nod agreement. Jason writes, "Both twins get the same."

SUMMARY

- Cooperative interaction requires the use of interpersonal, group, and organizational skills.
- The key principles of cooperative learning are individual responsibility—which involves commitment to the achievement of a common task—and accountability to the group.
- The best way to prepare your students to acquire cooperative learning skills is to build a classroom climate of trust.
- Teachers should use a variety of strategies, including peer tutoring and cooperative games, to teach cooperative learning.
- Cooperative learning results in a number of positive educational outcomes for students, particularly those challenged or disadvantaged in some way.

KEY WORDS

accountability

cooperative interaction

cooperative instruction

cooperative games

cooperative learning

group-effectiveness goals

group investigation (GI)

group self-evaluation

Jigsaw

observation
global
systematic

peer tutoring

positive interdependence

responsibility

self-concept

Student Teams and Achievement Divisions (STAD)

supportive intervention

RECOMMENDED READING

Bennett, B., Rolheiser-Bennett, C., & Stevahn, L. (1991). *Cooperative learning: Where heart meets mind*. Toronto: Educational Connections.

Brubacher, M., Payne, R., & Rickett, K. (1990). *Perspectives on small group learning: Theory and practice*. Oakville, ON: Rubicon. *Cooperative learning: The magazine for cooperation in education*. (Annual resource guide. See especially Vol. 11, No. 1, 1990.)

Clark, J., Wideman, R., & Eadie, S. (1990). *Together we learn: Cooperative small group learning*. Scarborough, ON: Prentice-Hall.

Curran, L. (1990). *Cooperative learning lessons for little ones: Literature-based language arts and social studies*. San Juan Capistrano, CA: Resources for Teachers.

Graves, N., & Graves, T. (1985). Creating a cooperative learning environment: An ecological approach. In R. Slavin et al. (Eds.), *Learning to cooperate, cooperating to learn*. New York: Plenum.

Orlich, T. (1982). *Cooperative sports and games book*. New York: Pantheon.

Slavin, R. (1991). Synthesis of research on cooperative learning. *Educational Leadership*, *48*(5), 71–82.

PART 5

Teaching for Learning:

Framing the Big Picture

■ ■ ■ ■ ■

The enormous variety of variable elements that make up the process of instruction might seem to suggest that teaching/learning is fragmented to the point where there is danger of "losing the forest in the trees." In fact, a highly important function of teaching is to help students integrate the various components of learning by choosing and planning appropriate instructional elements and sequences. Framing the big picture of the instructional process are two indispensable elements: unit planning, and assessment/evaluation. By examining these elements and preparing to add them to your repertoire of instructional skills, you will gain a useful perspective on instruction that will help you to integrate its virtually innumerable components.

Chapter 16 deals with the processes of assessment and evaluation. Assessment involves seeking and recording information concerning the learning progress of students. It should be an ongoing process based in the myriad activities that make up students' learning experiences during a designated period of instruction. Performance testing of many sorts can be used to provide grading that is codified in a number of systems or based on less structured but more personalized techniques such as narrative reporting or students' portfolios of work. It is highly important that all testing, assessment, and grading procedures be free of bias and discrimination, and that instruments and methods represent a balance of different approaches and forms.

Chapter 17 discusses the process of planning instructional units. An instructional unit is a cohesive portion of a prescribed course that centers on a particular topic, theme, or major concept. Unit planning is based on familiarity and experience with a very broad range of instructional variables, among which the planner must choose in order to separate, then integrate, essential learnings relating to the topic of choice. Lessons must also be presented in a logical sequence that will maximize students' learning opportunities. Careful planning of units consists of developing an outline or concept map of the topic to be studied. This outline or map covers all the processes of planning, preparing, delivering, monitoring, and evaluating lessons in terms of student learning objectives and teachers' professional development goals.

Appendix A provides a broad range of data collection forms that you will find invaluable as you reflect on and target aspects of teaching, both during your training period and throughout your professional practice.

Appendix B provides two sample lesson plans and a sample unit plan that should assist you in planning effectively a variety of lesson types.

CHAPTER 16

ASSESSMENT AND EVALUATION

■ ■ ■ ■ ■

Assessment should focus on students' abilities to integrate their learning into constructive action.

(COHEN, 1993, P. 794)

■ ■ ■ ■ ■

OVERVIEW

Classroom teachers are responsible for assessing, testing, and grading the performance of the students they teach. Assessment involves seeking information about students' progress in learning through observing, recording, and evaluating their performance. Information can be sought, recorded, and assessed in various ways through the use of various techniques and instruments, including tests of different sorts, contracts, and portfolios of students' work. Teachers can act alone in assessing students' progress, using a variety of methods, or share the process with their students, training them to make productive self- or peer assessments. Marking systems, too, are variable, ranging from systems that use letters and numbers to designate grades to systems that use narrative comments or simply a pass–fail decision. A combination of various approaches and methods is probably most satisfactory.

■ ■ ■ ■ ■

THE ASSESSMENT PROCESS

When you first began practice teaching, concerns about assessing students' performance were probably much farther from your mind than concerns about your own classroom performance. Now that you have gained much more experience and developed a much broader range of teaching techniques, you can focus more clearly on the levels of student performance, identifying where students need help, and using analysis to determine the kind of help they need. These procedures are aspects of the very broad process of student assessment, an integral and important part of the infinitely varied professional activity of teaching. Table 16.1 offers an overview of methods and techniques associated with student assessment.

Assessment: Seeking Information

Assessment is the process of seeking and obtaining information about student development. Audrey Cohen (1993, pp. 791–795) states that effective teaching and assessment stress the following five aspects of instruction:

- fostering students' problem-solving skills and their habitual exercise of flexibility and persistence as they study and learn a range of school subjects;
- promoting students' appreciation and application of the theoretical and practical aspects of values and ethics;
- enlarging students' intellectual and practical understanding of individual and group dynamics and social interactions;
- drawing on various disciplines to promote students' facility in becoming effective members of various systems (e.g., family, societal, political, economic, technological, environmental);
- fostering students' development of a broad range of specific basic skills (e.g., reading, writing) and the ability to perform tasks that demand facility in complex areas of learning (e.g., computer literacy, mathematics, science).

Assessment of these instructional targets or goals is integrative and based on performance. It moves beyond testing for cognitive awareness of learnings to evaluating their practical application in life at increasingly sophisticated levels.

Grounds of Assessment

Given the importance of the assessment process, how can you determine systematically the grounds on which you should base the assessment of your students'

TABLE 16.1

Student Assessment Methods and Techniques

Methods of Organization
- Assessment stations
- Individual assessments
- Group assessments
- Contracts
- Self- and peer assessments
- Portfolios

Methods of Data Recording
- Anecdotal records
- Observation checklists
- Rating scales

Ongoing Student Activities
- Written assignments
- Presentations
- Performance assessments
- Homework

Methods of Data Recording
- Oral assessment items
- Performance test items
- Extended open-response items
- Short-answer items
- Multiple-choice items
- True/false items

Source: Adapted from *Student Evaluation: A Teacher Handbook* by Saskatchewan Education, 1991, Regina, SK: Saskatchewan Department of Education.

performance? Most schools use a reporting system that provides an overall framework for an assessment process, but this process will not achieve the purposes outlined above if it is applied in haste in the midst of end-of-term or end-of-semester activities and pressures. It should be addressed systematically from the beginning of each school year or semester, and should form a regular part of your professional activities. Plenty of "raw material" for effective assessment is ready to hand! Some elements of this material are suggested below.

ONGOING STUDENT ACTIVITIES

Students engage in a wide variety of activities during a school day, week, and term. Activities may engage the whole class, a group, or individuals, during a lesson, after a lesson, in or outside the classroom. Some activities are routine, others vary with the content of the lesson and the judgment of the teacher. Student performance during these activities provides a wealth of material for you to observe, record, and assess. In planning classroom activities, consider the opportunities they suggest for assessment, and follow up those opportunities in systematic ways.

Written Assignments

You may have students, individually or in groups, plan, complete, and submit a written product. Examples of written assignments include essays, reports, journal entries, poetry, articles, short stories, interviews and analysis, and observation reports in science or other disciplines. Assessment may be made by a teacher only or be a combination of teacher- and self- and/or peer assessment.

Oral Presentations

Written products can be the basis for oral presentations by individuals or groups. Oral presentations are a useful means of involving students in any school subject and encouraging interest in a wide range of topics. A more structured form of oral presentation is debate. Both these formats provide opportunities for individual and group assessment.

Performance

Since the achievement of learning objectives is observable largely through performance, assessment necessarily focuses on performance. Sometimes performance must be assessed as it occurs (e.g., operating a microscope); at other times, it can be assessed by examining a product (e.g., a drawing). The criteria used to assess performance or a product should usually be limited to important factors, and students should be told what those factors are.

Homework

Homework consists of assignments that students are given to do independently, outside the classroom. To make homework an optimal learning experience, teachers must monitor completed homework consistently and systematically. Such monitoring helps teachers identify students' strengths and weaknesses, track their progress, and assess the effectiveness of the instruction they are receiving. Homework can also be self- or peer-assessed.

Key Concepts

Although this text will get you off to a good start in practicing assessment and evaluation, it cannot cover everything you will need to know about these processes. Since you will need to do more reading on these topics, it will be helpful for you to understand the key terms used in the literature. They are as folllows:

◆ **Assessment** usually involves collating information that gives a full picture of your students' performance. You will use the information you gather to frame an overall judgment on each student's progress in learning as demonstrated by performance (e.g., in playing the violin or participating in a debate).

◆ **Evaluation** is a process whereby you will assign a comparative standing or value to a performance level, measuring it in relation to a predetermined scale that runs from total inability to theoretical perfection. The evaluation process can be "formative" or "summative."

 ◆ **Formative evaluation** is a procedure used before or during a teaching/learning process to plan and/or adjust performance in order to promote learning. In integrating formative evaluation into a teaching process, instructors give pretests, observe and question students on task, assign seatwork or homework, and administer check-up tests. Frequent formative evaluation may be a useful instructional device to enlarge comprehension and to provide repetition that will extend the retention of learning. This type of evaluation should not be used, however, to determine grades.

 ◆ **Summative evaluation** is a procedure used to form a coherent judgement of a student's performance and progress over a given period of time. Its validity depend on the evaluator's careful and consistent observation. This type of evaluation is the basis for assigning grades.

 ◆ *Criterion-referenced evaluation* involves measuring student performance against an absolute criterion, or standard Teachers use this type of evaluation to help them decide if a student needs more instruction or practice. The criterion used might demand, for example, that a successful student meet a minimum standard of "7 out of 10 test answers correct" or, to pass a course, achieve a performance standard of 65 percent on a semester's work.

 ◆ *Norm-referenced evaluation* involves comparing each student's results with the results of all others in the same class or in a comparable group, and assigning a grade based on his or her performance level as compared with the performance levels of peers. A norm-referenced test is a standardized test that evaluates a student's performance as it relates to that of a large representative sample of learners called, for this purpose, the "norm group."

♦ *Measurement* is the application of a standard scale to data so that a particular aspect (e.g., frequency, magnitude, correctness) of performance required of more than one person can be compared in a fair and orderly fashion. For Example 16.1 compares measurement, assessment, and evaluation.

♦ *Teacher-made tests* should measure precisely what was taught and nothing else. When constructed properly, test items reflect classroom learning objectives and the teaching methods and classroom learning activities used.

♦ *Standardized tests* are usually commercially designed. They sample performance under uniform procedures (directions, time limits, and methods for scoring); they are usually meant for broad, often nationwide use, and include norms.

All tests should be valid, reliable, and authentic.

♦ *Validity* relates to the reliability of a test in measuring what it is intended to measure (e.g., a test that is intended to measure Grade 9 reading skills is valid if it measures reading skills at that level).

♦ *Reliability* relates to the consistency with which a test repeatedly yields virtually the same scores when given to the same individuals, under similar circumstances.

♦ *Authenticity* relates to the degree to which tests are congruent with reality. Authentic tests involve "real" problems that are transferable to life situations.

Assessing Performance

Teachers seek information about their own performance and that of their students in a variety of ways that have been classified as inquiry, observation, analysis, and testing (TenBrink, 1986).

FOR EXAMPLE 16.1

Measurement, Assessment, Evaluation

♦ Ms. X measures students' progress by using a pretest and a post-test in a lesson relating to the Riel Rebellion.
♦ Mr. Y assesses students' skill in basketball by forming intra-class teams and observing players' performance.
♦ Mrs. Z evaluates students' understanding of *King Lear* by having them write an essay on the tragic elements in the play.

INQUIRY

It will sometimes be appropriate for you to ask your students directly how they feel about themselves and their performance in class, what approaches to learning they like or dislike, and their opinion on certain matters, including how they would rate their success in handling a particular activity, assignment, or test. After you have trained your students to check their work, you might ask them to respond to such inquiries orally, in writing, or by using a checklist on which they record the strengths and weaknesses they think they have shown in carrying out an assignment.

You should use information gained in these ways carefully, since it may be incomplete or inaccurate. Combined with data that you have obtained through direct observation, however, information derived directly from individual students can suggest effective ways of helping them to improve their performance and become lifelong self-directed learners.

OBSERVATION

Observing your students as they participate in lessons and activities, respond to questions, and work individually and in groups at assigned tasks will inform you about their level of performance and allow you to provide prompt feedback. Watch for nonverbal signals (see Chapter 2) that may indicate a student's level of comfort and assurance with various instructional experiences. Record your observations unobtrusively on a regular and extended basis (throughout each term or semester) to build up a picture of each student's performance in a full range of learning situations. Though the process will be time consuming, and your observations will inevitably include a subjective factor, such records are an invaluable daily assessment tool.

ANALYSIS

You will need to analyze each student's performance, as well as your observation records, to discover what parts of a student's work have been well done, and where improvement should be made. You can make your analyses while students are engaged in completing an assignment or project, or when they have finished their work.

Analysis requires, first of all, surveying the sequential parts of a skill or process, or the organizational structure of a product. Your approach will vary, depending on the subject matter involved. In mathematics, for instance, you might survey the steps a student has taken to solve a problem; in science, you might check the parts of a model constructed to illustrate a scientific principle or phenomenon. This process should help you to determine what learning goals a student has achieved, and discover whether or where he or she is still having difficulty. You will use this information to help your students as necessary. The same process will help you to discover whether a number of students are having difficulty in the same areas: a signal that you may need to reteach some part(s) of an earlier lesson.

TESTING

Testing is a form of "controlled experiment": a systematic procedure for measuring student performance by applying a common set of instructions, scoring criteria, and methods of recording scores or achievement to a group of individuals to determine their relative degrees of success in learning a specified product or process. Tests may be made and administered by a classroom teacher or purchased by a school system to assess the performance of its students in relation to broader standards. Tests can measure learning achievement, skill levels attained in psychomotor performance, the attainment of instructional goals, or social attitudes.

AVOIDING BIAS AND DISCRIMINATION

In assessing students' performance, it is highly important that you be seen as fair and impartial. Huge discrepancies can occur in the grades awarded by different teachers to similar student performance on a given test or assignment. Be aware of how easy it is for teachers, even with the best of intentions, to make biased assessments of student performance. Broad student diversity within a classroom can create bias for or against some individuals in matters of test content, testing procedures, or test use (Eggen & Kauchak, 1993). Before giving a test, you will need to determine whether the students in your classroom have enough background knowledge to handle successfully the assessment items you plan to use. Teach students the knowledge and skills required for success *before* you test them.

Bias in test use or procedures can occur because minority students may not respond to a test in the same way that their majority peers do. Metaphors and idioms familiar to acculturated North Americans may leave other students totally confused. Problems are especially severe when students have limited command of standard English or come from a culture that stresses oral rather than written communication.

Different views of the purpose of testing can be another source of trouble. Students of Afro-American, Hispanic, or Aboriginal heritage may have a distinctly different perspective from that of other students on testing and the competitive nature of some assessment practices. Tests with time limits may be a problem for students who believe that it is best to work at their own pace instead of rushing through a task and doing it poorly.

Discrimination can result if tests do a poor job of measuring the performance of students with linguistic backgrounds other than standard English. Inappropriate test scores can affect their admission to postsecondary programs or their success in seeking employment.

Problems such as these are strong reasons for using a variety of assessment methods. Students from minority backgrounds should not be denied opportunities to achieve their potential. When you prepare tests for your students, use problem situations and stems familiar to all of them, providing for linguistic-minority students by allowing them to work in their first language as appropriate. (To make this possible, you may have to draw on resources available in the school system or the community.) Identify aspects of tests that are influenced by background, and try to keep these elements to a minimum. When you must include them, take up the tests in class and provide help as appropriate, or use an alternative testing method, such as oral testing (Eggen and Kauchak, 1993).

■ ■ ■ ■ ■

ASSESSMENT TECHNIQUES

Good assessment techniques show classroom teachers whether their students have achieved the instructional objectives set (see Chapter 3). Select techniques that are appropriate and varied to help you build up a complete picture of student performance and achievement. Teachers who consistently record student assessments can use those data to assess their own instructional approaches; to discover which objectives have been achieved; to decide whether the objectives were, in fact, appropriate; to identify instructional areas where remediation or reteaching are needed; and to place students in groups or in an alternative program.

Methods of Assessment

You will find that you can assess your students' performance through a variety of instruments and in a variety of ways: during a test, for instance, or during ongoing classroom activities. You can make the assessments yourself, or you can train your students to make self-assessments. The organizational approach that you select should be based on the type of information you wish to gather. Usually, it is better to combine methods of organization, techniques, and standards when assessing the progress of your students as individuals and as a class, for a combination of methods allows more flexibility and is fairer to individuals. Some of the methods sketched in the following discussion involve the use of assessment stations.

An *assessment station* is an area, inside or outside the classroom, identified by the teacher as the site to be used for voluntarily requesting and receiving assessments. Students, individually or in groups, go to this area to be assessed on academic performance or attitude and behavior. The provision of such an area allows students to seek assessment, during regular classroom time, of their work with ideas or materials. They might use such a station to demonstrate many types of performance, such as using a zoology display to classify a specimen, creating a chart on a computer, writing a story, or performing a gymnastic skill.

INDIVIDUAL ASSESSMENT

Individual assessment allows the teacher to examine the progress of each student in a class or group. To make such an assessment, you must decide whether to use **norm-referencing** (i.e., apply a group standard to all students of the same age, grade, or level of development), **criterion-referencing** (i.e., apply a predetermined standard to all students), or **self-referencing** (i.e., use a student's previous level of achievement as the standard against which to judge growth or performance).

GROUP ASSESSMENT

Group assessment is a way of collecting information about students working in group situations and determining their progress. The teacher may assign individual marks to group members or use a combination of group and individual marks; each approach has advantages and disadvantages. It is traditional for teachers to give individual marks, and some assessments are best done individually, but concerns do arise from the fact that

* the technique encourages competition; and
* it is hard to a measure an individual's contribution to a group project.

A compromise may be to combine individual and group assessment.

SELF- AND PEER ASSESSMENT

Self- and peer assessment give students the responsibility of assessing their own and their classmates' work. Before initiating this method of assessment, it is important for teachers to ensure that their students are mature enough to carry it out in a positive and productive way. Train your students to assess peer performance in a descriptive, nonjudgmental way. It will be helpful, too, for you to discuss assessment and its methods with your students in advance, pointing out that both the person being assessed and the person making the assessment can benefit from the exercise. Prepare checklists or rating scales for students to use, at least until you are sure that they can make productive written or oral assessments. Self- or peer assessment is best used when student self-knowledge is important. These methods lend themselves to projects or participation in group work. Ideally, students are involved in developing the assessment criteria.

Instruments of Assessment

You will find a number of devices useful for helping you gather and record data and assess your students' performance in a variety of situations. The most commonly used of these devices are probably quizzes and tests, but there are other devices as well.

CONTRACTS

A contract is an agreement between a student or group of students and the teacher. This agreement outlines what learning objective is to be achieved, who will do the work involved, how the work will be done, when the completed task is due, and how the performance or product will be marked. Students are involved in planning the contract, determining what the product is to be, and how it is to be evaluated. Products may include written assignments, displays, models, or portfolios. Before you organize a contract with your students, you may need to teach them how to plan contracts, motivate them to become self-directed learners (see Chapters 4 & 14), and give them practice in taking the responsibility required.

RATING SCALES

Teachers use rating scales of various extents (e.g., 1–5; 0–10) to record their assessment of the quality of performance or the degree of achievement of an individual's or group's learning objective, whether it be a concept, skill, process, or attitude. Rating scales may be useful, for instance, in assessing students' facility in using nonverbal communication (see Chapter 2) during an oral presentation; completing a written assignment; playing the piano at a recital; doing an experiment in a science laboratory; or making an item in a woodworking shop.

QUIZZES AND TESTS

Quizzes and tests are instruments to measure learnings or attitudes by presenting common situations for student response. Each quiz or test has common instructions and rules for scoring. Most subject-related quizzes and tests measure the degree to which students have achieved learning objectives; they allow students to show what they know or can do at a particular point in time. Teachers often use quizzes (which are usually shorter than tests because they are limited to material studied in one or two previous lessons) to determine whether their students are ready to go on to new material.

Setting Good Tests

Good tests are valid and reliable, and consist of items that relate appropriately to the learning outcomes to be measured (e.g., recall, understanding, application, analysis, creativity, and/or reasoning). The test items you select should seek information about material taught in the classroom, presenting questions and instructions in the ways used in class. They should require the same performance of students, and provide the same conditions, or "givens," that you identified in your instructional objectives; they should also be congruent with the activities students have engaged in to achieve the learning or performance objectives specified.

Although the primary purpose of tests is assessment of learning achievement and teaching effectiveness, tests should also be teaching and learning tools, and should be used to deepen understanding through a triple review—students review material before and during the writing of the test, and again when the teacher takes the test up—and improve learning through exercising recall and the other skills required.

When you are preparing a test, try to ensure that your students will understand what you are asking and how you want them to respond. Check to see that each item is free from clues and that its level of difficulty is appropriate. Some experienced teachers recommend framing a test as to the middle range of students in a class so that it will be neither too easy nor too difficult.

Plan to mark and return tests promptly. Students deserve to have prompt, clear feedback on their performance. This allows them to check what they know and what they still need to learn, and then to turn "deferred successes" into actual successes.

Selecting Test Items

Many types of test items are available, including oral, performance, extended open-response (essay), short-answer, matching, multiple-choice, and true/false tests. A first step in making appropriate selections is to decide precisely what you want to test.

◆ *Oral test items* evaluate what students say rather than what they write. You can use this type of test when you need to check students' ability to express themselves orally or to "think on their feet." You can also use it when a written test is unfeasible or inappropriate, or when you wish to supplement or check its validity. Oral tests allow you to ask more questions because students need more time to respond in writing than to respond orally. It also allows you to use rating scales or checklists.

You may find oral tests useful for teaching courses where the development of auditory comprehension skills is an objective, or in working with a student who is challenged by blindness or paralysis, or to help you recognize students who belong to a cultural minority or have a different language background. Depending on the circumstances, you might also use oral questions but require written responses.

If you use oral testing, however, be wary of the tendency you may experience to provide prompts, which might give some students an unfair advantage. You may also need to find ways to reduce the level of tension oral testing causes some students. Private sessions may be less stressful than class sessions.

◆ *Performance items* are used to assess how well a student performs a skill or process that he or she has practiced in order to achieve one or more learning objectives (e.g., using a computer, giving a speech, or operating a lathe). Performance tests may involve simulation (e.g., the simulated operation of a car). Such tests should usually assess both product and process.

◆ *Extended essay (open-response) items* generally require students to use complex cognitive processes or skills to compose a comprehensive, lengthy, or complex response on a given topic. No single response pattern is correct. Instead, students must organize information to solve problems, synthesize what they know, or draw on their creativity. Essay test items are useful to assess cognitive skills such as seeking a solution to a problem, synthesizing data from two or more sources, making comparisons, examining cause-and-effect relationships, developing an argument to support a position, and critically examining assumptions.

Although essay tests give students opportunities to demonstrate their command of learning objectives, they are time-consuming to write. This means that, in selecting test items, you must restrict the course content sampled, leaving important content untested. In addition, although you will have only a few items to prepare and mark, marking may be a long, laborious process that is hard to keep objective, and grading may become inconsistent. (Be aware of the tendency for teachers to grade essay items higher than objective items.) If, in addition to content and organizational and thinking skills, writing skill is part of the score, grading becomes even more complex. Some educators hold that essay items should be restricted to term papers or take-home tests.

◆ *Restricted-response (short-answer) items* direct students to supply, or complete, short written responses to specific questions. Students' answers may consist of a single word, a phrase, or a short paragraph or two. Your directions should specify response limitations, and you should provide evaluation criteria for scoring. Short-answer tests are relatively easy to construct, and their items are efficient for testing students' ability to recall, since knowledge of many facts can be tested in a short time. There is less guessing with this format than with other objective tests, but short-answer tests survey less content in a given time than do multiple-choice tests.

It is not easy to measure complex learning through restricted-response items. First, it is difficult to construct clear, unambiguous items; in addition, such testing may stress recall and encourage students to memorize trivial details. Scoring, too, may be difficult. Since there may be times, however, when it is practical to use short-answer tests, it is a good idea to develop a bank of short-answer (and other) items. If you want to use some of the items in future tests, arrange to collect the tests when your students have completed them, and keep them in a secure place. When you plan to reuse any items, check them to make sure that they are still appropriate.

♦ *Matching item questions* can test knowledge of facts, relationships, or associations. In using matching items, present your students with two lists of items, and ask them to select an item from one list (the premise list) that most closely matches an item in the other list (the response list). To prepare such a test, list items at random, making the response list longer than the premise list. Prevent confusion by making sure that the items are homogeneous (or related); keep the lists short—both lists should be on one page—and provide clear directions. Constructing lists that are free from clues takes time and can be difficult. Moreover, since students may begin to guess at answers as the process of elimination proceeds, matching-items tests are not suitable for assessing achievement of higher-level learning objectives.

♦ *Multiple-choice items* consist of questions or statements (stems) followed by a list of possible answers. Each answer should be plausible, and students should be told to pick the "best" response. Objective tests, such as multiple-choice tests, allow greater coverage of materials taught, and many educators think that multiple-choice is the best type of objective test: its items can be very reliable and objective; a large knowledge base can be tested in a short time; it is versatile and easy to mark; and it serves to evaluate learning at all cognitive levels.

Multiple-choice items are usually not suitable, however, for measuring capability in organization or composition. Measuring other higher-level thought processes by this method, though possible, is not easy: constructing good items is time-consuming and difficult, for great care must be taken to word items carefully so as to avoid giving clues. Because of these difficulties, such tests sometimes include an inordinate number of low-level items. Moreover, multiple-choice tests may promote guessing; in addition, they may give an advantage to students with above-average reading ability, even though students with poorer reading skills may know just as much content. Many more items are required to construct a multiple-choice test than an essay test. In sum, multiple-choice items should probably be used in conjunction with other types of items.

◆ *True/false (alternative-response) items* require students to indicate whether a statement is correct or incorrect. A large number of items increases their value. Items of this type seem easy to write, can test the greatest number of facts in the shortest time, and are the easiest to score. Although true/false items are usually used to test recall, they can measure a broad range of thinking skills.

True/false questions should rarely be the sole technique used in a test, however, since guessing is a problem: even a monkey has a 50 percent chance of getting the right answer to a true/false item. This means that care must be taken to reduce the effects of guessing. Since guessers tend to select "true" more often than "false," you should use more "false" items than "true" in such tests. A variation on the basic true/false test is to ask students to explain their choice or require them to revise statements that are false and give credit only if the revision is correct.

Writing Functional Assessment Items

To prepare for a performance test, you will need to frame clear criteria and inform your students of what they are. Make sure that in your plan for assessment items, you specify the learner behavior, conditions, and type of performance required (see Chapter 3) to measure the instructional outcomes intended. In wording essay test items, state clearly and precisely the performance skills required for response (e.g., "compare—that is, point out similarities *and* differences,"—"predict," "evaluate the merit of …," "use the following criteria" and "provide original examples"). Make sure that each item allows only one interpretation of the performance expected, for students may become confused when directions are too complicated, several possible answers may be correct, or items are to be arranged in an unspecified sequence or described in an unspecified way (Higgins & Sullivan, 1981). Check that assessment items specify the same performance that you stated as your students' learning objective, and that the conditions (or givens) specified are also the same (see For Example 16.2).

The stems of multiple-choice items should clearly state the central problem, and each choice offered should be plausible. Begin with clear directions and keep the lists of premises and responses homogeneous. Choices should be concise and grammatically consistent, and leading words in possible answers should be avoided. Avoid offering prompts or clues in the framing of questions, lists of equal length

FOR EXAMPLE **16.2**

Effective Assessment Items

PERFORMANCE OBJECTIVE 1: When presented with a newspaper or magazine advertisement, the student will be able to identify correctly the psychological influences on the consumer.

ASSESSMENT ITEM 1: The teacher provides clippings of magazine and newspaper advertisements and asks her students to identify which psychological needs each advertisement is appealing to.

PERFORMANCE OBJECTIVE 2: Given an atlas and a list of latitude and longitude coordinates, students will identify the names of nine out of the ten North American cities located at those coordinates.

ASSESSMENT ITEM 2: Students are given a list of the coordinates for ten cities, with a blank space beside each coordinate. Using their atlases as a reference tool, they are instructed to write the name of the city in the space beside the appropriate coordinates.

in matching questions, or illogical options in multiple-choice tests. Tests laden with such prompts are poor indicators of what students have learned. "Test-wise" students look for such hints to correct answers. Don't supply them! Even though a pattern of correct and incorrect responses for multiple-choice items (e.g., a "c-b-d-a-c-b-d-a" pattern) may make scoring easier, avoid it, for test-takers can "crack the code." For matching items, the list of responses should usually contain between five and fifteen items.

In true/false tests, every statement should be concise and completely true or completely false on the basis of important facts, not trivial details. Correct answers should be placed at random: there should be no pattern of correct answers.

Assessment items must not only be appropriate, but they must also be well written. Do not use items that are too broad, that leave students guessing, or that require reams of memorized information. Avoid choices if you want every student to write the same test.

Above all, *test only what you have taught!*

No matter how well a test is written, it may not assess what you intended it to assess if your students have not learned how to take tests. For instance, students who have not taken many essay tests during their schooling may not know how to respond to one. Teaching them how to prepare and use an outline before they write the test can increase their confidence and greatly improve their answers. If your students need help in taking tests successfully, let them practice with "dry run" tests that you give and take up with them, teaching them how to read the questions and explaining the steps involved in responding appropriately.

Making a Post-Test Analysis

After you have given a test and before you file it, evaluate the effectiveness of each item: examine its level of difficulty and its discrimination index (i.e., how well it identifies, as shown by the incidence of correct answers, students who know the work well and students who do not). Use the results of your analysis when you set other tests.

Recording Assessment Data

Information about student progress, including results of tests and observations of participation in activities, can be recorded in several ways. The techniques you select should be accurate and easy to use, and should fairly represent occurrences or developments. A number of techniques are outlined below.

ANECDOTAL RECORDS

Anecdotal records are narrative, day-to-day accounts of students' progress, based on teachers' observations and usually collected in a specific folder or book. These records usually consist of dated, descriptive, open-ended notes, often entered on forms that provide headings followed by spaces for recording observations. The notes may be formative (recording a student's progress and noting areas that require remedial attention) and/or summative (detailing a student's development over a definite period).

OBSERVATION CHECKLISTS

Observation checklists provide teachers with a way of making a minimal, on-the-spot record of a student's critical behaviors or key responses. Teachers usually complete these lists during class time. The lists, in which each entry represents a formative picture, can be used summatively to measure the extent to which a student gives performance evidence of achieving specified learning objectives, including concepts, skills, processes, or attitudes. Typical lists might record observations relating to students' use of problem-solving skills in mathematics, development of handwriting skills, development/problems in spelling, application of information to another context (transfer), development of logical thought in an essay or report, demonstration of attitudes and values, and participation in group or project work. A longitudinal profile of a student's progress may emerge if a checklist is used several times and then evaluated.

PORTFOLIOS

"A portfolio is a purposeful collection of student work that exhibits the student's efforts, progress, and achievements in one or more areas. The collection must include student participation in selecting contents, the criteria for selection, the criteria for judging merit, and evidence of student self-reflection" (Paulson, Paulson, & Meyer, 1991, p. 60). Portfolios, or representative items of students' work collected over an extended period for assessment according to present guidelines, eliminate any artificiality or pressure that tests might create. The best portfolios contain evidence of students' reflection on their work and progress in the form of free-expression logs or journals.

Portfolios assess students' learning in a different way from achievement tests, which measure specific outcomes that can be tabulated or counted. Portfolios allow teachers to observe students in a more complete way: they can be useful for assessing investigations reported through oral or written assignments or extended problem-solving activities in mathematics. They can also encourage students to be creative, to take risks, to become self-directed learners, and to practice self-evaluation.

■ ■ ■ ■ ■

GRADING AND MARKING SYSTEMS

Educational grading and marking systems have long been sources of controversy. Differences of opinion exist as to whether letters or other symbols, or percentages, or pass–fail systems should be used. Some educators have suggested the use of narrative reports, mastery reports, or student portfolios, which they believe can make assessment more authentic. Because each marking system has advantages and disadvantages, some school systems have adopted multiple (combined) systems, but some educators point out that, although combined systems, when used well, may be a reasonable compromise, teachers must then report double or triple the number of grades, and explaining the systems to parents is more difficult (Kubiszyn & Borich, 1987).

As a staff member in any given school, you may be required to use an established or generally accepted marking system, but you may also be allowed some flexibility. Whatever the system or combination of systems used, report cards should explain it clearly. Students and parents, not just school staff, have a right to understand the method(s) of assessment and reporting.

Many teachers believe that students and parents need marks as a form of feedback on students' academic achievement. Some educators argue that students need grades to provide **extrinsic motivation**, and that they will not work well without them. On the other hand, cheating on letter-graded and numerically graded tests is far more common than many educators would care to admit.

Letter Grading Systems

The most common symbol system uses letters to indicate grades. The letters used are usually A, B, C, D, and F. People generally are aware that A is the top mark, that D denotes marginal performance, and that F represents a failure. Numerical keys are often written on report cards that use a letter system (e.g., A+ = 90%–100%; A = 80%–89%; B = 70%–79%; C = 60%–69%; D = 50%–59%; and F = below 50%). Some teachers make finer distinctions by using plus and minus signs with letters (e.g., B+ or C–). Variations such as E, VG, G, S, and U (excellent, very good, good, satisfactory, and unsatisfactory) are used in some schools.

Letter grades that record and summarize a student's performance over a semester or a term are easy to record, and the standard five letters can represent as many as fifteen grades, if plus and minus categories are used. Letter grades reduce the amount of meaningless ranking of students that occurs with percentage grades (e.g., when a student with a grade of 69% is ranked below a student with a grade of 70%) and make unfair award decisions less common (e.g., when a student with an average of 96.29% does not receive a scholarship because it goes to a classmate with an average of 96.56% average).

Letter systems, however, have some disadvantages. Different school jurisdictions use different marking systems, which makes interpretation difficult when a student moves from one school system to another. Letter grades are arbitrary gross indicators of a student's level of mastery: there may be considerable difference, for instance, between a low C and a high C. (For that matter, differences can and do occur in the significance of marks assigned by two teachers in the same school or department.) Letters convey little information about a student's strengths and weaknesses. Some teachers think more precise differentiation between the achievement of different students is necessary, and so prefer a numerical system.

Numerical Grading Systems

Numerical grading systems are used less widely than letter systems. The most common numerical system involves percentages, with 100 percent as the highest mark. Numbers are a convenient way of recording a summary statement of work over a semester or term. Scores, or percentages, are easy to average, and ranking is more discriminating. Many parents think that numerical grades are meaningful and easy to understand, and some parents and teachers believe that they are extrinsic motivators.

The disadvantages of numerical grading systems include the difficulty of making, for example, 50 valid and reliable distinctions between 50 percent and 100 percent. Grading becomes arbitrary and communicates little information about student strengths and weaknesses. As with letter grades, numerical grades are not keyed to a common standard, and so considerable differences exist in the meaning of the designations between one school or district and another (e.g., a grade of 88% in one jurisdiction may be the equivalent of 78% in another). Remarkable differences can exist even in grades awarded by different teachers in the same school or department.

It is common for school systems that use letter or numerical systems to supplement assigned grades with checklists or brief comments because symbol systems do not describe a students' strengths, weaknesses, or performance ability. Checklists may also be used to describe nonacademic aspects of a student's behavior, such as social skills, responsibility, organization, or cooperation.

The Pass–Fail System

Another approach to grading is the pass–fail system. Variations are "pass–fail–incomplete" and "satisfactory–unsatisfactory." The pass–fail system is not common, though it is sometimes used to grade subjects with a high performance or finished product component. It can be argued, for instance, that letter or numerical grades are meaningless in performance-oriented (for example, phys-ed, typing), dance, drama, or visual arts classes or in relation to products in vocational classes.

An advantage of the pass–fail approach is that it reduces the negative effects of competition and test anxiety so that students are not afraid to take risks and are readier to help one another. Some educators claim that students learn more in a pass–fail system and are more likely to show improvement in their interpersonal and social skills. By contrast, others argue that students in such a system will do just as little work as it takes them to pass. Individual performance and ranking are difficult to indicate in a pass–fail system, and this may cause dissatisfaction among parents who wish to know how their child performed in comparison to other children.

Mastery Grading

Mastery grading can be useful for a course or part of a course. This system is based on the assumption that all students can master learning objectives if given enough instruction and time. Under the mastery learning system, content is broken into parts, and specific objectives and criteria for meeting them are designated for each part. If, on completion of a given part, a student fails to achieve a certain test grade (e.g., 80%) when tested, he or she is given more instruction and more learning time, and then retested. Grading under this system is usually pass–fail, but performance can be converted to marks.

CONTRACT GRADING

Contract grading, a variation of mastery grading, is often used with individual instruction. A contract generally specifies the type, quality, and amount of work the student will do to earn a grade of A, B, C, or D. In this system, learners choose the grade they will work to achieve, knowing exactly where they stand.

Narrative Grading Systems

In a narrative grading system, teachers describe and comment on students' learning. A narrative system can provide much more information than letter or numerical grading systems. Such information can help other teachers determine how they can best help a particular student. In addition to describing academic progress, narrative reports may include comments on students' work habits, level of effort, conduct, social skills, organization, and responsibility, as well as anecdotal information (i.e., brief objective descriptions of incidents or events with significant relevance to a particular student). Narrative grading systems can reduce test anxiety and the negative effects of competition, but they do not provide the grades that some parents and politicians require.

Some educators promote a variant of narrative grading in the form of reports that are essentially checklists of competencies. These reports are easier to prepare and, according to their proponents, do the job just as well as narrative reports. It is difficult, however, to prepare checklists that adequately describe a student's level of performance.

Portfolios as Assessment Tools

Many school systems are either using or considering using portfolios as assessment tools, with or without the use of other techniques. Many teachers, excited by the progress of their students under this system, are advocating its use, claiming that it gives them a sense of "professional renewal" and a "feeling of renewed commitment to improving learning in their classrooms" (Association for Supervision and Curriculum Development, 1993, p. 3). This growth in popularity seems to parallel the growing acceptance by teachers of the notion of authentic instruction.

Portfolios can be a useful tool for demonstrating students' progress to parents or guardians, since they provide much more information about students' strengths and weaknesses than do letter and numerical grading systems. They can also be used to supplement report cards and the results of standardized tests.

To use student portfolios, you must decide (since not all student work can be included) what goes into them and by what criteria to evaluate the quality of the work (Eggen & Kauchak, 1994, p. 666). Ideally, students are involved in making the selection, and assessing and evaluating it. This responsibility can motivate students to do quality work. The most common means of checking work against guidelines are checklists and rating scales.

Proponents must not ignore current criticisms of portfolios as an assessment tool—particularly if it is the one chiefly used—by some teachers, parents, business and industries, and political bodies. Critics object to portfolio assessment on the grounds that it is more time-consuming for teachers (who must examine and assess portfolios, and record and report the results of assessments); it focuses students' interest on their own work as the standard of performance; and it is difficult to rank students' work on this selective basis.

Self-Evaluation

Many school systems are placing more emphasis on self-directed learning, of which self-evaluation is an important aspect. Students share in determining their grades according to guidelines set by the teacher or through a cooperative process involving student and teacher. This approach may increase **intrinsic motivation** by encouraging students to develop ownership of and, consequently, accountability for, their own learning. Teachers must be aware, however, that students may over- or underrate themselves, and that self-evaluation can be used with other grading techniques.

Students are natural self-evaluators, and if they are to learn to think critically and make sound judgments, they need and should be given enough experience in self-evaluation (Bowd, McDougall, & Yewchuk, 1994). They can gain such experience by using checklists, rating scales, self-reporting forms, or learning logs or journals. These last devices are becoming popular as self-monitoring aids, particularly in language arts.

Logs or journals contain students' records of their reflections about themselves as learners, their feelings, their learnings, and their learning goals. To help your students use their logs to best advantage, you will have to teach them self-evaluation skills, and provide instruction and frequent feedback on the process of reflection. You should encourage your students, in using their logs, to be constructively analytical about both their successes and their "deferred successes."

Achieving a Balance

Each approach to testing and assessment has advantages and disadvantages. Differences of opinion as to the "best" approach exist and will continue to exist.

Some people strongly favor the letter- or numerical-grade approach to assessment, whereas others would jettison it and even do away with standardized testing. The best approach, in fact, may be a combination assessment procedure.

Reform-minded educators should realize that meaningful contexts and authentic assessment are not confined to only one type of assessment technique. Instruction and assessment processes are more meaningful and relate more fairly to the concerns and problems faced by students (i.e., have a greater degree of authenticity) when a combination of procedures is used. Instructors should jettison the mimetic approach to learning and use instructional practices that encourage students to search, think and rethink, and "do and show" (Brooks & Brooks, 1993). This should also be your target in selecting a mix of assessment techniques that will provide a range of benefits.

PRACTICE *and Projects*

1. a. Make lists of things you liked and disliked about the way your performance was graded during your schooling.
    b. Working in a small group, identify what you consider the three or four most important points that a teacher should communicate to parents when reporting students' progress. Try to reach consensus.
    c. Choose a group member to report your conclusions to the class.
    d. Discuss as a class any issues that arise. Form groups of five to discuss the meaning of each of the "Key Concepts" of assessment and evaluation listed on pages 367–368. Use paraphrasing and perception checking to reach consensus.

2. In some classrooms in Japan, students spend a part of every period practicing how to write tests. You are considering adopting this practice in your own classroom. Discuss the pros and cons with a small group of your "colleagues," then report your conclusions at a "general staff meeting."

3. a. Working with a teaching partner or a small group, and using Data Collection Form 16.1, analyze Mr. Turner's test and assess its suitability for use with his multicultural class.
    b. Join a subject-interest group and frame a test for a multicultural class at the level of your choice.

CASE STUDY 16.1

TESTING FOR BIAS

Mr. Turner has carefully prepared a test for his Grade 4 class in a large inner-city school. He thinks that he has made his test interesting and challenging. Because his students represent a variety of cultures and linguistic backgrounds—Japanese, Mexican, Somalian, English Canadian, East Indian, Polish—he has decided to use visual, as well as print, material.

But since Mr. Turner is just beginning his teaching career and is preparing his students for their first "major" language test, he has decided to use this first test as a pretest to learn more about his students' needs and to prepare them for a formal testing process at the end of term.

The first question of the pretest, which is based on a colorful illustration of a football game, checks students' ability to synthesize pictorial information with written description. Another question is based on a line drawing of a traditional French Canadian winter scene, showing a heavily muffled *Canadien* driving a sled across a frozen river. Students have been given a list of numbered items. They are to mark the number on the matching item in the picture, and then write a definition of each of the items. A third question asks students to compose a short verse of four to eight lines about "Fall" or "Winter."

Later, when Mr. Turner reads the completed tests, he realizes that many of his students are not yet ready for a test of this type. Most of the girls have had difficulty interpreting the football illustration. Three students have labeled the *Canadien*'s headgear a "toque," one has called it a "stocking cap," and the rest have simply called it a hat. Several students have made no attempt to write a verse.

"Tomorrow," Mr. Turner sighs, "I'll have to take this up with the class."

SUMMARY

◆ Assessment is the process of seeking and obtaining information about student development.

◆ Students' progress should be reported systematically from the beginning of each school year or semester; such reporting should form a regular part of professional activities.

- ◆ Student performance in a wide range of activities provides ample material for teachers to observe, record, and assess.
- ◆ Assessment, evaluation, measurement, and testing are key aspects of promoting and recording students' performance.
- ◆ Inquiry, observation, analysis, and avoiding bias and discrimination are important aspects of assessment and evaluation.
- ◆ Assessment techniques can operate through an individual or group approach that involves teacher and/or students.
- ◆ Instruments of assessment vary widely, and may be used singly or in combination.
- ◆ Data may be recorded in a variety of formats, from grading systems using letters or numbers to narrative reports and portfolios of students' work.
- ◆ Bias and discrimination in testing, assessing, and grading students' work are not always easy to identify, but a strong and continual effort should be made to avoid them.
- ◆ A variety of approaches to testing, assessment, and grading probably yields the most satisfactory results.

KEY WORDS

analysis
anecdotal records
assessment
assessment stations
bias
contract
discrimination
evaluation
    formative
    summative
    criterion-
       referenced
    norm-referenced

grading systems
    symbolic
    pass–fail
    mastery grading
    narrative grading
    portfolios
    self-evaluation
group assessment
individual assessment
inquiry
measurement
observation
observation checklists
oral presentations
peer assessment

portfolio
post-test analysis
quizzes
ranking
rating scales
reports
self-assessment
standardized tests
test criteria
    validity
    reliability
    authenticity
testing
written assignments

RECOMMENDED READING

Mitchell, R. (1992). *Testing for learning: New approaches to evaluation can improve American schools*. New York: Free Press.

Perrone, V. (1991). *Expanding student assessment*. Alexandria, VA: Association for Supervision and Curriculum Development.

Wiggins, G. (1993). Assessment, authenticity, context and validity. *Phi Delta Kappan*, 75(3), 200–214.

Testing Techniques

Hopkins, K., Stanley, J., & Hopkins, B. (1990). *Educational and psychological measurement and evaluation*. (7th ed.). Englewood Cliffs, NJ: Prentice-Hall.

Kubiszyn, T., & Borich, G. (1987). *Educational testing and measurement: Classroom application and practice* (2nd ed.). Glenview, IL: Scott Foresman.

CHAPTER 17

UNIT PLANNING: INTEGRATING INSTRUCTIONAL VARIABLES

■ ■ ■ ■ ■

[A course should be] divided into units ... that are structured and sequenced in ways that maximize clarity and ease of learning and minimize potential for confusion.

(GOOD & BROPHY, 1990, P. 273)

■ ■ ■ ■ ■

OVERVIEW

An instructional unit consists of a variety of variables that include teaching/learning domains, academic subjects, and a great variety of instructional elements, including curriculum objectives; instructional strategies, content or process; student routines, procedures, and activities; and formative and summative evaluation. In planning an instructional unit—that is, a relatively lengthy, cohesive segment of a curriculum outline—a basic task for teachers is to decide how far to separate or integrate the domains of instructional content.

Although the vast variety of instructional variables suggests that teaching/learning is a fragmented process, careful unit planning should integrate the components of learning through the choice of teaching strategies and methods. Only by integrating these variables can teachers make instruction effective.

Carefully planned units have common elements: a stated rationale, appropriate content, a concept map, a list of prerequisite student learnings, student learning objectives and targets for professional growth, an outline of teaching strategies and student activities, a list of materials and resources, and proposed evaluation methods. Though it must include all these elements, the planning process is not linear: teachers must be prepared to make decisions before, during, and after instruction.

■ ■ ■ ■ ■

DOMAINS OF INSTRUCTIONAL CONTENT

The three domains of instructional content are the cognitive/conceptual, the procedural, and the affective (see Chapter 3). Instruction in the cognitive/conceptual domain includes the teaching of declarative knowledge (i.e., facts, concepts, or relationships pertaining to an item). This domain requires instructional emphasis on word meanings and comprehension (see Chapter 8).

Instruction in the procedural domain includes the teaching of psychomotor, social, or cognitive skills and processes. Teaching in this domain involves presentation (through reading, lecture, demonstration, or modeling), followed by a cycle of practice and feedback that continues until learning is accomplished. Although the teaching of processes (e.g., problem solving or "discovering") usually links a number of skills, processes are broader and less patterned than skills, and instruction and practice are generally less specific (see Chapter 9).

Instruction in the affective domain involves helping students analyze, evaluate, and form or modify attitudes, interests, values, emotions, and feelings. Definite action can be taken to create a positive climate for learning affect (see Chapters 4 and 15), and definite teaching procedures can be used to teach for affective outcomes.

Though the vast variety of variable elements in education might suggest, at first glance, that teaching/learning is a fragmented process, teaching should, in reality, help to integrate the various components of learning as teachers choose and plan instructional procedures. Figure 17.1 diagrams the integration of learning components that occurs during this process.

FIGURE 17.1

Integration of Instructional Components

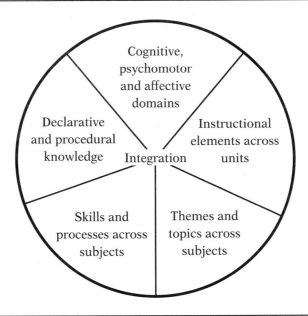

Separation and Integration

The procedure by which students learn and remember has been called **hypostatization**—that is, the laying of a solid foundation for learning (Davidson, 1976). Separation and integration are two fundamental and essential tasks of instruction; they parallel the processes of "simplifying" and "connecting" to make content teachable and memorable through the use of such means as analogies, examples, analyses, and syntheses. In planning and presenting lessons, all teachers must decide when to integrate/connect and when to separate/simplify; whether to analyze or synthesize; and whether to teach by part or by whole (see Chapter 9).

Historically, educators have argued over which process to emphasize: Should they teach reading, for example, by drilling phonics (separation) or by using a word-recognition approach (integration)? Similar questions arise in teacher education. The instructional process of modeling, for instance, supports **holistic** methods of learning (i.e., integrated methods), whereas task analysis and practice of parts support **analytic** methods of learning (i.e., separated or simplified methods). The key consideration in determining the optimum amount of separation or integration is the degree of **reality** or **artificiality** in the instructional process chosen.

The terms *reality* and *artificiality*, used in this sense, relate to the number of variables included in the content to be taught. The fewer variables you include in a teaching/learning experience, the more your students will be free to concentrate on a restricted number of specific aspects of the content or process. In some circumstances, this type of concentration may be necessary, but since "real life" situations are usually complex, the more restricted the variables in a learning process, the more "artificial" that experience becomes. By contrast, the higher the number of variables that are part of the lesson content or process, the higher becomes the degree of "reality" in the learning experience.

Firsthand experience is a condition that increases reality. You may choose experiential teaching strategies, such as field trips or interviews, when you want a learning situation to bring your students into the closest contact possible with the "reality" of the topic they are studying. Though vicarious experience, through such media as movies, pictures, or models, may approach the "real thing," it cannot provide the same degree of reality as can firsthand experience, through which all the domains of instructional content may be integrated.

Some cultures emphasize separation, while others prefer integration as the dominant element in instruction. Your choice should depend on a number of instructional variables, including your students' levels of development, their aptitude to learn in particular ways (see Chapter 6), the time and facilities available, and the purpose and type of instruction. Although your choices will depend on these and other variables, the need for planning will remain constant. The first step in this process is usually the planning of an instructional unit.

In planning to teach a curriculum unit, you should include the widest possible range of knowledge, competencies, and skills compatible with your own and your students' developmental levels.

Forms of Instructional Integration

So far, *Teaching* has presented the cognitive, procedural, and affective domains separately to simplify your learning process, but, in reality, the content of most lessons combines these elements. In integrated lessons, all domains are represented, though to achieve specific objectives, you will sometimes have to separate content into its component parts and integrate the parts later.

Of course, instructional integration can take a variety of forms. One might involve integrating in a single instructional unit general teaching strategies, skills, and processes, with content, materials, and subject-specific teaching skills and processes. Another might involve integrating a theme or topic across subjects such as music and science, or physical education and social studies. A third might involve integrating processes or skills such as problem solving or interpersonal or group relations across many subjects. Others might involve integrating components of the cognitive, procedural, and affective domains into instructional processes or content.

PRACTICING INSTRUCTIONAL INTEGRATION

To this point, you may not have planned or taught lessons specifically in terms of instructional integration, but you have already planned and practiced integrating teaching/learning principles, processes, and skills. In mathematics, for instance, while "ratio" is a concept, calculating a ratio is a skill, and working through a problem that requires calculating a ratio is a process. To teach a ratio lesson, therefore, you would need to know and practice procedures for teaching concepts, skills, and processes. You must integrate all these elements, as well as delivering any explaining and demonstrating required, in a way that creates meaning for your students.

INTEGRATING SUBJECTS: THE USE OF PROCESS

The same or similar instructional processes may be applied across a broad range of subject areas. Inductive reasoning, for instance, when used and reinforced in or adapted to a number of subject areas, provides a tool for learning academic content and using cognitive procedures and processes that integrate learnings across subject lines. At the same time, any given instructional process must be applied specifically to a particular subject area, and your planning must reflect this necessity.

Making Specific Decisions

In selecting certain teaching strategies or methods to teach facts, skills, and procedures, and others to help your students develop concepts, skills, and values, you make specific instructional decisions. A broad range of **instructional models**, strategies, and skills is available to teachers. Various strategies may be applicable, for instance, to direct and indirect instruction and to experiential learning. Lecture may consist largely of direct instruction, but it might elicit covert and even overt participation through questions that invite inquiry and discovery. In presenting your lessons, use a variety of instructional styles to complement your students' ways of learning (i.e., their preferred learning styles).

Table 17.1 lists some of the pre-instructional, instructional, post-instructional, and climate-related decisions that you will need to make in teaching specific subject areas.

PRACTICE *and Projects*

1. Bring to class a lesson plan that you have prepared or obtained from another source. Join a subject-interest group, and choose one of the plans available for analysis on the basis of its content (conceptual, procedural, and affective).

2. Prepare a lesson plan in a subject of your choice that integrates the three instructional domains. Share your plan with members of your teaching-specialization group.

3. When you have analyzed Case Study 17.1, answer the following questions:
   a. What parts of the lesson were directed toward declarative knowledge (understanding concepts)?
   b. What parts of the lesson were directed toward procedural knowledge (performing processes or skills) and practice of the forward roll?
   c. What teacher actions were directed toward establishing a positive attitude to safety in gymnastics?
   d. What should Mr. Barry do to ensure that his students will continue to develop a positive attitude toward safety?

4. Working in a subject-interest group, proceed as follows:
   a. Carefully review the teaching of concepts (see Chapter 8) and skills (see Chapter 9).

(continued)

(continued)

b. Discuss with other members of your group the interrelations involved in teaching concepts and skills, explaining and demonstrating, and teaching for affective growth. Brainstorm instances in your subject areas where integration of these elements must occur.

c. Select any topic identified in item 3, above, and prepare an eight- to ten-minute lesson that combines concept and skill teaching with appropriate affective aspects.

d. Choose a group member to present the lesson you have prepared to six peers. The lesson must not take more than ten minutes. Ask the rest of your class to act as data collectors, using Data Collection Forms 8.2, 9.2, 11.1, and 16.1 (Appendix A).

e. Ask class members to report the data collected, and debrief.

CASE STUDY 17.1

INTEGRATION

Mr. Barry is teaching a forward roll in gymnastics in his Grade 4 Physical Education class. He has explained the concept of a forward roll and has shown videotaped examples. To check his students' understanding of a forward roll, Mr. Barry has asked each one to write a brief definition. Finding that several students are confused, he has made a note to himself to work directly with these students as soon as he can.

Mr. Barry's chief lesson objective is that each student learn to do a forward roll, with appropriate placement of hands, tuck of head, and care for the safety of all. Mr. Barry describes and demonstrates the roll as a complete act, and then shows each of the steps separately. He allows time for each student to try each stage, to receive feedback from another student asked to observe specific behavior, to try the forward roll once more, and to receive feedback again. To observe and monitor this process, he appoints "spotters," whom he provides with a set of "teaching" notes.

Students' questions about the reasons for appointing spotters lead to a class discussion. One of the students asks why the procedure is called a roll. Mr. Barry explains the origin of the term and tells the class that there are other kinds of rolls.

Near the end of the period, Mr. Barry asks his students to suggest why there have been no injuries, and to specify the practices that have helped to ensure that no one has been hurt.

Table 17.1

Instructional Planning Decisions

Pre-Instruction Decisions

Content: What content will you teach and emphasize?

Time allocation: How much time will you give to each subject/topic?

Pacing: How rapidly should you cover the content?

Grouping: What grouping will interaction patterns require?

Activity structure: What student activities will be most appropriate?

Climate Decisions

Communication of expectations: How will you communicate your expectations to your students?

Developing the environment: What will you do to develop a safe, orderly, and academically focused environment?

Managing deviancy: How will you manage discipline procedures sensibly?

Developing cooperative environments: How will you foster appropriate cooperative group and interpersonal relationships?

Instructional Decisions

Structuring: What kind of organizers will you provide? What kinds of summaries will you or your students provide?

Time management: How much time will you give to each subject and topic? How much time will you allot to transition?

Questioning: What types and levels of questions will you pose?

On-task time: How much on-task time will your students need?

Academic learning time: How long will learners be engaged in activities that relate directly to learning-outcome?

Monitoring success rate: How will you monitor and ensure a high success rate?

Monitoring learning: How will you monitor your students during supervised and independent study? What individual teacher-student interactions are likely to occur?

Post-Instruction Decisions

Tests: How will you test the desired learning outcomes?

Grades: What kinds of grading and reporting systems will you use? How will you ensure that you grade your students' work objectively and judiciously?

Feedback: How can you make substantial corrective feedback and praise contingent on appropriate behavior? How can you use your students' ideas?

Source: Adapted from "The Half-Full Glass: A Review of Research on Teaching" by D. Berliner, 1984, in P. Hosford (Ed.), *Using What We Know about Teaching*, Alexandria, VA: Association for Supervision and Curriculum Development.

■ ■ ■ ■ ■

INTRODUCTION TO UNIT PLANNING

Every course, unit, or lesson that you teach is made up of a number of instructional variables that include content (product or process relating to one or more instructional domains), and modes, strategies, or methods of teaching. Planning an instructional unit requires reflection on all the basic teaching principles, practices, and skills as translated into the teaching competencies—such as writing objectives, planning and presenting set and closure, presenting content, questioning, and evaluating—that you have studied and practiced. Figure 17.2 diagrams this process.

Rationale for Unit Planning

How well could a contractor build a bridge without a blueprint? a pilot fly without a flight plan? a surgeon perform an operation without X-rays? a diamond

FIGURE 17.2

Unit-Planning Model

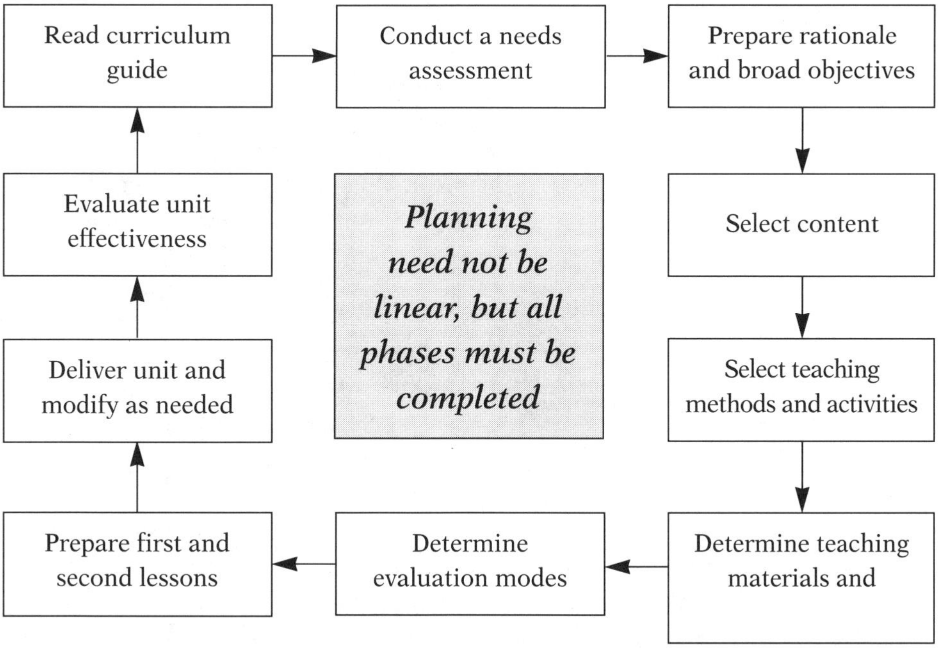

Read curriculum guide	→	Conduct a needs assessment	→	Prepare rationale and broad objectives

| Evaluate unit effectiveness | | *Planning need not be linear, but all phases must be completed* | | Select content |

| Deliver unit and modify as needed | | | | Select teaching methods and activities |

| Prepare first and second lessons | ← | Determine evaluation modes | ← | Determine teaching materials and |

Source: Adapted from *The Instructor's Survival Kit* (2nd ed.) (p. 97) by P. Renner, 1983, Vancouver, BC: PFR Training Associates.

cutter cut a rare stone at random? Like these other professionals, a teacher, too, needs to plan. It is simply not sufficient to "teach through" the chapters and pages of a text or workbook, for to benefit by instruction, students need constant and careful consideration based on planning for their group and individual needs. Good lessons do not spring out of thin air; they evolve only from focusing on the objectives of units planned to achieve course objectives.

In planning instructional objectives, you should follow guidelines derived from specific answers to the following questions.

Points to ponder...

- ❏ What tasks do curriculum guidelines specify?
- ❏ At what grade level are the students working?
- ❏ What are the students' ages, capabilities, cultural backgrounds, needs, interests, and preferred learning styles?
- ❏ How much can you and they accomplish in a day? a week? a month? a semester?
- ❏ What psychological learning principles, teaching methods, and student activities will best meet the students' needs? What materials and resources will best facilitate their learning?

As you plan instructional objectives, content, procedures, and evaluations, you should also plan professional targets and data-collection procedures. There is no short-cut to professional growth: research supports the connection between student achievement and teachers who organize instructional plans and teaching strategies.

Planning an Instructional Unit

An **instructional unit** is a cohesive portion of a prescribed course that centers on a topic, theme, or major concept. Units organize course content into manageable areas of investigation, focusing instruction and learning on specific course objectives.

A course should consist of a series of several units, each containing a series of three to twenty or more lessons that flow from one topic to another to form a logical whole by promoting integration of students' understanding and performance capabilities. Designing units and lessons to achieve the educational objectives prescribed for a course combines the art and applied decision-making science of teaching.

Different types of units have different functions. **Resource units** are usually collections or arrangements of materials and activities centered on a particular topic or theme. Well-planned **teaching/learning units** are more complex and more comprehensive than resource units.

LINEAR OR NONLINEAR?

The traditional view of instructional planning is that it is a **rational-linear planning** process: a process that begins with establishing goals and objectives, moves to planning instructional tactics to promote the achievement of those goals and objectives, and concludes with measuring their achievement. It is unrealistic, however, to believe that a unit plan should consist of careful lesson plans that must always follow closely, for **unit plans** should not be cast in concrete. You might plan the first lesson or two in a unit, but you might or might not execute the lesson(s) exactly as planned. You should be prepared to choose and use alternative content selections, teaching methods, and **introductory**, **developmental**, and **culminating student activities**; to vary emphasis; and to expand, add, or delete materials on the basis of your day-to-day classroom experiences. As you teach a unit, you may also, of course, adjust or add activities in response to your perception of your students' needs.

EXPERIENCE: GUIDE, NOT MASTER

By now, you have developed some proficiency in planning and delivering lessons, and your experience will help you to plan and prepare good teaching units. But mature people recognize that they are both beneficiaries and prisoners of experience, for although experience can be invaluable, it can also make them reluctant to alter ways that appear to work, keeping them in a comfortable rut, limiting their vision and their willingness to take risks, and blocking constructive adaptive change. Exciting teachers, while using experience as a guideline, are also willing to experiment—and do so with healthy curiosity, a positive attitude, and an open mind.

Your experience will show you that units and lessons are alike in several ways; indeed, their most notable difference is that lessons must preserve a sequence to achieve the outcomes planned, whereas more flexibility may be possible in sequencing units. In a sense, however, a unit plan is like a large lesson plan: whether units are **interdisciplinary** (integrating more than one subject area) or subject specific, unit plans, like lesson plans, include

◆ a rationale for instruction
◆ an assessment of students' needs;
◆ instructional goals and objectives;
◆ identifiable content;

- identification of resources;
- introductory, developmental, and culminating teaching methods and student activities; and
- evaluation procedures.

SOURCES OF INFORMATION

Major sources of information needed for unit planning are curriculum guidelines published by departments or ministries of education; goals and objectives published by departments or boards of education, school districts, and textbook publishers; professional information about learner characteristics and differences based on aptitude, past achievement, personality, home life, and peer influences; thorough knowledge of academic subjects; and knowledge of teaching models, strategies, and skills.

COMMON ESSENTIAL ELEMENTS

Good unit plans share certain common elements. All units should include common essential learnings relating to communication in terms of the language of the subject under study; numerical capability in terms of mathematical concepts, techniques, and applications; critical and creative thinking; technological literacy; personal and social values; and independent learning skills. Other common elements are listed in Table 17.2 as steps in effective unit planning.

A SUGGESTED UNIT-PLANNING SEQUENCE

In planning an instructional unit, many educators follow a sequence such as this:

- Select a unit topic, and prepare a **rationale statement** outlining the course objectives the unit is to address and the reasons they are important.
- Determine prerequisite student learnings and conduct a **needs assessment** to discover students' background for learning.
- Write appropriate unit objectives, ensuring that they are congruent with course objectives.
- Prepare a concept hierarchy and task analysis (i.e., a concept map, or web, as illustrated in Figure 8.3) of the concepts and skills to be learned.
- Prepare a content outline, arranging the content (facts, concepts, principles, skills, and processes) in a teaching/learning sequence.
- Brainstorm to select suitable teaching methods and student activities, organizing these as introductory, developmental, and culminating.
- Identify appropriate instructional resources and materials.
- Prepare a summative evaluation congruent with unit objectives and with student activities.

◆ Select personal professional targets and appropriate data collection forms.

◆ Prepare lesson plans for the first lesson or two of the unit.

These planning-cycle steps are shown in Figure 17.2. You may, of course, start at any point in this cycle, and go back and forth from one part of the plan to

TABLE *17.2*

Elements Common to Most Unit Plans

I.   Identification Data and Overview
   A. Unit title
   B. Subject and grade level
   C. Time allotment
   D. Overview statement (identifying broad objectives or purposes)
   E. Rationale statement (reason for teaching)
   F. Prerequisite student learning and pretesting

II.   Product and Process Objectives
   A. Cognitive
   B. Procedural (skills and processes)
   C. Affective (feelings, values, attitudes, appreciations, etc.)

III.   Content Outline
   A. Instructional (conceptual, procedural, affective)
   B. Subject content (declarative, procedural, affective; product and processes)
      Note: Construct a concept map.

IV.   Teaching Methods and Student Activities
   A. Introductory
   B. Developmental
   C. Culminating

V.   Resources and Materials
   A. For the teacher (books, pamphlets, periodicals, etc.)
   B. For instruction and student use (books, pamphlets, periodicals, audio-visual aids, community resources, etc.)

VI.   Evaluation
   A. Of the extent to which students achieve learning goals
   B. Of unit effectiveness

VII. Targets of Professional Growth
   A. Preparing a good unit
   B. Specific target for each lesson

another, adding or changing material as ideas come to mind. The important thing is to complete all the steps before you begin to teach a unit.

Choosing Instructional Variables

Your choice of instructional variables will depend, to some degree, on your identification of the prerequisite learnings necessary to the effective study of a new unit. To identify prerequisite learnings, you may have to select or construct a formal or informal pretest. In doing so, consider your students' levels of development, expectations, cultural backgrounds, and learning aptitudes.

In planning instructional units, you will need to do more than identify a range of variables: from a great variety of variables at your command, you must be able to choose and use those that are both appropriate to your students' developmental stage and experience and capable of arousing and maintaining their interest. Choosing is not easy, for some situations will not accommodate all the variables you might wish to include, and you will have to determine priorities and make compromises, while keeping variables congruent. At times, circumstances beyond your control may dictate your choice of variables. If, for example, your students are to be externally evaluated, you may need to "teach to" the evaluation process. At other times, the availability of requisite facilities or instructional materials may affect your choice.

Variables can sometimes be combined, but no matter what the combination, you and your students must be clear about the lesson objectives, the sequence of elements, the content or process to be learned, the activities that content suggests, the balance of teacher/student control or responsibility, the pattern of interactions, the preferred teaching/learning styles, the practical considerations relating to lesson delivery, the product or process by which students will demonstrate their learnings, and ways in which they can transfer and apply those learnings to new situations. Figure 17.3 diagrams these variables.

PRACTICE *and Projects*

1. Working with a subject-interest group, examine suitable unit plans, and analyze them in terms of the components of an effective unit plan and their logical flow from one element to another.

2. a. Using Data Collection Form 17.1 (Appendix A), prepare a unit teaching plan in a subject of your choice. Annotate your plan to show how you have applied the principles and practices of teaching that you have studied in earlier chapters.

   b. To check your unit plan and collect feedback on it, use Data Collection Form 17.2 (Appendix A).

FIGURE 17.3

Variables in Instructional Strategies

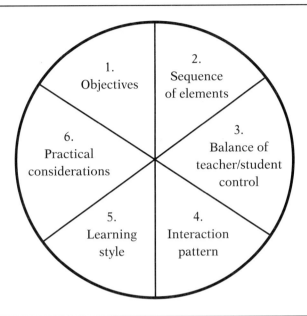

SUMMARY

- ◆ Instruction consists of a vast variety of teaching/learning components classified into the cognitive/conceptual, procedural, and affective domains.
- ◆ The teaching process, which devolves from unit planning, should help to integrate the various components of learning as teachers choose and plan instructional procedures.
- ◆ Separation and integration are two fundamental and essential tasks of instruction, paralleling the processes of "simplifying" and "connecting."
- ◆ Reducing the number of variables included in an instruction process simplifies teaching/learning, but also reduces the "reality" of the experience, since "real life" experiences are generally complex.
- ◆ The instructional integration process, which can take a variety of forms, requires that the teacher make specific decisions.
- ◆ Whereas lessons must preserve a given sequence to achieve the outcomes planned, more flexibility may be possible in sequencing units.

- Planning an instructional unit requires reflection on all the basic teaching principles, practices, and skills that you have studied and practiced.
- Good unit plans include a range of variables that reflect common essential learnings relating to communication skills, numerical or mathematical competencies, critical and creative thinking, technological literacy, personal and social values, and independent learning skills.

KEY WORDS

content	integration	separation
affective	"connecting"	analytic methods
declarative	holistic methods	"artificiality"
procedural	"reality"	analyzing
decision making	synthesizing	part, not whole
essential learnings	whole, not part	"simplifying"
instructional domains	product or process	teaching strategies
instructional unit		unit planning
instructional variables		

RECOMMENDED READING

Integrating Instructional Variables

Hosford, P.(Ed.). (1984). *Using what we know about teaching*. Alexandria, VA: Association for Supervision and Curriculum Development.

Kemp, J. (1985). *The instructional design process*. New York: Harper & Row.

APPENDIX A

DATA COLLECTION FORMS

```
┌──────────────────────────────────────────────────────────┐
│              DATA COLLECTION FORM 1.1                     │
├──────────────────────────────────────────────────────────┤
│  PROFESSIONAL PROFILE: PRESENT PERSONAL COMPETENCE        │
└──────────────────────────────────────────────────────────┘
```

O = Outstanding, V = Very Good, G = Good, F = Fair, U = Unsatisfactory, N = Not Rated
Please check what you believe to be the level of your *present* capability in each competency.

	O	V	G	F	U	N
☐ **A. PROFESSIONAL QUALITIES AND DEVELOPMENT**						
1. Subject knowledge		✓				
2. Professional target selection		✓				
3. Pre/post conferences						✓
4. Data-collection methods						✓
5. Analysis of data			✓			
6. Plans/commitment for growth	✓					
7. Reflection on experiences		✓				
8. Use of school/other resources		✓				
9. Extracurricular involvement	✓					
10. Interest in teaching	✓					
11. Relationship with colleagues		✓				
☐ **B. INTERACTION WITH LEARNERS**						
1. Respect for *all* pupils		✓				
2. Response to needs of *all*		✓				
3. Encouragement		✓				
4. Interpersonal skills		✓				
5. Group skills in classroom		✓				
6. Motivation		✓				
☐ **C. CLASSROOM MANAGEMENT AND DISCIPLINE**						
1. Classroom climate					✓	
2. Communicates expectations					✓	
3. Monitors expectations					✓	
4. Use of routines/procedures					✓	
5. Response to minor disruptions			✓			
6. Use of positive reinforcement			✓			
7. Discipline/problem solving					✓	
8. Consultation/referral					✓	
9. Fairness/consistency			✓			
10. Preventive management						✓
☐ **D. PLANNING AND ORGANIZATION**						
1. Daily plans					✓	
2. Long-term plans					✓	

AFFECTIVE DOMAIN (handwritten, above section C)

	O	V	G	F	U	N
3. Record keeping						✓
4. Assignments						✓
5. Testing						✓
E. TEACHING COMPETENCE						✓
1. Set and closure						✓
2. Methods: Variety and sequence			✓			
3. Activities: Variety and sequence			✓			
4. Media/resources		✓				
5. Content organization						✓
6. Methods specific to area of study			✓			
7. Instruction:						
a. Questioning techniques		✓				
b. Presentation/interaction skills		✓				
c. Thinking skills/processes		✓				
d. Common essential learnings	✓					
e. Concepts/explanations	✓					
f. Skills/demonstrations		✓				
g. Teaching of attitudes/values		✓				
h. Use of interactive methods	✓					
i. Use of direct methods		✓				
j. Use of indirect methods		✓				
k. Use of experiential methods	✓					
l. Attention to learning styles			✓			
m. Provision for transfer of learning	✓					
n. Provision for individual differences		✓				
o. Diagnosis and remediation			✓			⟨✓⟩
p. Evaluation methods						✓
q. Individual study (incl. seat/homework)			✓			
F. PERSONAL QUALITIES						
1. Professional image		✓				
2. Respect for others			✓			
3. Self-concept			✓			
4. Maturity and dependability			✓			
5. Initiative		✓				
6. Response to stress and/or conflict				✓		
7. Communication:						
a. verbal		✓				
b. nonverbal						✓
c. written			✓			
8. Creativity		✓				
Overall Evaluation						✓

DATA COLLECTION FORM 1.2
CONFERENCING CHECKLISTS

❑ **PRETEACHING CHECKLIST**   **NOTES**

____ Topic   _____

____ Target   _____

____ Approach to target   _____

____ Data-collection method   _____

____ Content   _____

____ Prerequisite knowledge/skills   _____

____ Materials/aids   _____

____ Introduction   _____

____ Development   _____

____ Closure   _____

____ Evaluation   _____

_____

_____

❑ **POST-TEACHING CHECKLIST** **NOTES**

____ Review of target and
        method of data collection   _____

____ Debriefing *re* pupils'
        achievement of objectives   _____

____ Presentation of data
        collected   _____

____ Your, (and your helper's)
        analysis of data   _____

____ Your opinion *re*
        significance of data   _____

____ Your commitment to
        specific future action   _____

DATA COLLECTION FORM 2.1
BASIC COMMUNICATION SKILLS

Please describe, in objective (nonevaluative) language, what you heard or observed.

❑ **VERBAL COMMUNICATION**

Audibility _____

_____

_____

_____

Clarity _____

_____

_____

_____

Enunciation _____

_____

_____

_____

Variety and emphasis _____

_____

_____

_____

Language use _____

_____

_____

_____

Mannerisms _____

_____

_____

❑ **NONVERBAL COMMUNICATION**

Facial expression _____

_____

_____

_____

Motion _____

_____

_____

_____

Gestures _____

_____

_____

_____

Eye contact _____

_____

_____

_____

Physical contact _____

_____

_____

_____

Pauses (silence) _____

_____

_____

Mannerisms _____

_____

_____

DATA COLLECTION FORM 2.2
INTERPERSONAL SKILLS

Please describe, in objective (nonvaluative) language, what you heard or observed, and how students reacted.

Paraphrasing

Perception checking

Behavior description

Feelings description

Other techniques for understanding others

Other techniques for helping others understand you

DATA COLLECTION FORM 2.3
MY BEHAVIOR IN GROUPS

This is a *personal and private* document. Please rate yourself on each point, circling the number that most nearly represents your typical behavior as a member of a class or small group. Only frank answers are valuable. The numbers indicate the following ratings: 1 – much more often than most; 2 – more often than most; 3 – about average for the group; 4 – once in a while; 5 – rarely or never.

❑ TASK FUNCTIONS

1. I offer facts, opinions, suggestions, ideas, and other
   relevant information.   1   2   3   4   5
2. I ask others for facts, opinions, suggestions, ideas, and feelings.   1   2   3   4   5
3. I am a starter who makes suggestions to initiate action in
   the group.   1   2   3   4   5
4. I help develop procedure plans to keep the group on task.   1   2   3   4   5
5. I summarize occurrences and the major points made
   in meetings.   1   2   3   4   5
6. I am a coordinator who pulls ideas together and harmonizes
   activities.   1   2   3   4   5
7. I diagnose the difficulties the group meets in working to
   achieve goals.   1   2   3   4   5
8. I stimulate the group to achieve a higher quality of work.   1   2   3   4   5
9. I apply the test of reality or practicality to ideas and options.   1   2   3   4   5
10. I evaluate and compare the standards and goals of the group
    with group decisions and achievements.   1   2   3   4   5

❑ MAINTENANCE FUNCTIONS

11. I accept others and encourage them to participate.   1   2   3   4   5
12. I listen actively to others and am receptive to others' ideas.   1   2   3   4   5
13. I support openness, encourage risk and individuality, and
    thus build trust.   1   2   3   4   5
14. I use interpersonal skills and make sure that others
    understand one another.   1   2   3   4   5
15. I observe the process the group is using and help to analyze
    its effectiveness.   1   2   3   4   5

16. I remind the group about its goals and standards, and help keep it on task.   1   2   3   4   5
17. I check group climate by determining how members feel about the group's progress and about one another.   1   2   3   4   5
18. I help cool tensions by joking and suggesting fun approaches or breaks.   1   2   3   4   5
19. I help solve conflicts and try to harmonize differences of opinion.   1   2   3   4   5

SOURCE: The contents of this form have been adapted from the summary of task and maintenance functions described in D. Johnson, and R. Johnson, 1975, *Joining Together: Group
Theory and group Skills*. Englewood Cliffs, NJ: Prentice-Hall.

DATA COLLECTION FORM 3.1
PROFESSIONAL TARGET: LESSON PLANNING

Please describe your observations of the teacher's success in implementing professional planning for the lesson presented.

Target _____

_____

_____

_____

Topic _____

_____

_____

_____

Objectives _____

_____

_____

_____

Content _____

_____

_____

_____

Materials and aids _____

_____

_____

_____

Set _____

_____

_____

Development _____

_____

_____

Closure _____

_____

_____

_____

Evaluation _____

_____

_____

_____

| DATA COLLECTION FORM 3.2 |
| PLANNING TEACHING OBJECTIVES AND TARGETS |

Subject _____   Date_____

Name_____

❑ **PLANNING FOR STUDENT LEARNING**

Topic _____

_____

Content _____

_____

Objectives

1. _____

_____

2. _____

_____

3. _____

_____

_____

Prerequisite student learnings _____

_____

_____

Presentation (teaching methods and student activities)

Set _____

_____

_____

Development _____

_____

_____

Closure _____

_____

_____

Material and aids _____

_____

_____

Evaluation _____

_____

_____

❑ **PLANNING FOR PROFESSIONAL DEVELOPMENT**

Data Collector _____ Date _____

Target topic _____

_____

_____

Professional target _____

_____

_____

Means of achieving target _____

_____

_____

❑ **DATA COLLECTION METHOD**

Check one: Please use the attached Target Topic sheet. ☐

Please use the attached blank sheet. ☐

Please collect data as described below. ☐

_____

_____

DATA COLLECTION FORM 3.3
PROFESSIONAL TARGET: STIMULUS VARIATION

Please describe what was said or done to vary stimuli, and how students reacted.

❑ **FOCUSING**

- ◆ Making statements _____

- ◆ Pointing, gesturing _____

- ◆ Using aids _____

_____

_____

_____

❑ **SHIFTING INTERACTION**

- ◆ Varying interaction patterns _____

    (teacher–class; teacher–student; _____

    student–student) _____

_____

_____

_____

❑ **PAUSING/SILENCE TO**

- ◆ gain attention _____

- ◆ emphasize a point _____

- ◆ provide time to think _____

- ◆ create suspense _____

- ◆ stop a minor disruption _____

_____

_____

_____

_____

❏ SHIFTING SENSES

- ◆ looking _____

- ◆ listening _____

- ◆ feeling _____

- ◆ tasting _____

- ◆ smelling _____

- ◆ doing _____

_____

_____

_____

_____

_____

❏ DESCRIBE STUDENT REACTIONS TO THE STIMULUS VARIATIONS:

_____

_____

_____

_____

_____

_____

DATA COLLECTION FORM 3.4

PROFESSIONAL TARGET: SET AND CLOSURE

Please describe the use of set and closure at the beginning and end of the lesson, respectively. On the reverse side of this sheet, please list and briefly describe each of the activities and instructional skills used in the development of the lesson.

❏ **SET**

Orientation set
_____

(focusing attention by
_____

motivating activity)
_____

_____

_____

_____

Transition set
_____

(smooth transition from
_____

known to new material)
_____

_____

_____

_____

Evaluation set
_____

(determining what students know
_____

about material taught before
_____

teaching new material
_____

_____

_____

_____

❑ Closure

Review closure

(reviewing material

just taught)

_____

_____

_____

_____

_____

_____

Transfer closure

(providing practice, or

alerting students about

future use of or link to

material covered)

_____

_____

_____

_____

_____

_____

_____

Serendipity closure

(taking advantage of

appropriate, unexpected

situation that provides

ideal closure)

_____

_____

_____

_____

_____

_____

_____

DATA COLLECTION FORM 4.1
DISCOVERING STUDENTS' INTERESTS

Name_____ Grade ____ Date_____

Please answer each of the following questions as completely as you can.

❏ **THINGS I LIKE TO DO**

Three things I like to do when I am at home are _____

_____

_____

_____

If I had up to $200 to spend on anything I wanted, I would buy _____

_____

_____

_____

If I could take a trip anywhere I liked, I would go to _____

_____

_____

_____

Three things I like to do at recess or during noon hour are _____

_____

_____

_____

Three things I like to do when I have finished my seatwork are _____

_____

_____

_____

Reasons I do well on an assignment or test are _____

_____

_____

_____

Reasons why I might not do well on an assignment or test are _____

_____

_____

_____

The person or persons whom I like the most or who are most important to

me are _____

_____

_____

_____

My reasons are _____

_____

_____

_____

DATA COLLECTION FORM 4.2
PROFESSIONAL TARGET: MOTIVATION

Please record your observations of instructional behavior, and describe the students' reactions.

❑ **EVIDENT PRECONDITIONS**

◆ Supportive environment? _____

◆ Appropriate level of difficulty? _____

◆ Relevant stated or implied objectives? _____

◆ Advance organizers, objectives stated? _____

_____

_____

❑ **SHOWING SUCCESS EXPECTATIONS**

◆ Student awareness of effort–success _____

connection? _____

◆ Attention to underachievers? _____

◆ Directions clear and logical? _____

_____

_____

❑ **EXTRINSIC INCENTIVES**

◆ Good performance rewarded? _____

◆ Improved performance rewarded? _____

◆ Competition used appropriately? _____

◆ Cooperation and mutual support _____

stressed? _____

◆ Everyday-life value of content _____

clarified? _____

◆ Student contributions valued? _____

❏ **APPEAL TO INTRINSIC MOTIVATION**

◆ Peer interaction? _____

◆ Game-like format? _____

◆ Fantasies, simulations? _____

◆ Tasks completed? _____

◆ Immediate feedback? _____

◆ Active choices of activities? _____

◆ Student choices of activities? _____

_____

_____

❏ **MOTIVATIONAL STRATEGIES USED**

◆ Modeling by teacher? _____

◆ Students expected to succeed? _____

◆ Performance anxiety reduced? _____

◆ Teacher enthusiasm? _____

◆ Curiosity aroused, suspense used? _____

◆ Content personalized? _____

◆ Student interests discovered? used? _____

◆ Content seen as important, useful? _____

◆ Sensitivity to self-concepts? _____

_____

_____

DATA COLLECTION FORM 5.1
PROFESSIONAL DEVELOPMENT TARGET: BASIC MANAGEMENT SKILLS

Please describe your observations relating to the professional development target and the students' reactions.

_____

Demonstrates awareness

(stands where he or she can see all

students; uses eye contact; gestures

at students; stands at angle to see

students while writing on board;

observes class while helping

individuals)

_____

_____

_____

_____

_____

_____

_____

_____

_____

Overlapping

(attends to student or deals with

minor disruption without

interrupting flow of lesson,

moving toward or standing beside

disruptive student(s); directing

question to disruptive student;

attending to needs of several

groups)

_____

_____

_____

_____

_____

_____

_____

_____

_____

Movement management

(reduces "dead time" through smooth
transitions from one part of lesson or
activity to another by having
demo materials or aids ready;
having materials distributed rapidly;
giving clear directions; ensuring well-
organized movement to various parts/in
and out of the room; making smooth
transitions to other activities or groups;
pacing the lesson appropriately)

_____

_____

_____

_____

_____

_____

_____

_____

_____

_____

_____

_____

Group focus

(keeps students alert and
accountable; keeps lesson
flowing while handling questions;
provides appropriate amount of
time for students to think;
distributes questions widely, both
to volunteers and nonvolunteers;
has students raise hand before
responding; does not repeat
questions or answers; does not permit
unsolicited responses; directs
responses to entire class)

_____

_____

_____

_____

_____

_____

_____

_____

_____

_____

_____

_____

DATA COLLECTION FORM 5.2
PROFESSIONAL DEVELOPMENT TARGET: HANDLING MINOR DISRUPTIONS

Please describe your observations relating to the professional development target and the students' reactions.

_____

Deterring

(firmly stopping unacceptable   _____

behavior by pausing; raising   _____

eyebrows; gesturing; making eye   _____

contact; walking toward student;   _____

reminding students of expected   _____

behavior; issuing desist; asking   _____

students to recall directions; giving   _____

individual attention; other)   _____

_____

_____

Checking/Monitoring

(preventing disruptions by   _____

gesturing; circulating in classroom;   _____

asking questions)   _____

_____

Reinforcing good behavior

(giving positive recognition to   _____

desired behavior of individuals/   _____

groups/whole class)   _____

_____

_____

_____

DATA COLLECTION FORM 7.1

PROFESSIONAL DEVELOPMENT TARGET: DISTRIBUTING QUESTIONS

QUESTION DISTRIBUTION PLAN

Enter student names in boxes. Place a check mark or the question number in the appropriate box as questions are asked.

Descriptive observations about the nature of question distribution _____

_____

_____

_____

_____

_____

_____

_____

Note: This observation form can also be used for recording eye contact, teacher movement, student off-task behavior, and so on.

DATA COLLECTION FORM 7.2
PROFESSIONAL TARGET: ANALYZING QUESTION PATTERNS

Please note the substance of each question asked. Later:

a. Classify each question as follows:

K—knowledge (facts or information)   An— analysis

C—comprehension   Syn—synthesis

Ap—application   E—evaluation

b. Note distinguishing features, such as whether each question was clear (cl); repeated (rep); "yes/no" (y/n); run-on (r-o); leading (ldg); or blanket (blk).

c. Classify each question as convergent (single correct answer expected); divergent or open-ended (no standard answer expected); or evaluative(relating to significance or worth)

d. Write a brief analysis of the questioning pattern you have identified.

❑ **NO. SUBSTANCE   DISTINGUISHING FEATURE   CLASSIFICATION**

1. _____

2. _____

3. _____

4. _____

5. _____

6. _____

7. _____

8. _____

9. _____

10. _____

11. _____

❏ **No.** **Substance** **Distinguishing Feature** **Classification**

12. _____

13. _____

14. _____

15. _____

16. _____

17. _____

18. _____

❏ **Analysis of Questioning Pattern**

_____

_____

_____

_____

_____

_____

_____

DATA COLLECTION FORM 7.3
PROFESSIONAL TARGET: EFFECTIVE QUESTIONING

For each question asked, please record the steps used, as follows:

  A—Attention of all secured   N—named responder
  Q—question posed   R—response from student(s)
  W—wait time   S—number of steps followed

Please note the number of seconds elapsed under "Wait Time," and enter a check mark for a prompt, a probe, or a redirect.

❑ **NO.   STEPS FOLLOWED   WAIT TIME   PROMPT   PROBE   REDIRECT**

1. _____

2. _____

3. _____

4. _____

5. _____

6. _____

7. _____

8. _____

9. _____

10. _____

11. _____

12. _____

13. _____

14. _____

❏ **No.** **Steps Followed** **Wait Time** **Prompt** **Probe** **Redirect**

15. _____

16. _____

17. _____

18. _____

19. _____

20. _____

21. _____

22. _____

23. _____

24. _____

25. _____

❏ **Description of Other Questioning Patterns**

_____

_____

_____

_____

_____

_____

DATA COLLECTION FORM 7.4
PROFESSIONAL TARGET: EXPLAINING

Please describe teacher activity and students' reactions.
_____

Nature of explanation

(brief? concise? involved? detailed?   _____

language suitability? motivating?)   _____

_____

_____

_____

_____

_____

Essential details (critical attributes)

(which covered? any omitted? stressed?   _____

definition provided? attributes and   _____

relationships? noncritical attributes)   _____

_____

_____

_____

_____

_____

Organization of explanation

(sequence used? clear?)   _____

_____

_____

_____

_____

_____

Examples used

(illustrations, analogies, visuals;

materials used)

_____

_____

_____

_____

_____

_____

_____

Checking for understanding?

_____

_____

_____

_____

_____

Practice provided/feedback provided?

_____

_____

_____

_____

_____

_____

DATA COLLECTION FORM 8.1
ANALYZING A CONCEPT

Name of Concept:

Kind of Concept (√):   Concrete ___   Abstract ___

  Conjunctive ___   Disjunctive ___   Relational ___

Presentation Mode: Observing/doing ___   Pictorial ___   Symbolic ___

Examples of concept (in sequence of presentation) _____

_____

_____

_____

Nonexamples of concept (in sequence of presentation) _____

_____

_____

_____

Critical attributes (in sequence of presentation) _____

_____

_____

_____

Noncritical attributes _____

_____

_____

_____

Concept definition _____

_____

_____

_____

Relationship to other concepts _____

_____

_____

_____

Superordinate concept _____

_____

_____

_____

(Some) Subordinate concepts _____

_____

_____

_____

(Some) Coordinate concepts _____

_____

_____

_____

DATA COLLECTION FORM 8.2
PROFESSIONAL TARGET: TEACHING A CONCEPT

Name of Concept:

Kind of Concept (√): Concrete ___ Abstract ___

Conjunctive ___ Disjunctive ___ Relational___

Presentation Approach: Enactive ___ Iconic (graphic) ___ Symbolic ___

Examples or analogies; cause and effect; behavior _____

_____

_____

_____

Nonexamples _____

_____

_____

_____

Nonanalogies _____

_____

_____

_____

Critical attributes identified and/or emphasized _____

_____

_____

_____

Noncritical attributes _____

_____

_____

_____

Attribute relationships identified _____

_____

_____

_____

Concept defined _____

_____

_____

_____

Related concepts identified (sub- or superordinate? coordinate? use?) _____

_____

_____

_____

Practice and transfer _____

_____

_____

_____

DATA COLLECTION FORM 9.1
PROFESSIONAL TARGET: TEACHING A SKILL

Detail each of the lesson elements for teaching a skill listed below.

❑ **APPROACH**

_____

_____

❑ **SET**

- ◆ Gains attention   _____
- ◆ Reviews prerequisite skills   _____
- ◆ Describes context for skill use   _____
- ◆ States skill objective   _____

_____

_____

❑ **DEVELOPMENT**

- ◆ Models or demonstrates skill   _____
- ◆ Cues or explains step by step   _____
- ◆ Focuses on essentials   _____
- ◆ Visual or verbal input   _____
- ◆ Maintains full attention   _____
- ◆ Leads students through skill   _____
- ◆ Checks students' performance   _____
- ◆ Models or explains again   _____
- ◆ Provides supervised practice   _____
- ◆ Provides feedback   _____
- ◆ Encourages transfer   _____

_____

_____

❑ CLOSURE

- ◆ Provides review of steps   _____

- ◆ Reinforces context of skill use   _____

- ◆ Assigns practice   _____

- ◆ Bridges to next step or lesson   _____

_____

_____

DATA COLLECTION FORM 9.2
PROFESSIONAL TARGET: TEACHING A SKILL LESSON

Skill _____

Task Analysis: Procedural __   Hierarchical __   Combination __

Check procedures for direct teaching of skills:

1. Objectives and set provided __   4. Guided practice provided __
2. Prerequisites reviewed __   5. Monitored practice __
3. Skill modeled __   6. Independent practice assigned __

Please describe each of the following elements in teaching the skill lesson.

Major subskills _____

_____

_____

_____

Related subskills _____

_____

_____

_____

Relationship of subskills _____

_____

_____

_____

Skills practice _____

_____

_____

_____

Feedback _____

_____

_____

_____

Use of skill identified _____

_____

_____

_____

Steps of presentation/demonstration _____

_____

_____

_____

DATA COLLECTION FORM 9.3
PROFESSIONAL TARGET: DEMONSTRATION

Please describe teacher's actions and students' reactions.

❑ **PREDEMONSTRATION PREPARATION**

◆ Materials and equipment ready   _____

◆ Good visibility and audibility   _____

_____

_____

_____

❑ **ESTABLISHING SET**

◆ Motivates students to learn   _____

◆ Conveys importance of skill   _____

_____

_____

_____

❑ **DEMONSTRATION**

◆ Gains and maintains attention   _____

◆ Describes/explains clearly   _____

◆ Gives nonverbal cues   _____

◆ Emphasizes key elements   _____

◆ Uses suitable materials   _____

_____

_____

_____

❑ **SKILLS PRACTICE**

- ◆ Gives directions clearly _____
- ◆ Students perform with teacher and _____

  receive feedback _____
- ◆ Checks for comprehension _____
- ◆ Guided practice and feedback _____
- ◆ Checks for comprehension _____
- ◆ Independent practice and feedback _____
- ◆ Reinforcement _____

_____

_____

_____

❑ **PROVIDES FOR TRANSFER**

| DATA COLLECTION FORM 9.4 |
| PROFESSIONAL DEVELOPMENT TARGET: GIVING DIRECTIONS |

Please describe your observations relating to the professional development target and the students' reactions.

Giving signals and securing attention _____

(using voice and body language to _____

secure students' attention; waiting _____

until all students are attending) _____

_____

_____

_____

_____

Alerting students _____

(allowing sufficient time; telling how much _____

time is left) _____

_____

_____

_____

_____

Giving clear directions _____

(brief, intelligible, complete; using chalkboard _____

or handout) _____

_____

_____

_____

_____

Checking up

(ensuring that students

understand and are working correctly)

Anticipating/attending

(anticipating problems; providing

post-assignment directions or

activities; keeping students on-task;

helping and reinforcing)

DATA COLLECTION FORM 10.1
PROFESSIONAL TARGET: TEACHING A THINKING SKILL

Please describe what you hear and see, and record how students reacted.

Provides skill label and definition

Provides rules or steps for using skill

Explains use of skill in the content studied

Models skill (demonstrates and explains)

Provides guided practice and context of practice

Provides independent practice

Evaluates use of skill and provides correctives _____

_____

_____

_____

Provides for transfer _____

_____

_____

_____

DATA COLLECTION FORM 10.2
PROBLEM-SOLVING CHECKLIST

Name(s)_____   Date _____

Problem   _____

_____

_____

_____

Causes of problem   _____

1. _____

2. _____

3. _____

4. _____

5. _____

6. _____

Most serious cause   _____

_____

_____

_____

Possible solutions   _____

1. _____

2. _____

3. _____

4. _____

5. _____

6. _____

Most likely solution _____

_____

_____

_____

_____

Action needed _____

_____

_____

_____

_____

_____

DATA COLLECTION FORM 11.1
PROFESSIONAL DEVELOPMENT TARGET: TEACHING VALUES AND ATTITUDES

Please describe teaching methods and students' reactions.

Discovering students' current values and attitudes _____

_____

_____

_____

Providing information or experiences _____

_____

_____

_____

Providing opportunities for reflection and understanding _____

_____

_____

_____

Checking for commitment _____

_____

_____

_____

(Plans for) checking for action _____

_____

_____

_____

_____

DATA COLLECTION FORM 12.1
PROFESSIONAL TARGET: LECTURE

Please describe what the teacher said and did, and students' reactions.

Organization: advance organizer, structure, post-organizer _____

_____

_____

_____

Relates present to past or future learnings _____

_____

_____

_____

Uses teacher or student summaries _____

_____

_____

_____

Stimulates students to participate overtly/covertly _____

_____

_____

_____

Varies stimuli _____

_____

_____

_____

Supplements instruction with visuals, discussion, question and answer _____

_____

_____

_____

Shows interest, enthusiasm for topic _____

_____

_____

_____

Uses examples to illustrate key ideas _____

_____

_____

_____

Delivery supports note taking _____

_____

_____

Seems to address each student _____

_____

_____

_____

Uses handouts _____

_____

_____

_____

Covers material inappropriate period of time _____

_____

_____

_____

DATA COLLECTION FORM 12.2
PROFESSIONAL TARGET: PRACTICE AND DRILL

Please describe what the teacher said and did, and students' reactions.

Determines entry level _____

_____

_____

_____

Ensures understanding _____

_____

_____

_____

Explains need for the information or skill _____

_____

_____

_____

Provides varied formsof practice _____

_____

_____

_____

Provides feedback, reinforcement, encouragement _____

_____

_____

_____

Similarity to conditions of use _____

_____

_____

_____

Emphasizes product or process _____

_____

_____

_____

Competition/self-competition _____

_____

_____

_____

Length and spacing of practice sessions _____

_____

_____

_____

Linking or application of skill to other content _____

_____

_____

_____

DATA COLLECTION FORM 12.3
PROFESSIONAL DEVELOPMENT TARGET: INDIRECT INSTRUCTION

Please describe what the teacher said and did and how students reacted.

Problem/objective understood? _____

_____

Adequacy and arrangement of _____

facilities, materials, references _____

_____

How and by whom were _____

data selected? _____

_____

How were data processed? _____

What thinking skills were used? _____

_____

Was the teacher "telling"? _____

_____

Was the teacher asking? _____

_____

_____

Questions open or closed? _____

   Convergent or divergent? _____

   Teacher- or student- initiated? _____

   Probes and redirects? _____

_____

_____

Was teacher supportive and _____

encouraging? _____

_____

_____

Were answers provided by _____

teacher? Students? _____

_____

_____

How were ideas tested and _____

evaluated? _____

_____

_____

What were the effects of new _____

data or new evidence? _____

_____

_____

Was a concept, principle, or _____

generalization applied to _____

new situations?

_____

_____

DATA COLLECTION FORM 13.1
PROFESSIONAL TARGET: LARGE GROUP OR CLASS DISCUSSION

Please describe the roles/behavior of students and instructor.

_____

❑ FOCUSING ON TOPIC

- ◆ Introduction of topic   _____
- ◆ Establishment of aims   _____
- ◆ Restatement of aims   _____
- ◆ Disposal of irrelevancies   _____
- ◆ Periodic summaries   _____
- ◆ Response to off-task behavior _____

_____

_____

❑ CLARIFICATION OF ANSWERS

- ◆ Paraphrasing   _____
- ◆ Summarizing   _____
- ◆ Probing   _____
- ◆ Elaborating   _____
- ◆ Analyzing   _____

_____

_____

❑ PROMOTING PARTICIPATION

- ◆ Use of students' ideas   _____
- ◆ Use of silence   _____
- ◆ Challenging   _____
- ◆ Key questions   _____
- ◆ Providing information   _____

❑ VARYING INTERACTION

- ◆ Setting ground rules _____

- ◆ Using eye contact _____

- ◆ Encouraging participation and _____

  interaction _____

- ◆ Seeking agreement _____

_____

_____

❑ CLOSING DISCUSSION

- ◆ Summarizing _____

- ◆ Evaluating discussion effectiveness _____

- ◆ Proposal(s) for follow-up _____

_____

_____

DATA COLLECTION FORM 13.2
PROFESSIONAL TARGET: GROUP PARTICIPATION

Assign each group member a number (*for your own record and use only*). When a member makes a contribution, enter his or her number after the appropriate heading below, with a brief descriptive note of the behavior identified.

Initiating

(initiating discussion, assisting organization,

helping group pursue goal)

_____

_____

_____

_____

Contributing

(offering opinions, facts, anecdotes,

or examples that help group solve

problems or pursue goal)

_____

_____

_____

_____

Clarifying

(helping ensure that all understand terms,

the problem, and members' contributions;

suggesting that more information is needed)

_____

_____

_____

_____

Summarizing

(ensuring that everyone understands

content and knows where each

person stands on a topic)

_____

_____

_____

_____

Evaluating

(keeping track of groups' progress

and identifying problems constructively)

_____

_____

_____

_____

Recording

(keeping and reading back to the group

a record of the main points, to help recall

what was done and to check for accuracy)

_____

_____

_____

_____

_____

Encouraging

(listening carefully, being friendly,

accepting and complimenting

good contributions or effort)

_____

_____

_____

_____

_____

Peace keeping

(relieving tension, settling disputes,

compromising)

_____

_____

_____

_____

DATA COLLECTION FORM 13.3
GUIDE TO PLANNING SMALL-GROUP ACTIVITIES

Subject and Grade Level _____

Unit Name _____ Lesson Topic _____

Group size _____

Method of group assignment _____

Time allotment _____

Materials needed per group _____

_____

_____

Work site of each group _____

_____

_____

Goals relating to interpersonal and group skills _____

_____

_____

Pre-instruction for skills goals _____

_____

_____

Evaluation criteria _____

_____

_____

Small-group tasks _____

_____

_____

Task objectives _____

_____

_____

Pre-task instructions _____

_____

_____

Method of task achievement _____

_____

_____

Evaluation criteria _____

_____

_____

DATA COLLECTION FORM 13.4
PROFESSIONAL TARGET: SMALL-GROUP INSTRUCTION

Please describe instructional behavior and students' reactions.

Set, objectives, and tie-in to lesson _____

_____

_____

_____

Method of group assignment _____

_____

_____

_____

Sites of group work _____

_____

_____

_____

Time allocation _____

_____

_____

_____

Task instructions _____

_____

_____

_____

Interpersonal and group skills instructions _____

_____

_____

_____

Students' behavior _____

_____

_____

_____

Teacher's interventions _____

_____

_____

_____

Group reporting and debriefing _____

_____

_____

_____

Groups' effectiveness _____

_____

_____

_____

DATA COLLECTION FORM 13.5
PROFESSIONAL DEVELOPMENT TARGET: EFFECTIVE GROUP FUNCTIONING

Please describe your observations on the behaviors and functions listed below, and report your findings to the group.

❑ **CHAIRPERSON**

◆ Sees that problem is clarified _____

_____

◆ Initiates and promotes discussion _____

_____

◆ Identifies all phases of problem _____

_____

◆ Keeps discussion on topic _____

_____

◆ Encourages all members to participate _____

_____

◆ Summarizes as required _____

_____

◆ Rephrases statements as needed _____

_____

◆ Maintains objectivity _____

_____

◆ Demonstrates listening skills _____

_____

◆ Treats all persons with respect _____

_____

◆ Accurately reports group process _____

_____

❑ PARTICIPANTS

◆ Contribute reasonably

_____

_____

◆ State ideas clearly and concisely

_____

_____

◆ Keep on task or on topic

_____

_____

◆ Do not show prejudices

_____

_____

◆ Avoid anecdotes, digressions,
  showing off

_____

_____

_____

◆ Paraphrase, clarify, encourage, listen

_____

_____

◆ Respect others' ideas and opinions

_____

_____

◆ Do not ridicule or ignore opinions

_____

_____

◆ Summarize, form conclusion(s)

_____

_____

DATA COLLECTION FORM 13.6
PROFESSIONAL DEVELOPMENT TARGET: EXPERIENTIAL EDUCATION

Please describe the instructor's and the students' actions.

Experiencing

(students experience an activity) _____

_____

_____

Sharing

(students share observations, reactions, _____

or feelings about their experiences) _____

_____

_____

Analyzing

(students "talk through" the shared experience, _____

identifying patterns and interactions) _____

_____

_____

Inferring

(students develop principles or _____

generalizations for future use) _____

_____

_____

Applying

(students plan application of their _____

learnings and/or individuals report their _____

application plans) _____

_____

_____

DATA COLLECTION FORM 14.1

PROFESSIONAL TARGET: ASSIGNED QUESTIONS

Please describe what was said and done and students' reactions.

Introduction of topic _____

_____

_____

_____

Directions about finding and recording answers _____

_____

_____

_____

Advance/post-organizers _____

_____

_____

_____

Nature of questions: domain, levels, convergent or divergent _____

_____

_____

_____

Circulation during seatwork; nature of help given _____

_____

_____

_____

Procedure in taking up questions; use of probes, redirects _____

_____

_____

_____

Tie-in to past and future learnings _____

_____

_____

_____

Integration of learning domains _____

_____

_____

_____

Use of encouragement and reinforcement _____

_____

_____

_____

DATA COLLECTION FORM 15.1

PROFESSIONAL DEVELOPMENT TARGET: USING COOPERATIVE LEARNING GROUPS

Please describe teacher's communication and behavior, and students' responses, with respect to the aspects of using cooperative learning groups listed below.

❏ **ARRANGING GROUPS**

◆ Group size   _____

◆ Heterogeneous assignments   _____

◆ Time allotments   _____

◆ Physical arrangements   _____

◆ Provision of materials   _____

_____

_____

❏ **POSITIVE INTERDEPENDENCE**

◆ Establishing group   _____

◆ Providing common goal   _____

◆ Requiring sharing of resources   _____

◆ Establishing individual rewards   _____

_____

_____

❏ **SKILLS DEVELOPMENT**

◆ Explaining roles   _____

◆ Identifying interpersonal and
  group skills   _____

◆ Practicing interpersonal and
  group skills   _____

_____

_____

❑ SETTING TASK AND GOAL STRUCTURE

- ◆ Stating task and goal structures _____

- ◆ Checking for understanding _____

_____

_____

❑ MONITORING AND GIVING FEEDBACK

- ◆ Circulating and observing _____

- ◆ Helping with task achievement _____

- ◆ Helping with group maintenance _____

- ◆ Providing and using group- _____

  effectiveness instruments _____

- ◆ Providing for student self-evaluation _____

_____

_____

❑ ASSESSMENT

- ◆ Providing quizzes and tests _____

- ◆ Assigning group and individual grades _____

- ◆ Using bonus marks _____

- ◆ Other kinds of recognition _____

_____

_____

DATA COLLECTION FORM 16.1
PROFESSIONAL TARGET: UNIT PLANNING

Unit Title _____

Grade Level and Subject Area _____

Time Estimate _____

_____

Does the rational statement adequately explain the importance to students of

the teaching unit?   Yes ___ No ___

Comments: _____

_____

_____

Are prerequisite student learnings identified?   Yes ___ No ___

Is provision made, as appropriate, for pretesting?   Yes ___ No ___

Comments: _____

_____

_____

Are unit objectives clear and measurable?   Yes ___ No ___

Comments: _____

_____

_____

Has an appropriate concept map (hierarchy) been prepared?   Yes ___ No ___

Have useful task analyses (procedural or hierarchical or combination) been

prepared?   Yes ___ No ___

Comments: _____

_____

_____

Has a clear content outline in appropriate sequence been provided?

Yes ___ No ___

Comments: _____

_____

_____

Is there a variety and balance of appropriate teaching methods and student

activities from which to select? Yes ___ No ___

Comments: _____

_____

_____

Has a suitable variety of resources and materials for students and teacher

been listed? Yes ___ No ___

Comments: _____

_____

_____

Are the formative and summative evaluation outlines congruent with the

lesson objectives? Yes ___ No ___

Comments: _____

_____

_____

Are professional growth targets clearly stated? Yes ___ No ___

Have suitable data collection instruments been provided? Yes ___ No ___

Comments: _____

_____

_____

Additional observations and comments: _____

_____

_____

DATA COLLECTION FORM 16.2
UNIT PLANNING FEEDBACK SHEET

Circle the appropriate numbers to indicate the extent to which requirements have been met: 1 Fully; 2 Quite well; 3 Adequately; 4 Only partially; 5 Insufficiently. Please supply the reasons for your ratings.

❑ **PLANNING AND ORGANIZATION**

1 2 3 4 5 Rationale statement

_____

1 2 3 4 5 Prerequisite learnings

_____

1 2 3 4 5 Concept/skills/processes map

_____

1 2 3 4 5 Declarative/procedural/ affective objectives

_____

❑ **SELECTION OF TEACHING METHODS AND STUDENT ACTIVITIES**

1 2 3 4 5 Use of competencies presented in Part 3 of this book

_____

1 2 3 4 5 Use of competencies presented in Parts 4 and 5 of this book

_____

1 2 3 4 5 Choice of teaching methods and student activities

_____

1 2 3 4 5 Selection of routines and procedures

_____

❑ **MEETING STUDENT NEEDS**

1 2 3 4 5 Motivation

_____

1 2 3 4 5 Varying teacher/student interactions and control

_____

1 2 3 4 5 Recognizing learning styles

_____

1 2 3 4 5 Recognizing cross-cultural needs

_____

1 2 3 4 5 Evaluation

_____

❏ GENERAL ASSESSMENT

1 2 3 4 5 Provision of appropriate teaching methods and learning activities for student growth in all three domains

_____

1 2 3 4 5 Meaningful sequence of experiences and components to accomplish the central purpose of the unit

_____

1 2 3 4 5 Interesting, relevant, and challenging, but achievable

_____

1 2 3 4 5 Teacher's understanding of his or her role as a decision-maker is evident

_____

❏ PERSONAL PROFESSIONAL DEVELOPMENT

1 2 3 4 5 Target selection and data collection (targets identified; a plan for achieving each target stated; a suitable data-collection method and instrument for each target selected or designed)

_____

APPENDIX B

SAMPLE LESSON AND UNIT PLANS

LESSON PLAN A
PLANNING FOR STUDENT LEARNING

Date: May 15, 1995   Grade/Subject: Grade 7 Science
Name: Tanya Bauman   Data Collector: Bobby Blackbird

1. TOPIC:

Dew Point—Earth Science

2. CONTENT IDENTIFICATION:

Formation of dew and relative humidity

3. OBJECTIVES:

a. Each student will list three situations in which he or she has seen dew.
b. Working in groups of three, and using a sling psychrometer, students will record the dew point.
c. Working in groups of three, and using the dew point charts in their textbook and dew point data, students will correctly determine and record relative humidity.

4. PREREQUISITE STUDENT LEARNINGS:

a. Use of thermometers and sling psychrometers.

5. PRESENTATION ACTIVITIES (METHODS):

a. Introductory (Set):
   ❑ Ask students: Have you noticed that sometimes when you get up early in the summer, cars are covered with moisture? Can you give other examples of moisture formation? Why do you think this happens early in the morning, but can occur in the evening too?
   ❑ Show photographs of fog formations.
b. Development:
   ❑ Explain the causes of dew formation and introduce the concept of dew point.
   ❑ With the help of two students, demonstrate how fog is formed.
   ❑ Distribute a handout that contains a step-by-step description of the procedure to be followed. Have the steps on a transparency

and, using progressive disclosure, review the steps. Follow with a brief class discussion on the procedures.

❑ Divide the class into groups of three to perform an experiment. Have groups determine dew point using a sling psychrometer, repeat the procedure three times, and compare results.

❑ After a brief lecture on the concepts involved and what students are to do, provide dew point data. Using temperature and dew point charts in the text, students practice using dew point data to determine relative humidity.

c. Closure:

❑ Through question and answer, review the definition of dew point and the steps in discovering relative humidity.

❑ Discuss why it is important to know about dew point and applications to life situations.

6. MATERIALS AND AIDS:

a. Thermometers; sling psychrometers; ether; bottles; text tables; photos of fog formations.

7. EVALUATION:

a. Responses to review questions on dew point and steps in discovering relative humidity.

b. Written lab reports by groups of three on relative humidity.

PLANNING FOR PROFESSIONAL DEVELOPMENT

1. TARGET AREA:

Classroom management

2. SPECIFIC TARGET(S):

a. "Withitness" (awareness of what each student is doing in the classroom)

3. HOW, SPECIFICALLY, WILL I GO ABOUT TRYING TO ACHIEVE THE TARGET?:

a. Stand and circulate while presenting, and during questions and answers, so that I can see every student.

b. Half-turned to the class while writing on the chalkboard, explain and illustrate; or use the overhead projector to present the steps of the experiment from a position where I can see all students.

c. When helping students with seatwork, keep as many students as possible in view.

4. DATA COLLECTION:

Please use the method described below and/or the data collection instrument that is appended.

LESSON PLAN B
PLANNING FOR STUDENT LEARNING

Date: November 15, 1994   Grade/Subject: Grade 7 Language Arts
Name: Kim Boyko   Data Collector: Beth Beshera

I. TOPIC:

Designing and writing an edition of a newspaper

2. CONTENT IDENTIFICATION:

a. *Concepts:* Typical components of a newspaper (news stories: local, national, international; sports section; business, market report; classifieds; editorial page; domestic issues; advertisements).

b. *Skills and processes:* Imagining, composing, collaborating, decision making, thinking, writing, planning format of a newspaper section.

c. *Attitudes and values:* Consideration for others, enjoyment of a creative task, performance of tasks involved in producing a paper.

3. OBJECTIVES:

a. Learners will use their knowledge of Cynthia Voigt's novel *Dicey's Song* to develop the format and content of a section of a newspaper.

b. Learners will work cooperatively, showing respect for others' ideas.

4. PREREQUISITE STUDENT LEARNINGS:

a. Familiarity with the novel *Dicey's Song.*

b. Knowledge of, and comfort with, group processes.

c. Groups were chosen last class and decisions made as to which newspaper section each group would prepare.

5. PRESENTATION ACTIVITIES (METHODS):

a. Introductory (Set):
   ❑ Tell students the class will prepare a newspaper; have them select a suitable name.
   ❑ Elicit from students the components of a typical newspaper.
   ❑ Remind students to practice effective group behaviors; assign roles and define tasks.

   b. Development: Each group
- ❑ assembles a set of materials relating to the newspaper component their group will work on;
- ❑ examines the material and records typical characteristics of the component from each sample; agrees on the material (and possible audience) for their component;
- ❑ uses the component characteristics and their knowledge of *Dicey's Song* as they brainstorm ideas for the newspaper section they will prepare;
- ❑ develops specific plans for that newspaper section, sharing responsibilities and composing a rough draft;
- ❑ decides what must be done after class, and who will do it.

   c. Closure:
- ❑ Groups spend five minutes evaluating group effectiveness. The recorder makes notes, reports the strengths of the group, and identifies aspects that need to be improved.
- ❑ The Task will be continued in the next class.

6. MATERIALS AND AIDS:

   a. Sections from a selection of newspapers, sorted into component groups.

7. EVALUATION:

   a. Observe newspaper components as they develop. Final copies will be evaluated according to previously specified criteria.

   b. Observe and monitor groups at work. Notes can be made about specific strengths or areas for improvement. Collect self-evaluation notes from groups.

   c. Observe participation during group work for level of interest, involvement, commitment, and enjoyment.

PLANNING FOR PROFESSIONAL DEVELOPMENT

1. TARGET AREA:

Indirect instruction

2. SPECIFIC TARGET(S):

   a. Guided inquiry

   b. Facilitating an indirect (inductive) learning experience

3. How, specifically, will I go about trying to achieve the target?:

    a. After receiving initial directions and instructions, groups will be responsible for their own planning and learning, and for generating new material.

    b. I will use questions to guide groups as I monitor their work.

4. Data Collection:

Please use the method described below and/or the data collection instrument that is appended.

    ❏ Verbatim record of my comments and questions as I monitor groups at work.

INTERDISCIPLINARY UNIT
NATIVE MYTHS AND LEGENDS

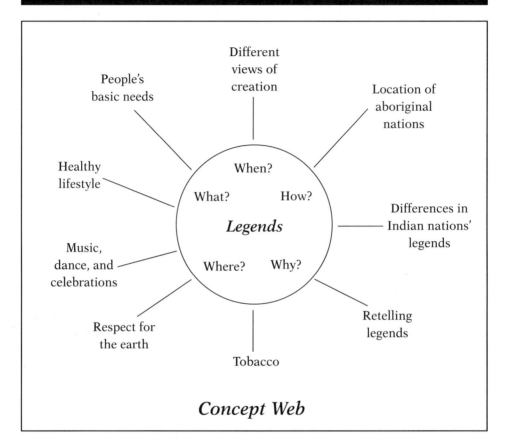

Concept Web

I. IDENTIFICATION DATA AND OVERVIEW

A. Unit Title:

Native Myths and Legends

B. Subject and Grade Level:

Integrated Unit, Grades 7 and 8

C. Time allotment:

Two weeks

D. Overview Statement:

A Native myth or legend may be found for almost any topic studied.

E. Rationale:

Students are interested in aboriginal cultures. They wish to understand traditional aboriginal beliefs and values. Presenting legends is one way to learn these traditions. Using legends to teach contemporary issues validates this approach to teaching.

Students in Grades 7 and 8 are developing self-identity. Having pride in their background, family, and heritage is important. This unit can have a positive influence on the lives of students.

F. Prerequisite Student Learning and Testing:

Students all have their own experiences in life. They come from different backgrounds, with varying beliefs and values. Some know a great deal about their background; some know very little. They have all been exposed to certain health and well-being issues. Through this unit, they will gain information and tools with which to address these issues.

II. PRODUCT AND PROCESS OBJECTIVES

A. Cognitive:

After reading legends, watching films, and participating in discussions, students will:

1. discuss/describe some traditional values and beliefs;
2. discuss/describe the effects of abuse of tobacco;
3. discuss/describe people's basic needs;
4. prioritize their own basic needs;
5. describe a healthy lifestyle;
6. list a number of different aboriginal nations;
7. label on a map the geographical locations of several nations.

B. Procedural:

As students participate in group projects, they will practice and develop:

1. communication skills;
2. thinking skills: interpreting, analyzing, critical thinking, decision making, evaluating, problem solving, summarizing;

3. group skills;
4. research skills: collecting data, organizing data;
5. working independently;
6. map-reading skills;
7. writing skills;
8. singing, dancing, using visual arts.

C. Values and attitudes:

While studying legends, listening to resource people, and participating in activities, students will

1. participate freely in the learning experiences of this unit;
2. demonstrate greater pride in themselves and their families through language and activities (e.g., inviting family members to visit the classroom, decorating the classroom with examples of traditional art and artifacts);
3. show respect for different cultures, particularly Native cultures as suggested in 2.

III. & IV. CONTENT, STUDENT ACTIVITIES, TEACHING METHODS

A. INTRODUCTORY

Content			Teaching/Learning	
Concepts	Skills and Processes	Attitudes and Values	Student Activities	Teaching Targets
Information about legends	Discussing Comparing	Valuing legends	Present examples of several different legends	Stimulus variation

B. DEVELOPMENTAL

Content			Teaching/Learning	
Concepts	Skills and Processes	Attitudes and Values	Student Activities	Teaching Targets
Traditional use of tobacco Tobacco can be abused	Communicating Interpreting Observing	Awareness of ceremonial use of tobacco Respect for traditions	Legend: "The Great Gift, Tobacco" Discussion Film: *Almost Everybody Does It* Discussion	Teaching for attitude change Analysis Teaching for thinking

Content			Teaching/Learning	
Concepts	**Skills and Processes**	**Attitudes and Values**	**Student Activities**	**Teaching Targets**
Effects of abusing tobacco Smoking as expensive Nicotine addiction	Evaluating Comparing Calculating	Respect for one's own body Responsibility for own health	Construct T-chart (traditional and contemporary uses of tobacco) Calculate smoking costs	Teaching for attitude change Thinking skills
Basic human needs remain the same	Communicating Analyzing	Respect for legends	Legend: "Gift of the Whale" (Caduto & Bruchac, 1991) Identifying basic needs	Discussion Teaching for attitude change Thinking skills
Urgency of needs	Group skills Prioritizing	Respect for others' opinions	Groups (3s)—list and prioritize 12 needs; move to 6s, and agree	Small-group learning
Maslow's hierarchy of needs led to self-actualization	Comparing	Cooperation	Compare lists of needs to Maslow's theory	Teaching for thinking
Goals can be derived from needs statements	Setting goals Making choices	Confidence Self-respect	Identify personal goals	Cooperative groups Teaching for attitude change
Dakota Indian people symbolized their goals in *Dream Catchers*	Following directions	Respect Valuing traditional ways	Diagraming construction of *Dream Catchers*	Giving directions Demonstrating
A legend can be presented visually	Observing	Interest in other ways of life	Introduce visual symbols Show examples of visual symbols	Cooperative groups Stimulus variation
Native people used visual symbols to communicate ideas	Constructing Composing	Taking pride in group effort	Groups create a visual-representation of legend and participate in storytelling	Thinking skills
Native legends about gift of food to the people	Communicating	Interest in traditional stories	Legend: "How Food Was Given" Discuss the value of good nutrition	Questioning
Medicine Wheel symbolizes knowledge	Listening Being courteous	Respect for traditional values and knowledge	Resource person for class discussion of four dimensions of wellness	Discussion Explaining

Content			Teaching/Learning	
Concepts	**Skills and Processes**	**Attitudes and Values**	**Student Activities**	**Teaching Targets**
Wellness; physical, emotional, intellectual, spiritual	Deciding Choosing Prioritizing	Valuing a different perspective	Goal setting for personal wellness	Thinking skills Attitude change
Traditional values include respect for Earth and the environment	Interpreting Summarizing Analyzing Group work	Appreciation and respect for traditional values	Research and write reports on effects of technological change on Earth	Explaining Independent learning
Technology severely damages the environment	Comparing Analyzing Evaluating	Working together	Create murals of Earth and environment before advent of technology	Giving directions Classroom management
Legends provide creation stories There are similarities and differences among the aboriginal nations	Gathering information Comparing data	Working together Accepting others' ideas	Groups choose a legend from a particular aboriginal nation. They research cultural practices and portray customs and values in a performance of the legend (using dance, drama, visual arts, or music) Groups select other legends from the nation as the basis for a Reader's Workshop	Giving directions Explaining Classroom management Cooperative groups
Native cultural heritage rich in music, dance, celebrations, ceremonies, and rituals	Observation Participating	Appreciation of Native arts	Legend: "Origin of Music" Resource people instruct students in appropriate traditional dances	Explaining Demonstrating
Aboriginal nations are located in many areas of North America	Gathering information Map reading	Valuing diversity	Construct class map of North America; mark locations of aboriginal nations. Discuss relationship of cultural traditions, livelihood, trading routes, physical features of the area	Questioning Discussion Thinking skills

C. Culminating Activities

1. Class debriefing
2. Preparation of displays and rehearsals of presentations
3. Display of work and performance during class exchange visit
4. Students make entries in their learning logs

V. RESOURCES AND MATERIALS

Allen, Paula Gunn. (1991). *Grandmothers of the light: A medicine woman's sourcebook.* Boston: Beacon Press.

Bierhorst, John. (1984). *The hungry woman: Myths and legends of the Aztecs.* New York: William Morrow & Company.

Bruchac, J. (1992). *Thirteen moons on Turtle's back: A Native American year of moons.* New York: Putnam.

Caduto, M., & Bruchac, J. (1989). *Keepers of the earth.* Saskatoon, SK: Fifth House.

Caduto, M., & Bruchac, J. (1991). *Keepers of the animals.* Saskatoon, SK: Fifth House.

Cameron, Anne. (1987a). *Orca's song.* Madiera Park, BC: Harbour Publications.

Cameron, Anne. (1987b). *Raven returns the water.* Madiera Park, BC: Harbour Publications.

Cameron, Anne. (1991a). *Raven and snipe.* Madiera Park, BC: Harbour Publications.

Cameron, Anne. (1991b). *Raven goes berry picking.* Madiera Park, BC: Harbour Publications.

Clark, Ella. (1960). *Indian legends of Canada.* Toronto, ON: McClelland & Stewart.

Desbarats, Peter. (1969). *What they used to tell about: Indian legends from Labrador.* Toronto, ON: McClelland & Stewart.

Epp, Henry. (1991). *Long ago today: The story of Saskatchewan's earliest people.* Saskatoon, SK: Saskatchewan Archeological Society.

Four Worlds. (1984). *The sacred tree: Reflections on Native American spirituality.* Alberta: Four Worlds Development Press.

Goble, Paul. (1992). *Crow Chief: A Plains Indian story.* New York: Orchard Books.

Henderson, Lucy. (1990a). *Opeyuko.* Lac La Ronge, SK: Lac La Ronge Indian Band Education Branch.

Henderson, Lucy. (1990b). *The wicked lady magician*. Lac La Ronge, SK: Lac La Ronge Indian Band Education Branch.

Highwater, Jamake. (1985). *The ceremony of innocence*. Toronto, ON: Harper and Row.

Highwater, Jamake. (1986). *I wear the morning star*. New York: Harper & Row.

Karras, A.L. (1970). *North to Cree Lake*. New York: Trident Press.

Martin, Rafe. (1992). *The rough faced girl*. New York: Putnam.

McLellan, Joseph. (1983). *Nanabosho, Soaring Eagle and the great sturgeon*. Winnipeg, MN: Pemmican Publications.

Miller, Jay. (1992). *Earthmaker: Tribal stories from Native North America*. New York: Perigee Books.

Millman, Lawrence. (1993). *Wolverine creates the world: Labrador Indian tales*. Santa Barbara, CA: Capra Press.

Milloy, John. (1988). *The Plains Cree: Trade, diplomacy and war, 1790 to 1870*. Winnipeg, MN: University of Manitoba Press.

Mills, W.G. (1992). *Legends of the Mississaugas*. Pickering, ON: Altona Editions.

Morton, Edward. (1988). *To touch the wind: An introduction to Native American literature*. Dubuque, IA: Kendall Hunt.

Ortiz, Simon (Ed.). (1983). *Earth power coming: Short fiction in Native American literature*. Tsaile, AZ: Navaho Community College Press.

Oughton, Jerrie. (1992). *How the stars fell into the sky: A Navaho legend*. Boston: Houghton Mifflin.

Pelton, M.H.W. (1992). *Images of the people: Tlingit myths and legends*. Englewood, CO: Libraries Unlimited.

Vandall, Peter. (1983). *Waskahikaniyiniw-Acimowina: Stories of the house people*. Lac La Ronge, SK: Lac La Ronge Indian Band Education Branch.

Whitehead, R. (1988). *Stories from the six worlds: Micmac legends*. Halifax, NS: Nimbus Publishing.

Wolfe, Alexander. (1988). *Earth Elder stories: The Pinayzitt path*. Saskatoon, SK: Fifth House.

Film and Video

Almost Everybody Does It [Film].

Indian Legends of Canada [CBC Video Series]. (1981). Thomas Howe.
Video, 15 legends.

VI. PRODUCT AND PROCESS OBJECTIVES

A. Degree to Which Students Achieve Objectives:

A variety of evaluation procedures and instruments will be used. Students
will keep a learning log throughout the unit. Work samples will be
collected and kept together. Evaluation will be based on students' perceptions as well as on teacher's observational records.

Objectives	Procedure	Instrument
Concepts	Observation of participation	Work samples Project checklists Learning logs Portfolios
Skills and processes	Observation of group processes Analysis	Anecdotal records Project work Criteria for performances Self-evaluation records Student–teacher conferences
Values and attitudes	Observation of participation Inquiry	Checklist Student conference Rating scale
	Analysis	Self-evaluation Learning logs

B. Unit Effectiveness

The effectiveness of the unit will be evaluated by the extent to which the
content objectives are met, taking into account the students' self-evalua-
tions and learning logs.

VII. PRODUCT AND PROCESS OBJECTIVES

The following teaching approaches, strategies, and skills will be practiced in this unit.

A. Direct Instruction:

Stimulus variation
Teaching for attitude change
Discussion
Giving directions
Demonstrating
Classroom management

Experiential Instruction:

Questioning
Explaining
Giving directions
Classroom management

Interactive Instruction:

Cooperative groups
Giving directions
Classroom management

B. Indirect Instruction:

Teaching for attitude change
Questioning
Teaching for thinking

Independent Study:

Giving directions
Questioning

Source: Adapted with permission from a unit by Lois Berard-Pearce, Saskatchewan *Urban Native Teacher Education Program* (SUNTEP) student.

■ ■ ■ ■ ■
GLOSSARY

abstract concept   A generalization pertaining to anything that cannot be directly perceived by the senses (e.g., democracy, beauty, truth).

academic learning time   The proportion of time during which students are engaged in constructive and meaningful learning.

active participation   Overt or observable involvement in a learning activity.

active teaching   See **explicit teaching**.

advance organizer   A brief statement that introduces and summarizes the main ideas of a lesson or unit and provides a structure for its content.

affect   Feelings, emotions, attitudes, and values.

affective content   The range of learnings relating to attitudes, interests, values, emotions, and feelings that is inherent in a lesson or unit.

affective domain   The domain of feelings, emotions, attitudes, and values that correspond to learning goals and that are carried through processes such as receiving, responding, valuing, organization, and characterization (see Krathwohl, Bloom, & Masia, 1968).

affective education   Education relating to values, attitudes, feelings, and emotions; its goals are to help learners build character, form personality and personal philosophies, reduce prejudices, encourage positive self-concept and healthy self-esteem, and promote personal and social adjustment and mental health.

affective skills   Procedures relating to forming and determining attitudes and values, such as perception checking, consensus seeking, and conflict resolution.

altruistic behaviors   Behaviors that are motivated or marked by a desire to benefit others rather than by self-interest.

analytic methods of learning   Learning methods that adopt a "parts" approach, simplifying skills and processes by separating them into their component parts.

"artificiality," instructional   An oversimplification of reality for the purpose of teaching specific aspects of a subject; reduction of the number of variables included in the content being taught.

assertive discipline   *See* **preventive discipline.**

assessment   Collecting information that provides a full picture of students' performance, creating a frame for judging each student's progress as demonstrated by performance.

assimilation   The absorption of minority groups or cultures into a majority culture.

assumption   Acceptance as fact of a proposition that has not been verified through observation or experiment.

attitude   A mental set, based on values and evolving from experience, that predisposes the person holding it to respond in a particular way to a person, object, situation, or event.

attraction   A force for positive social behavior that influences group members to like one another and to work or play well together.

authoritarianism (classroom-management approach)   An approach that involves careful monitoring of student behavior and control of the classroom through commands and rules that the teacher sets and enforces, disciplining students for infractions.

automaticity   Ready and efficient performance of a procedure without the need for conscious focus on the method.

behavior description   Verbal depiction of the behavior of another, told to the individual in order to inform him or her of its effect on others and thereby to promote personal awareness.

behavior modification   An approach to behavioral change that requires specific professional training in the use of positive reinforcement (e.g., praise, rewards, modeling, contingency contracts, prompts, signals) or negative reinforcement (e.g., signals, commands, response costs, and punishment) to promote desirable behavior and eliminate undesirable behavior.

behavioral norms   Accepted rules or commonly understood expectations for behavior.

behavioral objectives   Specific statements delineating exactly what students should be able to do as a result of a given lesson. They identify and specify the behavior that will provide evidence of achievement, the conditions under which that behavior is to occur, and the projected degree of anticipated student achievement.

belief   A proposition accepted as true by an individual or group.

bias   Unequal (positive or negative) depiction or treatment of persons based on their gender, culture, race, religion, or socioeconomic status, or for other reasons.

blanket questions   questions directed simultaneously to everyone in a class.

brainstorming   A technique used by individuals or groups to produce as many ideas or suggestions as possible within a few minutes, without initially judging the value or implications of the ideas suggested.

buzzing   Discussing, within small groups, the pros and cons of optional solutions for a problem with the goal of reaching consensus or taking a decision.

call-out answers   Unsolicited student responses to a question.

choral response   Response solicited from more that one student simultaneously or from the entire class.

classroom climate   The atmosphere and environment in which students and teachers work and relate to one another.

classroom management   A complex set of behaviors that teachers use to structure the classroom setting, and to create and maintain conditions that enable students to learn efficiently.

clinical supervision   *See* **conferencing.**

closure   Concluding statements or actions used to bring a lesson or unit to an appropriate end by highlighting, reinforcing, synthesizing, or summarizing key ideas.

cognitive domain   The field of learning concerned with ideas, knowledge, and intellectual skills and processes; it includes the categories of knowledge, comprehension, application, analysis, synthesis, and evaluation (Bloom et al., 1956).

cognitive skills   Specific intellectual procedures relating to learning or reasoning.

combination task analysis   A process useful for analyzing complex psychomotor skills and cognitive tasks, which combines procedural analysis (breaking down the sequence of steps involved) and hierarchical analysis (identifying the terminal skills and the associated enabling subskills involved).

communication   The sharing of thoughts and feelings through words or symbols that have approximately the same meaning for all involved.

communication congruence   The understanding of a verbal or nonverbal message in the same way by both the sender and the receiver.

communication skills   Specific procedures relating to the transmittal of information (e.g., listening and responding to promote verbal and nonverbal communication that reduces the possibility of discrepancy between messages sent and messages received.

communication skills, basic   Specific primary procedures relating to the transmittal of information verbally (through appropriate word choice, clarity, pronunciation, tonal variation, and pausing) and nonverbally (through gestures, eye contact, facial expression, posture, and body movement).

concept   A mental construct of a category or set of objects, abstract notions, conditions, events, or processes that can be grouped together on the basis of similarities and represented by a word or other symbol, image, or mental picture.

concept definition   A statement containing all the essential (critical) attributes of a concept and expressing the relationship of these attributes to one another.

concept hierarchy   A diagram showing the relationship of concepts or groups of concepts to one another, ordering them from broad to very specific or identifying them as superordinate, coordinate, or subordinate in relation to one another.

concept map   A graphic representation of the conceptual structure of a unit or units of knowledge in a given discipline.

concept name   The label associated with a concept as a symbol under which all instances of that concept are grouped or classified.

conceptual content   All declarative knowledge—whether about facts, concepts, or relationships—that is inherent in a lesson or unit.

conceptual knowledge   *See* **declarative knowledge**.

concrete concept   A general notion of a class of items perceived through one or more of the five senses.

conferencing   A cycle consisting of preconference discussion, observation and data collection, and postconference discussion that focuses on students' achievement of lesson goals and the teacher's achievement of a specific professional target (competency).

conflict resolution   A process for reconciling opposing or disparate views.

conjunctive concept   A concept that has an unchanging rule structure or a single set of characteristics or critical attributes, all of which are always present in any given example of the concept.

consensus   A common decision to support (though not necessarily agree with) a specific position, policy, or undertaking.

content   Instructional product or process relating to one or more of the three instructional domains: cognitive/conceptual, procedural, and affective.

convergent questions   Questions that require students to bring concepts together to achieve a single correct response.

cookbook classroom management   A random collection of dos and don'ts or a set of "how-tos" for classroom management, lacking any obviously consistent rationale.

cooperative games   Games that provide for maximum participation by players who play *with* rather than *against* one another, so that every player "wins." Such games are usually self-paced and fun, and players are not graded or assessed; common effort and helping others are important goals.

cooperative learning   A mode of learning that involves group participation and collective performance. Groups are often of mixed ability, and members are responsible for helping one another.

coordinate concept   A concept that has one or more unique critical attributes but shares some common critical attributes with other concepts, and can therefore be subsumed under a higher order.

creative thinking   Intellectual activity involved in forming new combinations of ideas to produce original and appropriate results.

criterion-referencing   An individual assessment process that involves applying a predetermined standard to an individual or group.

critical attributes   Characteristics essential to a given concept or item.

critical thinking   Fairminded interpretation, analysis, or evaluation of information, arguments, or experiences; also, the use of a set of reflective attitudes, skills, and abilities to guide thoughts, beliefs, and actions.

critical thinking skills   Techniques for exercising mental procedures that involve distinguishing between facts and values, warranted and unwarranted claims, and relevant and irrelevant information; determining the reliability of sources and the accuracy of statements; detecting bias; identifying assumptions and ambiguous or equivocal claims or arguments; recognizing logical inconsistencies in a line of argument; and determining the strength of an argument (Beyer, 1984).

cross-cultural   Relating to, functioning among, or interacting with diverse racial or ethnic groups.

cue   An indirect reminder that suggests information to students, without directly telling them, so that they can take a further step in reasoning and/or responding.

culminating student activities   Activities that are conducted at the end of a lesson or unit and that are designed to emphasize interrelationships, synthesize learnings, and examine a topic or problem in retrospect. They should help students to recognize what they have learned and what unsolved problems remain to be studied and researched. Summative testing is usually included in culminating activities.

culture   The unique lifestyle and ways of viewing the world that are manifested in the language and social behavior of a particular society or group of people.

decision making   The process of assessing the merits and possible consequences of actions, determining the most important factors, and then selecting a course of action.

declarative knowledge   The intellectual grasp of facts, concepts, and generalizations or relationships.

deductive reasoning   A logical intellectual procedure whereby the reasoner perceives a general concept and uses it to identify a number of specific examples. *Compare* **inductive reasoning**.

deferred success   An attempt that does not meet with immediate success but that allows the person making it to learn something that will promote a later success.

demonstration   Modeling and explaining a particular procedure to show a specific method of applying a skill.

developmental student activities   Activities planned and conducted by a teacher to promote specific learning goals.

dialectical thinking   The critical examination of one's own thinking, and the sympathetic use of a perspective different from or even opposed to one's own; also termed *reflective self-criticism*.

direct instruction   Teaching that focuses on the mastery of basic skills by means of clear content organization, direct student involvement, mastery of materials and procedures, and concentration on the task at hand. *Compare* **indirect instruction**.

direction giving   An instructional procedure that involves securing the attention of all; clearly stating any instructions; checking to discover whether all students understand the instructions before beginning work; making in-progress checks to ensure that students are following instructions.

discipline Control of student behavior by setting and enforcing rules and establishing consequences (rewards and punishments).

discipline, external A range of measures, or consequences, used by teachers to control students' behavior.

discipline, internal Students' acceptance of personal responsibility for behaving in ways that will promote learning.

discovery learning Exposure of students to specific examples from which they "discover" learning patterns, principles, or relationships on the basis of which to form conclusions.

discrimination The act of perceiving and identifying differences, and making distinctions on the basis of those differences.

disjunctive concept A concept that allows for two or more sets of critical attributes, each of which might independently define it (e.g., a noun is the name of a person *or* a place *or* a thing).

distributed practice Practice provided in several short sessions rather than in one or a few longer sessions.

divergent questions Questions that do not have a single correct response but that invite open-ended, creative responses.

enactive learning Learning at a "hands-on" or activity-oriented level.

ethnic group A group of people who share a common racial origin, history, language, religion, culture, value system, and social pattern.

ethnocentrism Evaluation of other races and cultures by criteria specific to one's own.

evaluation The process(es) whereby a teacher assesses the degree and kinds of learning that students have acquired.

evaluation set Use of motivational strategy to prepare students for and involve them in a review and assessment of newly acquired knowledge and skills.

evaluative questions Questions that require students to make carefully considered and clearly substantiated judgments.

exemplar A representative "pure" instance of a concept.

experiential education A learner-centered, integrated, holistic approach to teaching/learning that emphasizes firsthand encounters or direct involvement and participation, reflection on significance, and future application. Experiential education usually has an affective component.

experiential learning cycle The stages of experiential learning, including experiencing, sharing, analyzing, inferring, and applying.

explicit teaching A direct instructional strategy best suited for memorizing basic information and mastering well-defined performance skills. It emphasizes systematic organization, using small steps, checking for understanding, and ensuring active learner participation and learner success.

extrinsic motivation Inducement to perform generated by rewards or events not directly relating to the learning situation itself.

extrinsic reward A reward that is external to the learning experience itself, such as grades.

feedback, effective Informational data provided by an observer that is solicited, descriptive, nonjudgmental, focused on behavior that can be controlled, specific, and complete.

feelings description   Information that people give to one another to let them know their feelings and avoid possible misinterpretation.

field-dependent learners   Learners who view content globally; tend to impose personal structure on a task, and find it difficult to distinguish parts from the whole; prefer structured, teacher-centered, group-based approach to learning that is holistic rather than analytic.

field-independent learners   Learners who prefer an analytical, self-directed, independent approach to learning and who are capable of extrapolating a task from a pattern and devising an alternative pattern to make information comprehensible.

focusing   The act of gaining students' attention and directing it to specific lesson objectives.

formative evaluation   Evaluation made before or during a teaching/learning process.

generalization   A broad concept, often covering several particular ones.

generic principles and practices of teaching   Accepted concepts and methods of teaching that apply to a broad range of age and grade levels and subject areas.

global observation   General, unfocused remarking of activities or situations in the classroom.

group dynamics   Intragroup relationships and interactions that determine a group's functioning patterns and productivity.

group effectiveness   The capacity of a group to complete assigned tasks successfully through productive cooperative efforts.

group focus   A management skill used by teachers to maintain their awareness of *all* students; and to keep each student actively involved, through quick pacing of lessons, wide distribution of questions at varying levels, acceptance only of recognized responses, and individual assistance, feedback, and reinforcement.

group investigation (GI)   A cooperative learning model (Sharan and Lazarowitz, 1980) for teaching higher-order thinking skills by having students gather information and interpret it through discussion, synthesizing individual contributions into a group product.

group maintenance   Successful activities within a group to accommodate individual needs, get along with one another, and accomplish the work assigned. Behaviors supportive of group health include encouraging and listening to others, expressing group feelings, cooperating, creating harmony by compromising, and setting or applying standards.

group processes (classroom management approach)   An approach that involves maintaining teacher "withitness," setting reasonable expectations, promoting cooperative decision making, sharing leadership, initiating group-maintenance activities, resolving conflicts, and providing opportunities for role playing.

group skills   Interpersonal skills that apply to group situations, including group communication skills (techniques of giving and receiving messages to and from groups without distorting meanings) and group management skills (participating, problem solving, goal setting, conflict resolution, group-effectiveness monitoring).

group structure   The relationship patterns that develop in a group as a result of the positions and roles of its members.

guidance   Positive, focused, appropriate, and concise help in performing a skill, provided only as necessary, through cues, directions, demonstrations, or explanations.

guided discovery   A variation of discovery learning in which the teacher provides direction through leading questions and feedback to achieve previously determined learning objectives.

guided discussion   Discussion that is guided step by step by means of questions and timely interjection of information.

guided inquiry   An investigative process carefully structured, through the teacher's questions and selection of materials and activities, to lead students to make a specific discovery or generalization. *See also* **unguided inquiry**.

helping relationship   A relationship between a helper and "helpee" that involves empathy, trust, genuineness, and the provision of solicited, precise, nonjudgmental feedback.

hierarchical task analysis   The process of breaking a complex skill or task into component "enabling" subskills or subtasks, until a treelike structure of tasks and subtasks is clearly identified.

higher-order thinking   *See* **thinking, levels o**f.

holistic methods of learning   Learning methods that emphasize the integration and connection of elements.

hypostatization   Provision of a solid basis for learning.

hypothesis   A tentative statement or proposition that provides the basis for research or investigation.

iconic learning   Learning on the basis of visual representation.

indirect instruction   A learner-centered, "open" approach to education that facilitates practice of a range of thinking skills and encourages students to take responsibility for the inquiry process. *Compare* **direct instruction**.

individual accountability   Each student's acceptance of responsibility for completing an assigned task or following established rules and procedures.

individualizing   Adapting instruction to meet the needs, interests, and abilities of an individual.

inductive reasoning   A logical intellectual procedure whereby the reasoner perceives a number of specific examples and uses them to frame a general concept. *Compare* **deductive reasoning**.

inquiry   Investigation that leads to understanding or to finding solutions to problems. Its basic processes are observing, classifying, using numbers, measuring, using space–time relationships, predicting, inferring, defining operationally, framing hypotheses, interpreting data, controlling variables, experimenting, and communicating (see Orlich et al., 1985).

instruction (classroom management approach)   A method of classroom management that uses relevant content, reasonable routines and procedures, careful plans for student success, and appropriate instructional skills to motivate students to learn and reduce the incidence of problem behavior.

instructional model   A broad use of teaching/learning strategies and methods to promote information processing in the cognitive, procedural, and affective domains.

instructional objectives   Clear statements of teaching/learning intent that normally include a precise description of the student behavior expected, the conditions under which the expected behavior is to occur, and the degree (or level) of achievement or performance anticipated.

instructional strategies   Specific methods of promoting learners' achievement of planned learning goals.

instructional unit   A cohesive portion of a prescribed course that centers on a particular topic, theme, or major concept; an arrangement of content, materials, and activities around a central topic within a broad area of investigation.

intelligence   The innate intellectual ability to recall and process information and solve problems.

interactive instruction   A student-centered approach to instruction that relies heavily on guided discussion and sharing, often involving question-and-answer exchanges and cooperative small-group work.

interdisciplinary   Integrating more than one subject area.

interpersonal skills   Procedural facility in relating to others and communicating with them effectively, by means of making clear statements, paraphrasing their statements, describing one's own feelings, describing their behavior and one's own, and perception checking.

intimidation (classroom management approach):   Use of fear to control student behavior through threats, sarcasm, ridicule, disapproval, and/or physical force.

intrinsic motivation   Determination, exercised from within an individual or proceeding from a personal wish, to complete a task.

intrinsic reward   An internal reward, arising from satisfaction in the learning experience itself.

introductory student activities   tasks intended to set the stage and/or provide orientation or motivation for completing a learning assignment.

investigative group   *See* **group investigation**.

Jigsaw   A cooperative learning procedure, developed by Aronson, Blaney, Stephan, Sikes, and Snapp (1978), to encourage peer cooperation and tutoring. Students meet in "expert" groups to study assigned topics before returning to their heterogeneous "home" teams to teach their peers.

Jigsaw II   A variation of Jigsaw (Slavin, 1980b), in which individual test scores are totaled to form team scores, thereby intensifying student interdependence.

Johari Window   A model for self-awareness and awarenss of others (Luft, 1969) that facilitates learning and sharing information about oneself.

kinesthetic variation   A stimulus variation technique that relies on the movement of the teacher to draw or direct attention and arouse or maintain student interest.

knowledge of results   Feedback informing learners of their progress, specifying the aspects of their work that are correct, and those that need modification.

laboratory group   A learning group formed to investigate and complete a project or do experiments.

leading questions   Questions framed to contain a portion of, or to suggest, the answer.

learning   The acquisition of knowledge, skills, or affect that results in observable change in behavior or capability.

learning activities   Experiences in which students participate to achieve objectives.

learning experience   An occurrence or procedure during which a learner encounters and/or comprehends a particular reality.

learning goals   *See* **instructional objectives**.

learning modality   An innate approach to learning that may involve one or a combination of kinds of stimuli, as follows: visual (learning by watching or seeing), auditory (learning through listening), tactile (learning by touching or manipulating), or kinesthetic (learning through movement).

learning strategies   *See* **instructional strategies**.

learning style preferences   Individual's innate aptitude for specific modes of perceiving, grasping, and processing knowledge. Some educators relate these preferences to the individual's innate inclination to process learning with the right or the left hemisphere of the brain.

lesson planning   A complex procedure that takes into account both teaching and learning components, and involves the following elements: choice of lesson topic, content specification, prerequisite learnings, learning goals, presentation (set, development, and closure), choice of materials and aids, and evaluation methods; the professional development target and plans for its achievement may also be included.

low-profile control   A system of classroom management that involves smooth and discreet teacher handling, and avoids open and direct confrontations and constant orders that might cause a ripple effect, leading to further misbehavior.

management, classroom   *See* **classroom management**.

massed practice   Practice concentrated into one or a few longer sessions rather than several shorter sessions.

mastery learning   An approach to instruction that focuses on providing every student with appropriate activities and enough time to achieve specific learning goals.

microteaching   Teaching a lesson, or a portion of a lesson, to a small group of peers (teachers in training) in order to practice a specific professional development target.

modeling   Behaving in ways that provide examples for students to follow.

monitoring   Observing and checking student classroom performance and behavior.

motivation   Any condition or stimulus that induces, directs, and sustains desired performance and behavior.

movement management   Behaviors used by teachers to regulate the pace and flow of classroom activities, and to keep transitions smooth and "dead time" to a minimum.

multiple questions   A series of questions delivered rapidly, without the pauses necessary to allow respondents to answer any particular one.

needs assessment   The process of identifying the needs of groups of learners as a first step in planning an educational program.

negative reinforcement   The application of an aversive stimulus to deter an undesirable response and increase the frequency of a desired response.

noncritical attributes   Characteristics found in some but not all instances of a given concept; variable attributes.

nonexamples   Negative examples, or examples of what a concept *is not*.

norm-referencing   An individual assessment process that involves applying a group standard to students of the same age or grade.

norms for professional growth   Accepted behavior patterns including empathy, warmth, caring, openness, genuineness, positive regard and respect, and professional commitment.

objectives   Intended learning outcomes or goals. *See also* **behavioral objectives**, **instructional objectives**.

one-three-six consensus group   A sequential procedure that moves from individuals' recording their responses to an issue, to the forming of triads to seek agreement and acceptance of ideas, to the combining of triads into groups of six to achieve consensus.

open discussion   A free-flowing discussion wherein the teacher plans and monitors the degree of openess, and intervenes only to encourage, mediate, broaden participation, provide necessary information, or reinforce conclusions.

open discussion group   A group formed to discuss a controversial or emotionally charged topic.

open-ended questions   Questions that call for discussion or reflection rather than for a particular "right" answer.

orientation set   Use of a motivational strategy to introduce a lesson or topic in a way that stirs learners' interest and activates their desire to learn.

overgeneralization   Defining and applying a concept too broadly.

overlapping   Handling two or more instructional situations or activities simultaneously to promote productive use of classroom time and to minimize interruptions.

overlearning   Consolidating skills by practicing them beyond the required level of proficiency in order to ensure automaticity of performance and retention.

paraphrasing   Restating another person's words or providing an example to verify one's perception of that person's meaning.

participatory learning   *See* **enactive learning**.

"parts" approach to learning   An instructional approach normally associated with skills teaching that involves breaking lengthy or complex material into a series of component parts and having students learn one part at a time.

pausing   Using silence to gain or direct attention, provide an opportunity for covert practice, or invite participation.

pedagogy   The science and art of effective teaching and training of children.

peer tutoring   Instruction given by fellow students.

penalty   An undesirable consequence of inappropriate behavior.

perception checking   Verifying one's perception of another person's state of mind or intended meaning by describing that perception and asking the other person to confirm it.

permissiveness (classroom management approach)   Promotion of maximum student freedom in order to maximize the potential of individuals in instructional situations where the teacher acts as consultant rather than an authority figure.

personality integration   A personal adjustment to an environment that results in a positive self-concept, self-control, ethical behavior, social responsibility, and other characteristics beneficial to society and the individual.

positive interdependence   The productive reliance on the group and other members resulting among individual members from the belief that they are responsible for their own learning and the learning of all members of their group.

positive reinforcement   The application of a stimulus, such as approval or encouragement, that increases the frequency of a positive learner response.

postconferencing   A debriefing session after a lesson, conducted by a teacher and a teaching partner or cooperating teacher, to analyze the efficacy of the lesson with respect to student learning outcomes and the teacher's professional growth.

practice   Repeated performance of a task or skill, or recall of information, to perfect or consolidate the skill or knowledge for use in other contexts. Conscious, active, practice can be guided, monitored, or independent.

preconferencing   A lesson preview, conducted by a teacher and a helper, to clarify, confirm, or revise plans for achieving desired student learning outcomes and a professional development target.

prejudice   An attitude or belief formed or held on the basis of a bias or of insufficient or incorrect information.

preventive discipline   Classroom control based on a common-sense mix of praise and limit setting, and premised on the rule that no student has the right to prevent the teacher from carrying out duties or to prevent peers from learning. The teacher explains rules, and the logical consequences that will result from breaking them; students understand that they are responsible for accepting the consequences if they choose to break the rules, and that the teacher will be fair but firm.

probe   A technique whereby the teacher asks a series of step-by-step questions to help a student move through a reasoning process to frame a logical answer, or to elicit more detail or a higher-level response.

problem solving   A process of reasoning through a series of small, sequential steps to arrive at answers to questions or achieve a solution to a problem.

procedural knowledge   A grasp of skills that enables a person to perform efficiently an act that requires manipulation and coordination.

procedural task analysis   The identification of the steps that must be performed sequentially to complete a task.

procedures   Prescribed steps for helping students to participate in class activities and accomplish particular learning tasks.

processes   Procedures that link skills and concepts; they are less patterned and more extensive than skills.

professional development   A process of professional growth undertaken to achieve specific professional targets.

professional development journal   A personal professional development record involving description (a brief statement of what was experienced), impact (a specific statement of the learning acquired), and intent (a plan for future action).

professional target   *See* **target**.

prompt   A technique whereby the teacher provides a reminder to enable a student to work out a satisfactory answer, without exposing the answer.

prototype   The exemplar, or clearest example, of a category or concept.

psychomotor domain   The area of learning that involves sensory perceptions and conscious movement skills.

psychomotor skills   Procedural facility in manipulating objects or performing physical movements, as in crafts, typing, or physical activities.

punishment   The application of an unpleasant consequence to decrease or eliminate undesirable behavior.

questions, level of   The complexity of a question in relation to the academic maturity of the respondent. Levels of questions correspond to the levels of thinking.

racism   Prejudice against a particular racial group.

rational-linear planning   Planning that begins with establishing goals and objectives, moves to planning instructional strategies to promote achievement of those objectives, and concludes with measuring achievements.

rationale statement (unit)   A statement of the purpose of teaching a given unit that may provide an overview of the content and/or outline the major outcomes to be achieved, and state reasons why these are important.

reacting   Teacher behavior in response to student action.

"reality," instructional   Inclusion of a large number of variables in instructional content, approximating the complexity of real-life situations.

reality therapy   A remedial approach (Glasser, 1969) to behavior management that induces change by making clear to a student the consequence or outcome of current disruptive behavior.

redirect   The technique of passing a question to another student when the first student asked gives an incorrect or incomplete answer, or does not respond; sometimes used to confirm a response, invite comment, or stimulate discussion.

reinforcement   Teacher behavior that shows approval or confers a reward for correct or desirable behavior.

relational concept   A concept that is defined not by inherent attributes but by a comparison or fixed relationship between it and another or other concepts or attributes.

resource unit   A collection or arrangement of instructional materials and activities centered on a particular topic.

response costs   A kind of fine that can cost a student a reward that has already been earned.

review closure   Termination of a lesson or unit by summarizing its main points or relating them to an original concept or generalization.

reward   Compensation of some sort that students can earn for suitable effort, achievement, or behavior.

reward structure   The terms on which a reward is earned or made available.

rhetorical questions   Questions asked for rhetorical effect, and not to elicit a response.

ripple effect   A "contagious" spreading of desirable or undesirable behavior within a classroom.

role   The sum of the functions that a person is expected to perform in a particular situation or group; a set of behaviors adopted for a particular purpose.

role playing   An activity that involves playing an assigned part or dramatizing a designated event.

rules   Statements of standards or "dos and don'ts" that specify certain procedures or behaviors.

run-on questions   Questions that include confusing or unnecessary detail or are so long and involved that they may cause students to forget or misunderstand the point.

self-referencing   An individual assessment process that involves applying a student's previous level of achievement as the standard against which his or her growth or improvement is measured.

serendipity closure   Termination of a lesson by taking advantage of a highly suitable but unanticipated and unplanned opportunity.

set   A receptive frame of mind that results from motivation to learn.

set induction   The exercise of influence that moves students to adopt a receptive attitude toward learning new content or a new process.

shaping   An instructional technique by which a teacher reinforces responses that are progressively closer to the desired response.

shifting interaction   Maintaining student interest and involvement by continually adjusting participation to involve as many students as possible, thereby keeping the lesson lively.

shifting sense stimuli   The stimulus variation technique of requiring students to use more than one of their senses during the course of a lesson.

skilled performance   The performance of a skill with speed and accuracy while carrying out other brain functions.

skills   Knowledge of how to do something, as opposed to declarative knowledge; classified as cognitive, affective, and psychomotor.

social stratification   The hierarchical structuring of social classes according to their generally perceived political, economic, and social power.

socio-emotional (classroom-management approach)   Classroom management based on establishing a positive climate that stems from building healthy interpersonal relationships.

status   Position occupied in a group or society as a reflection of the degree of influence or power attributed to the holder.

stereotyping   The application of fixed ideas to all members of a group, denying them individual differences.

stimulus variation   The use of many different types of strategies and methods to develop and maintain student attention, and to increase learning and retention.

stocktaking   Assessing personal professional growth by comparing current levels of knowledge and skills with earlier levels, and determining what level of achievement still needs to be met.

Student Teams and Achievement Divisions (STAD)   A cooperative learning method (Slavin, 1978a) that involves cooperative competition.

subordinate concepts   Concepts that fall into a larger category because they share common critical attributes, but that have one or more unique critical attributes.

summative evaluation   Assessment of students' achievement of learning goals conducted at the end of a curriculum unit, usually in order to assign formal grades.

superordinate concept   A concept under which all others of one category are subsumed.

symbolic learning   Learning that is based on verbal or other symbols.

systematic observation   Focused remarking and recording (often by means of a checklist) of activities or situations in the classroom to provide or confirm information relating to essential learning behaviors or the need for teacher intervention.

target   A personal professional improvement or development toward which a teacher directs his or her intentions and energies.

task achievement skills   Group skills required for attaining specified academic goals.

task analysis   Identifying and ordering content as it relates to the sequence of steps or operations required to perform a task.

taxonomy   A rational, ordered classification system in which levels are arranged hierarchically.

teaching/learning strategies *See* **instructional strategies.**

teaching/learning unit *See* **instructional unit**.

testing A systematic procedure for measuring student performance by applying a common set of instructions, scoring criteria, and methods of recording scores to a group of individuals to determine their relative degrees of success in learning a specified product or process.

think, pair, share A small-group method that starts with having students think about an issue individually, then share and modify their ideas first in pairs, then among other pairs or the whole class.

thinking, levels of Cognitive levels from the simplest to the most complex, as follows: knowledge (recall), comprehension, application, analysis, synthesis, and evaluation.

transfer The application of learnings acquired in one area or one kind of activity to other contexts.

transfer closure Terminating a lesson or unit by focusing on its connections with previous or future learnings.

transition set Motivation designed to link knowledge already acquired to knowledge that is about to be acquired.

tutorial group A group formed to receive instructional remediation or enrichment.

undergeneralization Defining and applying a concept too narrowly.

unguided inquiry A learning process in which the student takes responsibility for investigating a topic and reaching conclusions about it.

unit *See* **instructional unit**.

unit evaluation An assessment of teaching methods and student activities conducted after completion of a curriculum unit to measure the degree to which students have achieved specific learning objectives.

unit plan A scheme for implementing a series of internally unified learning experiences that considers psychological learning principles; students' abilities, learning styles, levels of cognitive development, and cultural backgrounds; objectives; content; materials; teaching methods; activities; evaluation; and curriculum guidelines.

value Intrinsic worth attributed by virtue of experience or attitude.

values clarification A process whereby students are encouraged to identify and understand the values that inform their opinions, attitudes and behaviors.

variable An element that is subject to change with changing circumstances.

wait time "Thinking time" allowed a class after a question has been put and before an individual is asked to respond.

"whole" approach to learning A learning approach that focuses on an instructional entity as a whole rather than on the sequence of its parts.

"withitness" An instructor's state of constant alertness to all classroom activity (Kounin, 1970).

yes/no questions Questions to which the response is a simple yes or no.

■■■■■
BIBLIOGRAPHY

Alberta Human Rights Commission. (1978). *Human rights: Respecting our differences.* Teachers' Manual. Edmonton, AB: Alberta Department of Education.

Alderman, M. (1990). Motivation for at-risk students. *Educational Leadership, 48*(1)27–30.

Allen, J. (1986). Classroom management: Students' perspectives, goals, and strategies. *American Educational Research Journal, 23,* 437–459.

Anderson, L., & Block, J. (1987). Mastery learning models. In M. Dunkin (Ed.), *International encyclopedia of teaching and teacher education* (pp. 58–67). New York: Pergamon.

Anderson, L., & Pellicer, L. (1990). Synthesis of research on compensatory and remedial education. *Educational Leadership, 48*(1), 10–16.

Andrews, J., & Lupart, J. (1993). *The inclusive classroom: Educating exceptional children.* Scarborough, ON: Nelson Canada.

Arends, R. (1991). *Learning to teach.* New York: Random House.

Arnone, V. (1987). The nature of concepts: A point of view. In D. Lux (Ed.), *Theory into practice: Educational perspectives, then and now. Special 25th anniversary issue, 1962–1987.* Columbus, OH: Ohio State University.

Aronson, E., Blaney, N., Stephan, C., Sikes, J., & Snapp, M. (1978). *The jigsaw classroom.* Beverly Hills, CA: Sage.

Aronson, E., & Goode, E. (1980). Training teachers to implement jigsaw learning: A manual for teachers. In S. Sharan, P. Hare, C. Webb, & R. Hertz-Lazarowitz, *Cooperation in education* (pp. 47–81). Provo, UT: Brigham Young University Press.

Association for Educational Communications and Technology. (1986). Educational technology: Definition and glossary of terms. In F. Knirk & K. Gustafson, *Instructional technology: A systematic approach to education* (p. 17). New York: Holt, Rinehart & Winston.

Association for Supervision and Curriculum Development. (1993a, September). Are letter grades obsolete? *Update, 35*(7), 1, 4, 8. Alexandria, VA: Association for Supervision and Curriculum Development.

Association for Supervision and Curriculum Development. (1993b, October). Portfolio assessment bears the burden of popularity. *Update, 35*(8), 3, 8. Alexandria, VA: Association for Supervision and Curriculum Development.

Ausubel, D. (1960). The use of advance organizers in the learning and retention of meaningful verbal material. *Journal of Educational Psychology, 51,* 267-272.

Avery, P., & Walker, C. (1993). Prospective teachers' perspectives of ethnic and gender differences in academic achievement. *Journal of Teacher Education, 44*(1), 27–37.

Bailey, P. (1989). *Elements in effective teaching: Direct instruction.* Unpublished paper, University of Regina, Regina, SK.

Banks, J. (1980). Developing cross-cultural competency in the social studies. *Journal of Research and Development in Education, 13*(2), 113–122.

Banks, J. (1993). Multicultural education: Development, dimensions, and challenges. *Phi Delta Kappan, 25*(1), 22–28.

Banks, J., with contributions by Clegg, A., Jr. (1990). *Teaching strategies for the social studies: Inquiry, valuing and decision-making* (4th ed.). New York: Longman.

Barbe, W., & Swassing, R. (1979). *Teaching through modality strengths: Concepts and practices*. Columbus, OH: Zaner-Bloser.

Baron, J., & Sternberg, R. (1991). *Teaching thinking skills: Theory and practice*. New York: Freeman.

Baruth, L., & Manning, M.L. (1992). *Multicultural education of children and adolescents*. Boston: Allyn & Bacon.

Bauer, A., & Sapona, R. (1991). *Managing classrooms to facilitate learning*. Englewood Cliffs, NJ: Prentice-Hall.

Bellon, J., Bellon, E., & Blank, M. (1992). *Teaching from a research knowledge base: A development and renewal process*. New York: Merrill.

Belth, M. (1977). *The process of thinking*. New York: David McKay.

Bennett, B., Rolheiser-Bennett, C., & Stevahn, L. (1991). *Cooperative learning: Where heart meets mind*. Toronto: Educational Connections.

Bennett, C. (1979). Teaching students as they would be taught: The importance of cultural perspective. *Educational Leadership, 36*(4), 259–262.

Bereiter, C. (1991, April). Implications of connectionism for thinking about rules. *Educational Researcher*, pp. 10–16.

Berliner, D. (1984). The half-full glass: A review of research on teaching. In P. Hosford (Ed.). *Using what we know about teaching* (pp. 51–75). Alexandria, VA: Association for Supervision and Curriculum Development.

Berliner, D. (1985). Laboratory settings and the study of teacher education. *Journal of Teacher Education, 36*(6), 2–8.

Beyer, B. (1984). Improving thinking skills: Practical approaches. *Phi Delta Kappan, 85*(8), 556–560.

Blair, T. (1988). *Emerging patterns of teaching: From methods to field experiences*. Columbus, OH: Merrill.

Bloom, B. (1968). Learning for mastery. *Evaluation Comment, 1*(2), 1–12.

Bloom, B. (1982a). *Human interactions and school learning*. New York: McGraw-Hill.

Bloom, B. (1982b). The master teachers. *Phi Delta Kappan, 63*(10).

Bloom, B. (1985). *Developing talent in young people*. New York: McGraw-Hill.

Bloom, B. (1986). The hands and feet of genius: Automaticity. *Educational Leadership, 43*(5), 70–77.

Bloom, B., Englehart, M., Furst, E., Hill, W., & Krathwohl, D. (1956). *Taxonomy of educational objectives: The classification of educational goals. Handbook ONE: Cognitive domain*. New York: David McKay.

Borich, G. (1992). *Effective teaching methods* (2nd ed.). New York: Merrill.

Bowd, A., McDougall, D., & Yewchuk, C. (1994). *Educational psychology for Canadian teachers*. Toronto: Harcourt Brace & Company.

Brammer, L. (1985). *The helping relationship: Process and skills* (3rd ed.). Englewood Cliffs, NJ: Prentice-Hall.

Brandt, R. (1990a). If only we knew enough. *Educational Leadership. 48*(2), 3.

Brandt, R. (1990b). On restructuring schools: A conversation with Al Shanker. *Educational Leadership, 47*(7), 11–16.

Brennan, M., & Noffke, S. (1988, April). The dimensions of reflection: A conceptual and contextual analysis. Paper presented at the Annual Meeting of the American Educational Research Association, New Orleans, LA.

Brooks, J., & Brooks, M. (1993). *In search of understanding: The case for constructivist classrooms*. Alexandria, VA: Association for Supervision and Curriculum Development.

Brophy, J. (1984). Research on teaching and teacher education: The interface. In P. Grimmett (Ed.), *Research in teacher education: Current problems and future prospects in Canada* (pp. 76–92). Vancouver, BC: Centre for the Study of Teacher Education; Canadian Association for Teacher Education; Centre for the Study of Curriculum and Instruction, University of British Columbia.

Brophy, J. (1987). Synthesis of research on strategies for motivating students to learn. *Educational Leadership, 45*(2), 40–48.

Brown, C. (1963). *Understanding other cultures*. Englewood Cliffs, NJ: Prentice-Hall.

Brubacher, M., Payne, R., & Rickett, K. (1990). *Perspectives on small group learning: Theory and practice*. Oakville, ON: Rubicon.

Bruner, J. (1963). *The process of education*. New York: Vintage (Random House).

Bruner, J. (1966). *Toward a theory of instruction*. Cambridge: Harvard University.

Buchmann, M., & Schwille, J. (1982). *Education: The overcoming of experience*. (Occasional Paper #63). East Lansing, MI: Michigan State University, Institute for Research on Teaching.

Bullard, S. (1992). Sorting through the multicultural rhetoric. *Educational Leadership, 49*(4), 4–7.

Burke, S. (1989). The challenge of the future. *The Third Degree, 1*(2), 15–16.

Calderhead, J. (1988). The development of knowledge structures in learning to teach. In J. Calderhead (Ed.), *Teacher's professional learning* (pp. 51–64). London, U.K.: The Falmer Press.

Campbell, C., Cordis, L., McBeath, A., & Young, E. (1987). Implementing responsive supervision. *The Canadian Administrator. 26*(6), 10–22.

Carr, W., & Kemmis, S. (1986). *Becoming critical: Education, knowledge and action research*. London, U.K.: The Falmer Press.

Carroll, J. (1963). A model of school learning. *Teachers College Record, 64*, 722–733.

Cazden, C. (1988). *Classroom discourse*. Portsmouth, NH: Heinemann.

Chase, L. (1975). *The other side of the report card: A how-to-do-it program for affective education*. Glenview, IL: Scott Foresman.

Childcare. (1983). *Presenter's guide for the audio-visual program. Childcare shapes the future: Anti-racist strategies*. New York: Council on Interracial Books for Children, Inc., and the Multicultural Project for Communication and Education, Inc.

Cipywnyk, S., Pavolich, W., & Randhawa, R. (1983). *Early school leavers in Saskatchewan*. Report for the Saskatchewan School Trustees' Association and Saskatchewan Education. Saskatoon, SK: College of Education, University of Saskatchewan.

Civikly, J. (1992). *Classroom communication: Principles and practice*. Dubuque, IA: Wm. C. Brown.

Clark, J., Wideman, R., & Eadie, S. (1990). *Together we learn: Cooperative small group learning*. Scarborough, ON: Prentice-Hall.

Clark, R. (1989). Reconsidering research on learning from media. In L. Anderson (Ed.), *The effective teacher: Study guide and readings* (pp. 232–241). New York: Random House.

Clegg, A. (1971). Classroom questions. *The encyclopedia of education* (Vol. 2). New York: Macmillan.

Clifford, G., & Guthrie, J. (1988). *A brief for professional education: Ed school*. Chicago: University of Chicago Press.

Cohen, A. (1993). A new educational paradigm. *Phi Delta Kappan, 74,* 791–795.

Colangelo, N., Foxely, C., & Dustin, D. (1979). *Multicultural nonsexist education: A human relations approach.* Dubuque, IA: Kendal/Hunt.

Combs, A. (1982). *What we know about learning.* Presentation to an Educational Leadership Forum, Estes Park, CO.

Combs, A., Avila, D., & Purkey, W. (1974). *Helping relationships: Basic concepts for the helping professions.* Boston: Allyn & Bacon.

Coonan, H. (1987, April). *Teacher education: Research and practice, moving beyond practice.* Keynote Lecture presented at the Seventh Annual International Seminar in Teacher Education, Maastricht, The Netherlands.

Cooper, E. (1990, June). *Models of teacher education.* Paper presented to the Seminar in Teacher Education of the Regina-Yaoundi Teacher Education Project, Bomenda, Cameroon.

Cooper, H. (1989). Synthesis of research on homework. *Educational Leadership, 47*(3), 85–91.

Cooper, J. (Ed.). (1986a). *Classroom teaching skills: A handbook.* (3rd ed.). Lexington, MA: Heath.

Cooper, J. (1986b). The teacher as decision-maker. In J. Cooper (Ed.), *Classroom teaching skills: A handbook* (3rd ed.) (pp. 1–18). Lexington, MA: Heath.

Corno, L., & Snow, R. (1986). Adapting teaching to individual differences among learners. In M. Wittrock (Ed.), *Handbook of research on teaching,* (3rd ed.) (pp. 605–629). New York: Macmillan.

Costa, A. (1984). Mediating the metacognitive. *Educational Leadership, 42*(3), 57–62.

Costa, A. (1985). *Developing minds: A resource book for teaching thinking.* Alexandria, VA: Association for Supervision and Curriculum Development.

Cruickshank, D. (1984). *Models for the preparation of America's teachers.* Bloomington, IN: Phi Delta Kappan Educational Foundation.

Cruickshank, D. (1985). Applying research on teacher clarity. *Journal of Teacher Education, 36*(2), 44–48.

Cuban, L. (1989). The "at risk" label and the problem of urban school reform. *Phi Delta Kappan, 79,* 780–801.

Curran, L. (1990). *Cooperative learning lessons for little ones: Literature-based language arts and social studies.* San Juan Capistrano, CA: Resources for Teachers.

Curwin, R., & Mendler, A. (1988). *Discipline with dignity.* Alexandria, VA: Association for Supervision and Curriculum Development.

Cushner. K., McClelland, A., & Safford, P. (1992). *Human diversity in education: An integrative approach.* New York: McGraw-Hill.

Daines, D. (1982). *Teachers' oral questions and subsequent verbal behavior of teachers and students* (ERIC ED 225 979). Provo, UT: Brigham Young University.

Davidson, R. (1976). The role of metaphor and analogy in learning. In J. Levin & V. Allen (Eds.), *Cognitive learning in children: Theories and strategies* (pp. 135–162). New York: Academic Press.

Davis, G. (1983). *Educational psychology: Theory and practice.* Reading, MA: Addison-Wesley.

De Bono, E. (1983). The direct teaching of thinking as a skill. *Phi Delta Kappan, 64*(10), 703–708.

Derry, S. (1989). Putting learning strategies to work. *Educational Leadership, 46*(4), 4–10.

Dewey, John. (1933). How we think (Rev. Ed.). Boston, MA: Heath.

Dick, W. & Carey, L. (1978). *The systematic design of instruction.* Dallas, TX: Scott, Foresman.

Dickie, B. (1990). Toward critical teacher education. In International Society for Teacher Education, *Development in the next decade. Proceedings of the Tenth Annual International Seminar in Teacher Education.* Taipai, Taiwan Republic of China.

Dill, D., et al. (1990). *What teachers need to know: The knowledge, skills and values essential to good teaching.* San Francisco, CA: Jossey-Bass.

Dillon, J. (1984). Research on questioning and discussion. *Educational Leadership, 42*(4), 50–56.

Doyle, W. (1977). The uses of nonverbal behaviors: Toward an ecological model of classrooms. *Merrill-Palmer Quarterly, 23*, 179–192.

Doyle, W., & Carter, K. (1987). Choosing the means of instruction. In V. Richardson-Koehler (Ed.), *Educator's handbook.* New York: Longman.

Drefs, I. (1989). *Effective schools: Characteristics and outcomes.* Unpublished paper, University of Regina, Regina, SK.

Dunn, R., Beaudry, J., & Klavas, A. (1989). Survey of research on learning styles. *Educational Leadership, 47*(6), 50–58.

Dunn, K., & Dunn, R. (1987). Dispelling outmoded beliefs about student learning. *Educational Leadership, 44*(6), 55–62.

Dunn, R., & Dunn, K. (1979). Learning styles/teaching styles: Should they ... can they ... be matched? *Educational Leadership, 36*(4), 238–244).

Eggen, P., & Kauchak, D. (1994). *Educational psychology: Classroom connections* (2nd ed.). New York: Merrill.

Eisner, E. (1991). What really counts in schools. *Educational Leadership, 48*(5), 10–17.

Emmer, E., Evertson, C., Sanford, J., Clements, B., & Worsham, M. (1989). *Classroom management for secondary teachers* (2nd ed.). Englewood Cliffs, NJ: Prentice-Hall.

Evans, R. (1990). Making mainstreaming work through prereferral consultation. *Educational Leadership, 48*(1), 73–77.

Evertson, C., Emmer, E., Clements, B., Sanford, J., & Worsham, M. (1984). *Classroom management for elementary teachers.* Englewood Cliffs, NJ: Prentice-Hall.

Friesen, D. (1991, February). *Action research as professional development: Collaborative inquiry into teaching.* Paper presented to the Western Canadian Association for Student Teaching, Regina, SK.

Gage, N., & Berliner, D. (1984). *Educational psychology* (3rd ed.). Boston: Houghton-Mifflin.

Gagne, R. (1985). *The conditions of learning* (4th ed.). New York: Holt, Rinehart and Winston.

Gagne, R. (1987). *Instructional technology's foundations.* Hillsdale, NJ: LEA Publishers.

Gall, M. (1970). The use of questions in teaching. *Review of Educational Research, 40*, 707–721

Gall, M. (1984). Synthesis of research on teaching questioning. *Educational Leadership. 42*(4), 40–46.

Gall, M., Gall, J., Jacobsen, D., & Bullock, T. (1990). *Tools for learning: A guide to teaching study skills.* Alexandria, VA: Association for Supervision and Curriculum Development.

Gallen, V., & Bold, J. (1989). *Saskatchewan Teachers' Federation study of teaching.* Saskatoon, SK: Saskatchewan Teachers' Federation.

Gilstrap, R., & Martin, W. (1975). *Current strategies for teachers: A resource for personalizing instruction*. Santa Monica, CA: Goodyear Publishing Company, Inc.

Glasser, W. (1969). *Schools without failure*. New York: Harper & Row.

Glatthorn, A., & Baron, J. (1985). The good thinker. In *Teaching skillful thinking: A four-part video-based staff development program for educators*. Alexandria, VA: Association for Supervision and Curriculum Development, 1990.

Glickman, C. (1990). *Supervision of instruction*. Needham Heights, MA: Allyn & Bacon.

Goble, N. (1989). Task is to make excellent better. In Saskatchewan Teachers' Federation, *Saskatchewan Bulletin, 56*(6), 7.

Good, T.L., & Brophy, J.E. (1986). *Educational psychology: A realistic approach* (3rd ed.). New York: Longman.

Good, T.L., & Brophy, J.E. (1990). *Educational psychology: A realistic approach* (4th ed.). New York: Longman.

Goodlad, J. (1983). *A place called school*. New York: McGraw-Hill.

Gordon, L. (1975). *The consumer's handbook: 99 commercial rip-offs and how to spot them*. Toronto, ON: McClelland and Stewart.

Gordon, L., & Lee, S. (1972). *Economics for consumers* (6th ed.). New York: Van Nostrand Reinhold.

Goulet, L. (1987, February). *The development of racial attitudes in children*. Paper presented to the Western Canadian Association for Student Teaching, Saskatoon, SK.

Grambs, J., & Carr, J. (1991). *Modern methods in secondary education* (5th ed.). Toronto, ON: Holt, Rinehart and Winston.

Graves, N., & Graves, T. (1985). Creating a cooperative learning environment: An ecological approach. In R. Slavin et al. (Eds.), *Learning to cooperate, cooperating to learn* (pp. 403–436). New York: Plenum.

Gregorc, A. (1979). Learning/teaching styles: Potent forces behind them. *Educational Leadership, 36*(4), 234–236.

Gregorc, A. (1982). Learning style/brain research: Harbinger of an emerging psychology. In National Association of Secondary School Principals, *Student learning styles and brain behavior*. Reston, VA: National Association of Secondary School Principals.

Grimmett, P. (1988). *Implications of research in teaching and teacher education research for the content and delivery of teacher education programs*. Keynote Address to the National Conference on Extended Programs of Teacher Education, sponsored by the Canadian Teachers' Federation, Ottawa, ON.

Gronlund, N. (1974). *Stating behavioral objectives for classroom instruction*. New York: Macmillan.

Gronlund, N., & Linn, R. (1990). *Measurement and evaluation in teaching* (6th ed.). New York: Macmillan.

Gwin, S. (1985). *Teaching for learning style*. Unpublished paper, University of Regina, Regina, SK.

Hallahan, D., & Kauffman, J. (1991). *Exceptional children* (5th ed.). Englewood Cliffs, NJ: Prentice-Hall.

Halpern, D. (1984). *Thought and knowledge: An introduction to critical thinking*. Hillsdale, NJ: Erlbaum.

Harris, P., & Moran, R. (1979). *Managing cultural differences*. Houston, TX: Gulf.

Harrow, J. (1972). *A taxonomy of the psychomotor domain: A guide for developing behavioral objectives*. New York: David McKay.

Henderson, J. (1993). *Reflective teaching: Becoming an inquiring educator*. New York: Macmillan.

Henson, K. (1988). *Methods and strategies for teaching in secondary and middle schools*. New York: Longman.

Higgins, N., & Sullivan, H. (1978). *Writing worthwhile objectives*. Tempe, AZ: Teaching for Competence.

Higgins, N., & Sullivan, H. (1981). *Assessing student learning*. Tempe, AZ: Teaching for Competence.

Hopkins, K., Stanley, J., & Hopkins, B. (1990). *Educational and psychological measurement and evaluation* (7th ed.). Englewood Cliffs, NJ: Prentice-Hall.

Hosford, P. (Ed.). (1984). *Using what we know about teaching*. Alexandria, VA: Association for Supervision and Curriculum Development.

Houston, W.R. (1986). Foreword. In W.R. Houston (Ed.), *Guidelines for professional experiences in teacher education: A policy statement*. Reston, VA: Association of Teacher Educators.

Houston, W.R. (1988). Reflecting on reflection in teacher education. In H. Waxman, H. Freiberg, J. Vaughan, & M. Weil (Eds.), *Images of reflection in teacher education* (pp. 7–8). Reston, VA: Association of Teacher Educators.

Hughes, C., & Jones. B. (1988, March). *Integrating thinking skills and processes into content instruction*. Paper presented to the Forty-Third Annual Conference, Association for Supervision and Curriculum Development, Boston, MA.

Hunter, M. (1969). *Theory into practice: Teach more faster*. El Segundo, CA: TIP.

Hunter, M. (1971). *Theory into practice: Teach for transfer*. El Segundo, CA: TIP.

Hunter, M. (1982). *Mastery teaching*. El Segundo, CA: Cambridge University Press.

Hunter, M. (1984). Knowing teaching and supervising. In P. Hosford (Ed.), *Using what we know about teaching* (pp. 169–192). Alexandria, VA: Association for Supervision and Curriculum Development.

Hyde, A., & Bizar, M. (1989). *Thinking in context: Teaching cognitive processes across the elementary school curriculum*. New York: Longman.

Jackson, P. (1968). Life in classrooms. New York: Holt, Rinehart & Winston.

Jacobsen, D., Eggen, P., Kauchak, D., & Dulaney, C. (1985). *Methods for teaching: A skills approach* (2nd ed.). Columbus, OH: Merrill.

Johnson, D. (1986). *Reaching out: Interpersonal effectiveness and self-actualization* (3rd ed.). Englewood Cliffs, NJ: Prentice-Hall.

Johnson, D., & Johnson, F. (1975). *Joining together: Group theory and group skills*. Englewood Cliffs, NJ: Prentice-Hall.

Johnson, D., & Johnson, R. (1975). *Learning together and alone: Cooperation, competition and individualization*. Englewood Cliffs, NJ: Prentice-Hall.

Johnson, D., & Johnson, R. (1978). Cooperative, competitive, and individualistic learning. *Journal of Research and Development in Education, 1*(12), 3–15.

Johnson, D., & Johnson, R. (1980a). Cooperative learning: The power of positive goal interdependence. In V. Lyons (Ed.), *Structuring cooperative learning: The 1980 handbook*. Minneapolis, MN.: Cooperation Network.

Johnson, D., & Johnson, R. (1980b). The social integration of handicapped students into the mainstream. In M. Reynolds (Ed.) *Social environment of schools*. Reston, VA: Council for Exceptional Children.

Johnson, D., & Johnson, R. (1987). *Learning together and alone*. Englewood Cliffs, NJ: Prentice-Hall.

Johnson, D., & Johnson, R. (1987). Research shows the benefits of adult cooperation. *Educational Leadership, 45*(3), 27–30.

Johnson, D., & Johnson, R. (1989). Toward a cooperative effort: A response to Slavin. *Educational Leadership, 46*(7), 80–81.

Johnson, D., & Johnson, R. (1990). What is cooperative learning? In M. Brubacher, R. Payne, & K. Rickett, *Perspectives on small group learning: Theory and practice* (pp. 69–80). Oakville, ON: Rubicon.

Johnson, D., Johnson, R., Bartlett, J., & Johnson, L. (1988). *Our cooperative classroom*. Edina, VA: Interaction Book Company.

Johnson, R., & Johnson, D. (1990). *Cooperative learning: Warm-ups, grouping strategies and group activities*. Edina, VA: Interaction Book Company.

Jones, B., Palincsar, A., Ogle, D., & Carr, E. (1987). *Strategic teaching and learning: Cognitive instruction in the content areas*. Alexandria, VA: Association for Supervision and Curriculum Development.

Jones, J., & Pfeiffer, W. (1979). Role playing. In J. Jones & W. Pfeiffer (Eds.), *The 1979 annual handbook for group facilitators (The Eighth Annual)* (pp. 18–25). San Diego, CA: University Associates.

Joyce, B., Showers, B., & Rolheiser-Bennett, C. (1987). Staff development and student learning: A synthesis of research on models of teaching. *Educational Leadership, 45*(2), 11–23.

Joyce, B., & Weil, M. (1986). *Models of teaching* (3rd ed.). Englewood Cliffs, NJ: Prentice-Hall.

Junetune, J. (1985, December). *Teaching development strategies for the classroom teacher*. Paper presented at the Workshop on Creativity, The Creative Education Foundation, Whistler Creative Management Centre, Saskatoon, SK.

Kagan, S. (1985). *Cooperative learning resources for teachers*. Riverside, CA: University of California at Los Angeles, Psychology Department.

Kagan, S. (1992). *Cooperative learning*. San Juan Capistrano, CA: Resources for Teachers.

Kaplan, M. (1992). *Thinking in education*. Cambridge, U.K.: Cambridge University Press.

Kaplan, P. (1990). *Educational psychology for tomorrow's teacher*. St. Paul, MN: West.

Katz, L., & Chard, S. (1992). *Engaging children's minds: The project approach*. Norwood, NJ: Ablex Publishing.

Kauchak, D., & Eggen, P. (1992). *Learning and teaching: Research-based methods*. Boston: Allyn & Bacon.

Kaye, S., Trickett, E., & Quinlan, S. (1977). Alternative methods for environmental assessment: An example. *American Journal of Community Psychology, 5*, 367–377.

Keefe, J. (1979). Learning style: An overview. In National Association of Secondary School Principals, *Student learning styles: Diagnosing and prescribing programs* (pp. 1–17). Reston, VA: National Association of Secondary School Principals.

Keefe, J. (1982). Assessing student learning styles: An overview. In National Association of Secondary School Principals, *Student learning styles and brain behavior*. Reston, VA: National Association of Secondary School Principals.

Keller, J. (1983). Motivational design of instruction. In C. Reigeluth (Ed.), *Instructional-design theories and models: An overview of their current status* (pp. 383–434). Hillsdale, NJ: Erlbaum.

Kemp, J. (1985). *The instructional design process*. New York: Harper & Row.

Kennedy, M. (1991). Policy issues in teacher education. *Phi Delta Kappan, 9*, 658–665.

Kierstead, F., & Wagner, P. Jr. (1993). *The ethical, legal, and multicultural foundations of teaching*. Madison, WI: Brown & Benchmark.

Kindsvatter, R., Wilen, W., & Ishler, M. (1988). *Dynamics of effective teaching*. New York: Longman.

King, A. (1990). Enhancing peer interaction and learning in the classroom through reciprocal questioning. *American Educational Research Journal, 274*, 664–687.

Klausmeier, H. (1985). *Educational psychology* (5th ed.). New York: Harper & Row.

Knapp, M. (1972). *Nonverbal human communication*. New York: Holt, Rinehart and Winston.

Knapp, M., & Shields, P. (1990). Reconceiving academic instruction for the children of poverty. *Phi Delta Kappan, 71*, 752–758.

Knapp, M., Turnbull, B., & Shields, M. (1990). New directions for educating the children of poverty. *Educational Leadership, 48*(1), 4–9.

Knirk, F., & Gustafson, K. (1986). *Instructional technology: A systematic approach to education*. New York: Holt, Rinehart & Winston.

Knoop, R. (1986). Working with and in groups. *Education Canada, 26*(2), 16–20.

Knowles, M. (1970). *The modern practice of adult education*. New York: Association Press.

Kohn, A. (1990). *The brighter side of human nature: Altruism and empathy in everyday life*. New York: Basic Books.

Kohn, A. (1991). Group grade grubbing versus cooperative learning. *Educational Leadership, 48*(5), 83–87.

Kolb, D. (1984). *Experiential learning: Experience as the source of learning and development*. Englewood Cliffs, NJ: Prentice-Hall.

Kounin, J. (1970). *Discipline and group management in classrooms*. New York: Holt, Rinehart and Winston.

Kounin, J., & Doyle, P. (1975). Degree of continuity of a lesson's signal system and task involvement of children. *Journal of Educational Psychology, 67*, 159–164.

Krathwohl, D., Bloom, B., & Masia, B. (1968). *Taxonomy of educational objectives. Handbook 2: Affective domain*. New York: David McKay.

Kubiszyn, T., & Borich, G. (1987). *Educational testing and measurement: Classroom application and practice* (2nd ed.). Glenview, IL: Scott Foresman.

Kulik, J. (1983). Synthesis of research on computer-based instruction. *Educational Leadership, 41*(1), 19–21.

Lahey, B., & Johnson, M. (1978). *Psychology and instruction: A practical approach to educational psychology*. Dallas, TX: Scott, Foresman.

Lang, H. (1989). *Preparing the reflective teacher decision maker: A review of contemporary literature on preservice teacher education* (Draft 6). Unpublished manuscript, commissioned by the Dean, Faculty of Education, University of Regina, Regina, SK.

Lang, H. (1990). *Classroom management concerns of secondary teacher education preinterns*. Paper presented to the Western Canadian Association on Student Teaching, Brandon, MB.

Lang, H., & Scarfe, D. (1988). Group support during student teaching. In P. Holborn, M. Wideen, & I. Andrews (Eds.), *Becoming a teacher* (pp. 226–242). Toronto: Kagen and Woo.

Lasley, T. (1988). *Defining the knowledge base: Prescriptions and principles.* Unpublished paper, Department of Teacher Education, University of Dayton, Dayton, OH.

Leith, S. (1988). Using concept mapping as an aid to unit planning. In P. Holborn, M. Wideen, & I. Andrews (Eds.), *Becoming a teacher* (pp. 147–156). Toronto: Kagen and Woo.

Levin, T., with Long, R. (1981). *Effectiveness of instruction.* Washington, DC: American Association of Colleges of Teacher Education.

Lewin, K., Lippitt, R., & White, R. (1939). Patterns of aggressive behavior in experimentally created "social climates." *Journal of Social Psychology, 10,* 271–299.

Lewis, R., & Doorlag, D. (1991). *Teaching special students in the mainstream.* New York: Merrill.

Luft, J. (1969). *Of human interaction.* Palo Alto, CA: National Press Books.

Lyman, F. (1985). *Think-pair-share.* Mimeograph. College Park,MD: University of Maryland.

Maehr, M. (1974). *Sociocultural origins of achievement.* Monterey, CA: Brooks/Cole.

Mager, R. (1984). *Preparing instructional objectives* (2nd ed.). Palo Alto, CA: D.S. Lake.

Mancus, D. (1981, July). *Preparation and support of effective teachers for troubled times through self-knowledge development and improved sense of psychological well-being.* Paper presented at the International Seminar on Teacher Education, London, UK.

Manitoba Indian Brotherhood. (1977). *The shocking truth about Indians in text books.* Winnipeg, MN: Manitoba Indian Cultural Centre.

Manning, M.L. (1991). More than lip service to multicultural education. *Clearing House, 64,* 218.

Manning, M., & Lucking, R. (1991). The what, why, and how of cooperative learning. *The Clearing House, 64,* 152–156.

Marshall, C. (1991). Teachers' learning styles: How they affect student learning. *Clearing House, 64,* 225–227.

Martin, J. (1983). *Mastering instruction.* Boston: Allyn & Bacon.

Martorella, P. (1986). Teaching concepts. In J. Cooper (Ed.), *Classroom teaching skills:* A Handbook (3rd ed.) (pp. 181—224). Lexington, MA: Heath.

Marzano, R. (1992). *A different kind of classroom: Teaching with dimensions for learning.* Alexandria, VA: Association for Supervision and Curriculum Development.

Marzano, R., Brandt, R., Hughes, C., Jones, B., Presseisen, B., Rankin, S., & Suhor, C. (1988). *Dimensions of thinking: A framework for curriculum and instruction.* Alexandria, VA: Association for Supervision and Curriculum Development

Maslow, A. (1962). *Toward a psychology of being.* Princeton, NJ: Van Nostrand.

McBeath, A. (1986). *The complex act of teaching: Is it humanly possible?* Paper presented at the "Directions" Canadian Conference on Curriculum, Instruction, and Leadership, Saskatoon, SK.

McBeath, A. (1987, October). *A survey and analysis of the teaching skills employed by student teachers during the extended practicum at the University of Regina.* Paper presented at the Seventh Annual International Seminar in Teacher Education, Limburg, The Netherlands.

McBeath, A. (1989, March). Responses from an international perspective. *On the education of teachers: Responses to the Academic Review Task Force*. Regina, SK: Faculty of Education, University of Regina.

McBeath, A. (1990, February). *Basic principles of teaching*. Paper presented to the Summer Workshop of the University of Yaounde/University of Regina Project, Bamenda, Cameroon.

McCarthy, B. (1986). *Hemispheric mode indicator (HMI): Right and left brain approaches to learning*. Barrington, IL: Excel.

McCarthy, B. (1988). *The 4MAT system: Teaching to learning styles with right/left mode techniques*. Barrington, IL: Excel.

McCarthy, B. (1989, March). *Learning and teaching styles: The 4MAT system*. Paper presented at the Association for Supervision and Curriculum Development Workshop, Orlando, FL.

McCutcheon, J. (1983, May). Building from strength II: A suggested curriculum approach for the social studies. In *Contact 58*. Toronto, ON: Canadian Studies Foundation.

McGowan, M. (1988). Problem-solving initiatives. *Journal of Experiential Education, 11*(3), 15–17.

McKinney, C., Gilmore, H., Peddicord, H., & McCallum, S. (1987). Effects of a best example and critical attributes on prototype formation in the acquisition of a concept. *Theory and Research in Social Education 15,* 189–202.

McLaren, P. (1986). S*chooling as a ritual performance: Towards a political economy of educational symbols and gestures*. London, U.K.: Routledge & Kegan Paul.

McNeil, J., & Wiles, J. (1990). *The essentials of teaching: Decisions, plans and methods*. New York: Macmillan.

Medin, D., & Smith, E. (1984). Concepts and concept formation. *Annual Review of Psychology, 35,* 113—138.

Merrill, M., & R. Tennyson. (1977). *Teaching concepts: An instructional design guide*. Englewood Cliffs, NJ: Educational Technology.

Mitchell, R. (1992). *Testing for learning: New approaches to evaluation can improve American schools*. New York: Free Press.

Montague, E. (1987). *Fundamentals of secondary classroom instruction*. Columbus, OH: Merrill.

Moore, J., Mintz, S., & Berriman, M. (1988). Reflectivity: The Edsel of education? In H. Waxman, H. Frieberg, J. Vaughen, & M. Weil (Eds.), *Images of reflection in teacher education*. Reston, VA: Association of Teacher Educators.

Moore, K. (1989). *Classroom teaching skills: A primer*. New York: Random House.

Morine, H., & Morine, G. (1973). *Discovery: A challenge to teachers*. Englewood Cliffs, NJ: Prentice-Hall.

Morris, B. (1982). A conceptualization of education in the future. *Canadian Journal of Education, 2,* 16–23.

Murgio, M. (1969). *Communication graphics*. New York: Van Nostrand Reinhold.

Negin, G. (1987). *A primer in inferential reasoning for teachers*. Dubuque, IA: Kendall/Hunt Publishing.

Nickerson, R. (1989). On improving thinking through instruction. *Review of Research in Education, 15,* 3–37 (Edited by E. Rathkoph).

Noffke, S., & Brennan, M. (1988, April). *The dimensions of reflection: A conceptual and contextual analysis*. Paper presented at the Annual Meeting of the American Educational Research Association, New Orleans, LA.

Norris, S. (1989). Can we test validly for critical thinking? *Educational Researcher, 18*(9), 21–26.

Olmstead, J. (1970). *Theory and state of the art of small group methods of instruction.* Alexandria, VA: Human Resources Research Organization.

O'Neill, G. (1988). Teaching effectiveness: A review of research. *Canadian Journal of Education, 13*(1), 162–185.

Orlich, D. (1991). A new analogue for the cognitive taxonomy. *The Clearing House, 64*(3), 159–161.

Orlich, D., Harder, R., Callahan, R., Kravas, C., Kauchak, D., Pendergrass, R., & Keogh, A. (1985). *Teaching strategies: A guide to better instruction* (2nd ed.). Lexington, MA: Heath.

Orlich, D., Harder, R., Callahan, R., Kauchak, D., Pendergrass, R., & Jeighm A. (1990). *Teaching strategies: A guide to better instruction* (3rd ed.). Lexington, MA: Heath.

Orlich, T. (1982). *Cooperative sports and games book.* New York: Pantheon.

Ornstein, A. (1985). Research of teaching: Issues and trends. *Journal of Teacher Education, 36*(6), 27–31.

Orpwood, W., & Souque, J. (1984). *Science education in Canadian schools, Vol. 1: Introduction and analysis* (Background study No.52) Hull, PQ: Canadian Government Publishing Centre.

Palincsar, A., & Brown, A. (1984). Reciprocal teaching of comprehension-fostering and comprehension-monitoring activities. *Cognition and Instruction, 1,* 117–175.

Parker, J., & Rubin, L. (1966). *Process as content: Curriculum design and the application of content.* Chicago, IL: Rand-McNally.

Parker, W. (1987). Teaching thinking: The pervasive approach. *Journal of Teacher Education, 38*(3), 50–55.

Paul, R. (1990). *Critical thinking: What every person needs to survive in a rapidly changing world.* Rohnert Park, CA: Sonoma State University.

Paulson, F., Paulson, P., & Meyer, C. (1991). What makes a portfolio a portfolio? *Educational Leadership, 48*(5), 60–64.

Perkins, D. (1984). Creativity by design. *Educational Leadership, 42*(3), 18–25.

Perkins, D., & Salomon, G. (1989). Are cognitive skills context bound? *Educational Researcher, 18*(1), 16–25.

Perrone, V. (1991). *Expanding student assessment.* Alexandria, VA: Association for Supervision and Curriculum Development.

Peterson, D., Kromrey, J., Borg, J., & Lewis, A. (1990). Defining and establishing relationships between essential and higher order teaching skills. *Journal of Educational Research, 84*(1), 5–12.

Peterson, R., Bowyer, J., Butts, D., and Bybee, R. (1984). *Science and society: A source book for elementary and junior high school teachers.* Columbus, OH: Merrill.

Pfeiffer, J., & Goodstein, L. (Eds.). (1982). *The 1982 annual handbook for group facilitators* (Vol. 8). San Diego, CA: University Associates.

Porter, A. (1988). *Defining the knowledge base: Prescriptions and principles.* Unpublished paper, Department of Teacher Education, University of Dayton, Dayton, OH.

Porter, A., & Brophy, J. (1988). Good teaching: Insights from the work of the Institute for Research on Teaching. *Educational Leadership, 45*(8), 74–85.

Pressley, M., & Harris, K. (1990). What we really know about strategy instruction. *Educational Leadership, 48*(1), 31–34.

Provost, R. (1991). The value of ideas: The immersion approach to the development of thinking. *Educational Researcher, 20*(2), 3–10.

Raths, L., Wasserman, S., Jonas, A., & Rothstein, A. (1967). *Teaching for thinking: Theory and application*. Columbus, OH: Merrill.

Reed, S., & Sautter, R. (1990). Kappan special report. Children of poverty: The status of 12 million young Americans. *Phi Delta Kappan, 71*(10), 785—790.

Renner, P. (1983). *The instructor's survival kit* (2nd ed.). Vancouver, BC: PFR Training Associates.

Resnick, L. (1987). *Education and learning to think*. Washington, DC: National Academy Press.

Resnick, L., & Kloper, L., (Eds.). (1989). *Toward the thinking curriculum: Current cognitive research*. Alexandria, VA: Association for Supervision and Curriculum Development.

Roehler, L., Duffy, G., & Johnson, J. (1988, April). *A creative tension between content and process: The instructional challenge in developing self-regulated readers*. Paper presented to the American Educational Research Association Annual Conference, New Orleans, LA.

Rosenshine, B. (1987). Explicit teaching and teacher training. *Journal of Teacher Education, 38*(3), 34–36.

Rosenshine, B. (1986). Synthesis of research on explicit teaching. *Educational Leadership, 43*(7), 60–69.

Rosenshine, B., & Stevens, R. (1986). Teaching functions. In M. Wittrock (Ed.), *Handbook of research on teaching* (3rd ed.) (pp. 376–391). New York: Macmillan.

Rosser, R., & Nicholson, G. (1984). *Educational psychology: Principles in practice*. Boston, MA.: Little, Brown.

Rothstein, P. (1990). *Educational psychology*. New York: McGraw-Hill's College Review Books.

Rowe, M. (1986). Wait time: Slowing down may be a way of speeding up. *Teacher Education, 37*(1), 43–50.

Royal Bank. (1989). The importance of teaching. *Royal Bank Letter, 70*(5), 1–4.

Rudinow, J., & Paul, R. (1987). A strategy for developing dialectical thinking skills. In M. Heiman & J. Slomianko (Eds.), *Thinking skills instruction: Concepts and techniques* (pp. 92–97). Washington, D.C.: National Education Association.

Russell, T. (1988). Introduction. In J. Calderhead (Ed.), *Teacher's professional learning*. London, U.K.: The Falmer Press.

Sadker, M., & Sadker, D. (1986). Questioning skills. In J. Cooper (Ed.), *Classroom teaching skills: A handbook* (3rd ed.) (pp. 143—184). Lexington, MA: Heath.

Sadler, W., & Whimbey, A. (1985). A holistic approach to improving thinking skills. *Phi Delta Kappan, 67*(3), 199–202.

Sanders, N. (1966). *Classroom questions: What kinds?* New York: Harper & Row.

Sanford, J., & Emmer, E. (1988). *Understanding classroom management: An observation guide*. Englewood Cliffs, NJ: Prentice-Hall.

Saskatchewan. Department of Consumer Affairs. (1972). *Consumer expertise test*. Regina: Saskatchewan Department of Consumer Affairs.

Saskatchewan Education. (1984). *Directions: The final report*. Report of the Minister's Advisory Committee, Curriculum and Instruction Review. Regina, SK: Saskatchewan Department of Education.

Saskatchewan Education. (1985). *Future directions in curriculum and instruction*. Report of the Minister's Advisory Committee, Curriculum and Instruction Review. Regina, SK: Saskatchewan Department of Education.

Saskatchewan Education. (1988). *Understanding the common essential learnings: A handbook for teachers*. Regina: Saskatchewan Education. Regina, SK: Saskatchewan Department of Education.

Saskatchewan Education. (1989). *Evaluation in education*. Regina, SK: Saskatchewan Department of Education.

Saskatchewan Education. (1991). *Student evaluation: A teacher handbook*. Regina, SK: Saskatchewan Department of Education.

Saskatchewan Teachers' Federation. (1988). Saskatchewan educators gear up to stem the tide of school leavers. *Saskatchewan Bulletin*, May 27, 1988.

Schmuck, R., & Schmuck, P. (1992). *Group processes in the classroom* (6th ed.). Dubuque, IA: Wm. C. Brown.

Schon, D. (1983). *The reflective practitioner*. New York: Basic Books.

Schon, D. (1990). *Educating the reflective practitioner*. San Francisco, CA: Jossey-Bass.

Schuck, R. (1985). An empirical analysis of the power of set induction and systematic questioning and instructional strategies. *Journal of Teacher Education, 36*(2), 38–43.

Seaman, D., & Fellenz, R. (1989). *Effective strategies for teaching adults*. Columbus, OH: Merrill.

Sergiovanni, T. (1989). Science and action in supervision and teaching. *Journal of Curriculum and Supervision, 4*(2), 93–105.

Shanker, A. (1985). Newsnotes: Leading educators outline training needed by future teachers. *Phi Delta Kappan, 67*, 321.

Sharan, S., (1980). Cooperative learning in small groups: Recent methods and effects of achievement, attitudes and ethnic relations. *Review of Educational Research, 50*, 240–71.

Sharan, S.,& Lazarowitz, R. (1980). A group investigation method of cooperative learning in the classroom. In Sharan et al. (Eds.), *Cooperation in education: Based on the proceedings of the first international conference on cooperation in education*. Provo, UT: Brigham Young University Press.

Sharan, S., & Sharan, Y. (1976). *Small group teaching*. Englewood Cliffs, NJ: Educational Technology Publications.

Shostak, R. (1977). Lesson presentation skills. In *Classroom teaching skills: A handbook*, Cooper, J. (Ed.) Lexington, MA: Heath.

Shostak, R. (1982). Lesson presentation skills. In J. Cooper, P. Martorella, Morine-Dershimer, J. Pfeifer, D. Sadker, M. Sadker, R. Shostak, S. Sokolove, T. TenBrink, & W. Weber, *Classroom teaching skills: A handbook*. Lexington, MA: Heath.

Shostak, R. (1986). Lesson presentation skills. In J. Cooper, P. Martorella, Morine-Dershimer, J. Pfeifer, D. Sadker, M. Sadker, R. Shostak, S. Sokolove, T. TenBrink, & W. Weber (Ed.), *Classroom teaching skills: A handbook* (3rd ed.) (pp. 111–138). Lexington, MA: Heath.

Shulman, L. (1987). Knowledge and teaching: Foundations of the new reform. *Harvard Educational Review, 57*(1), 1–22.

Shulman, L. (1988). The dangers of dichotomous thinking in education. In P. Grimmett & G. Erickson (Eds.), *Reflection in teacher education* (pp. 31–37). New York: Teachers' College Press.

Siedentop, D. (1983). *Developing teaching skills in physical education* (2nd ed.). Palo Alto, CA: Mayfield.

Silberman, C. (1966). Technology is knocking at the schoolhouse door. *Fortune, 74*, 120–125.

Simon, A., & Byram, C. (1984). *You've got to reach 'em to teach 'em.* Dallas, TX: Training Associates Press.

Skon, L., Johnson, D., & Johnson, R. (1981). Cooperative peer interaction versus individual competition and individualistic efforts: Effects on the acquisition of cognitive reasoning strategies. *Journal of Educational Psychology 73*, 83–92.

Slavin, R. (1978a). Student teams and comparison among equals: Effects on academic performance and student attitudes. *Journal of Educational Psychology, 70*, 532–538.

Slavin, R. (1978b). Student teams and achievement divisions. *Journal of Research and Development in Education, 12*(1), 39–49.

Slavin, R. (1980a). Cooperative learning. *Review of Educational Research, 50*, 315–342.

Slavin, R. (1980b). *Using Student Team Learning* (Rev. Ed.). Baltimore, MD: Center for Social Organization of Schools, Johns Hopkins University.

Slavin, R. (1983). *Cooperative learning: Research on teaching monograph series.* New York: Longman.

Slavin, R. (1987). Cooperative learning and the cooperative school. *Educational Leadership, 45*(3), 7–13.

Slavin R., (1991). Synthesis of research on cooperative learning. *Educational Leadership, 48*(5), 71–82.

Slavin, R., Sharan, S., Kagan, S., Lazarowitz, R., Webb, C., & Schmuck, R. (Eds.). (1985). *Learning to cooperate, cooperating to learn.* New York: Plenum.

Sleeter, C., & Grant, C. (1993). *Making choices for multicultural education: Five approaches to race, class, and gender.* New York: Merrill.

Smith, B.O. (1985). Research bases for teacher education. *Phi Delta Kappan, 66*, 685–690.

Smith, B. O. (1987). On teaching thinking skills: A conversation with B. Othanel Smith. *Educational Leadership, 45*(2), 35–39.

Smith, H. (1984). *Nonverbal behavior: Perspectives, applications, intercultural insights.* New York: C.J. Hogreve.

Stanford, G. (1977). *Developing effective classroom groups: A practical guide for teachers.* New York: Harper & Row.

Stanford, G., & Roark, A. (1974). *Human interaction in education.* Boston, MA: Allyn & Bacon.

Stanley, W. (1984). Approaches to teaching concepts and conceptualizing: An analysis of social studies methods textbooks. *Theory and Research in Social Education, 11*(4), 1–11.

Stanley, W. (1985). Recent research on concept learning: Implications for social education. *Theory and Research in Social Education, 12*(4), 57–71.

Stavin, R. (1986). *Educational psychology: Theory into practice.* Englewood Cliffs, NJ: Prentice-Hall.

Steinaker, N., & Bell, R. (1979). *The experiential taxonomy: A new approach to teaching and learning.* New York: Academic Press.

Sternberg, R. (1985). Teaching critical thinking. Part 1: Are we making critical mistakes? *Phi Delta Kappan, 67*, 194–198; Part 2: Possible solutions. *Phi Delta Kappan, 67*, 277–280.

Sternberg, R. (1990a, August). *Problem solving: Teaching for thinking.* Paper presented to the Regina Board of Education Teachers, Regina, SK.

Sternberg, R. (1990b). Thinking styles: Keys to understanding student performance. *Phi Delta Kappan, 71*, 366–371.

Strong, R., Silver, H., & Hanson, R. (1986). New strategies, new visions. *Educational Leadership, 44*(2), 52–44.

TenBrink, T. (1974). *Evaluation: A practical guide for teachers*. New York: McGraw-Hill.

TenBrink, T. (1986). Writing instructional objectives. In J. Cooper (Ed.), *Classroom teaching skills: A handbook* (3rd ed.) (pp. 67–110). Lexington, MA: Heath.

Tennyson, R., & Park, O. (1980). The teaching of concepts: A review of instructional design research literature. *Review of Educational Research, 50*(1), 55–70.

Thomas, B. (1984). *Principles of anti-racist education*. Toronto: Urban Alliance on Race Relations.

Tiedt, P., & Tiedt, I. (1979). *Multicultural teaching: A handbook of activities, information, and resources*. Boston: Allyn & Bacon.

Tobin, K. (1980). The effect of an extended teacher wait time on science achievement. *Journal of Research on Science Teaching, 17*, 469–475.

Tobin, K., & Capie, W. (1982). Relationships between classroom process variables and middle-school science achievement. *Journal of Educational Psychology, 74*, 441–454.

Travers, J., Elliott, S., & Kratchowill, T. (1993). *Educational psychology: Effective teaching and learning*. Madison, WI: Brown & Benchmark.

Trimarco, T. (1986). Cultural diversity in teacher education programs: Intercultural understanding and appreciation are imperatives. In Yoost Yff (Ed.), *Cultural diversity and global interdependence: Imperatives for teacher education. International Yearbook on Teacher Education* (pp. 79–83). Washington, DC: International Council on Teacher Education (ICTE).

United States Department of Education. (1986). *What works: Research about teaching and learning*. Washington, DC: United States Department of Education.

University of Regina, Faculty of Education. (1988). *Internship seminars for interns and cooperating teachers*. Sponsored by the Faculty of Education, University of Regina; the Saskatchewan Teachers' Federation; and the Saskatchewan Department of Education. Regina, SK.: Faculty of Education, University of Regina.

Vallet, R. (1986, November). Developing thinking skills. *Academic Therapy*, pp. 186–193.

Walberg, H. (1990). Productive teaching and instruction: Assessing the knowledge base. *Phi Delta Kappan, 71*, 470–478.

Wang, M., Haertel, G., & Walberg, H. (1990). What influences learning? A content analysis of review literature. *Journal of Educational Research, 84*(1), 30–57.

Wang, M., & Walberg, H. (Eds.). (1985). *Adapting instruction to individual differences*. Berkeley, CA: McCutchan.

Wasserman, S. (1978). *Put some thinking in your classroom*. San Diego, CA: Coronado.

Weber, W. (1983). Weber's major advocated and condemned strategies keyed for empirical evidence. In W. Webber, L. Roff, J. Crawford, & C. Robinson (Eds.), *Classroom management: Reviews of the teacher education research literature* (p. 42). Princeton, NJ: Educational Testing Service.

Weber, W., and Roff, L. (1983). A review of teacher education literature on classroom management. In W. Webber, L. Roff, J. Crawford, & C. Robinson (Eds.), *Classroom management: Reviews of the teacher education research literature* (pp. 7—41). Princeton, NJ: Educational Testing Service.

Weber, W., Roff, L., Crawford, J., & Robinson, C. (Eds.). (1983). *Classroom management: Reviews of the teacher education research literature*. Princeton, NJ: Educational Testing Service.

Weil, M., & Murphy, J. (1982). *Instructional processes. Encyclopedia of educational research* (5th ed.). New York: Macmillan.

Weinstein, C., & Mayer, R. (1986). The teaching of learning strategies. In M. Wittrock (Ed.), *Handbook of research on teaching* (3rd ed.) (pp. 315–327). New York: Macmillan.

Weinstein, C., Ridley, S., Dahl, T., & Weber, S. (1989). Helping students develop strategies for effective learning. *Educational Leadership, 46*(4), 17–19.

West, C., & Foster, S. (1976). *The psychology of human learning and instruction in education*. Belmont, CA: Wadsworth.

West, C., Farmer, J., & Wolff, P. (1991). *Instructional design: Implications from cognitive science*. Englewood Cliffs, NJ: Prentice-Hall.

Wideen, M., & Holborn, P. (1986). Research in Canadian teacher education: Promises and problems. *Canadian Journal of Education, 11*, 557–583.

Wiggins, G. (1993). Assessment, authenticity, context and validity. *Phi Delta Kappan, 75*, 200–214.

Wilen, W., & Clegg, A. (1986). Effective questions and questioning: A research review. *Theory and Research in Social Education, 14*, 153–161.

Willis, S. (1993). Quality by design through portfolios. *Update, 34*(5), 2.

Wilson, S. (1990). Globalization and teacher education. In International Society for Teacher Education, *Development in the next decade: Proceedings of the Tenth Annual International Seminar in Teacher Education*. Taipai, TW: Republic of China.

Winzer, M., & Grigg, N. (1992). *Educational psychology in the Canadian classroom*. Scarborough: Prentice-Hall.

Womack, J. (1966). *Discovering the structure of the social studies*. New York: Benzinger Brothers.

Woolfolk, A. (1987. *Educational psychology*, (3rd ed.). Englewood Cliffs, NJ: Prentice-Hall.

Woolfolk, A. (1990). *Educational psychology*, (4th ed.). Englewood Cliffs, NJ: Prentice-Hall.

Yakel, N. (1985). *Choices: Saskatchewan student opinions on education*. Regina, SK.: Faculty of Education, University of Regina.

Zemelman, S., Daniels, H., & Hyde, A. (1993). *Best practice: New standards for teaching and learning in America's schools*. Portsmouth, NH: Heinemann.

INDEX

■ ■ ■ ■ ■

PHOTO CREDITS

Cathie Archbould   2, 3, 6, 12, 13, 15, 16, 18, 19, 20, 21, 23, 25, 28, 30

Brett Lamb   1, 4, 7, 9, 10, 11, 26

Birgitte Nielsen   5, 8, 14, 17, 22, 24, 27, 31, 32

Paul Till   29

■ ■ ■ ■ ■

READER REPLY CARD

We are interested in your reaction to *Teaching: Strategies and Methods for Student-Centered Instruction* by Hellmut Lang, Arthur McBeath, and Jo Hébert. You can help us to improve this book in future editions by completing this questionnaire.

1. What was your reason for using this book?

    ☐ university course ☐ college course ☐ continuing education course

    ☐ professional ☐ personal interest ☐ other_____
    development _____

2. If you are a student, please identify your school and the course in which you used this book.

3. Which chapters or parts of this book did you use? Which did you omit?

4. What did you like best about this book? What did you like least?

5. Please identify any topics you think should be added to future editions.

6. Please add any comments or suggestions.

7. May we contact you for further information?

NAME: _____

ADDRESS: _____

PHONE: _____

(fold here and tape shut)

- -

MAIL ⮞POSTE

Canada Post Corporation / Société canadienne des postes

Postage paid
If mailed in Canada

Port payé
si posté au Canada

**Business
Reply**

**Réponse
d'affaires**

0116870399   01

0116870399-M8Z4X6-BR01

Heather McWhinney
Publisher, College Division
HARCOURT BRACE & COMPANY, CANADA
55 HORNER AVENUE
TORONTO, ONTARIO
M8Z 9Z9